Outrageous Fortune

Outrageous Fortune
Capital and Culture in Modern Ireland

Joe Cleary

Field Day Files 1

Series Editors: Seamus Deane and Breandán Mac Suibhne

Field Day Publications
Dublin, 2007

ISBN-10 0-946755-35-3
ISBN-13 978-0-946755-35-6

Published by Field Day Publications in association with the Keough-Naughton Institute for Irish Studies at the University of Notre Dame.

First published 2006
Second edition 2007

Field Day Publications
Newman House
86 St. Stephen's Green
Dublin 2
Ireland

Set in 10.5pt/13.5pt Quadraat
Designed and typeset by Red Dog Design Consultants
Printed on Freelife Vellum

For Gemma and Conor

Contents

Contents

Acknowledgements

The essays that constitute this book were written over many years and as interventions in different debates. Though never conceived as a single project, there are continuities of topic and theme, and in many cases arguments in the margins of one essay later became central in another. My first thanks is to Seamus Deane who invited me to gather these pieces into a single volume, and who has been an exceptionally patient and thoughtful and generous editor throughout the process. Breandán Mac Suibhne worked assiduously on all aspects of the final production, and the book is considerably the better for his care, acumen and persistence. I am indebted to them both.

Several of the pieces were first sketched out as lectures for The Irish Seminars convened in Newman House, Dublin, by the Keough-Naughton Institute for Irish Studies at the University of Notre Dame. These drafts were invariably improved by the lively responses offered by the other contributors and students who attended these events. My thanks to the three directors of the programme, Seamus Deane, Luke Gibbons and Kevin Whelan, for the repeated invitations to be involved. The scholarship and company of several of the other participants, particularly Amy Martin, David Lloyd, Siobhán Kilfeather and Richard Bourke, have been an invaluable stimulus. I am also grateful to Hilary Bell for copy-editing the book and to Cormac Ó Duibhne for compiling the index.

Special thanks are owed to two friends. Emer Nolan took the time to read several of the chapters in draft and her cogent commentaries, friendly scepticism and encouragement were always helpful. Conor McCarthy shares an interest in many of the issues debated here, and I have learned a great deal from our discussions over the years.

My colleagues and students in the Department of English at NUI Maynooth have helped in more ways than either they or I can always tell. The lively collegiality offered by the Department is a pleasure to acknowledge. I also want to record my debts to the staff and students connected to the 'Culture and Colonialism' postgraduate programme at

NUI Galway, and especially to Tadhg Foley, Lionel Pilkington and Sean Ryder. The many
Galway conferences on colonialism have done much to sharpen the analysis of Ireland
and the imperial world, and all scholars interested in such matters are indebted to the
labours of the organizers of those conferences. Above all, thanks to all the members of
the Red Stripe Seminar and to the Twentieth Century Irish Studies Society. The fortnightly
seminars conducted by these organizations have been models of intellectual debate and
exchange.

I have benefited from the kindness and expertise of many friends. They include Kevin
Honan, Yumna Siddiqi, Colleen Lye, David Pickell, Sinéad Kennedy, Heather Laird,
Raymond Deane, Colin Coulter, Michael Cronin, Honor Fagan, Catherine Morris, Claire
Connolly, Ray Ryan, John P. Waters, Mark Quigley, Rebecca McLennan, Jean Howard,
John Archer, Qadri Ismail, Conrad Brunström, Peter Denman, Aamir Mufti, Dermot Dix,
Chandana Mathur and Joseph Massad.

Gemma Murphy has, as ever, given her care unstintingly and with matchless generosity.
Conor Cleary teaches me something useful everyday. They make everything possible, so
no words can thank them sufficiently.

The receipt of a Senior Fellowship in 2004–05 from the Irish Research Council for the
Humanities and Social Sciences allowed me to complete this project; I deeply appreciate
the time to research and to write which that fellowship enabled.

Though most have been updated, extended or revised for this volume, versions of several
of the essays have appeared elsewhere. I would like to thank the editors and publishers of
those earlier versions for permission to include the following pieces in this volume:

'Into which West? Irish Modernity and the Maternal Supernatural', in Brian Cosgrove,
    ed., Literature and the Supernatural (Dublin: Columba Press, 1995), 147–73;
'Modernization and Aesthetic Ideology in Contemporary Irish Culture', in Ray Ryan, ed.,
    Writing in the Irish Republic: Literature, Culture, Politics, 1949–1999 (London: Macmillan
    Press, 2000), 105–29;
'Domestic Troubles: Tragedy and the Northern Ireland Conflict', The South Atlantic
    Quarterly, 98, 3 (2000), 501–37;
'Misplaced Ideas? Locating and Dislocating Ireland in Colonial and Postcolonial Studies',
    in Neil Lazarus and Crystal Bartolovich, eds., Marxism, Modernity and Postcolonial Studies
    (Cambridge: Cambridge University Press, 2002), 101–24, reprinted in abbreviated form
    as 'Misplaced Ideas? Colonialism, Location and Dislocation in Irish Studies', in Claire
    Connolly, ed., Theorizing Ireland (Houndmills: Palgrave Macmillan, 2003), 91–104, and
    in an extended version as 'Misplaced Ideas? Colonialism, Location and Dislocation
    in Irish Studies', in Clare Carroll and Patricia King, eds., Ireland and Postcolonial Theory
    (Cork: Cork University Press, 2003), 16–45;
'Toward a Materialist-Formalist History of Twentieth-Century Irish Literature in English',
    boundary 2, 31, 1 (2004), 207–41;
'The Nineteenth-Century Irish Novel: Some Notes and Speculations on Irish Literary
    Historiography', in Jacqueline Belanger, ed., The Irish Novel in the Nineteenth Century
    (Dublin: Four Courts Press, 2005), 202–21.

Introduction

This volume is about Irish cultural history from 1800 to 2000. Among the topics covered are debates about Ireland's colonial status; the historiography of the nineteenth-century novel; the conditions that contributed to the emergence and waning of literary modernism; the evolution of literary naturalism from the 1890s to the 1990s; and modes of aesthetic ideology in late twentieth-century theatre, fiction, film and popular music. The book is self-consciously essayistic in approach and interrogative and exploratory in spirit. It seeks less to offer definitive new interpretations of this author or that text than to map the intersecting forces that structure the field of modern Irish literary and cultural production, and to query some of the received modes of thinking about the period that inform Irish cultural studies. Broadly speaking, it is an historical materialist work that diagnoses how socio-historical forces converge to shape particular aesthetic ideologies and forms, and how the latter in turn coalesce to mould conceptions of the histories that initially stimulated them. Thus, it moves between local readings of individual authors and texts and broader historical surveys that track the fortunes of particular literary modes over an extended period.

Though it ranges across a long historical period, the volume's main focus is on the second half of the twentieth century, and its concerns throughout are obviously shaped by contemporary cultural and historical debates in Irish studies. Irish cultural criticism in the late twentieth century has been invigorated by the social volatility of the country as it has made the long, difficult transitions from postcolonial economic depression to consumerist opulence in the South, and from a strange late colonial war to an even stranger and still-unsettled 'peace' in the North. In the course of the accelerated overhauls of state and society conducted on both parts of the island during the later decades of the last century especially, many older belief-systems and structures of feeling have been obviously disaggregated. The extended social legitimacy crises, North and South, triggered in these decades have inevitably generated intellectual and cultural debates more often characterized by short-term tactical skirmishing than by long-range structural analyses. But, on the positive side, these crises also opened fertile space for lively debates about the vicissitudes of modern Irish history and about the direction of Irish society. The intellectual and cultural debates of the period between 1960 and 2000 can now sometimes seem to be distempered by a society too shaken by conflict, too haunted or daunted by a sense of failure. Today, in the early years of the twenty-first century, the greater risk may be that elation at overcoming a difficult history will serve only to reduce the space for debate, and to consolidate new orthodoxies as disabling as any that prevailed in the past. It used to be joked that in Soviet historiography the future was always certain and only the past remained to be predicted. Now, in a post-Cold War climate where it is conventional to assume that the social templates of the future are already given, since all serious alternatives to liberal capitalism have been eliminated from the world stage, that sense of dogmatically stupefied certainty seems to apply more to the artistic and intellectual worlds of affluent Western societies, including Ireland, than to any others. Several essays here consider how this 'end of history' structure of feeling weighs upon late twentieth-century Irish literary and cultural production, and on cultural criticism.

Three broad scholarly formations have commanded the field of Irish literary and cultural studies for some time now: revisionism, feminism, and what is now commonly called postcolonial studies. Many of the most substantive works of literary and cultural scholarship here in recent times have emerged from one or other of these intellectual formations or, more accurately, from the contentions between them. These are inevitably crude descriptive categories for large and mobile bodies of scholarship. They can also be obfuscating ones, when they forcibly conscript works by critics who would not identify themselves with any of these formations, or when they occlude the debts that many scholarly projects owe to more than one of these sources. Patently, the cultural and intellectual field is divided along multiple lines of fracture and in response to multiple sources of conflict, not all of which are contained by, or will line up neatly in, these terms. Some strands of contemporary Irish literary or cultural feminism, for example, clearly share much common ground with revisionism; others lean in a more postcolonialist direction; others still are characterized by a scepticism or indifference towards both.[1]

---

1 The extended debates around The Field Day Anthology of Irish Writing, 5 vols. (1991, 2002) offer a good example of the complexities of the cultural field and of the (mis)identifications possible within it. The fourth and fifth volumes of the anthology, on Irish Women's Writing, were famously stimulated by a feminist critique of the initial Field Day Anthology. Insofar as it ascribed that initial Anthology's under-representation of women to the supposed nationalism of the initial editors, and to the anthology's supposedly nation-building and canon-making intentions, that critique intersected with the revisionist critique of Field Day. Yet the fact that the team of scholars that edited these two volumes was prepared to associate this major late twentieth-century feminist undertaking with a 'completion' of the original Anthology might seem to have identified cultural feminism more broadly, however critically, with the 'anti-revisionist' Field Day. Indeed, the enterprise drew some revisionist fire on precisely these grounds.

Similarly, there are versions of Irish postcolonialist critique that comport comfortably with a revisionist political outlook whereas other more republican-minded or left-wing versions do not.[2] There is every reason, then, to avoid overly tidy schematizations of Irish cultural criticism. Nevertheless, the broad impress of revisionist, postcolonial and feminist studies on the production of knowledge in the humanities in recent decades is indisputable, and most conceptualizations of modern Irish social and cultural history are now indebted to one or other, or to some combination, of these formations.

This study's affiliations within this larger field are clear enough. Still, the individual essays maintain a certain agnosticism towards the scholarly sources (and attendant 'worldviews') to which they are most indebted, even if only in the interests of critical self-reflexivity. It is one of the more curious features of Irish cultural criticism that all of the scholarly formations mentioned above represent themselves in fundamentally adversarial terms. Thus, since the 1970s at least, Irish revisionism has presented itself as a dissident intellectual formation dedicated to debunking the reactionary and supposedly obdurately entrenched 'mythologies' that cultural nationalism fashioned in the nineteenth century and then institutionalized in the post-independence state education system.[3] However, for postcolonial critics, revisionists are less the anti-establishment dissidents they mistake themselves to be than the avant-garde fraction of a new state intelligentsia determined, firstly, to free historiography from its earlier subordination to militant nationalist agendas and, secondly, to liberalize Irish society (or at least southern society) in ways that upset and provoked the old value-systems of revolutionary nationalism and conservative Catholicism.[4] For revisionists, postcolonial studies in its turn is merely a project of intellectual restoration, a rearguard effort to rescue the old Sinn Féin worldview under a new 'postmodern' camouflage. Though Irish feminism sometimes finds itself fractured along this revisonist-postcolonialist axis, it nonetheless shares with both formations a fundamentally adversarial disposition. For many feminists, revisionism and postcolonial studies are both deeply masculinist scholarly formations, neither of which addresses itself sufficiently to the patriarchal

---

2 Interestingly, although revisionist scholarship generally is methodologically conservative and is thus normally dismissive of postmodern or poststructuralist theories, it is often the most poststructuralist versions of postcolonial theory that have most in common politically with revisionism. Where both converge, despite methodological differences, is in their tendency to regard nearly all forms of Irish nationalism as inherently reactionary, or at least in their common disinclination to distinguish between the progressive and retrograde elements in the more militant forms of nationalism.

3 Some of the standard surveys of Irish historical revisionism include Ciaran Brady, ed., *Interpreting Irish History: The Debate on Historical Revisionism 1938–1994* (Dublin, 1994) and Máirín Ní Dhonnchadha and Theo Dorgan, eds., *Revising the Rising* (Derry, 1991). There is as yet no major study of Irish revisionism in either the world of the arts or in that of literary and cultural criticism, though its influence in both is substantial.

4 Terry Eagleton's 'Revisionism Revisited' in his *Crazy John and the Bishop and other Essays on Irish Culture* (Cork, 1998), 308–27, offers a cogent marxian critique of revisionism. For a more 'subalternist' critique, see David Lloyd's 'Outside History: Irish New Histories and the "Subalternity Effect"' in his *Ireland After History* (Cork, 1999), 77–88.

dimensions of Irish society (or academia). By critiquing those forms of gender oppression that others fail to take seriously, feminists claim for themselves an adversarial stance not only vis-à-vis state and society, but also vis-à-vis those other 'radical' intellectual formations within the cultural field that understand themselves in dissident terms.

When every intellectual grouping in Irish studies looks to its opponents and sees essentially 'potentates of the establishment' (residual or emergent) and gazes into its own mirror to discover only anti-establishment 'dissidence,' the potential for intellectual circus is considerable. In this din of dissent, it is easily forgotten that intellectual and cultural debate, however conducted, is monopolized in modern Ireland (as elsewhere of course) by reasonably well-to-do middle-class women and men who typically share a great deal in common despite the constitutive divisions of the intellectual field. Such sibling commonalities include similar modes of education and professional training, shared forms of cultural taste and cultural capital, and, more significantly, a collective structural positioning and vantage-point within the larger social system conferred by their occupation as intellectual workers. These shared experiences and interests surface in relatively standardized languages of argument and analysis, repeated reworkings, via a rather narrow band of methodologies, of relatively small sets of key authors and topics, and reciprocated tolerances for certain modes of licensed ignorance.[5]

Where literary and cultural studies specifically are concerned, these sibling identities across divisions register above all in terms of a widespread tendency to equate political engagement and analysis with thematizing 'the political' in literary or other cultural texts. Conceived thus, political analysis in the cultural sphere essentially amounts to producing new readings of cultural texts or artefacts that foreground political and social themes. The analytical idioms in such cases will undoubtedly be very-up-to-the-moment, but the actual practice (whether in revisionist or postcolonialist or feminist or queer studies, and so on) will still remain largely consonant with the older modes of 'ethical' criticism characteristic of the discipline of literary criticism in its bourgeois meridian.[6] Whether the object of analysis is a high modernist literary text or popular film, a work of visual art or music, the debate in such instances will predictably be conducted mainly at the level of the semiotic content of the text. This means that more

5 The most obvious form of licensed ignorance across the intellectual field has to do with the Irish language. A capacity in Latin or French, or both, as well as English would be regarded as part of the normal professional competence of any historian or literary critic working on the medieval period in Ireland. However, the same standard of competence in the Irish language is not usually expected of scholars in these disciplines working on the period 1600–1845, even though Ireland was then predominantly Irish-speaking. To give a rather different example, any literary critic working in the field of twentieth-century Irish literature who did not have some knowledge of Shakespeare would almost certainly be considered somewhat philistine by his or her colleagues. But to profess a complete ignorance of, say, economic history or world systems theory might well be considered unremarkable, even a sign of sophistication, since these are commonly viewed within literary circles as vulgar 'sociological' competences.

6 My argument here is much indebted to John Guillory's provocative essay 'Literary Critics as Intellectuals: Class Analysis and the Humanities', in Wai Chee Dimock and Michael T. Gilmore, *Rethinking Class: Literary Studies and Social Formations* (New York, 1994), 107–49.

complex 'sociological' questions about how works of art of any kind, or indeed academic analyses of such works, can actually effect change, go almost totally unexamined. Irish cultural criticism attends remarkably little as a rule to the sedimented, and mostly only slowly-changing, aesthetic ideologies that regulate the production of individual artistic works.[7] It investigates even less the operations of the institutional networks (of schools and universities; circuits of publishing and performance; cinemas, theatres, museums, galleries; ministries of culture and culture industries) that organize the cultural field and mediate how texts are disseminated to the public and achieve meaning. The changing ways in which cultural and intellectual institutions negotiate their relationship with the domains of the state and the market in late capitalist conditions are equally ignored.[8] In fine, the Irish universities promote and reward certain textualist modes of humanistic research, and even if they do not actively discourage or legislatively exclude other modes, they don't support them much either. This study cannot claim any great innovative quality for itself in this respect. But in moving things beyond individual author studies and towards the survey of how aesthetic forms and ideologies shape literary production, part of its agenda is to at least nudge cultural criticism in such directions.

Within the existing cultural field, issues of tradition and modernity have been a key site of debate in recent times. Because revisionism, postcolonialism and feminism all conceive of themselves as dissident intellectual formations and even as intellectual avant-gardes of a kind, none, naturally, casts itself as a defender of 'tradition.' Yet whereas revisionists are nearly always enthusiasts of the modernizing thrust of Irish society since the 1960s, postcolonial critics are typically much warier. This is because while modernization in some of its forms may be entirely welcome (as in the various kinds of social liberalization attained in recent decades), the term also clearly serves as alibi for the increasing subjection of nearly every aspect of Irish society (including artistic, academic and intellectual work) to the logic of market forces. But if postcolonialists have good reason to be cautious of the jargon of 'modernization,' a term now almost entirely appropriated by liberals and neo-liberals, they have equal reason to be sceptical about any appeals to 'tradition,' since that latter term has long been the preserve of social conservatives. As a consequence, postcolonial studies has generally found itself

7   Some distinguished exceptions include Seamus Deane's long-range surveys of the intersections of the histories of ideas and aesthetics, especially in *Celtic Revivals: Essays in Modern Irish Literature* (London, 1985) and *Strange Country: Modernity and Nationhood in Irish Writing since 1790* (Oxford, 1997) and Terry Eagleton's studies of form in *Heathcliff and the Great Hunger: Studies in Irish Culture* (London, 1995). This is not to dismiss strong readings of individual authors or texts, a staple and pleasurable component of any cultural criticism; it is the tendency in Irish studies to treat such readings as the primary site of sociopolitical engagement and analysis that might be questioned.

8   The fact that Raymond Williams's *The Sociology of Culture* (Chicago, 1995) or Pierre Bourdieu's many works dealing with academics and intellectuals, most famously perhaps *Homo Academicus*, trans. Peter Collier (Stanford, 1988), have had such little 'take up' in Irish cultural studies tells its own story. Despite the pioneering efforts of Terence Brown in *Ireland: A Social and Cultural History, 1922–1985* (London, 1981), comprehensive studies of Irish intellectual and artistic life in the twentieth century have scarcely ever been attempted by a later generation.

reduced either to repeated deconstructions of the tradition/modernity dichotomy or to valorizing 'alternative modernities,' meaning recuperating repertoires of possible developments in the past never realized at the time.[9] But however valuable such exercises may be, they translate poorly into the praxis-orientated world of the public sphere where the language of modernization governs almost all discussion of social change. Nor does a commitment to 'alternative modernities' usually provide much by way of structural analysis or cognitive mapping of the wider global conjunctures that any collective political movement must be able to diagnose to situate itself strategically.[10] Feminists confront a not dissimilar bind. Since feminism was one of the major agents of social modernization in the late twentieth century, and since Irish women have apparently been among the major beneficiaries of both social and economic modernization, feminism in general has been (like marxism or liberalism for that matter) enthusiastically 'modernizing' in its general thrust. The more left-wing and postcolonial strands of feminist analysis may share the usual reservations of the contemporary intellectual left about the ways in which 'modernization' has come to mean capitalist modernization. But this means that they share, too, the difficulties of articulating a viable alternative to the capitalist modernity from which Ireland has reaped so many rewards in recent times.

Yet however much cultural critics might be at odds about the discourses of modernization, some broadly homologous conceptualizations of the Irish twentieth century seem nonetheless to prevail across these various intellectual formations. They might disagree on other matters, but feminists, revisionists and postcolonialists would seem at least to agree that the society that emerged in (southern) Ireland between independence and the 1960s was overwhelmingly disappointing and unattractive.[11] Of course, in many ways this disillusioned sense of the southern state has been around since its inception and on both the left and the right of the political spectrum. Thus, for unionists (north and south), it was axiomatic from the start that post-independent twenty-six county Ireland was intrinsically insular, impoverished, oppressive and theocratic.

9   In the Irish context, arguments about the history and value of alternative possibilities foreclosed by the dominant versions of modernity are most fully developed by Luke Gibbons in *Transformations in Irish Culture* (Cork, 1996) and Lloyd in *Ireland After History*.

10 The extent of the dilemma involved here, evident as much in the Irish cultural field as any other, is pithily summarized by Fredric Jameson: 'If free-market positions can be systematically identified with modernity and habitually grasped as representing what is modern, then the free-market people have won a fundamental victory which goes well beyond the older ideological victories. To call this a media victory is to underestimate the displacement onto language and terminology of political struggle today. The point is that the holders of the opposite position have nowhere to go terminologically. The adversaries of the free market, such as the socialists, can only be classed in the negative or privative category of the unmodern, the traditionalist, or, even, ultimately, since they clearly resist progress and modernity, of the hardliners.' See Jameson, *A Singular Modernity: Essays on the Ontology of the Present* (London, 2002), 9–10.

11 Where social and cultural life is concerned, far more attention has been devoted to the southern than to the northern state in 1920–60 especially. Terence Brown's *Ireland: A Social and Cultural History* is typical of the scholarship generally in its concentration on the twenty-six county state, and it is notable that there is no equivalent for its six-county counterpart.

Much of this could be dismissed as mere anti-Catholic bigotry and resentment at the diminution of the Union. But even before Max Weber or R. H. Tawney had identified Protestantism with economic individualism and with a generally modernizing, entrepreneurial and capitalist mentality, it had been conventional in secular intellectual circles to regard Catholicism as an impediment to social or economic progress.[12] So, in many ways the new, largely rural and non-industrialized, and overwhelmingly Catholic Irish Free State came into the world tailor-made to accommodate not just crude Unionist prejudices, but also more respectable sociological and intellectual ones as well. On the left, too, many radical republicans also held that the new state was by definition a failure since it fell so far short of the one-island radical democratic republic they had hoped for. Inveterate antagonists otherwise, the unionist right and the republican left more or less converged on this point at least.

In their different ways, the contemporary revisionist, postcolonialist and feminist critiques of post-independent Ireland are all late twentieth-century legatees to these originary critiques, which they now inflect in their own directions. Thus, for revisionists, the failures of the new state in this period are conventionally charged to its economic and cultural nationalism, to its anti-modern clericalism, and to its incapacity to overcome a 'romantic' commitment to some sort of rural, Gaelic or Catholic utopia. For marxists and the more left-wing postcolonialists, the stress falls instead on the ways in which 'the revolution' was stymied by a comprador bourgeoisie, which repressed more radical social constituencies and concentrated its efforts on keeping the country safe for some form of dependent capitalist development. In feminist analyses, the emphasis falls heavily on the patriarchal dimensions of the new state, and on the ways in which women's agency was written out of the revolutionary period even as the new regime set about disempowering women and confining them, where possible, to the private sphere.

Needless to say, each of these analytics captures real and significant aspects of the harsh and oppressive realities of postcolonial Ireland. If the epoch between 1920 and 1960 has a negative image, it is not without cause. Yet however different they may be in origin and purpose, all of these different critiques of Ireland in this period seem to meet up somewhere in the liberal centre of the intellectual-cultural field at least to create an iconic version of what is now commonly called 'de Valera's Ireland.' In that iconic version, the whole post-independence epoch before the Lemassian turn has become practically a byword for a soul-killing Catholic nationalist traditionalism and in the parlance of much contemporary cultural debate 'de Valera's Ireland' now serves as a reflex shorthand for everything from economic austerity to sexual puritanism, from cultural philistinism to the abuse of women and children.[13] In many ways, the reaction that led to this stark

12 Max Weber, *The Protestant Ethic and the Spirit of Capitalism*, trans. Talcott Parsons (London, 1930 [1904–05]); R. H. Tawney, *Religion and the Rise of Capitalism* (London, 1926)

13 No equivalent shorthand exists to designate the oppressiveness of the Northern state in the same period. For a shrewd discussion of what she terms 'de Valera's' overdetermined and somewhat contradictory symbolic potency', see Elizabeth Butler Cullingford, 'Re-Reading the Past: *Michael Collins*

image of the post-independence state was probably not only inevitable but also even radical and progressive in most of its post-1960s versions. As Fredric Jameson has noted, every strong moment of rupture with an old order seems to require 'a powerful act of dissociation whereby the present seals off its past from itself and expels and ejects it; an act without which neither the present nor past truly exist, the past not yet fully constituted, the present still a living on within the force field of a past not yet over and done with.'[14] In this sense, the now-conventional negative image of 'de Valera's Ireland' may be understood not just as a creation of post-1960s 'Lemass's Ireland,' but also as a necessary condition for the latter's self-constitution. For 'contemporary Ireland' to emerge, in other words, it had first to create the 'de Valera's Ireland' that would be its repudiated antithesis.

The difficulty is, though, that if 'de Valera's Ireland' has become a magnet-term around which to constellate every negative inference of the word 'tradition,' the term 'Lemass's Ireland' or, more commonly, just 'contemporary Ireland', likewise accrues to itself all of the uncritically positive connotations of the word 'modernity.' Thus, if one period is conventionally agreed to mean nationalist stagnation and repression, the other, by reflex, comes to mean post-nationalist dynamism and tolerance. These are caricatures of the two epochs, of course, and widely recognized as such, yet their symbolic potency is not necessarily diminished for all that.[15] And when the trajectory of twentieth-century Irish development is configured in this repression-modernization dyad, all sorts of things get drastically simplified. 'De Valera's Ireland' may well have been overwhelmingly repressive, but its repressions were always unequally allocated across classes and genders. Likewise, 'contemporary Ireland' may well be dynamic and reforming, but the benefits of such have been as unevenly distributed as were the repressions before. Too often, the dyadic conception of these two eras serves only as a bulwark to sustain inherited modes of dissent, and as a lazy substitute for the more difficult labour of working out the calculus of class and gender power operative in both periods. In other words, the liability of 'de Valera's Ireland' is that even if it began as a tool of critique that enabled a break with the past, today it serves more effectively as a tool to muffle critiques of the post-1960s social and political order. And while cultural critics may readily agree

and Contemporary Popular Culture', in Robert J. Savage, ed., *Ireland in the New Century: Politics, Culture and Identity* (Dublin, 2003), 174–88. See also Caitríona Clear, 'Women in de Valera's Ireland 1932–48: A Reappraisal', in Gabriel Doherty and Dermot Keogh, eds., *De Valera's Ireland* (Cork, 2003), 104–14

14 See Jameson, *Singular Modernity*, 25.

15 An exemplary instance of this conception of things is Paul Durcan's poem, 'Making Love outside Áras an Uachtaráin', in which the young poet and his girlfriend make love in the grass outside Áras an Uachtaráin where an aging, blind de Valera reproves them, or is imagined to do so, for their intercourse. In a manner conventional to much post-independence Irish literature, the poem associates nationalist figures with repressiveness, sexual prudery and violence (in a classically Freudian sequence), and equates radicalism with a supposedly audacious transgression of sexual taboos. See Paul Durcan, *Sam's Cross* (Dublin, 1978), 47. This whole conception of things rests not only on a now commonplace view of de Valera but also on a vulgarization of Freudian theories of sexual repression and liberation.

that the terms 'tradition' and 'modernity' are diagnostically clumsy, the familiar habits of dividing twentieth-century Ireland into 'de Valera's Ireland' and 'Lemass's Ireland' (or 'contemporary Ireland') effectively smuggles that tradition/modernity schema back into our temporal conceptualizations of the whole post-independence period. What gets deconstructed semantically at one level returns to organize conceptions of the century at the level of periodization.

The proper business of any critical theory is not to validate a pregiven political position, whether to the left or right. It is, rather, to track the matrix of oppressive and emancipatory forces at work in every period of modernity, and indeed to be attentive to how even the most emancipatory developments can sometimes collude with or be commandeered by the regressive. Several essays here investigate the aesthetic and intellectual forces that go into the making of 'de Valera's Ireland.' The object of these pieces is not to revise the revisionists, which would be to remain tied to revisionism, even if only oppositionally. Nor is the main motive to salvage that period from what an English historian famously called 'the enormous condescension of posterity,' though this in itself might be a worthy project.[16] Certainly, the intention is not to take issue with the many valuable works that have made it their business to try to understand the more repressive and exploitative realities of the post-independence period. But the aim is to challenge some of the lazier habits and reflexes — operative both in the worlds of art and cultural criticism alike — induced by conceptualizing the century in a manner that associates one whole epoch with static repressiveness and another with dynamic reformism. Beyond that, the broader goal is to locate twentieth-century Irish cultural developments in a more materialist and broader comparativist analytical frame than either nationalist or revisionist cultural scholarship has usually managed to do.

If the interrogative nature of this book risks appearing too indulgent towards an abusively oppressive past to some, it will as likely seem much too grudging of the real achievements of the present to others. However one makes sense of the last century, it can hardly be disputed that most of the people on the island of Ireland now are materially better off and have more social rights and liberties than did their antecedents either when the two states were founded in the early 1920s or even in the early 1960s. This, surely, must be the definitive litmus test of the generally 'progressive' character of the modes of capitalist modernization supervized by the ruling classes in Northern and Southern Irish society in recent decades? Leftists, feminists, and left-of-centre-liberals will rightly argue that if the two Irish states and societies are generally-speaking more socially liberal now than they once were, these boons have not been gifted to them by capitalism in any of its forms, whether autarkic, dependent or neo-liberal. Instead, radical movements from below have had to struggle hard to win such freedoms. These have been secured in recent decades chiefly by the women's liberation movement, trade unions, community organizations, and left-wing or radical democratic campaigns in

---

16 The phrase is E. P. Thompson's in *The Making of the English Working Class* (New York, 1963), 12.

the South. They have been won, at higher cost (because more fiercely resisted), mainly by the civil rights movement, constitutional nationalist reformism, and republican militancy in the North. To this, the defenders of neo-liberal capitalist modernization will argue that however they were won, only the capitalist mode of production can now generate the material affluence needed to sustain those freedoms and to guarantee those liberties. The advances wrested by the various constituencies of what might broadly be called 'the liberal left' since the 1960s, in other words, presuppose the very capitalism that these constituencies take as the object of their critique.

Yet even if a great deal of contemporary cultural criticism of whatever kind (postcolonialist, feminist, revisionist) is still struggling conceptually to catch up with Celtic Tiger Ireland and its modes of consumption, some fundamental structural problems of the wider capitalist dispensation are evident.[17] Can capitalist consumerism of the kind that Ireland now enjoys be generalized to the less fortunate peripheries in Asia or South America or devastated Africa or the war-racked Middle East? If it can, then it might well be argued that the Irish experience can serve as a template for other postcolonies, offering them a shining example of transition from the economic destitution and cultural damage of the colonial era to the capitalist land of plenty that lies beyond. Some of the more liberal strands of Irish postcolonial studies now seem disposed towards this roseate view. But what if — as the prevailing conditions of the modern era seem amply to attest — consumerist wealth cannot be globalized and that it is, rather, as Perry Anderson has termed it, an 'oligarchic wealth,' the existence of which depends on its restriction to a small minority? As Anderson notes in one of the more considered leftist responses to Francis Fukuyama's encomium to the historical achievements of liberal capitalism in 'The End of History?': 'Less than a quarter of the world's population now appropriates eighty-five per cent of world income, and the gap between the shares of the advanced and backward zones has widened over the past half century.'[18] And even if one were to assume, against all appearances, that the extraordinary consumerist affluence of the prevailing capitalist core regions could indeed be generalized to the impoverished peripheries, could the world sustain such

17 The 'weakest' critiques from the left — but the most common in artistic, literary and cultural circles — are of the 'quality of life' variety, which argue that although capitalism may create materially wealthy societies, it produces modes of social being that are spiritually- or culturally- or time-poor. There may well be much truth to this, but such modes of argument typically treat society as a homogenous bloc and fail to distinguish between the classes which are the beneficiaries and those which are the most exploited in the system. Distributionist critiques are 'stronger,' since these at least seek to diagnose how wealth is apportioned across classes and constituencies. But even distributionist critiques are limited because, even when they demonstrate how exploitatively capitalist wealth is generated and how unevenly it is divided, this does not in itself establish that some other mode of production would necessarily fare better. Unless harnessed to a conception of how some non-capitalist society would do better, the main effect, whatever the intention, of distributionist critiques is reformist.

18 Perry Anderson, 'The Ends of History', in A Zone of Engagement (London, 1992), 279–375, 353. See also Francis Fukuyama, 'The End of History?', The National Interest, 16 (1989), 1–18, a longer version of which later appeared in Fukuyama, The End of History and the Last Man (New York, 1992).

extension in any event? Doesn't the overwhelming immediate evidence seem to indicate, to cite Anderson again, that 'If all of the peoples of the earth possessed the same number of refrigerators and automobiles as those of North America and Western Europe, the planet would become uninhabitable. In the global ecology of capital today, the privilege of the few requires the misery of the many, to be sustainable.'[19]

Even within those core zones that currently monopolize the world's wealth, greater affluence commonly goes hand-in-hand with greater levels of inequality between classes. The defenders of capitalism normally reply that even the poorest underclasses in the West are vastly better off now than were the modestly well-to-do middle classes of yesteryear. But this ignores the economic logic of late consumer capitalism, which requires a mode of production that generates not only affluence but also endemic frustration and dissatisfaction. Only by manufacturing a perpetually dissatisfied sense of want can consumer capitalism sustain the continual demand for the unlimited volumes of goods it needs to sell in order to reproduce itself. In the more harshly puritanical capitalist societies of the past, religious value-systems had tried to subordinate individual need to some supposedly higher collective purpose.[20] Even if the underclasses of the modern Western world are in fact moderately better off than earlier generations of their kind, the consumerist breakdown of the older religious or secular-left value-systems that valorized things other than wealth accumulation may well have negated any such material advance. Lacking now either the consolations of religion or that sense of collective purpose that the socialist conception of the proletariat's historical mission had once conferred on them, the underclasses are at once exposed to the most rawly exploitative aspects of the consumer society and yet are normally the recipients of only its most low-grade material benefits. Today, Irish society as a whole may be extravagantly wealthy compared to what it was a few decades ago, but what may be revised out of existence is not just the old economic or cultural nationalism of an earlier epoch, but also the old republican credo of liberty, equality, fraternity. In the new neo-liberal Ireland, is liberty — however construed — the only term in that trinity now recognized as a social value? How much of the republican commitment to equality and fraternity (meaning collective solidarity in contemporary idioms) — whether these latter values are defined in national or global terms — is the Republic of Ireland prepared to trade off in the name of its dynamic capitalist competitiveness?

The basic point at issue here is that if 'contemporary Ireland' has escaped the miseries of 'de Valera's Ireland' to secure the benefits of 'the Celtic Tiger,' it has done so essentially by hitching its fortunes to global capitalism. To say as much is not to moralistically indict the society for having done so; in a world that offers so little viable alternative, to have opted otherwise would have been perverse. But far from it being, as its Fukuyamian

19 Anderson, 'The Ends of History', 352–53
20 For a useful critical review of the literature on consumerism, see Don Slater, *Consumer Culture and Modernity* (Cambridge, 1997) and for a broad historical survey, see Peter N. Stearns, *Consumerism in World History: The Global Transformation of Desire* (London, 2001).

defenders suppose, a system whose long-term viability has been definitively attested by its capacity to see off its twentieth-century rivals, the central case against capitalism today is that it breeds on a global scale social polarization and ecological crisis of a magnitude that portend disasters as great as any that afflicted the last century. Contemporary Ireland, in short, may have escaped the crises of the autarkic capitalism of 'de Valera's Ireland,' but the new neo-liberal version it has embraced has its own structural crises in abundance.

However, the quandary for the contemporary left now is that capitalism's difficulty is not necessarily socialism's opportunity. While the fundamental socialist critique of capitalism's systemic contradictions seems as cogent as ever, the left's capacity to elaborate some kind of viable order that could replace capitalism was probably never weaker. The problem is not that it is difficult to imagine a world better than the current one. It is rather that it has become difficult, in the wake of socialism's own catastrophic historical failures, to make a persuasive case that socialist modernization does not simply offer either a less functional form of modernization than capitalism (as in the Soviet model) or else only some more democratically-tempered or moderately-restrained versions of capitalism, which would still be vulnerable in any case to the consumerist contradictions and ecological destructiveness of capitalism proper. After all, the triumphal post-Cold War neo-liberal claim registered in Fukuyama's 'The End of History?' was not that liberal democracy was or would ever be a perfect system; only that all attempts to elaborate a superior alternative had failed, and thus historically eliminated themselves. As Anderson's response to Fukuyama reminded its readers, an effective critique of 'The End of History?' could not just be content to point out the manifold problems that liberal capitalism seems unlikely to resolve. It must also be able to show that there are powerful systemic alternatives available that Fukuyama had discounted.[21]

To date, very little Irish writing, Irish film, or Irish art generally, can be said to have contemplated with much distinction the vagaries or vicissitudes of the new global order of which Ireland is a constituent part. Nor have literary or cultural criticism distinguished themselves in this regard. For all the talk of a new postnationalism, multiculturalism and cosmoplitanism in Irish society, all of the intellectual formations in Irish studies are remarkably localized and narrowly anglocentric or eurocentric in their funadamental dispositions. Time alone will not guarantee a qualitatively better response, since time is only an index, not an agent of change, and some radicalizing transformation in the ideologies and modes of Irish cultural production and analysis will be necessary if positive developments are to occur.[22] It remains to be seen whether (or how) revisionist,

---

21 Anderson, 'The Ends of History', 336, 357–58
22 It is sometimes argued that Irish literature and art have been so habituated to dealing with poverty and backwardness that it will take time for them to catch up with the new realities of Irish society. Such arguments simply presuppose positive change, but they cannot identify either the means by which it will come about, or the valence it might have. Is there any reason to presuppose that cultural change must be radical or inflected in any broadly left direction? Is not the converse as likely?

feminist or postcolonialist cultural criticism can evolve to meet the new challenges of the emergent domestic and international conjuncture. If the colonial and autarkic modes of capitalism visited forms of outrageous fortune on Ireland in the past, neoliberal capitalism visits as bad and much worse on many other places today. In such a world, even the best of good fortunes will always have its outrageous dimension.

Irish Studies, Colonial Questions:
Locating Ireland in the Colonial World

Questions about Ireland's colonial status, and about the country's relationship to the British Empire, did not begin in the 1980s. However, for reasons both domestic and international, these topics began to receive sustained academic attention and became the focus of considerable controversy in Irish studies in that decade. In retrospect, the Field Day Theatre Company's staging of Brian Friel's *Translations* in 1980 might be seen as a constitutive moment in the emergence of postcolonial studies in Ireland. The play raised a cluster of issues about British state expansion in nineteenth-century Ireland, about the politics of cultural collision and language change, and about the role of knowledge in the imaginative appropriation of territory, that would subsequently become key issues for an emergent Irish postcolonial studies as well. Later in the decade, Field Day also published a number of pamphlets that implicitly situated modern Irish culture within a colonial framework.[1] The small but growing body of work that shared this critical perspective received further stimulus in 1988 when Field Day commissioned pamphlets by Edward Said, Fredric Jameson and Terry Eagleton, each of which examined some aspect of modern Irish culture within the context of colonialism, imperialism and anti-colonial nationalism.[2] In the same year, David Cairns and Shaun Richards published their seminal *Writing Ireland: Colonialism, Nationalism and Culture*, the first extended historical survey of Irish literature to draw explicitly on the wider international body of postcolonial cultural

1   See especially Seamus Deane, *Civilians and Barbarians* (Derry, 1983), and Declan Kiberd, *Anglo-Irish Attitudes* (Derry, 1985), both reprinted in *Ireland's Field Day* (London, 1985).
2   Edward Said, *Yeats and Decolonization* (Derry, 1988), Fredric Jameson, *Modernism and Imperialism* (Derry, 1988), and Terry Eagleton, *Nationalism: Irony and Commitment* (Derry, 1988), later republished in Seamus Deane, introd., *Nationalism, Colonialism and Literature* (Minneapolis, 1990)

criticism inspired by Said's *Orientalism*.[3] The increasing significance that postcolonial theory was beginning to assume in Irish cultural studies was indicated in the early 1990s with the inclusion of essays by Luke Gibbons, David Lloyd and Clair Wills in a special issue of the *Oxford Literary Review* on colonialism.[4] All three essays explored Ireland's particular place within the categories of British nineteenth-century colonial and racial discourse. Since then a substantial body of criticism by some of Ireland's leading cultural critics has appeared that draws extensively on the theoretical resources of postcolonial studies. Key works include Thomas Boylan and Timothy Foley's, *Political Economy and Colonial Ireland* (1992); David Lloyd's *Anomalous States: Irish Writing and the Postcolonial Moment* (1993) and *Ireland After History* (1999); Declan Kiberd's *Inventing Ireland* (1995); Luke Gibbons's *Transformations in Irish Culture* (1996); and Seamus Deane's *Strange Country* (1997).[5]

Postcolonial studies in Ireland is sometimes conceived as an offshoot of literary or cultural studies, but the scholarship and controversies emerging from the 1980s onwards were indebted not only to the wider international emergence of postcolonial studies but also to concurrent developments in British and Irish historiography. The development of the historical enterprises sometimes referred to as the 'the Atlantic archipelago' and the 'new British history' are noteworthy in this context.[6] Both challenged, in various ways, twentieth-century British historiography's insular amnesia about the British imperial enterprise. The new British history took as its object the interconnections between English state formation and the extension of English control over the rest of the British Isles, while the Atlantic model investigated the wider connections between developments in the British Isles and Britain's westward expansion into North America and the Caribbean. Long before the 1980s, Irish historians, notably David Beers Quinn and Nicholas Canny, working with the Atlantic model of history had been busily publishing on the connections (personnel, trade, practices, and *mentalités*) that linked the early modern English plantations in Ireland with the contemporaneous establishment of British colonies in North America.[7]

3 David Cairns and Shaun Richards, *Writing Ireland: Colonialism, Nationalism and Culture* (Manchester, 1988)
4 Luke Gibbons, 'Race Against Time: Racial Discourse and Irish History', *Oxford Literary Review*, 13, 1–2 (1991), 95–113, subsequently republished in Gibbons, *Transformations in Irish Culture* (Cork, 1996); David Lloyd, 'Race Under Representation', *Oxford Literary Review*, 13, 1–2 (1991), 62–94; Clair Wills, 'Language Politics, Narrative, Political Violence', *Oxford Literary Review*, 13, 1–2 (1991), 20–60
5 Thomas A. Boylan and Timothy P. Foley, *Political Economy and Colonial Ireland* (London, 1992); David Lloyd, *Anomalous States: Irish Writing and the Post-Colonial Moment* (Durham, 1993) and *Ireland After History* (Cork, 1999); Declan Kiberd, *Inventing Ireland: The Literature of the Modern Nation* (London, 1995); Gibbons, *Transformations in Irish Culture*; Seamus Deane, *Strange Country: Modernity and Nationhood in Irish Writing Since 1790* (Oxford, 1997). Other book-length contributions include Fintan Cullen, *Visual Politics: The Representation of Ireland 1750–1930* (Cork, 1997) and Gerry Smyth, *Decolonisation and Criticism: The Construction of Irish Literature* (London, 1998).
6 For some suggestive overviews on the development of the 'New British' and 'Atlantic' models of historiography, see the special forum on 'The New British History in Atlantic Perspective' in *American Historical Review*, 104 (1999).
7 Quinn's works include *The Elizabethans and the Irish* (Ithaca, 1966) and *Ireland and America: Their Early Associations, 1500–1640* (Liverpool, 1991). Among Canny's numerous publications, see: 'The Ideology of

The historical research agenda pioneered by Quinn and energetically developed by Canny has generated considerable dispute in its own right. Its critics have suggested that early modern Ireland was culturally less alien to the British than the more remote and only recently 'discovered' Americas and that Ireland's constitutional relationship to the British crown was more ambivalent than that of the American colonies.[8] For such critics, Ireland must be considered 'a constitutional anomaly, neither the "kingdom" of England nor a "colony" in north America'.[9] Nevertheless, despite the controversy that Canny's work provoked, the emergence of postcolonial studies in the 1980s generated more intense academic heat for several reasons. First, the disputes provoked by the work of Beers Quinn and Canny had been restricted to historians, but postcolonial studies extended the debate about Ireland's colonial condition across several disciplines, thus lending the controversies more interdisciplinary and methodological dimensions. Second, while the Atlantic and (to a lesser extent) the new British histories unsettled the state-centrism of the dominant strains within both Irish and British nationalist historiography, both modes of scholarship remained concentrated on the early modern period, whereas the works that appeared under the rubric of postcolonial studies in the 1980s asserted that colonialism was not simply a remote historical phenomenon but something that remained critical to the development of Irish society until the twentieth century, and that its consequences continued to shape developments in the post-partition period as well. To many, such claims represented not only an unwarranted exaggeration of the importance of colonialism but also an unwelcome 'politicization' of Irish scholarship.[10]

However, the emergence and reception of postcolonial studies in Ireland must ultimately be linked not only to domestic and international intellectual cross-currents, but also to the socio-political climate on the island at the time. The social toll of the

English Colonization: From Ireland to America', William and Mary Quarterly, 30, 4 (1973), 575–98; The Elizabethan Conquest of Ireland: A Pattern Established (New York, 1976); Colonial Identity in the Atlantic World, 1500–1800 (Princeton, 1987); and Kingdom and Colony: Ireland and the Atlantic World, 1560–1800 (Baltimore, 1988). See also the contributions by Canny and others in K. R. Andrews, N. P. Canny and P. E. H. Hair, eds., The Westward Enterprise: English Activities in Ireland, the Atlantic, and America 1480–1650 (Liverpool, 1978) and in Nicholas Canny, ed., The Oxford History of British Empire, 1, The Origins of Empire (Oxford, 1998).

8   For representative critiques, see T. C. Barnard, 'Crisis of Identity Among Irish Protestants, 1641–1845', Past and Present, 127 (1990), 39–83; Karl Bottigheimer, 'Kingdom and Colony: Ireland in the Westward Enterprise 1536–1660', in Andrews, Canny and Hair, Westward Enterprise, 45–64; Ciaran Brady, 'The Road to the View: On the Decline of Reform Thought in Tudor Ireland', in Patricia Coughlan, ed., Spenser and Ireland; An Interdisciplinary Perspective (Cork, 1989), 25–45; Hiram Morgan 'Mid-Atlantic Blues', The Irish Review, 11 (1991–92), 50–55; and Steven G. Ellis, 'Writing Irish History: Revisionism, Colonialism, and the British Isles', The Irish Review, 27 (1994), 1–21.

9   Ciaran Brady and Raymond Gillespie, eds., Natives and Newcomers: Essays on the Making of Irish Colonial Society, 1534–1641 (Dublin, 1986), 17

10 Examples include Denis Donoghue, 'Fears for Irish Studies in an Age of Identity Politics', Chronicle of Higher Education, 21 Nov. 1997; David Krause, 'Review Article: The Reinvention of Ireland', Irish University Review, 27, 2 (1997), 236–44; and Edna Longley, The Living Stream: Literature and Revisionism in Ireland (Newcastle upon Tyne, 1994), 22–44.

long economic recession that had continued in the South since the early 1970s and the political deadlock, hunger strikes, and military conflict in the North created an aggravated political and intellectual atmosphere in which the word 'colonial' carried a volatile historical and semantic baggage that disturbed many. Since the 1970s, the dominant intellectual responses to the economic and political conflicts that afflicted the island had been shaped by variants of modernization theory and revisionist historiography. Based on a crude dichotomy between 'traditional' and 'modern' societies, modernization theories sought to explore the institutional arrangements, cultural values and other social variables that might allow traditional societies to become modern as quickly and effectively as possible.[11] From this perspective, the problems that bedevilled Irish society — whether political violence and sectarianism in the North or conservative Catholic nationalism and economic inefficiency in the South — were understood to mean that Ireland remained a dysfunctional traditional society that had still to make the necessary transition to a properly modern social order.

The popularity of modernization discourse in both political and academic milieux is at least partially explained by its discursive suppleness, and by its consequent capacity to lend itself to a wide range of political positions and agendas.[12] 'Modernity as such,' Francis Mulhern comments, 'has no necessary social content: it is a form of "temporalization", an invariant production of present, past and future that "valorizes the new" and, by that very act, "produces the old", along with the characteristic modes of its embrace, the distinctively modern phenomena of traditionalism and reaction.'[13] Irish liberals, genuinely concerned to secularize the Catholic-dominated official culture consolidated in the Irish Republic after independence, had used the tradition/ modernity dichotomy very effectively to argue that Irish social legislation needed to be modernized to bring the country into line with the rest of Western Europe. However, the same dichotomy could equally well be used to advance the rather different interests of neo-liberals less concerned with social emancipation than with the emancipation of international capital from all sorts of traditional constraints such as state or trade-union regulation. Modernization discourse also exercised considerable attraction for some sections of the Irish left on both sides of the border. Some liberals and leftists, dismayed that the Irish political landscape did not conform to the right–left divisions common to most Western European societies, seemed to believe that only when a European

11 For a more detailed analysis of modernization theory, see Jorge Larrain, *Theories of Development: Capitalism, Colonialism and Dependency* (Oxford, 1989), esp. 85–110. For an incisive critique of the limits of modernization theory as a mode of comparative social analysis, see Dean C. Tipps, 'Modernization Theory and the Comparative Study of Societies: A Critical Perspective', *Comparative Studies in Society and History*, 15 (1973), 199–226.

12 For an incisive critique of modernization discourse in the Irish context, a discourse he terms 'the cultural dominant of the nineties' and 'the preferred code of advocacy and dissent', see Francis Mulhern's *The Present Lasts a Long Time: Essays in Cultural Politics* (Cork, 1998), 1–28, 20.

13 Mulhern, *The Present Lasts a Long Time*, 20. Mulhern's critique draws on Peter Osborne's *The Politics of Time: Modernity and Avant-Garde* (London, 1995).

modernization had enabled Ireland to overcome 'the idiocy of rural life' in the South and the 'atavism' of sectarianism in the North, would Irish social democracy finally make its belated rendezvous with history.[14]

For many, one of the main attractions of postcolonial studies as it took shape in Ireland in the 1980s was its capacity to destabilize the regnant intellectual assumptions of both modernization discourse and revisionist historiography. Like modernization theory, postcolonial studies seeks to articulate the systemic connections between the various crises that affect Irish society, north and south, but it does so in a manner that disputes crucial tenets of the older orthodoxy. From the perspective of postcolonial studies, modernization discourse is simply a contemporary variant on the nineteenth-century bourgeois ideology of evolutionary progress, the occluded side of which has always been European imperialism and the colonial subordination of the greater part of the world to metropolitan domination. By focusing overwhelmingly upon variables relating to indigenous aspects of social culture and structure, modernization theories generally display indifference to the wider systemic dimensions of economic and political imperialism. Even in those cases where they do accord significance to external forces, modernization theorists tend to evaluate 'impact' in terms of the diffusion of ideas, values and expectations, but rarely attend to the structural composition of the wider world system that constrains and conditions such interactions. Where modernization discourse consistently locates modern Ireland within an apparently self-contained Western European context and a foreshortened time span in which the past is reductively coded as 'tradition', the latter conceived as a negative force that acts mainly as an impediment to progress, postcolonial discourse insists on the need to understand Irish historical development in terms both of the *longue durée* and of the wider geographical span of Western colonial capitalism. Both modernization discourse and Irish revisionist historiography stress the reactionary nature of Irish nationalism, especially its more militant versions, but postcolonial discourse has suggested that Irish nationalism can only be understood contextually as the complex outcome of local interactions with an aggressively-expanding imperialist world economy. Revisionist historiography and modernization studies have both been obsessed with the 'high' history of nation and state formation, with the narrative of the political élites that shaped Irish state apparatuses. Postcolonial discourse, in contrast, has sought to develop a more

14 For a revisionist-leftist overview of southern Irish society informed by a modernization perspective, see Ellen Hazelkorn and Henry Patterson, 'The New Politics of the Irish Republic', *New Left Review*, 207 (1994), 49–71. See also Tom Nairn, 'The Curse of Rurality: The Limits of Modernisation Theory', in John A. Hall, ed., *The State of the Nation: Ernest Gellner and the Theory of Nationalism* (Cambridge, 1998), 107–34, 107–08. For both articles, what Nairn calls the 'curse of rurality' seems to be the determinant explanation for conservatism and violence in Irish society, and Ireland's entry into the European Union is undialectically conceived in each case as an unequivocal moment of emancipation. Nairn's thesis that the upsurge of ethno-nationalist violence around the globe in recent decades can be traced to 'the spell of rurality' displays a remarkable lack of interest in issues of imperialism and state oppression in many of these regions.

critical understanding of the various forms of subaltern social struggles largely written out of the dominant modes of Irish historiography, whether in bourgeois nationalist or revisionist versions.[15]

For a variety of reasons, then, the applicability of postcolonial studies to the understanding of Irish culture and society, and the question as to whether Ireland was or was not a colony, have never been 'purely' scholarly or academic issues. Methodological differences, different disciplinary protocols and practices, and extra-academic political ideologies and allegiances all came into contentious, and sometimes confused and confusing, play with each other on this issue. For some, to use the word 'colonial' in an Irish context in recent decades has been tantamount to giving intellectual succour to the Provisional IRA; for others, the word emphasized only the negative aspects of Ireland's relationship to the United Kingdom at a time when it was important to build new and better relations with that state. The terms 'colonial' and 'postcolonial' also seemed to controvert the idea, shared by nearly all political parties in the South especially, that Irish people should forget the past and get on with integrating themselves into European mainstream culture where their future now lay. Differences about whether or not Ireland should be regarded as a colony do not tidily organize themselves along conventional 'right' and 'left' fault-lines and render the ensuing controversies more intricate and acrimonious, even if not always more enlightening. It is against this complex socio-political and intellectual-methodological background that any attempt to weigh questions about Ireland's colonial status must be evaluated.

2

The question about Ireland's colonial status can be posed and inflected in a variety of ways. For some critics, the essential question is whether Ireland can legitimately be considered a colony just like Britain's other overseas possessions. For others, the more pressing issue is whether colonialism played a significant role or not in Irish historical development and in what periods (if any) its significance was most consequential. Does the situation in Northern Ireland, for example, represent the continued salience of a colonial dimension in Irish politics or has colonialism long since ceased to be relevant to contemporary matters? If colonialism has actually left any substantive socio-cultural legacies in its wake, what form do they take and how are they to be addressed?[16]

---

15 This aspect of the postcolonial studies project is developed most forcefully by David Lloyd in 'Regarding Ireland in a Postcolonial Frame' and 'Outside History: Irish New Histories and the "Subalternity Effect"'; both essays are in *Ireland After History*.

16 This essay was completed prior to the publication of Stephen Howe's *Ireland and Empire: Colonial Legacies in Irish History and Culture* (Oxford, 2000). Since any substantive engagement with Howe's study would require a separate essay in its own right, this will not be attempted here. The most comprehensive review of Irish scholarship on the colonial question to date, Howe's book has been widely welcomed by revisionist critics especially as a decisive critique of Irish postcolonial studies. While it does usefully critique some of the

For sceptics, the contention that the Irish historical experience resembles that of other colonized countries is simply a species of auto-exoticism with little conceptual merit. Three key objections to the conception of Irish history in colonial terms are consistently cited. The first is that the Irish situation is much more usefully compared to those of other Western European societies, especially to other small peripheral societies dominated by more powerful neighbours, than it is to those of colonized societies in more distant quarters of the globe. In geographic, religious, racial, cultural and economic terms — so this argument runs — Ireland was always an intrinsic part of Western Europe. Hence attempts to consider its historical development in terms of non-European colonized countries tend inevitably to eclipse the intricate network of connections that bind Ireland to its immediate geo-cultural locale. This line of argument has essentially to do with propinquity: its operative assumption is that countries tend inevitably to be shaped by developments in their immediate environs and that Western Europe thus provides the appropriate, indeed inevitable, framework for any comparative analysis of Irish society.[17]

more tendentious arguments about Ireland's colonial status, Howe's overall grasp of contemporary Irish cultural theory is weak and many of his arguments about Irish nationalism, which are heavily indebted to revisionist scholarship in the first instance, are quite debatable. Moreover, revisionists who dispute the whole idea that Ireland can be considered a colony in any sense will hardly find much comfort for their own positions in Howe's conclusion that Ireland has had: 'A colonial past, then, yes; though one that took unique hybrid forms, involving extensive integration and consensual partnership as well as exploitation and coercion. And only as part, and not on all levels the dominant part, of an extremely complex and unusual set of legacies shaping the historical present' (232). The circularity and shadow-boxing inherent in this mode of argument should be evident. As the present essay will indicate, many colonial situations could be characterized as 'hybrid forms'; there is nothing aberrant or unique about this and, therefore, to say that Ireland was a colonial hybrid is not to say very much one way or the other. Nearly every mode of colonial power also involved elements of co-operation and 'consensual partnership' on behalf of some sections of the colonized peoples; there is nothing specifically Irish about this either, though the way the sentence highlights the matter seems to infer that this was at least somehow unusual. Colonialism by definition also implies some form of 'integration' of colony and metropole; perhaps Howe wishes to suggest that the degree of integration was exceptional in the Irish case. But even were this the case, and it probably was, then it would not thereby follow that the consequences of integration were any less 'colonial' — indeed, the most successful modes of colonialism might well be those where the colonized society is disaggregated to the degree that very little of it remains intact and 'integration' into the colonizing society on the latter's own terms is the only option left to the 'natives'. Finally, in no colonial situation, even in undisputed instances like those of India or Africa, would one argue that colonialism was the whole story or, as Howe puts it, more than 'only as part, and not on all levels the dominant part' of the historical legacies shaping the present. In sum, the effect of Howe's passage is to suggest that Ireland can be considered colonial only in a highly qualified sense, but what he says of Ireland might be said of many (if not indeed all) colonies. In passages such as this, Howe seems implicitly to assume some 'classical' colonial situation to which Ireland fails to correspond, even though, elsewhere in the study, he dismisses the idea that there is some 'classical' colonial model.

17 The objection based on ideas of physical propinquity is developed in Barnard, 'Crisis of Identity Among Irish Protestants 1641–1685', 43. The emphasis on propinquity in Irish studies displays a conceptual indebtedness to 'area studies' modes of scholarship.

A second objection is that Irish nationalists seldom conceived of their historical experience in colonial terms and even more rarely identified their own situation with that of other non-European colonized peoples in Asia and Africa or elsewhere. It is argued that the terminology of 'colonialism' and 'imperialism' did not appear in Irish nationalist or unionist discourse until comparatively recent times, and that those opposed to British rule in Ireland used instead the political languages derived from their immediate European surrounds. The language of Irish dissent to British rule, that is, was coded variously in the languages of Jacobitism, of English radicalism and French republicanism and was even shaped by anti-slavery and abolitionist discourses that dominated European politics at specific historical moments. Only rarely was it coded in a specifically anti-colonial vocabulary. It is also argued that where Irish nationalists before the twentieth century did locate Ireland within a wider imperial frame, they tended in the main to compare their situation with those of white settler peoples in the British Empire, not with those of the indigenous peoples. Thus, for example, Irish nationalists writing in the *Nation* in the early nineteenth century frequently drew analogies between their own situation and that of French Catholics in British Canada, not with that of the native Canadians. Similarly, at the start of the twentieth century, many Irish nationalists sympathized with the revolt of the Dutch Boers against British imperialism in South Africa but not with the struggles of native African peoples in the region.

A third objection is that not only did the Irish usually fail to identify with the subaltern indigenous peoples of the British Empire, but that they were in effect, like the Scots, enthusiastic co-partners and beneficiaries in the British imperial enterprise. The massive emigration from Ireland to colonies such as Australia, Canada and New Zealand and the country's significance as a supplier of manpower to the British imperial military machine as well as its extended contribution to the Catholic missionary enterprise in Latin America, Asia and Africa are usually cited to support this argument. Given its involvement in such enterprises, 'then surely Ireland,' Thomas Bartlett has queried, 'so far from being a colony, should be considered a mother country in her own right?'[18] From this perspective, even if not formally an imperial metropole like Britain, France, the Netherlands, Belgium, Portugal or Spain, Ireland nevertheless shares more in common with these adjacent colonizing powers than it does with the colonized peoples of the European empires.

All of these arguments carry some weight and collectively they serve as useful reminders of the dangers of facile identifications between Ireland and 'Third World' colonial situations. But none constitutes a decisive objection to the proposition that Ireland was a colony. I will deal with the question of Ireland's place within Europe here; the other objections will be engaged later in the essay. With regard to the issue

---

18 These objections are succinctly outlined in Thomas Bartlett, '"What Ish My Nation?": Themes in Irish History, 1550–1850', in Thomas Bartlett et al., eds., *Irish Studies: A General Introduction* (Dublin, 1988), 44–59, 47. See also Tom Dunne, 'New Histories, Beyond "Revisionism"', *The Irish Review*, 12 (1992), 1–12.

of location, it is important to note that the thesis that Ireland was a British colony does not at all rest on the assumption that the country was somehow, culturally or otherwise, 'outside' of Europe and hence part of the 'Third World'.[19] It is transparently the case that the major intellectual and cultural transformations that have shaped Western Europe — the Reformation and Counter-Reformation, the Enlightenment, French republicanism and German Romanticism, ultramontane Catholicism, European literary modernism, among them — have also exercised a decisive role in the development of Irish society. For those who would contend that Ireland was a colony, however, what matters is that these wider European currents were mediated through a society that was in its structural composition — class and ethnic relations, land tenure systems, relationship with England, and so on — objectively colonial in character.

In a classic essay, 'Misplaced Ideas', the Brazilian cultural critic Roberto Schwarz discusses what he describes as the besetting 'experience of incongruity' that continually obsesses commentators on Brazilian society.[20] Schwarz's attempt to account for this 'experience of incongruity' centres on a contrast between the ideological function of liberal ideas in Europe (their location of origin) and Brazil (one of their places of adoption). In Europe, he suggests, liberal ideology was the expression of a triumphant bourgeoisie in its successful struggle against the *ancien régime*. In Brazil, where the fundamental productive relationship in the nineteenth century continued to be based on slavery, an ideology that proclaimed the autonomy of the individual, the equality of all men, the universality of the law and the disinterest of culture was patently out of place. For Schwarz, an ideology is 'in place' when it constitutes an abstraction of the social processes to which it refers. In Europe, liberal ideology constituted, therefore, an abstraction of industrial capitalism; the import of liberal ideas to Brazil, however, created a situation where these ideas were put to work in a social order of a very different kind. The contrast between, on the one hand, the material realities of the slave trade, economic dependency, and a political system based on clientilism and favour and, on the other, a liberal discourse that proclaimed universal equality before the law and the virtues of the impersonal state, created an effect of ill-assortedness, dissonance and distortion. This distortion, Schwarz contends, contributed simultaneously to the debasement of Brazilian intellectual life and to an almost reflex scepticism where matters of ideology were concerned, since the disjunction between ideology and material reality was so vast. According to Schwarz, then, the 'experience of incongruity' that obsesses commentators on Brazil ought not to be construed in terms of a clash between European 'modernity'

19 See, for example, Longley, *The Living Stream*, 30.
20 Roberto Schwarz, 'Misplaced Ideas', in *Misplaced Ideas: Essays on Brazilian Culture*, edited with an introduction by John Gledson (London, 1992), 19–32, 25. My reading of Schwarz's essay has been informed by several commentaries. See especially Adriana Johnson's 'Reading Roberto Schwarz: Outside Out-of-Place Ideas', *Journal of Latin American Cultural Studies*, 8, 1 (1999), 21–33, and Neil Larsen, 'Brazilian Critical Theory and the Question of Cultural Studies', in his *Reading North by South: On Latin American Literature, Culture and Politics* (Minneapolis, 1995), 205–16. See also the comments by Francis Mulhern in *The Present Lasts a Long Time*, 159–60.

and Brazilian 'backwardness', nor explained away by a poststructuralist relativism that assumes that the real problem has to do with the inadequacies of the European sciences and methodologies and not with Brazilian reality itself. Instead, that experience must ultimately be attributed to the constitutive paradox of the Brazilian social order: a local slave-owning latifundist economy structurally integrated on a dependent basis into the 'liberal' capitalist world economy.

From a postcolonialist perspective, Irish history discloses a constitutive paradox of a rather similar kind. The suggestion is not, patently, that nineteenth-century Ireland was like nineteenth-century Brazil. What is suggested, rather, is that although Ireland belonged to the same geo-cultural locale, the same orbit of capital, as the major European imperial powers, it was integrated into that orbit of capital in a very different way to its main European neighbours. Those who contend that Western Europe represents the appropriate comparative framework for the evaluation of Irish society assume an essentially homologous relationship between the country's spatial location, its socio-economic composition, and its cultural dynamics. Conceived in this way, differences between Ireland and Europe are invariably structured by the conceptual couplet of 'backwardness' and 'advance'. The postcolonialist perspective, in contrast, suspends the notion that geography, economy and culture are all neatly homologous with each other, and attempts to investigate the *discrepant* ways in which Irish political and cultural life, which were obviously shaped and textured by wider European developments, were at the same time overdetermined by the country's dependent socio-economic composition. Contrary to what its critics would claim, then, postcolonial studies is neither misplaced nor out of place in Irish circumstances. On the contrary, it might be argued, following Schwarz, that an obsessive 'experience of incongruity' — occasioned by the fact that dependent cultures are always interpreting their own realities with intellectual methodologies created and validated somewhere else and whose bases lie in other social processes — is indeed a typical characteristic of postcolonial societies.[21]

In an insightful survey essay, Joseph Ruane has demonstrated that a *theoretical haziness* about whether or not Ireland should be considered a colony extends across all the major disciplines within the Irish academy. Discussing Irish historiography, Ruane notes that colonial themes have been paramount in the writings of historians of the late medieval period in Ireland, covering such topics as the coming of the Anglo-Normans, the displacement of the native Gaelic lordships, the introduction of English concepts of sovereignty and legality, and so forth. In the case of early modern Ireland, colonial themes continue to occupy a central place in the historical literature. The arrival of new classes of British settlers in the Tudor, Cromwellian and Williamite conquests, the massive confiscation of lands by the settlers and the displacement of native élites of both Irish and Old English descent, the deliberate destruction of Gaelic society and the opening up of the economy to capitalist accumulation, as well as the perception of the

21 Schwarz, 'Beware of Alien Ideologies', in *Misplaced Ideas*, 33–40, 39

Gaelic Irish as wild and uncivilized, have encouraged many historians to use the language of colonialism to characterize developments in this period. Ruane notes, however, that the analytical model that governs Irish historical writing alters quite dramatically for the nineteenth and twentieth centuries: the language of colonialism suddenly drops from mainstream historiography at this juncture 'without explicit justification or discussion' to be replaced by the language of 'modernization'.[22] For many historians, he comments, the Act of Union in 1801 puts a remarkably speedy end (apparently by the magic wand of parliamentary statute) to whatever colonial features may have existed in Irish society over previous centuries.[23]

Given Ireland's location within Europe, its geographical distance from other British colonies, and its integration into the United Kingdom, it is scarcely surprising that some scholars have attempted to settle the controversial issues involved by way of various 'intermediate' solutions. These generally work from the assumption that Ireland's experience was colonial to some degree but that it was always 'anomalous' or 'atypical' and hence by inference too 'exceptional' to be usefully considered alongside the overseas colonies. Hence while some will allow that the Irish experience of British rule may share some similarities with that of other acknowledged colonies, the differences are ultimately held to weigh more heavily than any similarities. Alternatively, it has also been proposed

22 Joseph Ruane, 'Colonialism and the Interpretation of Irish Historical Development', in M. Silverman and P. H. Gulliver, eds., *Approaching the Past: Historical Anthropology Through Irish Case Studies* (New York, 1992), 293–323, 318. Ruane's essay offers a comprehensive overview of the treatment of the colonial theme in Irish studies across a range of disciplines, including history, geography, sociology, economics and political science. For subsequent comments, see also Joseph Ruane, 'Ireland, European Integration, and the Dialectic of Nationalism and Postnationalism', *Études Irlandaises*, 19, 1 (1994), 183–93, and 'Colonial Legacies and Cultural Reflexivities', *Études Irlandaises*, 19, 2 (1994), 107–19.

23 The question as to whether Ireland should be considered a colony or a small European nation has a great deal to do with the categorization of Irish nationalism. For those who doubt the validity of the colonial model, Irish national struggles are better considered in terms of those of other Western or Central European movements such as Young Italy or Hungarian or Polish nationalism rather than in terms of movements in the 'Third World'. David Lloyd has observed that there are compelling arguments on either side of this debate, but it is the dichotomy between 'Europe' and the 'Third World' that subtends this controversy that must ultimately be queried. David Lloyd, 'Outside History: Irish New Histories and the "Subalternity Effect"', in Shahid Amin and Dipesh Chakrabarty, eds., *Subaltern Studies IX* (New Delhi, 1996), 261–80, 262. When contemporary scholars of whatever hue discuss colonialism they invariably refer to British, French and Iberian *overseas colonies* in Asia, Africa and Latin America. The great Habsburg, Ottoman and Tsarist Russian European *land empires* that stretched from Siberia across Central Europe to the Middle East until World War I are routinely passed over in silence. A lack of comparative research makes it difficult to say whether or how the practices developed by these land empires differed and in what ways to those developed in the overseas colonies of maritime empires. Whether or not a territory was geographically contiguous to the dominating power or a distant overseas possession does not seem the decisive issue. From a materialist standpoint, the fact that the Western European maritime empires (England, France, Holland) that eventually displaced the older Iberian empires were advanced capitalist countries, while the Central and Eastern European land empires were much less so, seems more important. Were the modern European land empires to be taken into account, then the either/or compartmentalization that structures debates as to whether the nineteenth-century Irish experience was closer to that of Europe or the so-called 'Third World' might be less compelling.

that Ireland should be considered an example of 'internal colonialism' whereby England came to dominate the Celtic peripheries as distinct from its overseas colonial enterprises. Neither of these intermediate 'solutions' is theoretically compelling. The conception of Ireland as somehow anomalous or exceptional rests on the untenable assumption that there is such a thing as a standard colonial experience, a classic colonial order of things replicated almost everywhere across the world, while the concept of internal colonialism depends on a categorical distinction between geographically contiguous and overseas colonization processes that has never adequately been theorized.[24]

If matters are to be advanced beyond the controversies that have attended the initial emergence of postcolonial studies in Irish scholarship, it is imperative to understand that the issue about whether Ireland can be considered a colony can be posed on two *analytically* discrete levels that require different methods of investigation: one that has to do essentially with matters of consciousness, systems of representation and discursive régimes; the other with 'objective' structural and socio-cultural correspondences — though of course ultimately the relationship between these two 'levels' also needs to be theorized. This essay will deal briefly with both levels individually, setting aside for the present the more complex question of their mediation. In doing so, it will work with the hypothesis or proposition that Ireland was indeed a colony and that there are compelling arguments to support this case. However, its objective is not to 'prove' that it was so, but rather to consider some of the theoretical matters that need to be addressed if the colonial question is to be advanced in some reasonably satisfactory way. As Ruane has rightly observed, comparativist studies in the Irish humanities are poorly developed, and neither those who advocate that Ireland is best compared to its smaller European neighbours nor those who propose a colonial framework of analysis have conducted much comparative research to substantiate their cases.[25] In the absence of extensive comparative research of these kinds, it would be premature to leap to conclusions; the priority of this essay, therefore, is to elucidate some of the ways in which a comparativist colonial research agenda might be constructed and developed.

On the first level, when we ask, 'Was Ireland a colony?', the question that is essentially being posed is: To what extent did those charged with British government in Ireland, as well as Irish nationalists, unionists and others, consciously consider the Irish situation a colonial one? Since British rule in Ireland extended over several centuries, during which time the British Empire changed dramatically in economic character and geographical composition, and since conceptions of empire and colonialism also changed from one epoch to another, what is called for here is a very challenging kind of intellectual history:

---

24 The argument that Ireland's constitutional circumstances makes it an 'anomaly' is asserted in Brady and Gillespie, *Natives and Newcomers*, 17. The concept of Ireland as 'internal colony' is developed in Michael Hechter, *Internal Colonialism: The Celtic Fringe in British National Development, 1536–1966* (London, 1975). For a succinct critique of Hechter's work, see William N. Sloan, 'Ethnicity or Imperialism? A Review Article', *Comparative Studies in Society and History*, 21, 1 (1979), 113–25.

25 Ruane, 'Colonialism and the Interpretation of Irish Historical Development', 318

one capable of tracing the shifting ways in which the various British governing classes, Irish political élites and insurgent social movements conceived of the Irish situation over an extended period of time. Whereas most historiography, imperialist, nationalist and post-nationalist, has focused on the more élite classes competing for position within the state — in other words, privileging those classes that leave behind the most extensive written archives — postcolonial studies has shown greater interest than most in the histories and structures of feelings of those subaltern classes and organizations that were more difficult to conscript into state-and-nation-building movements. Even so, the task of reconstructing the ways in which the more subaltern sectors of society viewed their situation is a difficult one, and a great deal of work remains to be done in this area. While the value of a history of *mentalités* and systems of representation of this sort can hardly be questioned, some caveats need to be entered. As mentioned earlier, it is commonly argued that Ireland cannot be considered a colony at some or other stage because the Irish did not deploy the language of colonialism and that opposition to British domination was coded instead in the language of tyranny and denied citizenship or argued on the constitutional grounds that the country was a separate kingdom. The difficulty with this line of argument, as David Lloyd has pointed out, is that it assumes already the historical development of a concept whose full range of meanings emerged only gradually through the nineteenth and twentieth centuries.[26] The fact that 'peasants' in late medieval England, Spain or Russia did not consciously think of themselves as oppressed by a 'feudal' social system does nothing to diminish the theoretical value of the term 'feudalism'. For the same reason, the objective theoretical value of the term 'colonialism', which historically emerges as a conceptual rationalization of European overseas rule and only later as part of a wider oppositional critique of that enterprise, can never be made to rest solely on the subjective consciousness or the available political rhetorics of the colonized.

The argument that eighteenth- and early nineteenth-century Irish nationalists looked mostly to the white settler colonies to highlight their own grievances, and less so to the indigenous native peoples of America or Africa or wherever, also needs to be weighed in this context. It is often forgotten that in the period between the eighteenth and the late nineteenth century (perhaps even later) the most difficult struggles of the European imperialist metropoles were not for the most part with the native peoples in their colonies but with their own white settlers.[27] The transformations of the whole structure of the contemporary capitalist world system as a consequence of Britain's disputes with her restive white setters in North America and Spain's with her creole populations in South America in the late eighteenth century testify to the world-systemic significance of such conflicts. In other words, the earliest and most successful anti-colonial nationalisms

---

26 Lloyd, *Ireland After History*, 7
27 See Arghiri Emmanuel, 'White-Settler Colonialism and the Myth of Investment Imperialism', *New Left Review*, 73 (1972), 35–57. Emmanuel does not mention some significant exceptions such as the slave rebellion in Haiti or the so-called Great Indian Mutiny.

were those of the white settlers and creole populations in the Americas and, given the wider global significance of such movements, it is not particularly surprising that their influence was most acutely registered in Ireland at the time. The fact that many prominent Irish nationalists — John Mitchel and Arthur Griffith are frequently cited cases — considered it outrageous that Ireland should be treated as a colony, because to do so was to put an ancient and civilized European people on the same level as non-white colonial subjects in Africa or Asia, is well established. Numerous examples of Irish nationalists — such as Michael Davitt or Patrick Ford — who did identify the Irish predicament with that of non-white colonized peoples can always be produced to counter the examples of those who did not. But to try to determine the ratio of those individuals who did and who did not is only to compound the conceptual confusion and futile point-scoring inherent in this whole mode of argument. The extent to which *some* versions of anti-colonial nationalism (throughout the world and not just in Ireland, as some Irish revisionists seem fondly to imagine) assimilate and replicate elements of the racist and imperialist mentalities they set out to oppose is a well-developed theme in postcolonial studies, and Irish nationalism in this and other respects thus shows the conventional limits of nationalism as an oppositional discourse. Yet the fact that some Irish nationalists or some versions of Irish nationalism were capable of only a very limited and conservative critique of British imperialism is not in itself an argument that Ireland was not a colony. Were the class-consciousness and solidarity of the oppressed not something that has continuously to be struggled for, educated and directed, rather than something that automatically attends the subaltern condition, then oppression would not be the problem it is in the first instance.

If the concept of colonialism has a theoretical value that cannot be reduced to the subjective consciousness of the colonizer or the colonized, this might well beg the question as to why it matters at all whether either the Irish or the British conceived of Ireland in colonial terms. Even if some British administrators or some Irish nationalists discerned parallels between the situation in Ireland and that in various British colonies, this obviously does not establish that the actual conditions were indeed always commensurable. Nevertheless, these things do matter, since, as Luke Gibbons has argued, it is always the case that understanding communities or cultures does not consist solely in establishing 'neutral' facts and 'objective' details: 'it means taking seriously their ways of structuring experience, their popular narratives, the distinctive manner in which they frame the social and political realities which affect their lives'.[28] Once it is allowed that language and culture are the spheres through which conflicts are experienced and evaluated, then it is clear that the attempt to trace the shifting ways in which Ireland was conceived in relation to other parts of the colonial world does have its own intrinsic historical value and scholarly interest. There is now also a steadily accumulating body of work that attempts to trace the shifting mentalities and

28 Gibbons, Introduction in *Transformations in Irish Culture*, 17

ideologies of settlement and resistance in sixteenth- and seventeenth-century Ireland.[29] A good deal of this scholarship is centred (no doubt disproportionately) on the writings of Edmund Spenser, but the range of materials covered is constantly expanding.[30] For the post-Union period, the parallels between British attitudes to Ireland and India in the nineteenth century are discussed by Scott B. Cook, while Perry Curtis's and R. N. Lebow's books on the racialized constructions of the Irish in British and American popular culture in the Victorian period are important contributions to any understanding of nineteenth-century attitudes towards the Irish.[31] To date at least, the scholarly material on the subject of colonialism is concentrated overwhelmingly on English language sources. The historical response of the subaltern Gaelic community to British rule in Ireland is consequently still seriously underresearched, though Joep Leerssen's work and especially Breandán Ó Buachalla's *Aisling Ghéar* represent pioneering attempts to excavate this material.[32] The kinds of scholarship referred to here clearly suggest that

29 Some important book-length studies on the representational systems that shaped British rule in Ireland and Irish responses to that rule lend considerable support to the idea that the Irish situation can usefully be viewed within the wider context of European colonization and imperialism. Much of the most valuable work on this issue concentrates on the early modern period. For its scope and authority, Nicholas Canny's work on how Ireland's colonial experience in the Tudor and Stuart period was of a piece with the greater European westward colonial thrust at the time, represents the outstanding contribution in the field. In a suggestive work of historical jurisprudence, *The American Indian in Western Legal Thought* (Oxford, 1993), Robert A. Williams Jr. has also argued that Elizabethan colonial projects in Ireland drew extensively upon Spanish colonial doctrine in the Americas. More recently, valuable studies in the early modern period, notably those of Clare Carroll and Patricia Palmer, have extended this kind of research in new directions, examining the ways in which discourses of civility and barbarism in sixteenth- and seventeenth-century Ireland were developed in dialogue with, and sometimes shaped, parallel sets of discourses then being fashioned by English and other European powers in the New World. See Clare Carroll, *Circe's Cup: Cultural Transformations in Early Modern Ireland* (Cork, 2001) and Patricia Palmer, *Language and Conquest in Early Modern Ireland: English Renaissance Literature and Elizabethan Imperial Expansion* (Cambridge, 2001).

30 On Spenser, see Anne Fogarty, ed., *Special Issue: Spenser in Ireland: The Faerie Queene 1596–1996*, Irish University Review, 26, 2 (1996); Andrew Hadfield, *Edmund Spenser's Irish Experience: Wilde Fruit and Salvage Soyl* (Oxford, 1997); Christopher Highley, *Shakespeare, Spenser and the Crisis in Ireland* (Cambridge, 1997); and Willy Maley, *Salvaging Spenser: Colonialism, Culture and Identity* (London, 1997). For works that look beyond Spenser, see Brendan Bradshaw et al., eds., *Representing Ireland: Literature and the Origins of the Conflict, 1534–1660* (Cambridge, 1993) and the anthology of travel writing edited by Andrew Hadfield and John McVeigh, *Strangers to that Land: British Perceptions of Ireland from the Reformation to the Famine* (Gerrards Cross, 1994).

31 Scott B. Cook, *Imperial Affinities: Nineteenth Century Analogies and Exchanges between Ireland and India* (New Delhi and London, 1993); L. Perry Curtis Jr., *Apes and Angels: The Irishman in Victorian Caricature*, rev. edn. (Washington and London, 1997); R. N. Lebow, *White Britain and Black Ireland: The Influence of Stereotypes on Colonial Policy* (Philadelphia, 1979). See also Tadhg Foley and Sean Ryder, eds., *Ideology and Ireland in the Nineteenth Century* (Dublin, 1998) and Keith Jeffery, ed., *'An Irish Empire?': Aspects of Ireland and the British Empire* (Manchester, 1996). Other useful analyses of nineteenth-century discourse include Angela Bourke, *The Burning of Bridget Cleary: A True Story* (London, 1999) and David Cairns and Shaun Richards, 'Discourses of Opposition and Resistance in Late Nineteenth- and Early Twentieth-Century Ireland', Text & Context, 2, 1 (1988), 76–84.

32 Joep Leerssen, *Mere Irish and Fíor-Ghael: Studies in the Idea of Irish Nationality, its Development and Literary Expression prior to the Nineteenth Century*, rev. edn. (Cork, 1996); Breandán Ó Buachalla, *Aisling Ghéar: Na Stíobhartaigh agus an tAos Léinn, 1703–1788* (Baile Átha Cliath, 1996)

connections between Ireland and other colonial sites were a reasonably consistent feature of both British administrative and Irish oppositional discourses. What is still much less well established, though, is the extent to which discursive identifications between the Irish and other colonial situations remained scattered, opportunistic and unsystematic or to what degree, or at what moments especially, they acquired systematic force. The shifting trajectories and mutations of such discourses as they are transformed over the longer term from one historical epoch to another also remain unmapped. An authoritative genealogy of the discourses of British rule in Ireland from the early modern period to the twentieth century, and of the discourses of Irish response and resistance to such rule, is something that has yet to be achieved.

3

Discourses that construe Ireland in colonial terms help us to understand how political agents and communities structured their own experience, but no historical materialist could be content to pose the question 'Was Ireland a colony?' simply at the level of systems of representation. To do so would be to allow a one-sided concern with semiotics and matters of ideology and political consciousness to dispose with the question of deciding whether or not the putative correspondences between Ireland and other colonies are compelling as an explanatory historical framework. For this reason, the question must also be posed at a level that tries to determine if there are compelling or illuminating socio-cultural correspondences or similarities between Ireland and other colonial situations. But this immediately leads to the question: With which colonies and with what kinds of colonial processes elsewhere might the Irish situation productively be compared? Naïve objections to the proposal that the Irish historical experience can be considered a colonial one, often assume that there is such a thing as a typical colony and a standard or one-size-fits-all colonial experience against which Ireland's claims might be weighed and measured. The real difficulty, on the contrary, is that colonial practices, structures and conditions around the globe have been of the most varied and heterogeneous kinds. The sheer diversity of lands that comprised the British Empire alone has caused scholars to question whether any substantive similarities between colonial polities can be deduced, and some have even queried whether the term 'colonialism' itself has any analytical value.[33] To avoid surrender to such positivism, which reduces everything to a catalogue of disconnected singularities, Irish studies might do well to devote more attention to the task of generating a serviceable historicized typology of colonies.

The conservative historian of empire D. K. Fieldhouse and George Fredrickson, an American comparative sociologist of race relations, have divided overseas colonies into

---

33 See Robert J. Hind, '"We Have No Colonies" — Similarities within the British Imperial Experience', *Comparative Studies in Society and History*, 26 (1984), 3–35.

four categories: administrative, plantation, mixed settlement and pure settlement.[34] Though often the most prized imperial possessions, administrative colonies aimed at military, economic and administrative control of a politically strategic region and were never settled by Europeans on a mass scale. What usually destined a particular region to be an administrative colony rather than one of the settler types, Fredrickson suggests, was the presence of a dense, settled, agricultural population with a complex social and economic system, considerable military capacity, and relative immunity to the diseases of European origin of the kind that wreaked demographic havoc on the native peoples of the New World. Where such factors obtained, European conquest would normally be difficult and costly and little land was readily available for white settlement. Hence, once they had attained dominance in the region, the European powers could economically benefit most by extracting economic surplus or valuable mineral resources from these lands without systematically destroying their traditional societies. Colonial control in such instances could best be exercised by means of indirect rule exercised by co-opting indigenous élites or by newly constructed colonial bureaucracies staffed by European administrators and civil servants, or by way of some combination of the two. This category includes the colonies of South Asia as well as most of Africa and the Middle East.

In contrast to the administrative colonies, where power was exercised through a relatively small, sojourning group of primarily male European administrators, settlement colonies were characterized by much larger settler European populations of both sexes whose intentions were for permanent settlement. These fall into three general types. Plantation colonies usually attracted relatively small numbers of white settlers, but these acquired large tracts of land, found that the indigenous population did not meet their labour needs, and imported a slave or indentured and usually non-European labour force to work the mono-cultural plantations. In the plantation colonies, the mode of economic production rested essentially on the forced labour of imported workers to produce specialized staples for the world market. The paradigmatic instances in this case are the mono-cultural plantations in the West Indies and in the southern region of the United States.[35]

In the mixed settlement colonies, of which the clearest examples are the highland societies of Latin America, the indigenous peoples were not annihilated. Still, the Iberian settler culture and social structures nonetheless became dominant. When Europeans first intruded, these regions already had large populations and complex sedentary societies. But the drastic losses suffered by the native population as a result of epidemics,

34 D. K. Fieldhouse, *The Colonial Empires: A Comparative Survey from the Eighteenth Century* (London, 1965), 7–13; George Fredrickson, *The Arrogance of Race: Historical Perspectives on Slavery, Racism and Social Inequality* (Middletown, 1985), 216–35. My own taxonomy borrows heavily from Fredrickson's reworking of Fieldhouse's scholarship. For another attempt at a typology, see Jürgen Osterhammel, *Colonialism: A Theoretical Overview*, trans. Shelley L. Frisch (Princeton, 1997), 10–12.

35 On the plantation colonies, see Philip D. Curtin, *The Rise and Fall of the Plantation Complex: Essays in Atlantic History* (Cambridge, 1990) and David Watts, *The West Indies: Patterns of Development, Culture and Environmental Change since 1492* (Cambridge, 1987).

warfare and brutal exploitation allowed the European settlers, Fredrickson suggests, to monopolize control of the land and to replace native political and cultural institutions with their own. Though the racial and class strata that emerged in such situations were typically very complex, miscegenation normally occurred and gave rise to racially mixed groups that served as buffers between those of settler and indigenous descent. Labour was exploited in such situations usually by way of coercive landlord–peasant relationships — with the indigenous peasantry left in place but required to pay tribute to European landlords or political authorities in the form of labour or commodities.[36]

In the pure settlement colonies, of which the United States, Canada and Australia are the exemplary instances, the native peoples were either exterminated altogether or their remnants pushed onto reservations in remote or unproductive regions. European exploitation in these regions did not take the form of the coercion of native labour. Instead, an expanding settler frontier was constantly pushed back as the indigenous peoples were displaced to make way for new waves of settlers. The North American and Australian colonial economies of this kind depended in their initial phases on indentured or bonded labour and even at later stages cheap 'coolie' labour from Asia especially continued to play a major role in their development. But because land in such instances was usually relatively cheap by contemporary European standards, and labour consequently comparatively expensive, the pure settlement economies were not structured in terms of the 'feudal' tenurial systems that characterized mixed settlement and plantation colonies, where a small landed oligarchy dominated peasant masses. Instead, farmer-settlement and free white labour became the social dominant. Because of the rigid social separation between settler and displaced native and comparatively low levels of miscegenation, these societies usually became homogeneously European in cultural character. Nevertheless, since land was cheap and white labour expensive, and because there were fewer inherited institutional restraints than in Europe, these societies were also often less rigidly socially differentiated and considerably more egalitarian — at least for white settlers — than their European counterparts.[37]

Used crudely, typologies such as these can freeze into Weberian ideal types. But they can also be used productively to highlight dominant settlement patterns, economic systems, labour forms, and state structures that emerged in particular colonial situations, and they can be adapted to account for historical transformations within a given colonial situation in response to the larger global mutations of the world capitalist system. Moreover, it is also clear that many colonial situations must be construed as composites or hybrids of the basic types rather than simply as varieties of them. The case of the

36 For overviews of colonial South America, see James Lockhart and Stuart B. Schwarz, *Early Latin America: A History of Colonial Latin America and Brazil* (Cambridge, 1983) and Mark A. Burkholder and Lyman L. Johnson, *Colonial Latin America* (Oxford, 1994).

37 On these issues, see R. Cole Harris, 'The Simplification of Europe Overseas', *Annals of the Association of American Geographers*, 67, 4 (1977), 469–83, and R. Cole Harris and Leonard Guelke, 'Land and Society in Early Canada and South Africa', *Journal of Historical Geography*, 3, 2 (1977), 135–53.

United States, which can be described as a composite of a pure settlement colony in the North and a plantation type in the South, is a case in point — though several other major examples such as South Africa or Palestine might also be mentioned.[38] The chief value of such typologies is that they can help to distinguish the new and varied compositions of land, labour and capital (and the attendant class, racial and cultural relations) that typically emerged and predominated in different colonial situations. As such, they may have at least the potential to take us beyond the ungrounded theoretical abstractions for which postcolonial theory is sometimes rightly criticized.

4

Viewed in this frame, some elements essential to any evaluation of Ireland in comparative colonial context become evident. First, Ireland was systematically colonized on a modern proto-capitalist basis in the early modern period, roughly contemporaneous with the establishment of the Spanish and Portuguese colonies in South America and the English ones in North America. None of the expanding European colonial powers in that period was a stranger to conquest and colonization when it reached the New World: all had been engaged in extensive offshore colonization schemes before undertaking longer-range overseas colonial enterprises. Portugal had already occupied the islands of the Azores and Madeira, and was establishing trading colonies on the coast of West Africa, while Castile had taken the Moorish kingdom of Granada and was completing its conquest of the Canary archipelago. Both Iberian kingdoms had also been engaged for centuries in the struggle to expel the Moors from the Iberian peninsula. Many of the techniques developed to settle and defend great tracts of underpopulated territory, as well as the spirit of religious crusade that inspired this reconquest, were to be carried over in due course to the New World.[39] By the same token, England had been engaged for centuries in various attempts to subjugate Ireland when it established its first colonies in North America. In the sixteenth century efforts to establish comprehensive schemes of plantation by Englishmen in the Gaelic areas of the country were already under way, and Ireland was gradually redefined at this time as a crucial strategic site in the European struggle to control the Atlantic and the New World. In the same period, the island also became what William J. Smyth describes as one of the epic battlegrounds in the struggle between Reformation and Counter-Reformation Europe.[40] For this reason, it has been

---

38 See George M. Fredrickson, *White Supremacy: A Comparative Study in American and South African History* (Oxford, 1988). On Palestine, see Gershon Shafir, *Land, Labor and the Origins of the Israeli–Palestinian Conflict, 1882–1914* (Cambridge, MA, 1989).

39 On these continuities, see Edwin Williamson, *The Penguin History of Latin America* (London, 1992), 55–75.

40 See William J. Smyth, 'Ireland a Colony: Settlement Implications of the Revolution in Military Administrative, Urban and Ecclesiastical Structures, c.1550 to c.1730', in Terry Barry, ed., *A History of Settlement in Ireland* (London, 2000), 158–86.

suggested that religion, not ethnic descent or cultural identity, became the major index that distinguished between colonizer and colonized in early modern Ireland, with the Old English settler-descended communities from the pre-Reformation period ultimately relegated by the New English Protestant arrivals in the early modern period to the same inferior social status as the Gaelic Irish.[41] Because colonial processes change over time, however, the indices that distinguished between colonizer and colonized changed also, and hence the ways in which religion, culture and ethnicity were articulated with each other to demarcate the divide varied considerably from one conjuncture to the next.

The dominant economic system that shaped early modern colonial development was state-regulated merchant capitalism (or mercantilism). Like the West Indies and the American colonies, Ireland in this period underwent an exceptionally violent and accelerated process of colonial modernization in which every aspect of the indigenous society was almost wholly transformed in a very short space of time. All of these colonial sites were commercially oriented towards the emerging Atlantic economy, but imperial mercantilist policy was designed to prevent the colonies from developing independent trading links with each other. Instead, trade had to be channelled through the British and Spanish imperial centres, inhibiting independent economic development and diversification within the colonies over the longer term and thereby establishing the structures that would condition future economic dependence.[42] One of the distinguishing characteristics of the colonial outposts of this emergent Atlantic economy is the velocity of their transition from various forms of pre-capitalist society to mercantile capitalist modernity, without experiencing what Kevin Whelan has called the long conditioning of other medieval European societies.[43] Thus, at the beginning of the seventeenth century, Ireland was a very lightly settled, overwhelmingly pastoral, heavily-wooded country, with a poorly integrated, quasi-autarkic and technologically backward economy. By the end of the century, all that had changed. As it was commercially reoriented to service

41 Raymond Crotty has argued that where religion became the index between colonizer and colonized, it has proved more durable as a mode of social differentiation than race: 'Colonizers and colonized in Ireland were distinguished ... by their religions. The former were Protestant; the latter were Catholic. The inevitable miscegenation between white colonizers and black or brown colonized produced sub-classes of mestizos, mulattos and Eurasians, who occupied the middle ground and eroded in time the sharp distinctions between black/brown and white. But successive generations born in Ireland, whether of mixed parentage or not, were Catholics and Protestants, with no diminution over the centuries of the fine theological distinctions between them.' Crotty, *Ireland in Crisis: A Study in Capitalist Colonial Underdevelopment* (Dingle, 1986), 38. Crotty fails to comment on the ways in which the Catholic Church itself assumed the role of 'middle-man' or 'buffer' between British rulers and Irish masses for much of the nineteenth century. The subject of religion has received little attention in Irish postcolonial studies.

42 Immanuel Wallerstein's *The Modern World System, II, Mercantilism and the Consolidation of the European World-Economy, 1600–1750* (New York, 1980) is the classic study of this development. For an alternative account, which seeks to remedy the theoretical weaknesses in Wallerstein's work and to correct its North European bias, see Giovanni Arrighi, *The Long Twentieth Century: Money, Power, and the Origins of Our Times* (London, 1994).

43 Kevin Whelan, 'Ireland in the World-System 1600–1800', in Hans-Jürgen Nitz, ed., *The Early-Modern World-System in Geographical Perspective* (Stuttgart, 1993), 204–18, 205

the expanding English mercantilist state and concurrently integrated into the world of North Atlantic trade, Ireland, Whelan argues, underwent 'the most rapid transformation in any European seventeenth century economy, society and culture'.[44]

In all the colonial sites that constituted this new Atlantic world this precociously accelerated modernization process was accompanied by what would ultimately appear from the perspective of a more fully developed industrial capitalism, with its 'liberal' emphasis on free labour and free trade, to be apparent economic and legal-juridical 'archaisms'. These include the slave plantations in the West Indies, the southern United States and Brazil; the encomienda and hacienda system in South America; and the oligarchic landed estates system in Ireland — by the nineteenth century the last would be regarded by political economists of all shades as the single greatest impediment to 'proper' capitalist development in the country. In nearly all these situations, moreover, the native populations were subjected for extended periods to legal and political constraints — though these, as might be expected, varied in kind enormously — designed to exclude them from civil and political society and to secure the privileges of the immigrant settler communities. To schematize, then, colonialism in these areas, based on the monopoly of land maintained by state structures controlled by classes mostly of settler origin, was corollary to a globally expanding commercial capitalism and hence all of these economies were deeply integrated into the emergent world capitalist system. But basic productive relationships in all of these situations continued to depend on overwhelmingly rural workforces subjected to various modes of coerced labour.

The discrepancy between the precocious modernity of these colonial societies and the extent of their integration into the emergent capitalist world system, on the one hand, and some of their more 'archaic' *ancien régime* characteristics has generated considerable theoretical controversy among Marxists. One position, associated with the work of Paul Baran, André Gunder Frank and Immanuel Wallerstein, holds that capitalism as a mode of production can be equated with the penetration of capitalist market relations. From this perspective, as capitalism comes into contact with other modes of production through trade, all economic activity is increasingly subordinated to the profit-maximizing imperatives of the market. Hence all essential distinction between the capitalist mode and modes initially outside the capitalist sphere is rapidly eroded and the problem that then poses itself is that of analysing the relationships of unequal exchange that subsequently emerge between capitalist core and periphery. An alternative position, associated with Ernesto Laclau and Robert Brenner, holds that while capitalist expansion is often accompanied by the extension of capitalist class relations, it may also result in the combination of capitalist and non-capitalist modes of production in ways that contribute to underdevelopment. Brenner, for example, contends that capitalist expansion may result in 'merely the interconnection of capitalist with pre-capitalist class forms, and indeed the strengthening of the latter'. Alternatively, it may also lead

---

44 Whelan, 'Ireland in the World-System 1600–1800', 204

to 'the transformation of pre-capitalist class relations, but without their substitution by fully capitalist social-productive relations of free wage labour, in which labour power is a commodity'. For Brenner, accounts such as Wallerstein's, that equate capitalism with the extension of the capitalist market

> fail to take into account either the way in which class structures, once established, will in fact determine the course of economic development or underdevelopment over an entire epoch, or the way in which these class structures themselves emerge: as the outcome of class struggles whose outcomes are incomprehensible in terms merely of market forces.[45]

These different theoretical methodologies point to strikingly different conceptualizations of Irish history. From the first perspective, a hallmark of the Irish economy as it developed in the seventeenth century is the accelerated velocity of its enforced capitalist modernization through conquest and colonization and the extent to which the country is incorporated as a producer of agricultural exports into an emergent Atlantic economy. The sweeping aside of existing feudal custom and moral economy during the successive conquests that displaced the old Gaelic systems is viewed in this context as leading to an unfettered capitalist exploitation of peasant labour in Ireland. Unrestrained by the hereditary rights and established moral economies that conditioned landlord–tenant relationships in Britain, the Irish situation in this view constitutes not a more retarded but rather a less regulated form of capitalism that lacked the customary checks and balances that made its British counterpart more politically stable. Moreover, Ireland's specialized and dependent economy, oriented towards international export, made it more vulnerable to the cyclical vagaries of international markets and this in turn aggravated the political volatility of a region already fissured by colonially-structured ethno-religious cleavages.

From the alternative perspective, which has been argued by Eamonn Slater and Terrence McDonough, the British conquest of Ireland allowed for the creation of a landlord class that controlled the Irish legal and political system to a degree unparalleled in England. In this account, conquest led to the emergence of a kind of bastardized feudalism that allowed the landlords to extract rental payments from tenants by means of extra-economic coercion. Notwithstanding the fact that it was constitutionally integrated into the most advanced industrial capitalist economy of the time, Irish society remained essentially feudal or quasi-feudal in character in this view until the very end of the nineteenth century. It was not, they argue, primarily the dynamics of the capitalist market but rather the development of class struggle within what remained an essentially

---

45 Robert Brenner, 'The Origins of Capitalist Development: A Critique of Neo-Smithian Marxism', *New Left Review*, 104 (1977), 25–92, cited in Eamonn Slater and Terrence McDonough, 'Bulwark of Landlordism and Capitalism: The Dynamics of Feudalism in Nineteenth-Century Ireland', *Research in Political Economy*, 14 (1994), 63–118, 64–65. My account of these Marxist debates rehearses the account offered in Slater and McDonough.

feudal mode of production that eventually propelled the demise of this system. After the late nineteenth-century collapse of landlordism, peasant proprietorship replaced it with a small farmer régime, and only then was the stage set for actual capitalist production in agriculture.[46]

Depending on the theoretical model applied, it is argued then that Ireland either underwent an extremely rapid enforced transition to a form of dependent capitalism constrained within a colonial relationship mediated through London or, alternatively, that it evolved by way of a bastardized variety of colonial feudalism that allowed only for a very late development of capitalism by Western European standards. The differences here do not simply reduce to matters of different chronologies of capitalist development; different conceptions of the character and role of the Irish state are also at issue. Despite such divergence, both models suggest that Irish historical and economic development poses theoretical questions for Marxism that cannot be slotted into the feudalism–absolutism–capitalism sequence usually applied to the core centres of Western European imperialism. Though modern Ireland emerges in the same orbit of capital as the Western European imperial states, its social development and functional role within that orbit seems in crucial respects very different.

What both theoretical models suggest, therefore, is that the assumption that Western Europe constitutes the natural frame of comparative analysis within which Ireland should be located is open to question. The importance of Europe as the source of many of the economic, political, cultural and intellectual stimuli that shaped Irish society is not in doubt here — though these stimuli were also felt, to varying degrees, in all the major colonies of European settlement in the Atlantic world. What a postcolonialist methodology would suggest, though, is that it is the disjunctive way in which these metropolitan influences are articulated in a socio-economic context different to those in which they originally emerged, that constitutes one of the real interests of the Irish situation.

If Ireland is included in the category of settlement colonies as outlined above, then it evidently belongs to a quite limited set of situations where the settler population did not over time become a demographic majority. South Africa (partially settled in the same historical epoch as Ireland was), Algeria, Rhodesia, Kenya and Palestine (all settled in a much later epoch when industrial capitalism had already developed in Europe) are other major examples. As in the South American colonies, in Ireland the native population was not expelled but was retained as a peasant labour force within a land system now almost totally monopolized by the settler élite. But in contrast to South America, where the indigenous Indian population suffered a drastic decline, in Ireland the native population actually increased in the early modern colonial period and remained a demographic majority in most parts of the island except in the north-east.

46 Slater and McDonough, 'Bulwark of Landlordism and Capitalism', 111

The fact that Ireland was a settlement rather than an administration colony is of some significance. Within the administrative colonies, concentrated mostly in Asia and Africa, colonialism did not create new societies by destroying the native élites and installing European ones in their place — instead it intervened to restructure existing 'traditional' societies. Within the system of domination maintained by the colonial state in such cases, two distinct social communities came into contact with each other, but the social distance between the metropolitan rulers who remained a tiny demographic minority and the majority indigenous society was clearly marked. In such instances, the metropolitan society was a mere bridgehead of the metropolis and had no local 'creole' identity. The settler colonies, in contrast, were characterized by a much larger and more socially mixed metropolitan-affiliated population and in such cases the colonist and indigenous societies were more closely intermeshed. In these situations, the settlers became an independent third factor that intervened between the imperial mother-country and the colonized native peoples.

These settler communities were typically engaged throughout their history in a struggle on at least two fronts. On the one side, they were determined to maintain their control over the natives of the occupied territories since these constituted the most immediate threat to their privileged position within the colony; on the other, they also struggled, sometimes violently, against the metropolitan mother-state whenever the latter's trade monopolies threatened their interests or whenever metropolitan policies seemed to favour the natives in ways perceived to jeopardize settler control. On the political plane, the relative weight of the settlers and their capacity to act independently differed widely from one situation to the next, but their structural positions are nonetheless often very similar.[47] Because their relationship and manner of integration into the colonial society was different, settlers defended their position, which was based on immobile property, much more aggressively than administrators did. For this reason, the emancipation of settlement colonies was generally a much more violent and protracted affair than that of their administrative counterparts. For the imperial metropole, the democratization and political independence of a colony did not always threaten its economic control over the region. From the point of view of minority settler communities, however, the same processes would inevitably have much more immediate and drastic consequences since they spelled an end to their monopoly of power within the colonial state.

In Irish nationalist discourse it is regularly asserted that Ireland was the first British colony to win independence, setting an example that India and the other colonies would later follow. The claim has some validity: in his theoretical survey of colonialism, Jürgen Osterhammel states, for example, that '[t]he endorsement of "home rule" in Ireland in 1922 may be regarded as the first major act of colonial liberation of the twentieth century'.[48] Nevertheless, this emphasis on Irish precedence in the twentieth century can

47 See Emmanuel, 'White-Settler Colonialism and the Myth of Investment Imperialism', 39–40.
48 Osterhammel, *Colonialism*, 37

occlude or misconstrue some curiosities of the Irish situation in comparative colonial terms. After all, the twentieth-century decolonizations were only the third phase in the wider territorial dismantling of the European overseas empires. The first wave of decolonization saw the national emancipation of most of the European possessions in the New World between 1776 and 1825.[49] The second wave began in Canada in 1839 and inaugurated the slow transformation of the pure settlement colonies in places such as Australia and New Zealand into *de facto* autonomous states, generally known as 'dominions' within the British Empire after 1907.[50] Since Ireland was colonized during the first phase of European expansion, it might be argued that the real question that calls for explanation is why the development of colonial-settler nationalism in Ireland did not follow the same trajectory as in the American colonies that had their genesis in the same historical epoch. Had this occurred, then Ireland might have been expected to win its independence in the first wave of decolonization when the American colonies all the way from the United States to Argentina, as well as Saint-Dominique in the West Indies, won theirs. The creole nationalisms pioneered in the American colonies constitute, as Benedict Anderson suggests in *Imagined Communities*, the first successful anti-colonial independence movements.[51]

As is well known, an Irish 'patriot' Protestant nationalism did indeed emerge precisely in this period, on cue with that in the other settler colonies. Nevertheless, unlike the movements in the Americas, this nationalism did not succeed in winning independence and, after the 1798 rebellion, Ireland's semi-autonomous colonial parliament was abolished and the country integrated into the British state.[52] Why did Irish settler nationalism falter when its American counterparts prospered? This is not the place to tackle this issue in any depth but some speculative comments may be entertained.

When considering the two situations, one major difference between Ireland and the South American colonies at this time was that Spain was overrun by Napoleon's armies and cut off from naval access to its colonies by British blockade. While Spain could thus offer little support to its colonial loyalists, Britain suffered no such fate and emerged after the Napoleonic Wars as the supreme European power.[53] Spain's weakness in this

49 Decolonization in this instance obviously refers to the political independence of the European settler peoples. Though inadequately enforced, laws had existed under European imperial rule to protect indigenous peoples; so for them and for slave populations in these regions, the severing of links with the metropolitan mother-state usually led to intensified oppression rather than to emancipation.

50 For this periodization, see Osterhammel, *Colonialism*, 37.

51 Benedict Anderson, *Imagined Communities: Reflections on the Origin and Spread of Nationalism*, rev. edn. (London, 1991), 47–65

52 The literature on this period is vast and interpretations diverse. For some important recent contributions, see Thomas Bartlett, 'The Rise and Fall of the Protestant Nation 1690–1800', *Éire-Ireland*, 26 (1991), 7–18; James Kelly, *Prelude to Union: Anglo-Irish Politics in the 1780s* (Cork, 1992); Dáire Keogh, *The French Disease: The Catholic Church and Radicalism in Ireland 1790–1800* (Dublin, 1993); Jim Smyth, *The Men of No Property: Irish Radicals and Popular Politics in the Late Eighteenth Century* (Houndmills, 1992); and Kevin Whelan, *The Tree of Liberty: Radicalism, Catholicism and the Construction of Irish Identity* (Cork, 1996).

53 For a succinct overview of this period in the Spanish colonies, see Burkholder and Johnson, *Colonial Latin*

period must be seen in any case as part of a much longer process of decline whereby it ceded its place as a centre of colonial trade to more successful capitalist imperial rivals. Despite Spanish metropolitan weakness, some of the Hispanic American creole struggles for independence were still constrained by a fear of what would happen if the masses revolted, and in some instances the memory of recent insurrections from below acted as a considerable deterrent to the drive for full autonomy. Creole attitudes were often indecisive and even after they had seized control from the royal governors in several South American capitals after Spain was occupied by Napoleon in 1808 many of the local élites continued to proclaim their loyalty to the Spanish throne. It was only when the Spanish monarchy, restored in 1814, attempted to restore the *status quo* after a period in which the colonies had already enjoyed *de facto* autonomy, that many creoles finally opted for complete independence.[54]

The mixture of creole anxiety concerning the dangers of mass insurrection from below and increasing self-assertiveness in the face of imperial crisis has some suggestive parallels with Irish Protestant nationalism in the same period. The long eighteenth century between 1690 and 1829 is often considered the era of the Protestant nation in Ireland. During this period the Protestants of Ireland became a politically confident class that completely monopolized state power. Throughout the period between 1650 and 1778, however, the Protestant parliament in Dublin had fewer powers than most of the avowedly colonial assemblies in Britain's North American colonies. The American struggle for independence, and its attendant rhetoric of 'democracy' and 'representation' and 'uniting', exerted an enormous impact on Irish Protestant nationalism. In addition, Britain's losses in the American war made it uniquely vulnerable to Irish pressures at that moment. When the American colonies declared themselves independent, 'patriot' members of the Irish parliament, backed up by volunteer militias, managed to have the constitutional relationship between Ireland and England adjusted and, as Thomas Bartlett observes, 'succeeded in giving Ireland for the first time something that looked like an independent parliament'.[55] The experiment was short-lived however. Mounting popular unrest in the aftermath of the French Revolution culminated in the emergence of a more radical republican nationalism determined to sever the link with Britain and committed to establishing an Irish republic that would extend civil and religious liberties to Irish Catholics. The threat posed by the republican rising in 1798 and the dangers of French invasion induced Britain to reassert its control over Ireland. It also persuaded the Protestant interest to surrender the parliamentary independence it had long defended rather than risk the loss of its political control over the country.

America, ch. 8.

54 This point is made in Peadar Kirby, *Ireland and Latin America: Links and Lessons* (Dublin, 1992), 32–33. For a more extended account of the Latin American revolutions, see Lockhart and Schwarz, *Early Latin America*, 405–26.

55 Bartlett, '"What Ish My Nation?"', 46

Thus, the intellectual stimulus to Irish Protestant nationalism in the late eighteenth century may have come from the North American colonies, but, it may be argued, the social conditions in which that nationalism developed were more like those in Latin American societies — a narrow oligarchy and culturally distinct peasant mass. In such conditions, the demand for independence had to be weighed against the danger of mass insurrection from below. Given the decline of Spanish imperial power, South American creole nationalisms ultimately opted for political independence. Confronted by an economically and militarily stronger imperial centre closer to hand, as well as by the dangers posed by the threats of a Catholic majority and the new French-inspired republican creed, Irish Protestant nationalism took a different route and opted instead for political integration into an expanded United Kingdom. It is perhaps a telling sign of the times that it was Daniel O'Connell, the hero of the struggle for Catholic emancipation in the early nineteenth century, who came to bear the title 'The Liberator', originally coined for Simón Bolívar, the great architect of South American independence.[56]

As mentioned earlier, the fact that Ireland became part of the British state after 1801 is the main reason why many Irish historians find it difficult to accept that Ireland can be regarded as a colony from this time onwards. It is true that its integration into the United Kingdom granted Ireland privileges enjoyed by no other colony. Ireland sent MPs to Westminster, something that neither the British white settler colonies nor the Asian and African colonies did. Irish migrants to the outposts of empire, or to former British colonies such as the United States, could also profit from what David Roediger has called, in a ground-breaking study, 'the wages of whiteness'.[57] They could, in other words, be integrated into the settler society labour forces or into the colonial bureaucracies in ways rarely open to non-European peoples. The scale of Irish immigration to the United States and several British colonies is regularly cited nowadays as evidence that Ireland effectively 'behaved' culturally as another European imperial centre, even if it was not formally one. But Roediger's work does not support this claim. For him, Irish immigrants in America serve as a paradigmatic case for understanding 'whiteness', not as an always-already given biological or epidermal 'reality', or as an index of automatic cultural kinship, but as a socially constructed project. In The Wages of Whiteness, therefore, the 'whitening' of Irish immigrants is conceived as a compensatory 'wage' that worked to disrupt possible black/Irish or Irish/Chinese identifications in the context of industrial exploitation, thereby pitting race against class alliances in ways that

56 On O'Connell and Bolívar, see Oliver MacDonagh, O'Connell: The Life of Daniel O'Connell 1775–1847 (London, 1991), 171. My thanks to Margaret Kelleher for alerting me to this point. The spectre of the South American revolutions can also be detected in some of the Anglo-Irish literature of the period such as Sydney Owenson's Florence Macarthy (1811) in which the hero returns from the Spanish American revolutions in a ship portentously named 'Il Librador'. Owenson's The Wild Irish Girl (1806) also alludes to South America, as, for example, in the long footnote in the third volume of that novel when Owenson refers to Garcilaso de la Vega, el Inca, the mestizo son of a Spanish father and Inca mother who had written a history of pre-Hispanic Peru which treated the defeated Inca rulers with sympathy and respect.
57 David Roediger, The Wages of Whiteness: Race and the Making of the American Working Class (London, 1991)

have haunted working-class struggles ever since. From this perspective, the fact that the Irish in America would often play an extremely reactionary role in that country's race wars is not adduced as evidence that the Irish were culturally preconditioned to behave the same as other imperialist Europeans from the same part of the world.[58] Instead, the story of the Irish immigrants is offered as key to the demonstration of the historically constructed nature of 'whiteness'; racialized Irish subjects of British colonial rule set out actively to pursue the status of whiteness to negotiate their way out of their subaltern structural position into mainstream American society. Though the historical upshot is the same — the Irish identified with white supremacy rather than with the non-European oppressed and exploited — there is a substantive distinction between an analytic that stresses an enthusiastic embrace of either 'whiteness' or imperialism on the basis of a pre-supposed common European identity, and one that stresses that it was precisely because they could not automatically assume such 'whiteness' in the United States or in the British Empire that the Irish were so anxious to disclaim identifications with non-Europeans who also occupied subaltern positions in the social hierarchy.[59]

Whatever the situation of the Irish abroad, the assumption that Ireland simply ceased to be a colony as a consequence of its constitutional integration into the United Kingdom runs up against some considerable difficulties — not least the catastrophic dimension to Irish development in the century subsequent to the Act of Union. Historians seem largely to agree that an extended period of modest economic development and prosperity which had begun about 1660 stalled after 1815. It has been argued that in 1700 Ireland seemed set for a brighter economic future than Scotland, the other country within the United Kingdom that stood in roughly the same historical relationship to England.[60] Yet by the 1840s, when Scotland was well on the way to becoming an advanced industrial economy, Ireland was still overwhelmingly agricultural and held fast in the grip of an extended economic crisis that would culminate in the Great Famine, the last great subsistence crisis in Western Europe. The devastating consequences of that famine were both immediate and long-term. In the short-term, about a million people died and a million and a half emigrated. In the course of a single decade between 1841 and 1851 the country's population was reduced by 20 per cent. Over the longer term, in a sustained stream of emigration, more than 4 million people left Ireland between the Famine and World War I. Many European countries experienced high emigration rates in the latter

---

58 Roediger's work offers an instructive contrast in this respect to Donald Akenson's *If the Irish Ran the World: Montserrat, 1630–1730* (Liverpool, 1970).

59 For other works on the 'whitening' of Irish immigrants to the United States, see Theodore Allen, *The Invention of the White Race*, vol. 1 (London, 1994) and Noel Ignatiev, *How the Irish Became White* (New York, 1995).

60 L. M. Cullen and T. C. Smout, eds., *Comparative Aspects of Scottish and Irish Economic and Social History 1600–1900* (Edinburgh, 1978), 4. For a later revised view by the same authors, see L. M. Cullen, T. C. Smout and A. Gibson, 'Wages and Comparative Development in Ireland and Scotland, 1565–1780', in Rosalind Mitchinson and Peter Roebuck, eds., *Economy and Society in Scotland and Ireland, 1500–1939* (Edinburgh, 1988), 105–16.

half of the nineteenth century, but its size and duration distinguished the Irish outflow.[61] So great was the volume that Ireland in this period can reasonably be described, in Jim Mac Laughlin's words, as a 'global emigrant nursery' which supplied several of the core industrial centres of the world economy, especially Great Britain and North America, with cheap labour.[62]

The volume of emigration served ultimately to reorganize the whole structure of Irish class relations: it devastated the rural labouring class and impeded the growth of an urban working class. For the most part, with the exception of Belfast, the Irish industrial proletariat in this period was concentrated in urban centres outside rather than within Ireland. In places such as England, Scotland, the United States and Australia, Irish workers would later become key constituencies in the emergent Labour-oriented parties, but in nineteenth-century Ireland itself it was the rural lower and middle classes that remained the motor of radical social change. The consequences of the Famine, however, were not simply economic. Demographic disaster was compounded by cultural trauma, as English, long the language of state and economic power, quickly displaced an already declining Gaelic as the spoken language of the mass of the population. This in turn lent impetus to a cultural nationalism determined to salvage what it could from the shipwreck of the old civilization and to reverse what was conceived, no doubt often simplistically, to be a deliberate state-supported policy of anglicization and cultural assimilation. One does not have to interpret the period in apocalyptic terms to conclude that many of the long-term social patterns conditioned in one way or another by the Famine would continue to reverberate across most of the twentieth century in Ireland.

It was this catastrophic dimension to nineteenth-century Irish history that persuaded many Irish nationalists at home and abroad that, whatever its constitutional position, Ireland's relationship to England continued to be a colonial one. Economic stagnation, famine and flight, industrial underdevelopment, the superimposition of English on Gaelic culture, the spread of new pseudo-scientific racialist doctrines to legitimate Empire and notions of British superiority all lent force to that conception. So too did the fact that despite the constitutional merger, a whole series of Irish institutions — the police and legal systems, Dublin Castle and the Lord Lieutenancy, systems of education and local government — either had no counterpart in the rest of the United Kingdom or operated in ways quite different to their British counterparts. Irish nationalists were not alone in drawing conclusions about the colonial nature of the relationship. On return from a visit to Ireland, Friedrich Engels observed in a letter to Karl Marx in 1856 that: 'Ireland may be regarded as the first English colony and as one which because of its proximity is still governed exactly in the old way, and here one can already observe that

---

61 Timothy W. Guinnane, The Vanishing Irish: Households, Migration, and the Rural Economy in Ireland, 1850–1914 (Princeton, 1997), 101
62 Jim Mac Laughlin, 'Emigration and the Peripheralization of Ireland in the Global Economy', Review: A Journal of the Fernand Braudel Center, 17, 2 (1994), 257

the so-called liberty of English citizens is based on the oppression of the colonies.'[63] Ireland and India would become the two key sites for Marx's speculations on the nature of colonial capitalist development, and it was his conception of conditions in Ireland that prompted Marx's strongest comments about the regressive (rather than progressive) consequences of colonial rule.[64] By the second half of the century, Indian nationalist movements were taking a keen interest in Irish struggles, and in 1886 complaints were made to Lord Kimberley, the secretary of state for India, that 'all the arts of Irish agitation had come to India'.[65]

Thus, the thesis that it is Ireland's geographical proximity to Britain or its constitutional merger with the United Kingdom that renders its condition completely different to those of Britain's distant overseas colonies, runs directly contrary to Engels's comments of 1856 cited above. For Engels, we recall, 'Ireland may be regarded as the first English colony and as one which *because of its proximity* is still governed exactly in the old way.' Following this lead, it is at least arguable that the Union, far from ending Ireland's colonial status, actually served to make the Irish situation, politically at least, considerably more difficult than that of other colonies. The constitutional merger did not undo either the deep ethno-religious cleavages or the Protestant colonial nationalism that matured in the epoch that preceded the Union. Instead, the latter might be argued to have mutated in different directions. In one line of development, an erstwhile colonial-settler nationalism with tentative separatist inclinations was now transmuted into a rearguard imperialist nationalism whose central dogma was that any concession to Irish demands for autonomy (however modest) was bad for Ireland, Britain, and the Empire. There was another line of Whiggish liberal unionism which collapsed as a political force only when the extension of mass suffrage and the rise of Irish nationalism undermined the paternalist structures of social control on which it depended. A third line would see many Irish Protestants, from Thomas Davis to John Mitchel to Isaac Butt to Charles Stewart Parnell to Douglas Hyde and W. B. Yeats, assume decisive roles as political leaders and cultural intellectuals in the development of several different modalities of Irish nationalism.

As the nineteenth century proceeded, however, Irish nationalism was now opposed by powerful forces in Westminster because concessions might create a domino effect throughout the Empire, especially in India, and because they might stimulate the break-up of Britain itself. Nevertheless, as time progressed, the British position in Ireland became increasingly untenable. Since it was formally part of the British state, Ireland could not consistently be denied British liberal and democratic standards, despite the fact that these undermined the privileged position of the Protestant Anglo-Irish élite on whose support the Union largely depended. In the north-east, the capacity to maintain the

63 Engels, cited in Seamus Deane, 'The Famine and Young Ireland', in Seamus Deane, ed., *The Field Day Anthology of Irish Writing*, vol. 2 (Derry, 1991), 115–21, 118–19
64 See the collection of writings gathered in Karl Marx and Friedrich Engels, *On Ireland* (London, 1971).
65 Cited in Crotty, *Ireland in Crisis*, 221

Union was strongest, since this was the only region where the Protestant population was a demographic majority and where there was a broad-based Protestant working class. In this region alone Protestant-unionist power had a wide populist base and did not simply rest on the monopoly of landed estates or on the control of command positions within the state apparatus. The uneven development of capitalism had also opened up economic cleavages between the more industrialized north-east and the rest of the island in ways that had generated compelling economic incentives in the north-eastern region to maintain the link with Britain. The intricate clash of domestic and metropolitan interests ultimately created a triangular conflict — one that simply cannot be accommodated within a reading of history as a bilateral conflict between English imperialism and Irish nationalism still sponsored by some Irish postcolonial critics — that catapulted the whole of Ireland into military conflict. Only in the later case of Algeria, perhaps — where questions of the integrity of the French Republic and settler resistance to both anti-colonial nationalism and metropolitan betrayal were intertwined in an analogous concatenation — did another colonial independence movement stimulate such severe political convulsion in the *domestic* politics of a metropolitan European imperial state.[66] India was undoubtedly a more important imperial possession than Ireland and its loss had more far-reaching consequences for Britain's place in the world. Yet when India was finally 'released' by Britain in 1948, there were no army revolts such as the Curragh Mutiny in Ireland and no internal splits within any of the major British political parties such as the one that sundered the Liberal Party over Irish Home Rule. The fact that Irish independence generated such sharp crisis within the United Kingdom might be construed as evidence that the relationship between the two countries was simply more 'intimate' than that between Britain and its more distant colonies. But the emphasis on 'intimacy' serves only to displace the more crucial structural point. For those committed to Empire, to the territorial centralization of the United Kingdom of Great Britain and Ireland, and to the class interests vested in the House of Lords, which twice exercised its veto over Home Rule, the democratization of Irish society was consistently conceived as a threat. That democratization and the preservation of Empire, the Union and the interests of the Irish Ascendancy and British aristocracy were construed to be so at odds, is ultimately the strongest evidence that the structural relationship between the two countries was indeed a colonial one.

5

Irish postcolonial studies presents a considerable challenge to Irish studies as currently constituted. Too often reduced on all sides to a drama between nationalism and its critics,

---

66 For a careful comparative analysis of Ireland and Algeria, see Ian Lustick, *Unsettled States, Disputed Lands: Britain and Ireland, France and Algeria, Israel and the West Bank-Gaza* (Ithaca, 1993).

the real novelty of this new field of scholarship may well lie elsewhere. To determine how Irish social and cultural development was mediated by colonial capitalism is the goal of postcolonial studies. From its inception, the colonial process was never simply a matter of the subjugation of this or that territory. It was, rather, an *international* process through which different parts of the globe were differentially integrated into an emergent world capitalist system. Once this premise is accepted, then it follows that the determination of a specific national configuration must be conceived as a product of the global: to borrow Neil Larsen's phrase, the *part* must be thought through the *whole* and not vice versa.[67] In contrast to a nationalist conception of Irish studies, obsessed with the discovery of chimerical 'national' identities, and a liberal area studies alternative that hesitates to look beyond the horizon of the British Isles or Western European state formation, postcolonial critique impels Irish studies in the direction of conjunctural global analysis. From such perspective, the national arena still remains a crucial site for social struggles, but a true understanding of those struggles can only be grasped contextually within a wider global frame.

For the most part, debates about whether Ireland was or was not a colony have rarely got beyond questions of geo-cultural location and constitutional statute. These are important, but not the decisive issues. If colonialism is conceived as an historical process in which societies of various kinds and locations are differentially integrated into a world capitalist system, then it is on the basis of the comparative conjunctural analysis of such processes that debate must ultimately be developed. Cultural analysis has an important role here, since this is the decisive area where social conflicts are experienced and evaluated, but it is ultimately the contradictions of the wider capitalist system that shape those conflicts, whether cultural, political or economic. While I have suggested that typologies of colonialism can serve as a useful heuristic device for the analysis of colonial situations, any taxonomy that loses sight of the fact that colonialism is an historically changing process will also be reductive. As Francis Mulhern has remarked, Ireland's colonial history, by virtue of its sheer duration, can read like a history of colonialism itself.[68] In the late medieval period the country was, like Scotland and Wales, one of the ragged frontiers of English state expansion and contraction; in the early modern period, a commercial settlement plantation was developed in the same westward thrust as European expansion into the New World. At the moment of the southern state's independence, it was constitutionally configured as a white 'dominion' like Canada, Australia, New Zealand or South Africa. But this status was conferred against the backdrop of a triangulated military conflict between nationalist, unionist and metropolitan British forces — in some ways a precursor to the situation involving a similar tangle of forces that would later emerge in Algeria — that split the island into two states. The situation in contemporary Northern Ireland is sometimes compared to

---

67 Larsen, *Reading North by South*, 214–15
68 Mulhern, *The Present Lasts a Long Time*, 24

that of the Basque region in Spain or to ethnic conflicts in Central Europe. But Northern Irish republicans have also construed and evaluated their situation in terms of African-American civil rights campaigns and late anti-colonial struggles in South Africa and Palestine.[69] The recent 'peace process' is also repeatedly compared to roughly concurrent processes in the Middle East and South Africa. Even the term 'Celtic Tiger', adopted to describe the late twentieth-century economic boom in the Irish Republic, implicitly associates that phenomenon with the small handful of East Asian 'tiger' economies that have emerged from a colonial history to attain levels of economic development comparable to those in the West. While the term infers, on the one hand, that Ireland had by the close of the century attained levels of economic development comparable to those in the rest of Western Europe, it also infers, on the other hand, that the trajectory of that development finds its closest parallels with other non-European histories. The point, finally, is not to adduce whether Ireland is or is not really 'just like' any of these situations, since no two colonial sites are ever completely identical. It is, rather, to think of the ways in which specific national configurations are always the product of dislocating intersections between local and global processes that are not simply random but part of the internally contradictory structure of the modern capitalist world system.

69 Several works in comparative sociology locate Northern Ireland within a wider colonial settler context. In addition to Lustick cited above, see Ronald Weitzer, *Transforming Settler States: Communal Conflict and Internal Security in Northern Ireland and Zimbabwe* (London, 1990); Michael MacDonald, *Children of Wrath: Political Violence in Northern Ireland* (Oxford, 1986); Hermann Giliomee and Jannie Gagiano, eds., *The Elusive Search for Peace: South Africa, Israel, Northern Ireland* (Cape Town, 1990); and Pamela Clayton, *Enemies and Passing Friends: Settler Ideologies in Twentieth-Century Ulster* (London, 1996). Some leading political scientists and sociologists of the Northern Ireland conflict have also attributed some importance to settler colonialism as a shaping influence on the contemporary period, though the degree of salience they attach to it varies. See Liam O'Dowd, New Introduction to Albert Memmi, *The Colonizer and the Colonized*, trans. Howard Greenfeld (London, 1990); John McGarry and Brendan O'Leary, *Explaining Northern Ireland: Broken Images* (Oxford, 1995); Joseph Ruane and Jennifer Todd, *The Dynamics of Power in Northern Ireland: Power, Conflict and Emancipation* (Cambridge, 1996). For a related view, which situates Northern Ireland in terms of other 'ethnic frontiers' in Europe and elsewhere, see Frank Wright, *Northern Ireland: A Comparative Analysis* (Dublin, 1987).

The National Novel in an Imperial Age:
Notes on the Historiography of the Nineteenth-Century Novel

Literary history used to be impossible to write; lately it has become much harder.

Lawrence Lipkin[1]

The extensive scholarly activity invested in nineteenth-century Irish studies in recent decades has prepared the ground for the elaboration of substantive new empirical and theoretical questions about the nineteenth-century Irish novel. As our understanding of nineteenth-century Irish culture becomes more sinuous and complex, a sense of the difficulties of literary history may become proportionately more acute. That is to say, as our knowledge of neglected authors, of the material infrastructures of publication, circulation and reviewing, of the dynamics of print and popular culture, or the politics of nationalist and unionist anthologizing and canon-building in the period grows, the sheer volume of new data to be reckoned with forces us to ask if the old-style synoptic histories that would track the development of the novel over the course of a century can any longer compel at all.

Nevertheless, we cannot do without literary history of some kind and our increasingly 'globalized' world may, in fact, ultimately require more rather than less expansive kinds of cultural history and cognitive mapping. Though subjected to vigorous poststructuralist challenge a few decades ago, literary history has, moreover, undoubtedly witnessed a remarkable revival in more recent times and, with that, new opportunities present themselves as well. New feminist and queer histories have appeared as supplements or alternatives to older nationalist canons; postcolonial scholarship has opened up

1   Lawrence Lipkin, 'A Trout in the Milk', in Marshall Bown, ed., *The Uses of Literary History* (Durham, 1995), 1

new theoretical questions about the dynamics of cultural domination, emulation and resistance that operate across metropolitan and colonial societies; more recently, the globalization and 'world literature' debates have taken such concerns in new directions, and have tabled issues about circuits of cultural exchange between literary 'cores' and 'peripheries', and about the dynamics of nationalized competitions for the accumulation of cultural capital and prestige. Given these wider intellectual developments, the moment may well be opportune for some critical speculation not just on the nineteenth-century Irish novel, but on those modes of literary historiography that have to date shaped our conceptions of that form. The aim here is not to produce some new history of the nineteenth-century Irish novel; instead, what I want to suggest is that the ongoing work of research and recovery needs to be supplemented at this stage by some critical examination of the established modes of writing the history of the nineteenth-century Irish novel.[2] The object of this chapter, then, is to essay some scattered speculations towards this end.

Studies of the nineteenth-century Irish novel have long been conditioned by the search for an Irish *Middlemarch* and by the attempt to explain why there is not one.[3] It might equally be the case, though, that Irish literary historians have approached the nineteenth-century Irish novel in ways that seem to be conditioned by their attempts to produce an Irish equivalent of Ian Watt's spectacularly successful and influential *The Rise of the Novel: Studies in Defoe, Richardson and Fielding* (1957).[4] In Irish literary history, as in other forms of history writing, the tendency to think of Irish history as a somewhat anomalous or strange regional variant of a British (read English) historical 'master narrative' is settled and pervasive. Hence the predictable and recurrent emphasis in Irish history generally on the manifold ways in which Irish society 'failed' to reproduce the social and cultural patterns of its more 'modern' neighbour. This sense of Irish deficiency, measured against an English model taken to be normative, has certainly informed the historiography of the nineteenth-century Irish novel: indeed, it might be said to be one of its constitutive features.

To be fair, the more sophisticated Irish literary historians have never simply laboured in Watt's tracks to manufacture an Irish realist tradition or to lament its absence. While almost all have indeed regretted the lack of a consolidated realism along English lines, they have also gone on to try to deduce the historical and sociological reasons that would explain this deficiency. We can detect as early as Thomas Flanagan's *The Irish Novelists, 1800–1850* (1959), moreover, the emergence of an alternative critical current that begins

---

2   The most important contribution to this project remains David Lloyd's 'Violence and the Constitution of the Novel', in his *Anomalous States* (Durham, 1993), 125–62.

3   Margaret Kelleher, 'How to Define the Irish Novel', paper delivered at 'The Nineteenth-Century Irish Novel: Facts and Fictions', Cardiff University, 16 Sept. 2001, later published as '"Wanted an Irish Novelist": The Critical Decline of the Nineteenth-Century Novel', in Jacqueline Belanger, ed., *The Irish Novel in the Nineteenth Century: Facts and Fictions* (Dublin, 2005), 187–201

4   Ian Watt, *The Rise of the Novel: Studies in Defoe, Richardson and Fielding* (Berkeley, 1957)

to view the more fragmented, ruptured, distressed Irish novel forms less as deficiencies to be mourned than as interesting anticipations of twentieth-century modernism or even postmodernism. From this perspective, interest shifts from asking why there was no Irish *Middlemarch* to an examination of the conditions that did produce an Irish *Ulysses*. Viewed thus, there has been a distinct tendency in some quarters at least to identify realism with Englishness, and to identify the Irish novelist tradition — as it extends from Swiftian satire, the popular folk tale, and Ascendancy gothic through to the glories of Irish modernism — as inherently 'fantastic' or 'anti-realist' in its essential line of development. But perhaps this nationalized realist/anti-realist dichotomy conceals a renovated version of the obdurate Arnoldian distinction between the orderly and empirical Saxon and the more flighty but imaginative Celtic national characters within our historical conception of the novel.

However, even where Irish literary historians have worked towards conceptions of the nineteenth-century Irish novel that stress lineages of development different to that traced by Watt, a great many of the governing concerns and conventions that distinguish Watt-type historiography continue to structure Irish literary histories. In the first instance, these would include an obsession with the importance of origins. Thus, as many scholars have noted, the early history of the Irish novel is much more extensively studied than that of the middle or later part of the century, this despite the fact that levels of literacy in English in Ireland were much lower in the early 1800s, so that the national tales universally taken to inaugurate the Irish novel tradition must have had a rather limited national readership at that time. Is it, then, its national subject matter, or the depth of its readership and its capacity to secure a place for itself within the popular imagination or on the education syllabus, that makes the novel a national form? Without a substantive socio-cultural history of the Irish literary marketplace as it evolved over the nineteenth century, something that would allow us to establish the relative importance of the novel, or of particular types of novel, within that marketplace relative to other modes of writing, we can scarcely begin to answer such questions. Attempts to construct nationalized histories of the rise of the nineteenth-century Irish novel along the lines given to us by English literary histories tend by their nature to take a great many questions as already answered. To whom, for instance, did the nineteenth-century Irish novel actually matter? What was its public and to what extent did the scope and composition of that public change across the century? How was its readership distributed across class or gender or religious lines? What were the marketing strategies used by publishers to reach their audiences? We have many quite accomplished textual histories that study nineteenth-century Irish novels and novelists, but not a single socio-cultural history of Irish novel readers or of their reading practices.[5]

5   Some important studies of the development of English publishing and the English literary marketplace include John Sutherland, *Victorian Novelists and Publishers* (London, 1976) and *Fiction and the Fiction Industry* (London, 1978); Richard Altick, *The English Common Reader: A Social History of the Mass Reading Public, 1800–1900* (Chicago, 1957); Peter McDonald, *British Literary Culture and Publishing Practice 1880–1914* (Stanford,

Second, there is a preoccupation with identifying a single, continuous linear model of novelistic evolution: hence the tendency to isolate Ascendancy gothic as the defining nineteenth-century Irish novelistic alternative to English realism. To date at least, the gothic is the only line of nineteenth-century novelistic development for which we have something like a discrete extended or longitudinal history. Discrete studies that track other forms, such as the historical novel, the picaresque novel, the travel narrative, the novel of agrarian unrest, melodrama, and so forth, over an extended period across the century have as yet to emerge.[6]

Third, there is an uncritical tendency to assume that the automatic fate of the novel is to 'rise': in other words, that the novel ought naturally to be expected to eliminate or subordinate competitive species en route towards its inevitable command of the narrative field. Perhaps the established emphasis here needs to be reversed such that it is not the 'failure' of the realist novel to rise in Ireland so much as the resilience of a diverse ecology of pre-or non-realist forms (ballads and aislings, chronicles and histories, fairy tales and folk tales, memoirs and melodramas, political pamphlets and sermons, travel narratives or jail journals) that needs to be explained.

Finally, there is a tendency to think of the development of the novel almost exclusively within a self-contained national frame or with reference to one single dominant external tradition against which it defines itself (in this case, the English tradition). The history of the Irish novel is always assessed in terms of its English counterpart; never in terms of other peripheral societies that were also struggling in the same period against strong metropolitan rivals for literary recognition. Were they to look further afield, Irish literary historians might find that they may have as much to learn from Scottish, American or Canadian as from English literary history, or that the dilemmas of the Irish novel are closer in some ways to those of nineteenth-century Belgian or Swiss novels in French or to Latin American novels than they are to those of English or French metropolitan fiction. Even though an Irish/English axis of comparison seems absolutely useful and inevitable for any analysis of Irish fiction, there is still every reason to rethink the history of the Irish novel in terms other than those conferred on us by the dominant models of English literary historiography. But to think beyond those models, which may exert a pressure on contemporary Irish literary historians no less than English realism did on nineteenth-century Irish novelists, we must first try to comprehend their inherent forms and assumptions.

1990); John Feather, *A History of British Publishing* (London, 1988); and Paul Delany, *Literature, Money and the Marketplace: From Trollope to Amis* (Houndmills, 2002). On Irish fiction, see Rolf Loeber and Magda Stouthamer-Loeber, in collaboration with Anne M. Burnham, *A Guide to Irish Fiction, 1650–1900* (Dublin, 2006).

6   Seamus Deane, ed., *The Field Day Anthology of Irish Writing*, vol. 2 (Derry, 1991) is a useful index of the state of current scholarship on these matters: there is an extended section on 'Poetry and Song 1800–1890' but the only novelistic lineage to receive its own section is 'Irish Gothic and After (1820–1945)' (though this includes non-novelistic modes of gothic as well).

2

The contemporary study of the modern novel is conditioned by a whole variety of methodologies: Marxist, feminist, Bakhtinian, Foucauldian, Bourdieuian, discourse analysis, and many others. Nevertheless, it can be argued that at least where the history of the English novel is concerned two particular lines of development have proved particularly compelling. One of these lines, broadly Marxist-sociological, includes landmark works such as those by Ian Watt and Michael McKeon. Another more recent but enormously productive line is a Foucauldian one, and especially perhaps a feminist-Foucauldian one that, building on decades of feminist scholarship on women-centred and women-authored fiction, includes decisive works such as Nancy Armstrong's and Catherine Gallagher's.[7]

Despite some fundamental differences, the ways in which these Marxist-sociological and feminist-Foucauldian histories narrate the story of the rise of the novel share considerable common ground. First, for both, the origins of the English novel are temporally modern. The *longue durée* approach that conceives the novel more inclusively and which comprehends the term to include ancient, medieval and Renaissance romance narratives is simply disregarded by both.[8] One of the functions of this conception of the origins of the novel is not only to detach the form from earlier or ancillary genres, but to ascribe it an essentially Northern European rather than a Mediterranean provenance or pedigree. Second, for both of these kinds of history, the novel is conceived essentially as an autonomous and indigenous English product and its later development is tracked within an hermetically self-enclosed and narrowly-nationalized framework.[9] Third, the construction of the novel as a peculiarly English invention is more than a simple act of Anglocentric parochialism; the gesture carries with it considerable ideological freight, since the idea that the novel is an eighteenth-century English invention effectively ties

7   Watt, *Rise of the Novel*; Michael McKeon, *The Origins of the English Novel, 1600–1740* (Baltimore, 1987); Nancy Armstrong, *Desire and Domestic Fiction: A Political History of the Novel* (Oxford, 1987); Catherine Gallagher, *Nobody's Story: The Vanishing Acts of Women Writers in the Marketplace, 1670–1820* (Berkeley, 1994)

8   Studies that allow for a longer history of the novel that encompasses Greek and Roman versions of the form include Mikhail Bakhtin, *The Dialogic Imagination: Four Essays* (Austin, 1981) and Margaret Ann Doody, *The True Story of the Novel* (New Brunswick, 1996).

9   It was by way of nineteenth-century multi-volume anthologies and critical studies of the novel — such as Letitia Barbault's *The British Novelists* (1810), and, above all, Hippolyte Taine's *History of English Literature* (1871) — that the thesis that the modern English novel owed little or nothing to earlier novel or romance forms, or indeed to Italian, Spanish or French precursors, was first consolidated. Later, the shift within the university system towards the institution of separate disciplines and departments for the study and teaching of European national literatures consolidated this process. By the time Watt's *Rise of the Novel* appeared, the supposedly indigenous and autonomous rise of the distinctive English novel was already taken for granted. Indeed, in Watt's title, as William Warner notes, the modifier 'English' is implied but erased; the clear inference is that 'the rise of the (English) novel' takes priority in the emergence of the modern novel *per se*. See William B. Warner, *Licensing Entertainment: The Elevation of Novel Reading in Britain, 1684–1750* (Berkeley, 1998), 19–32.

the genre to the economic, political and cultural rise of the English middle class and hence to a larger set of assumptions about Protestantism, individuality and democracy (in other words, English liberty). The nationalized grand narrative of the rise of the novel thus acquires a distinctly Whiggish cast in its institutionalization from Taine to Watt, and the Marxist-sociological and feminist-Foucauldian histories are both, in their diverse ways, legatees of this Whiggish history, even if they dispute its more triumphalist assumptions and much of its specific content.

For both Marxist and Foucauldian literary historiographical models, for example, the rise of the English middle class, and its eventual acquisition of hegemony over (or class compromise with) the aristocracy, is grasped within a securely self-enclosed domestic English frame, despite the fact that England in the century associated with the rise of the novel was engaged in an almost continuous series of European and colonial wars. The period between the Glorious Revolution (1688–89) and the end of the Napoleonic Wars (1815) witnessed the rise and fall of the 'first' English Empire in the Atlantic world; after the independence of the American colonies, British imperial ambitions underwent a decisive swing to the East into the Indian and Pacific oceans. (The Caribbean islands, Canadian North America, and Ireland, which had all been part of the 'first' English empire, also continued to be part of the 'second'.) Whether the development of English society and capital and the dynamics of the class struggle between the aristocracy and the new 'middle' classes are conceptualized within this wider geographical and imperial frame or an hermetically domestic English one, makes a great difference. Viewed in an imperial frame, the whole assumption that the gradual ascent of the English manufacturing, merchant and middle classes represented a generalized expansion of democracy and a liberating transition away from age-old feudalistic violence into a pacific new era of le doux commerce seems, to put it mildly, doubtful. In other words, while the triumph of the bourgeoisie over the aristocracy can be construed within a domestic English frame as an heroic narrative of middle-class emancipation, in a wider global frame the new dispensation that emerged from the shell of absolutism cannot be detached from the extension of an aggressively expansionist imperialism or from the attendant rise of a host of reactionary ideologies — such as forms of 'muscular Christianity', social Darwinism and scientific race theory — to legitimate this enterprise.[10]

There can be little doubt that in nineteenth-century Ireland different perceptions of the temporality of history of this sort were critical to the century-long conflict between nationalists and unionists. The latter largely subscribed to a Whig view of history that saw the Williamite Wars as securing a decisive expansion of modern liberties over

---

10 Interpretations of modern British history tend to stress either (a) the dramatic changes brought about in the established class structure as a consequence of the early development of capitalism in England and especially as a result of the Industrial Revolution, or (b) the remarkable stability and persistence of the old aristocratic order. In recent times, the latter interpretation seems to be the more dominant. For further discussion, see Mike Savage et al., *Property, Bureaucracy, and Culture: Middle-Class Formation in Contemporary Britain* (London, 1992), ch. 3.

absolutist despotism and 'old corruption'; the former were more inclined to view these wars as a consolidation of a deeply oppressive process of domination. Where the novel is concerned, it was not just that Irish nationalists and unionists had different takes on various episodes of Irish history; on a deeper level, their respective senses of temporality were deeply at odds with each other, and hence the task of accommodating any kind of nationalist narrative to the structural morphology of an English realist plot was never going to be straightforward.

Finally, in the conventional English histories of the form, the 'novel' is essentially equated with the realist novel. All other types of novelistic narrative are expelled, either by dismissing them as residual hangovers of some pre-modern, pre-industrial aristocratic culture or by construing them as sub-novelistic forms associated with the degraded and vulgar tastes of commercial popular culture. As a consequence, the whole concept of the novel is narrowed and homogenized. The sub-genres constituting the novelistic system as a whole — the historical novel, the adventure novel, oriental tales, the philosophical novel, the gothic novel, the detective novel, novels of sensation and melodrama, marriage novels, the novel of manners, the erotic novel, the pornographic novel — are expelled from consideration and our sense of the dynamics of evolution within the form are considerably weakened.

The object here is not to debunk this particular mode of literary historiography (the conception of the rise of the novel that it advances is in some ways unsurpassed in its sophistication), but rather to disclose its provisional nature and to underscore some of the typical limits, silences and occlusions on which it rests. One of the effects of this version of literary history is that when the realist novel is identified as the exemplary form of bourgeois liberal-capitalist modernity, the 'mature' modern novel is effectively severed from the whole pre-bourgeois, pre-capitalist history of antecedent and cognate narrative forms. It may well be the case — as this version of literary history contends — that the novel in eighteenth-century English capitalist society underwent such substantive transformation as to become effectively an almost wholly new literary form, with only very limited resemblance and tenuous connection to any earlier novelistic-type narratives. Nevertheless, it should be stressed that — especially from a colonial or postcolonial perspective — some significant losses are incurred by asserting an absolute correspondence between the novel and advanced capitalist modernity, and by asserting too rigid a demarcation between the mature modern novel and its earlier historical antecedents.

For this kind of demarcation confines the study of narrative to its developed form (the realist novel as practised by Defoe, Fielding, and Richardson and their successors) within developed capitalist society (eighteenth-century England). Hence, questions of what kinds of longer narrative fictions flourished within pre- or non-capitalist societies, and of what their functions might be are sidelined. This tendency to equate the novel with bourgeois modernity became a characteristic feature of the dominant forms of continental European Hegelian-Marxist historiography, represented especially by Georg

Lukács, and also of the more Anglocentric sociological versions, represented by Watt and McKeon. (There were many Marxist literary historians who resisted this development, and who argued that it was a mistake to sever the study of the modern developed novel from the study of its earlier pre-capitalist antecedents, but theirs were not the dominant voices.[11])

For our purposes here, it is worth mentioning that the identification of the novel with developed metropolitan capitalism in both of these strands of Marxist scholarship would seriously diminish the capacity of Marxist literary historiography to deal with the novel and other cognate narrative forms in the European colonies. The colonies were not non-capitalist but, in the societies created by colonialism, combinations of capitalist and various non-capitalist elements were structurally quite different to those that emerged in the advanced centres of European capitalism. Had the history of the novel been construed in a more historically expansive and inclusive manner, then the theoretical equipment necessary to 'think the question' of the novel when it was transported via colonial routes beyond the capitalist centres of Northern Europe might well have been considerably better developed in Marxist literary criticism than it is today. However, this was a road not taken in Marxist and sociological histories of the novel. Hence when Marxist theorists, such as Fredric Jameson, have tried in recent times to theorize the condition of the novel in the 'colonial world' or on the peripheries of the modern world system, their attempts to do so have consequently tended, for lack of a developed tradition in this area, to be rather abstract.[12]

3

The past decade or so has witnessed the emergence of a substantial body of postcolonial scholarship that sets out to undo Eurocentric models of historiography and to write the question of empire back into the history of the European novel. Within this field of scholarship, a number of different models of enquiry have developed. The first and

11 For a fascinating account of the Soviet debates in the 1930s on the history of the novel, see Galin Tihanov, *The Master and the Slave: Lukács, Bakhtin and the Ideas of their Time* (Oxford, 2000). Tihanov's account suggests that while the thesis that the emergence of the novel should be attributed to bourgeois capitalist society — a position associated with Lukács — would be triumphant in this debate, and thus become part of official Soviet literary historiography, there were some Marxist-identified scholars — most notably Valerian Pereverzev — who resisted this conception of things. Bakhtin's work, Tihanov suggests, tacitly refuses the official Soviet line on this issue and is closer to Pereverzev's position, which allows for greater continuity between pre-capitalist (Greek and Roman) and capitalist versions of the novel.

12 See Fredric Jameson's 'Third World Literature in the Era of Multinational Capitalism', *Social Text*, 15 (1986), 65–88, and Aijaz Ahmad's response, 'Jameson's Rhetoric of Otherness and the "National Allegory"', reprinted in Ahmad's *In Theory, Classes, Nations, Literatures* (London, 1992). For a brilliant examination on the ways in which Jameson's essay has been damagingly misread in postcolonial studies, see Neil Lazarus, 'Fredric Jameson on "Third World Literature": A Qualified Defence', in Douglas Kellner and Sean Homer, eds., *Fredric Jameson: A Critical Reader* (Houndmills, 2004), 42–61.

most commonly practised model — developed in formative works by Benita Parry, Martin Green, and Patrick Bratlinger — deals with English novels that engage directly with the subject of empire.[13] A second model starts with the apparent insularity of the canonical English novel (its tendency, on the whole, to remain somewhat detached from questions of empire), and sets out to disclose something that might be called the imperial unconscious at work within the form, demonstrating the ways in which major texts by Austen, Dickens, Thackeray, George Eliot and others presuppose the macro-economics and macro-politics of empire even when direct engagement with empire seems peripheral to their more immediate domestic concerns. This model, best exemplified to date by Edward Said's *Culture and Imperialism* (1993), considerably widens the scope of analysis by dealing not just with matters of content or representation, but also with more complex questions about the relationships between the form of the novel, or the novel as cultural institution, and the consolidation of empire.[14]

A third and more recent — and much less widely practised — model is that exemplified by Katie Trumpener's *Bardic Nationalism: The Romantic Novel and the British Empire* (1997).[15] Whereas Said's study works within the established canon of the English novel, Trumpener's work (much more attuned to feminist and non-metropolitan scholarship of recovery) attempts a more ambitious rewriting of the conventional rise-of-the-novel grand narrative by decentring its standard English framework. *Bardic Nationalism* does this by refusing to privilege the realist novel over other contemporary genres and by trying to reinsert the fictions written in Ireland, Scotland, and Britain's other overseas colonies into its account of the early nineteenth-century novel.[16] Watt's and McKeon's works assume a discrete eighteenth-century English origin for the modern realist novel and then track the gradual development, refinement and sophistication of the form; Trumpener's study, by contrast, traces a much less linear history that involves not only a constant traffic between genres (for example, the national tale, the adventure novel, the travel narrative, and the historical novel) but also multilateral circuits of cultural exchange between the English literary centre and its colonial or semi-colonial peripheries. For Trumpener:

> An empire lives from its peripheries; its economy and trade depend on their underdevelopment in relationship to the imperial center. Yet the large-scale social displacements that result from such economic unevenness, and from the need to anchor colonial authority with imperial armies and administrations, bind the

---

13 Benita Parry, *Delusions and Discoveries: Studies on India in the British Imagination* (London, 1988 [1972]); Martin Green, *Dreams of Adventure, Deeds of Empire* (New York, 1979); Patrick Bratlinger, *The Rule of Darkness: British Literature and Imperialism* (Ithaca, 1988).

14 Edward Said, *Culture and Imperialism* (New York, 1993)

15 Katie Trumpener, *Bardic Nationalism: The Romantic Novel and the British Empire* (Princeton, 1997)

16 Methodologically, Trumpener's work seems to represent an overdue grafting of the New British and Atlantic models of historiography onto what has been a very nation-centred field of early nineteenth-century literary history.

peripheries to one another, as well as to the center. On one level empires function by fixing a hierarchy of place and by instituting laws that keep colonized subjects in their respective places; on another level they function only by perpetual motion.[17]

Whereas the Watt/McKeon histories inscribe a singular linearly-conceived, nationally-enclosed English rise of the novel, Trumpener's work conceives of the development of the form in terms of a multilinear series of lateral or transverse exchanges of ideologies and genres across the wider domains of empire.

The cultural traffic between imperial centre and periphery, moreover, is not, as is sometimes imagined, a uni-directional one in which the periphery simply mimics the more culturally advanced centre. Trumpener's thesis indeed is that

English literature, so-called, constitutes itself in the late eighteenth and early nineteenth centuries through the systematic imitation, appropriation and political neutralization of antiquarian and nationalist literary developments in Scotland, Ireland, and Wales. The period's major new genres (ballad collection, sentimental and Gothic fiction, national tale, and historical novel), its central models of historical scholarship and literary production, and even its notions of collective and individual memory have their origins in the cultural nationalism of the peripheries.[18]

In Trumpener's model (borrowing productively from Benedict Anderson's *Imagined Communities*, which sees creole colonial nationalisms in the Americas as antecedent to metropolitan European official nationalisms), cultural nationalisms of various kinds develop initially in England's Celtic peripheries in opposition to imperialist projects of conquest and modernization.[19]

Despite its remarkable achievements, Trumpener's study, like Said's, is largely text-based. As might be expected, the extension in the geo-historical scope of her survey comes at the expense of the kind of sociological depth more nationalized studies such as Watt's and McKeon's attain. Their detailed sociological accounts insert the novel into wider histories of the book, print technologies, libraries and circulation systems, categories of readers, changing reading and publishing practices, and so on. Trumpener is undoubtedly right to stress that intellectual and literary innovation stems from the imperial periphery as well as from the metropolitan centre, and this is a very useful corrective to the general bias of some 'world systems' cultural theorists, such as Franco Moretti, who tends to see the metropoles as consistently innovative and the peripheries

17 *Bardic Nationalism*, 244
18 *Bardic Nationalism*, xi
19 Benedict Anderson, *Imagined Communities: Reflections on the Origin and Spread of Nationalism*, rev. edn. (London, 1991)

as innovative only in very sporadic, exceptional cases.[20] But Trumpener sometimes appears to scant the fact that cultural innovation and the steady accumulation of cultural capital are not the same thing. The English and French literary traditions, with their large stocks of inherited literary capital, with their substantial publishing industries and command of commercial trade routes, enjoyed support bases not easily replicated in the colonies. The comparative strength and stability of the English publishing industry, the capacity of its library, archive and circulation systems, the cultural prestige of the idiolects of the English upper classes as a consequence of Britain's global pre-eminence, all allowed England a capacity to accumulate and consolidate symbolic capital in ways its colonies (whether settler, plantation or administrative) or even its sister-countries could rarely match. No matter how innovative colonial authors might prove themselves, the economic underdevelopment of the colonies had real material consequences for the production of culture generally and the development of the novel particularly in these sites. While Trumpener's insistence that intellectual and cultural exchange between colony and metropolitan centre operated in more than one direction is salutary, the uneven and asymmetrical material conditions that regulated such exchange ought not to be forgotten either.

4

Even in metropolitan sites the notion of an autonomous evolution of the novel is dubious, but in the colonies the novel self-evidently originates as a metropolitan import and the reading habits and generic expectations based on the European novel usually antecede the development of local versions of the genre. As Roberto Schwarz puts it, the novel had existed in Brazil well before there were Brazilian novels.[21] Extending Schwarz's point, Moretti has remarked that 'in cultures that belong to the periphery of the European literary system ... the modern novel first arises not as an autonomous development but as a compromise between a Western formal influence (usually French or English) and local materials'.[22] In most of the world, Moretti surmises, the attempted compromise between the conventions of the imported Western novel and local materials proved radically unstable. In those instances where such compromises succeeded, genuine formal revolutions were achieved, but these were rare. The evidence for this, Moretti notes, can be seen in the widely shared perception in histories of the novel almost everywhere beyond the European metropolitan centres that local nineteenth-century novels are

20 See Franco Moretti, 'Conjectures on World Literature', New Left Review, 1 (2000), 54–68, 59 and, for a
    somewhat revised case, Moretti, 'More Conjectures', New Left Review, 1 (2003), 73–81.
21 Roberto Schwarz, 'The Importation of the Novel to Brazil and Its Contradictions in the Work of Alencar',
    Misplaced Ideas: Essays on Brazilian Culture (London, 1992), 41–78
22 Moretti, 'Conjectures on World Literature', 58

clumsy, imitative, and second-rate compared to their British and French counterparts.[23]

Moretti's assumption — that in the peripheries innovation is the exception and imitation the rule — must be questioned. But it must also be allowed, to some degree, if only because the perceived deficiency of the nineteenth-century Irish realist novel in relation to its British counterpart is a staple element of commentary on the form by both nineteenth-century novelists themselves and by twentieth-century commentators. The fact that this same sense of comparative deficiency is so regular a feature of other national surveys everywhere in the colonial and non-metropolitan world — from nineteenth-century South America (and indeed the United States) to twentieth-century Africa, Asia, the Middle East or Eastern Europe — may not be of much comfort to Irish literary historians bent on discovering or inventing a strong indigenous novel tradition. Nevertheless, a greater appreciation of the fact that, where the early development of the novel is concerned, the Irish situation is the peripheral or colonial norm rather than a Western European exception, might compel some useful rethinking of the topic. Once we accept that the development of Anglo-French realism in the nineteenth century is really quite idiosyncratic in terms of the wider development of the world novel, then the development of the nineteenth-century Irish novel can no longer be understood as any kind of aberration. It might better be studied in the light of the development of the form in colonial and agrarian peripheries, such as South America or Eastern Europe, which may in fact offer closer parallels to the Irish situation.

A postcolonial history of the nineteenth-century Irish novel would have to take some account of the issues raised in recent world literature debates about the ways that the rise of nineteenth-century cultural nationalism consolidated the development of a modern international literary system within which nations and national literatures compete for cultural precedence and prestige.[24] Even allowing for the rudimentary nature of the current world literary systems models of cultural analysis, there are implications here for how Irish literary critics understand the development of the Irish novel. Modern Irish literature in English developed as a dependent offshoot of the literature of a European mother-country. As happened elsewhere, that literature was developed, especially in its initial stages, primarily by intellectuals descended from what was historically a creole colonial settler community. These writers typically displayed either a mixture of alienation

23 Moretti's essay cites an extended list of South American, Turkish, Arabic, Japanese, Yiddish and West African histories of the novel that seem to verify this point. Moretti's work tends to privilege the development of British and French realism and to downplay the significance of Russian realism. This seems odd since Russia ought to excite attention, one would think, precisely because it did develop a significant realist novel tradition, even though it was not an advanced capitalist state.

24 The leading work on world literature to date has been Pascale Casanova's *The World Republic of Letters*, trans. M. B. De Bevoise (Cambridge, MA, 2004) and several essays on the topic by Franco Moretti cited earlier. For a useful examination of the issues involved, see the essays collected in Christopher Prendergast, ed., *Debating World Literature* (London, 2004). For a review of Casanova's work that develops its significance for Irish studies, see Joe Cleary, 'The World Literary System: Atlas and Epitaph', *Field Day Review*, 2 (2006), 197–219.

from, or contempt for, the local indigenous culture, as well as considerable anxiety about the anti-modern backwardness of the colony compared to the mother-country. But in many cases the colonial settler élites, sensitive to the rise of mass democracy and cultural nationalism across Europe, were also compelled to attempt imaginative appropriations of the indigenous cultures to bolster their own national legitimacy. At a time when other European intellectual élites were conscripting their ancient epics and sagas — Beowulf, the Nibelungenlied, the Eddas, La Chanson de Roland — as the foundational Ur-texts of their respective national literatures, the colonial settlers, conscious of themselves as relative historical newcomers without a comparable indigenous body of ethnic epic of their own, often laid claim, via translation, to those of the local native culture to make good the deficiency. But while they typically appropriated material from the domestic pre-colonial cultures, the colonial settler intellectual communities — in North or South America, Ireland, or, later, in places such as South Africa, Canada or Australia — were also acutely conscious of the much more prestigious cultural forms of the mother-countries, and wrote as if their ideal public was in Europe. Writers from the various classes of the native community in the colonies were not exempt from this alienation; they too were distanced by education and acculturation from the masses of their own community; they too almost invariably took Europe or the imperial mother-country as the lodestar of cultural reference, the arbiter of cultural taste and norms.

Everywhere in the peripheries this condition generated persistent problems of a public and addressees. In Ireland, the fact that the nineteenth-century Anglo-Irish novel takes Ireland as its subject matter but is commonly addressed to an English audience has been a recurrent topic of comment from relatively early historians of the form, such as Stephen Gwynn and Daniel Corkery, to more recent writers, such as Seamus Deane and Joep Leerssen.[25] As these critics have variously noted, the disjunctions that attend this condition are consistently manifest in the form and structure of the novel itself in a variety of ways, from the device of placing an English traveller (a metonymic substitute for the intended English reader) at the centre of the narrative to the extensive paratextual apparatuses, the ethnographic descriptions, and the sudden shifts in stylistic register and address. More importantly perhaps, the condition of writing for an external target audience also gives rise to recurrent dilemmas at the level of narrative voice. The narrator in the novel is the pole of value, comment, and evaluation, the mediator inserted between the tale and its readership. In a situation where the material is local but the ideal reader conceived to be external to that culture, the narrator is constantly either applying metropolitan worldviews to recalcitrant local conditions or else polemically explicating, excusing, defending, deprecating or exploiting the local for the edification or amusement of the external reader. The condition of constantly negotiating between

25 See Daniel Corkery, Synge and Anglo-Irish Literature (Cork and London, 1931), Stephen Gwynn, Irish Literarture and Drama in the English Language: A Short History (London, 1936), Seamus Deane, A Short History of Irish Literature (London, 1986), and Joep Leerssen, Remembrance and Imagination: Patterns in the Historical and Literary Representation of Ireland in the Nineteenth Century (Cork, 1996).

two distinct cultures (the local and the metropolitan) can be deployed to considerable comic, satiric or auto-exotic effect, but it is conducive also to a habitual instability of narrative voice — one of the primary reasons, surely, why the kind of cool authoritative omniscience that is one of the major features of the nineteenth-century English realist novel was so difficult to replicate in Ireland.

To speak of cultural centres and peripheries in this way always runs the risk of restoring by the back door the excessively restricted Anglocentrism decried earlier, but it need not do so. Writers within the colonies and peripheries were not at all indifferent to their cultural dependence and many sought ways to alleviate or escape it. The Brazilian critic Antonio Candido has remarked, for instance, that in their effort to escape the burden of cultural dependency on Spain, Latin American writers often bypassed their own imperial mother-country and looked instead to France as alternative cultural model. A not altogether dissimilar 'transfer of dependency' from Britain to alternative European centres is certainly discernible in the Irish case, and Irish appropriations of continental cultural movements, from German Romanticism in the early part of the century to French naturalism in the later period, might well be considered in this light. Moreover, to recall Trumpener, it must also be remembered that an empire depends on the economic underdevelopment of its peripheries, and this economic unevenness produces its own large scale displacements of population, something that also establishes new circuits of economic and cultural contact between periphery and centre. The obvious example of this in the Irish case is the massive migrations to English industrial cities and to North America. This Irish-American diasporic circuit, however, is patently quite different in character to the 'high cultural' one in which nineteenth-century London and Paris vie with each other as competing cultural capitals. Nonetheless, especially after the watershed of the Famine, the establishment of a major Irish emigrant community in the United States, at a time when that country was emerging as a new world power, undoubtedly had consequences for Irish cultural and literary development — though these have been the object of surprisingly little investigation to date. One might speculate that the existence of this Irish-American community, and the consequent redrawing of literary circuits and relations, may well have impacted more slowly on the Irish novel than on other cultural forms such as the Irish theatre (though by the late twentieth century the significance of an American readership for Irish fiction is certainly striking), but even were this shown to be the case, it would still be significant.[26] Theatre, closer in many ways to popular ritual (given its communal and carnivalesque dimensions) and to oral culture and melodrama, could perhaps hope to access a mass Irish audience at home and abroad, whereas the novel demanded not only greater levels of print literacy in English, but also a more individualized reading experience and a privatization of cultural consumption

26 For a discussion of Irish theatre and America, see Chris Morash, A History of the Irish Theatre, 1601–2000 (Cambridge, 2002). On the Irish-American novel, see Charles Fanning, The Exiles of Erin: Nineteenth-Century Irish-American Fiction (Chester Springs, 1997).

that was historically linked to the development of middle-class forms of socialization, subjectivity and leisure. Because the novel could reach only a more restricted audience, it was destined to play a subsidiary cultural role to theatre and other less individualized cultural practices until at least the late nineteenth century.

5

The previous section has argued that there are compelling reasons to think of the development of the nineteenth-century Irish novel in terms that widen beyond the usual exclusive focus on England to include a complex series of cultural negotiations conducted between several alternative and shifting centres that would include continental Europe, the wider world of the British Empire, and the North American migration settlements. As the century progressed, the *lingua franca* of this imperial and Atlantic world would become increasingly, indeed overwhelmingly, anglophonic. The adoption of English as the language of instruction by an increasingly powerful Catholic Church in Ireland diminished intellectual links between Ireland and continental Europe established in earlier centuries, while at the same time the virtual obliteration of Gaelic culture, especially after the Famine, consolidated the trend towards anglicization at the level of Irish popular culture. Moreover, as Ireland was becoming increasingly anglicized, England was becoming increasingly xenophobic and hostile to continental European culture. Eighteenth-century English writers seem to have been more familiar with French books than were their Victorian counterparts, and translations of classic European novels into English in the latter era were considerably slower than those into other major European languages.[27] By a curious twist of historical dialectic, then, even as Irish society was opening out towards the wider world of the Americas and Empire, culturally it was subsumed into an increasingly mono-lingual anglophonic world that was — despite or because of its imperial extension — itself becoming more culturally autarkic, chauvinist and isolationist.

Crucially, this Anglo-American world into which Ireland was absorbed was culturally not only English-speaking but also overwhelmingly Protestant in its reflexive structures of feeling. No part of this English-speaking world was religiously monolithic, but in all of its major centres in the nineteenth century, Protestantism was the dominant religion of state — the crucial difference in Ireland being, of course, that Catholicism was the religion of the majority and, because of its long history of colonial conquest, the legitimization and contestation of social and political structures were religiously coded, as the increasing deployment of the term 'Protestant Ascendancy' in the period suggests. The consequences of Ireland's status as a Catholic enclave within an overwhelmingly

---

27 On the increasing insularity of English culture in the nineteenth century, see Franco Moretti, *Atlas of the European Novel, 1800–1900* (London and New York, 1998), 156–58.

Protestant Anglo-American-imperial world, or of the peculiar imbrication of religion and social status in Ireland, for the development of the Irish novel have attracted surprisingly little investigation — a matter of some curiosity given that the links between Puritanism, Protestantism and the rise of the English novel are universally remarked in the histories of the form from Watt to Armstrong.

Given the intimate connections between Protestantism and the development of the novel, the difficulties of translating the form into a largely Catholic — but religiously divided — society must have been quite formidable. In nineteenth-century Anglo-American society, Catholicism was a byword for despotism, dogmatism, benightedness, treason and superstition — in short, for the fundamentally anti-modern. In such circumstances it was possible to believe that Catholicism and the novel were in fact almost wholly inimical. Sir Hugh Walpole once commented that he was opposed to the spread of Catholicism because it was bad for the novel, and in the twentieth century, George Orwell (ignoring Cervantes) could still argue that 'The novel is practically a Protestant form of art; it is a product of the free mind, of the autonomous individual.' For Orwell, any kind of ideological orthodoxy is inimical to the creative process, and hence Catholicism, through its authoritarian hold on its writer-believers, could not produce first-rate novelists. (The few distinguished Catholic novelists, Orwell asserted, were not 'good Catholics'.[28])

If Orwell is right to believe that the novel is a form to which nothing is more sacrosanct than the self-realization of the individual subject, then this would certainly explain why the Irish novel would have to await James Joyce to find its place in international literature. Whereas the nineteenth-century Irish novelists struggle to produce heroes who somehow represent the popular values (religious or political or cultural) of the collective, Joyce's Stephen Dedalus repudiates his religion, flees his nation, and scorns the Gaelic language, even if he also feels English to be an alien tongue. Yet although it rightly highlights the deep connections between the (English) novel and Protestantism, Orwell's statement rests on a cluster of 'English' prejudices that might themselves call for scrutiny: namely, that Catholicism is invariably authoritarian; that the 'serious' novel is essentially realist; that the veneration of the freethinking 'autonomous individual' as the fundamental unit of social creativity is not itself a product of a kind of liberal orthodoxy or dogma. Whatever the truth of the matter, it is undoubtedly the case, as several critics have observed, that a variety of pressures have combined to impel Catholic writers away from classic realism. Within Anglo-American Protestantism, especially as it became less puritanical and more liberal, the assumption that individual redemption and fulfilment are achieved not so much by divine grace as by individual effort, self-improvement and moral decency became axiomatic, and this worldview finds expression in the realist novel, where moral responsibility and worldly fulfilment are usually mutually

28 For the comments by Walpole and Orwell on Catholicism and the novel, see Thomas Woodman, *The Catholic Novel in British Literature* (Milton Keynes, 1991), ix.

complementary. Catholicism, anglophone Catholicism especially, tended to see this as Protestant complacency, however, and located sin at the centre of spiritual life; without sin, the drama of salvation and the redemptive role of the Church could not be fulfilled.[29] In addition, the realist novel equates 'the real' with the empirically observable, palpable, everyday world of the senses, but Catholicism (like all strong forms of revealed religion) resists the notion that the everyday world is sufficient to itself.[30] Given the hostility of the realist novel to this kind of theocentric or transcendent worldview, with its innately different modalities of time, and the inherent tendency of the low mimetic realist aesthetic to eschew the exceptional and to rationalize the miraculous, Catholic writers have often been drawn towards other forms of fiction, such as romance, fable, the supernatural tale, the philosophical novel, or the novel of ideas. In nineteenth-century British culture, however, where the regulative power of the realist novel was securely established, such genres were almost by definition assigned to the sidelines of the mainstream tradition.

The rejection of the idea of salvation exclusively through individual effort; the critique of liberal secular democracy; a belief in the reality of supernatural intervention and in sacred time: these all have implications for form, and may go some way to explaining why the classic realist novel might be difficult to develop even in the more bourgeois strata of nineteenth-century Catholic Ireland. At issue, in short, was a struggle between two opposed versions of 'the real', which meant that the inherent ethos of the classic realist novel and central elements of the whole Catholic ethos were rather at odds. For its own reasons, Irish Protestantism — itself an embattled minority enclave within an embattled Catholic enclave — was also resistant to realism. Feeling its historical hegemony eroding right across the century (from the successive shocks of 1798, Catholic emancipation, the disestablishment of the Church of Ireland, and then the Land Wars), the Irish Protestant middle class could not share with its English Protestant counterpart the same sanguine faith in historical progress and evolution through gradual reform. In England, such reform could be welcomed because it advanced the position of the middle classes relative to the established élite and simultaneously safeguarded it from working-class threat from below, but in Ireland any substantive reform threatened to bring the Catholic middle classes to power and, in so doing, completely to scupper Protestant dominance. Much more immediately threatened by Catholicism, Irish Protestantism was situationally prone to be darker in temper, more fundamentalist and less optimistically liberal than its English counterpart. Hence it was the gothic novel — with its characteristically paranoid atmospherics, its sense of historical guilt, its climate of degeneration and impending collapse — and not classical realism that would become the most successfully realized form of the Ascendancy novel in nineteenth-century Ireland.

29 For this point, see Theodore P. Fraser, *The Modern Catholic Novel in Europe* (New York, 1994), xv.
30 See Malcolm Scott, *The Struggle for the Soul of the French Novel: French Catholic and Realist Novels, 1850–1970* (Houndmills, 1989), 50.

   While it is important to recognize its significance, there are, however, reasons to resist
the investiture of this Ascendancy gothic line as the long-unidentified 'great tradition'
of the nineteenth-century Irish novel, not least because it occludes a century-long
succession of Catholic novelists mostly working in modes quite different to the gothic.[31]
But if the Protestant middle and upper classes could not share the historical confidence
of their English counterparts, it remains the case that the Irish Catholic middle class,
which was in this period slowly but surely — like its English counterpart — climbing to
power, did still not develop its own internationally distinguished realist or non-realist
narrative traditions.

   The wider intellectual milieu within which nineteenth-century Irish Catholic culture
developed may be the telling factor here. At that time, Ireland's nearest (culturally
speaking) and most influential Catholic European neighbour was France, and 'the
Catholic novel', as it is known today, is usually held to have originated in nineteenth-
century French literature.[32] In the first half of that century, committed French Catholic
writers such as Chateaubriand, de Maistre, Lacordaire and others directed their energies
against the rationalist, atheistic, secular republican philosophy that they considered
the legacy of the hated French Revolution. Their intellectual worldview was fiercely
anti-modern and anti-Enlightenment. After the revolutions of 1848, and Pope Pius
IX's *Syllabus of Errors* of 1864, the reactionary, centralized and ultramontane forms of
Catholicism became even more pronounced. The intellectual climate in Protestant
England was equally hostile to the French Revolution's republican legacies, but English
Protestantism could embrace rationalism, democracy and the liberal state, since these
were considered to be not the terrible spawn of the revolution, but the wholesome
fruits of native English genius. Within this English world — where Catholicism had
been ostracized and oppressed for centuries, and where (unlike in France) Catholics
remained isolated and alienated from the intellectual mainstream of their own society
— the primary aspiration of the Catholic Church was not to undo the revolution, but,
much more modestly, to achieve a status within the state that approached that of the
major Protestant denominations.

   But, if from the French (and Italian) side, Irish Catholic culture absorbed some of
the hostility to radical republicanism and liberal democratic modernity and the cult of
reactionary (medievalist, corporativist) Romanticism, from the English (and American)
side it absorbed Victorian mass-culture sentimentalism, philistine anti-intellectualism,
and the assiduous pursuit of bourgeois respectability. In her history of the nineteenth-
century American novel, Ann Douglas notes that there is a vast gulf between English
and American Protestants of 1800 and those of, say, 1875. On the whole, she suggests,
Protestants before 1800 subscribed to a rather complicated and rigidly defined body of

---

31 The standard work on nineteenth-century Irish gothic is W. J. McCormack's *Ascendancy and Tradition in
   Anglo-Irish Literary History from 1789 to 1939* (Oxford, 1985).
32 See Fraser, *Modern Catholic Novel*, 1.

dogma and attendance at a certain church had a distinctive theological significance. But by 1875 Protestants as a whole were much more likely to define their faith in terms of family morals, civic responsibility, and, above all, in terms of the social function of churchgoing. As its more Calvinist inheritance declined, this liberal Protestantism, Douglas argues, acquired in its place a populist anti-intellectual sentimentalism conditioned partly at least by its adjustment to the still relatively new mass-culture industries.[33] Encompassed within this Anglo-Atlantic world, determined indeed to be accommodated to it, Irish Catholicism absorbed many of its literary values and standards as its own.

Irish Catholics faced many difficulties in strategically positioning themselves within this wider transatlantic world in which Protestantism was dominant. In Ireland, the Catholic middle classes were challenging the long-established Protestant hegemony and very gradually coming to be the new ruling élite, though this transfer of power would not be secured, and then only in the South, until the foundation of the Irish Free State. For this reason, it was the Irish Catholic middle classes, not their Irish Protestant counterparts, who had most to gain by subscribing, politically speaking at least, to liberal democratic values. Indeed, the alliance between Catholicism and democracy, especially as represented by O'Connellism, fascinated French liberal Catholics in the early nineteenth century, no doubt because that alliance seemed to them so historically unusual and promising.[34] From an English, Irish and American Protestant standpoint, however, Catholicism by definition was fundamentally despotic and anti-modern and no matter how avidly the Irish middle-class Catholics laboured to display their respectable liberal credentials, their religion and their liberalism seemed, from this perspective, ultimately at odds.

Located, geographically and culturally, in the cross-current of this world of intellectually reactionary French and Vatican Catholicism, on one side, and intellectually complacent and sentimental Anglo-American Protestantism, on the other, Irish Catholicism, developed an intellectual compromise that combined the worst elements of both. Lacking either the outright rejection of Western modernity that would elsewhere produce a Dostoyevsky or a Melville, or the confident endorsement of progress, liberalism and evolution epitomized by a Jane Austen or George Eliot, Irish Catholic culture displayed neither the rebarbative intellectual combativeness that characterized the former nor the reformist establishment assurance that typified the latter. Instead, a politically expedient but not necessarily inspiring compromise between a European Catholic reaction to modernity as such (confused with theologically orthodox rejection of 'this world' for a higher spiritual universe) and an Anglo-American anti-intellectual sentimentalism gave nineteenth-century Irish cultural Catholicism its distinctive stamp. Or, one could argue that the emergent Irish Catholic middle classes, painfully seeking to be admitted

33 Ann Douglas, *The Feminization of American Culture* (London, 1996 [1977])
34 On this topic, see Seamus Deane, 'Burke and Tocqueville: New Worlds, New Beings', *boundary 2*, 31, 1 (2004), 1–23, 16–19.

into British and American democracy, were not likely, on the one hand, to find in the fiercely anti-liberal French Catholic novel anything like a 'useful tradition' serviceable to their own aspirations, while, on the other hand, the English and American novel traditions were so constitutively Protestant that they, too, were difficult to appropriate. The choice within the established decorum of the literary marketplace of the times was to be acceptably modern and civilized but only timorously Catholic and Irish nationalist, or to be more assertively Catholic and Irish nationalist but then to be accused of being anti-British and by extension, in nineteenth-century terms, unacceptably anti-modern and backwardly provincial as well.[35] Joyce's solution to this dilemma was not to try to reconcile English Victorianism and Irish Catholicism, as most of his predecessors had done, but to repudiate both one and the other. This may have represented a literary breakthrough of enormous significance, but even here matters were far from resolved. For most commentators in the twentieth century, it was precisely Joyce's rejection of both his Catholicism and Irish cultural nationalism that was the acid test that certified his modernity — thus demonstrating the obduracy of the thesis that Irish Catholicism and/or Irish nationalism and modernity (and modernism) are fundamentally antithetical to each other.[36]

Finally, some remarks on class might also be ventured here. For many critics, the supposed absence of a strong and independent Irish middle class, both as reading public and narrative subject, is taken to be the crucial explanation for the weakness of the nineteenth-century Irish novel. David Lloyd has diagnosed the many limitations of this thesis, at least as it is usually formulated. As Lloyd points out, traditional conceptions of a nineteenth-century Irish society dualistically divided between 'the wealthy and the wretched', landlords and peasants, Anglo-Irish and Gaelic stock, have been refuted by recent research, which posits a much more complex class stratification that included landless labourers, cottiers, farmers, middle-men, and landowners. The principal difference between England and Ireland was not, then, that the former had an expanding and increasingly hegemonic middle class while Ireland simply lacked a middle class (or had only a very attenuated one). The more crucial difference, Lloyd contends, hinges on the ownership of property. Essential to the notion of the middle classes as a force for social and political stability, he suggests, is the notion that this class owns property:

35 Herman Melville's *Moby-Dick* exemplifies the fate that any radical attempt to buck the English-American liberal Protestant cultural consensus was likely to incur in the nineteenth century. Now widely considered the greatest American novel of that time, it was poorly received when it appeared and had to await the modernist 1920s to receive its belated recognition. A deeply Calvinistic work that represents, as Ann Douglas has observed, an 'implicit critique of liberal Protestantism' that attempts 'to put the shark back into religion', as well as a searing investigation of the brutal acquisitiveness of (American) capitalist society, *Moby-Dick* flouted not only the temper but also the conventional form of the established novel traditions of its day and was hence greeted with incomprehension or hostility or both. See Douglas, 'Herman Melville and the Revolt Against the Reader', in *Feminization*, 289–326, 305–06.

36 Emer Nolan's *James Joyce and Nationalism* (London, 1995) discusses some of these issues with reference to the Western European and North American critical reception of Joyce.

it is this assumption that confers on the English yeoman farmer his exemplary iconic status in British political theory, whether liberal or conservative. For Lloyd, the whole formation of the middle classes in colonial Ireland is markedly different, since the vast proportion of middling and even large farmers were landholders, or tenants, rather than actual proprietors. This makes the nineteenth-century Irish middle class — vulnerable to extreme economic fluctuations in a dependent export economy and affiliated at one moment with the landowners, at another with the landless in those periods of agrarian struggle that continued across the century — a site of maximum instability in Irish social life. Hence this class was unable to serve as exemplars of stability, social harmony and progressive class reconciliation — the role typically attributed to their counterparts across the Irish channel in the English realist novel.[37]

The difference here, it should be noted, is not (as one reading of Lloyd's account might imply) that England was a nation of small rural landowners while in Ireland the occupants of the land were rent-paying tenants rather than proprietors. Indeed, most accounts of English rural history suggest that as a consequence of an exceptionally early programme of land enclosure there were only a very small number of independent, self-employed farmers in England. Eric Hobsbawm, for example, contends that nineteenth-century 'England was a country of mainly large landlords, cultivated by tenant farmers, working the land with hired labourers.'[38] In contrast to most of continental Europe, the rural petite bourgeoisie was of only small importance in the English rural class structure. Lloyd's argument could be extended and complicated, therefore, perhaps by studying not simply the different characters of the English and Irish middle classes, but the different relative weight of urban and rural petite bourgeoisie in each and the different economic composition of the two societies as well.

Historians seem now generally agreed that in England the development of modern industrial capitalism cannot be conceived in terms of a straightforward contest between a (falling) feudal aristocracy and a (rising) urban capitalist middle class. Instead, English capitalism traces its origins to a dynamic early modern agrarian economy, which saw the active early involvement of a substantial sector of the aristocracy and landlord class in capitalist commerce, and relatively little clear-cut opposition between bourgeoisie and aristocracy. Many of the larger English industrialists came from a landed, aristocratic background; indeed, studies suggest that almost 90 per cent of the leading steel magnates between 1850 and 1925 were drawn from that class.[39] In place of an openly revolutionary struggle between these two classes (imagined in terms of the French model) there appears, rather, to have been a long class compromise — which took the form of the establishment of commercial, political and marriage alliances between

---

37 Lloyd, 'Violence and the Constitution of the Novel', 138–41
38 E. J. Hobsbawm, *Industry and Empire* (London, 1968), 98
39 See J. Foster, *Class Struggle in the Industrial Revolution* (London, 1974) and C. Erikson, *British Industrialists: Steel and Hosiery 1850–1950* (Cambridge, 1959). Both authors are cited in Savage et al., *Property, Bureaucracy, and Culture*, 37.

the aristocratic and financier, mercantile and manufacturing capitalist élites, and a correspondent construction of a shared British patrician culture. At the apex of English society, then, was a highly cohesive propertied class: as some recent commentators have observed, 'whatever the social divisions between aristocrats, merchants, financiers, and industrialists, they all drew upon property assets to secure their dominant position in British society — usually as a means of securing rentier income'.[40]

In this context, the English novel can be regarded as a crucial literary form through which cross-class cultural compromise is negotiated. In *Desire and Domestic Fiction*, for example, Nancy Armstrong argues that middle-class values find their initial existence in literature and only later, through extended processes of socialization, in historical actuality. The English domestic novel, she contends, typically stages a class compromise that takes the form of a sexual or marriage drama in which a feminized representative of the middle orders (Pamela, Elizabeth Bennett, Emma, Jane Eyre) eventually persuades a male aristocrat (Mr. B., Darcy, Knightley, Rochester) to recognize the superiority of the middle-class values, modes of conduct and forms of subjectivity that she represents. The novel, in this view, can be seen as an engaged social form that actively participates in the elaboration of a new type of class subject; the form does not so much contest the old social hierarchies as to systematically redefine new ones. Its end, in Armstrong's words, was to create 'a new linguistic community, a class that was neither gentry nor nobility as the eighteenth century knew them, yet one that was clearly a leisure class and thus a paradoxical configuration that can only be called a middle-class aristocracy'.[41] The novel, in other words, was a vehicle for the remodelling of social authority: through the embourgeoisement of the aristocracy and the gentrification of the middle classes, a more unitary and integrated British élite culture was elaborated.

Nineteenth-century colonial Ireland, in contrast, was essentially a dependent, and chronically unstable, agrarian export economy, which, with the exception of the north-east, experienced no industrial revolution. Hence, the Irish middle class was concentrated in agriculture, shopkeeping, the professions, and in servicing the expanding imperial and domestic state bureaucracy, rather than in industrial factory manufacture or high finance. In these conditions, the kind of élite class compromise that was secured in England could never be realized. Whereas in England that compromise worked by way of mutually beneficial exchanges of entrepreneurial wealth for cultural distinction and by a sense of common participation in England's imperial modernizing mission, in Ireland trade-offs of capital and status in these terms were simply much more difficult. In a struggling agrarian economy, the Irish middle classes, composed mainly of a petite bourgeoisie that lacked substantive industrial or financier sectors, did not possess the economic capital that made their English counterparts attractive class partners for alliances with the landed élite. To compound matters, the Catholicism of

---

40 Savage et al., *Property, Bureaucracy, and Culture*, 37
41 Armstrong, *Desire and Domestic Fiction*, 160

the Irish middle classes meant that in the overall context of the British state they did not have the right cultural capital either. Moreover, in the absence of a strong industrial base, the primary generator of wealth was land, and hence the Irish middle and upper classes were essentially destined to wrestle unto death with each other over the same crucial commodity. This dilemma also extended to the state, where the interests of the Irish landed and middle classes were no less fundamentally at odds. To retain their power in Ireland, the mainly Protestant landlord class needed to maintain the Union with Britain. However, Irish bourgeois nationalism was impelled to release middle-class economic interests from their subordination under the Union to a much stronger English capitalism.

Given all these structural impediments, the competing strata of the aristocratic and upper middle classes in Ireland were incapable of welding together a cohesive class bloc or a securely integrated establishment culture of the English kind. It would be neither the old Protestant Ascendancy (which found its political expression in constructivist Unionism) nor the Catholic upper middle classes (that found its political vehicle in Redmondite Home Rule), but rather the Catholic lower middle class (that eventually threw its political weight behind a separatist Sinn Féin) that would give a political and cultural lead to the new Ireland that slowly emerged in the wake of the Land Wars. The fact that in nineteenth-century Ireland no single novel genre ever attains the consolidated, durable hegemony over other genres that the realist novel did in England may be symptomatic of the fact that a common élite culture of the English kind could not be replicated in Ireland; the constant slippage from one genre to another is evidence of a quest for such a common or cohesive patrician class culture that was in the end never really secured. In nineteenth-century Ireland, in marked contrast to England at any rate, no single novel species ever commands the literary field for very long. Instead, the Irish novel 'evolves' very episodically: the national tale attains a short vogue at the start of the century; then gothic and historical novel forms come to the fore; then the melodrama and assorted tales of peasant life; then French naturalist or decadent modes; the last, in turn, eventually to be moulded, in Joyce's hands, towards a high modernism that attained unprecedented international recognition but which was perhaps also unable to generate any sustained lineage either.

When one compares the respective drives towards reconciliation in the Irish and English novels in this context the differences are suggestive. In the novels of Richardson, Austen and Charlotte Brontë described by Armstrong, marriages are exclusively English and Protestant affairs; class boundaries may be crossed, but national or religious ones almost never are. In contrast, in the Irish and Scottish novels of the same period — such as those by Edgeworth, Owenson and Scott — the marriages are invariably between partners of different nationalities: in these novels the heroes are typically English, their brides Irish or Scottish. By all accounts, intermarriage between the 'Celtic' and English aristocracies was increasing dramatically in the early nineteenth century. Whereas in the Tudor and Stuart eras the landed establishments in England, Scotland, Wales and

Ireland had been substantially separate and discrete, the last quarter of the eighteenth and the first quarter of the nineteenth century saw the consolidation of a genuinely pan-British ruling élite that shared a common culture.[42] But even in the works of later less patrician, more middle-class, Catholic Irish authors such as Griffin, the Banims, and others, marriage plots continue to be frequently interdenominational, attesting to the durability of the religious cleavage as a real obstacle to the creation of a common élite national culture. In these narratives, the aim is clearly to imagine various alliances between Ireland's Anglo-Irish, English and Gaelic (or Catholic and Protestant) élites that might deliver a successful ruling class compromise after the English kind. In the Irish situation, the drive to reconcile through interdenominational marriage is certainly not a case of art imitating life: the recurrent Catholic–Protestant marriages in nineteenth-century Irish novels seem to be in inverse proportion to social reality, where in fact all churches were determinedly hardening the obstacles to 'mixed marriages'.[43] In England, the marriage novel — inaugurated by Richardson, perfected by Austen, brought to a conclusion by Trollope — proved itself a very durable vehicle for the exploration of the complex nexus where love, kinship, class and economic interests came into play. That form goes out of fashion in England only towards the end of the nineteenth century, when the whole substratum of sexual and economic interests on which it thrived was dissolved.[44] By the end of the century, Austenesque marriages between the English worlds of commerce and landed gentry no longer compel in the way they once did and two different vectors of development take its place: in the hands of Henry James, interest is shifted instead towards transcontinental marriages between American capital and European aristocracy; in those of Flaubert, the 'new women' writers, Ibsen and Joyce, the sanctity of marriage begins to be disenchanted altogether. The English marriage novel, in other words, was never just a compendium of arbitrary literary devices; it was a literary form that, like all literary forms, was an abstract expression of real social relations. It might be only a very short distance geographically from London to Dublin or Belfast, but the divergence between the social compositions of English and Irish nineteenth-century society was nonetheless very considerable indeed and the take up of the marriage novel in Ireland, therefore, offers an instructive example of what happens when forms developed in advanced capitalist societies find themselves transported to socially different situations.[45]

42 See Linda Colley, *Britons: Forging the Nation, 1707–1837* (New Haven, 1992), 159, 161, 164.
43 See David Harmon Akenson, *Small Differences: Irish Catholics and Irish Protestants, 1815–1922: An International Perspective* (Kingston and Montreal, 1988).
44 Social changes relevant to the dissolution of the older form include the Married Women's Property Act of 1882, which granted women control over their own property after marriage, and the Property Settlement Act, also of 1882, which freed landowners from the obligation to keep land in trust for future generations and allowed them to release it on to the market in their own lifetimes.
45 The notion of a class identity detachable from all other status considerations (such as race, religion, ethnicity) is perhaps a peculiarly English fiction — a consequence of the monolithically (even if schismatically) Protestant nature of that culture in the nineteenth century. In this respect at least,

It can scarcely be mere coincidence that the efflorescence of literary production that brought the Irish nineteenth century to a close on such a high note, after what is generally regarded as the relative doldrums of the long mid-century, should have occurred more or less concurrently with the disintegration of the material infrastructure of the high Victorian literary system and, with it, of the cultural authority of the British realist novel. It might of course be the case that the relative poverty of mid-nineteenth-century Irish literary production, especially in the novel, is a retrospective construction, a view of things established by the Irish Literary Revival, many of the tutelary figures of which, especially Yeats, were temperamentally disposed to prefer poetic to novelistic forms, the latter deemed the medium of a dully prosaic and empiricist and generally debased modern age. Nevertheless, even allowing for the propensity of all cultural revivals to mythologize their own efforts by downplaying those of precursor generations, there were some seismic shifts in the material bases of late nineteenth-century cultural production that may have been decisive to the cultural breakthrough that we now call the Irish Literary Revival. Under the presiding cultural conditions of high Victorian culture, this might have been much more difficult to achieve. Ironically, the expansion of market forces that Yeats and the Revivalists generally deplored may well have had no small part in creating this opening.

According to the sociologists of cultural production, one of the more decisive shifts in the whole apparatus of English cultural production in the late nineteenth century was the collapse of the three-decker novel form and of the subscription libraries, Mudie's and W. H. Smith's, on which that whole enterprise had depended. As Paul Delany and others have noted, in the period between 1840 and 1870 all the major novels in the United Kingdom were put out by seven publishers, and in this system two main libraries, but especially Mudie's Select Library (the word 'select' here meaning that Mudie himself would screen out in advance any works deemed offensive to taste and decency), might order more than half of any novel's print run. Under such conditions, the novel market was effectively supplied and controlled by Mudie, something which meant that his company had not only an enormous capacity to maintain cultural norms, but also that in this period the novel enjoyed a stability of form and a degree of cultural authority that was to be drastically eroded in the less-regulated and more diversified literary marketplace that emerged in the last two decades of the century.

When Mudie's system collapsed (George Moore's energetic campaign against it in the 1880s in the interests of promoting French naturalism and his own naturalistic novels might be remembered in this context) in the 1890s, novels began to appear instead in one-volume units of diverse length, the cost of these reduced to about a third of previous rates.

nineteenth-century Ireland now appears in some ways more 'modern' than England, where questions of race, religion, ethnicity would only seriously trouble the question of national identity after World War II when inwards migration from the ex-colonies created a multi-racial, multi-religious society and the decline of Britain as an imperial superpower loosened the cultural bonds that had once cemented its English, Scottish, Irish and Welsh élites in a common British imperial identity.

Novelists now had to earn their success on the basis of thousands of individual consumer decisions rather than on the bulk purchases of a handful of subscriber libraries.[46] (The term 'individual decisions' needs to be understood in the context of the rise of new marketing and advertising industries in this period as well.) Initially, the collapse of the three-decker system made the market for fiction more disorderly, though things were soon enough restructured by the appearance of new genres. In one way or another, however, the disintegration of a central support of the high Victorian literary régime led to a recentring of literary authority and allowed for a relaxation of long-established generic and moral constraints. It seems likely that this can only have been an enabling development for all minority literati groups, such as the Irish, who might have been seeking out reading publics rather different to the restricted one maintained under the previous régime.

But if the Irish Revival may have owed something to the increased capitalization of culture that brought about an end to the high Victorian literary régime, it may also have benefited from the dissolution of Irish popular culture — a process speeded by the Famine and by the emergence of modern mass culture, itself facilitated by the extension of compulsory primary education and the greater availability of cheap newspapers and other forms of commercial entertainment. The Revivalists were much disposed to regret and to romanticize the decline of Irish popular or folk culture and much of their efforts were bent on salvaging what they deemed to be its residual vestiges. Nonetheless, by transmuting what was largely an oral culture into print, with all of the attendant shifts in everything from modes of transmission and reception to the restructuring of subjectivity that this involved, the Revivalists themselves became the beneficiaries of the death of the very culture they lamented. Indeed, one way to read the Revival would be to see it (whether in the form of the Abbey Theatre, the Gaelic League or the Gaelic Athletic Association), not as the backward-looking movement its detractors usually take it to be, but rather as an opportunistic move to insert into the space between a dying popular and an expanding commercial zone a form of nationalist high literary culture that had previously lacked the social conditions and institutional vehicles to secure it. Not until the force of popular culture had diminished, perhaps, could this national 'literature' (with all of the connotations of the autonomy of the artist, the individualization of production and consumption, the separation of literary from other 'non-creative' modes of writing, and so forth, that this word connotes) achieve the national authority to which it aspired.

While the demise of Irish popular culture and the domestic decentring of the high Victorian literary marketplace may both have helped to create openings within which the Revival could find room for itself, it is also important to remember that Irish writers at the start of the twentieth century, in contrast to those in the long interval between the Battle of Waterloo and the death of Victoria, were operating in an international arena where

---

46 For a more extended discussion of the issues discussed here, see Delany, 'The New Literary Marketplace, 1870–1914', in his *Literature, Money and the Marketplace*, 97–124.

the authority of English literature was less secure than it had been. At the start of the nineteenth-century, American cultural nationalism was still only a weak force in terms of literary production and offered only a very timorous challenge to the regulative force of English cultural authority. By the closing decades of the century much had changed. In the period after Twain and Whitman especially, American literature acquired a much more confident and vigorously assertive note and the American vernacular had been much more fully liberated from the idioms and idiolects of English high culture.

The English language enjoyed enormous global expansion concurrent with the spread of the British Empire, and this expansion came at the cost of a drastic sweeping aside of indigenous languages everywhere from Ireland and Scotland to North America, Australia and New Zealand. Nevertheless, as English expanded, regional anglophone vernaculars (abetted in no small way by the continuing force of Romanticism) would eventually emerge to challenge the idiolects and value-systems represented by Home Counties English and received pronunciation. Literary Australians, Canadians, South Africans or New Zealanders might have been slower, for historical reasons, than their American, Irish or Caribbean counterparts to challenge English cultural hegemony, but in many respects the story of twentieth-century anglophone literature is the decentring of English literary authority. This generated the widespread belief that English literature has itself suffered a steady decline. One does not have to subscribe entirely to this story to see, nonetheless, that, starting with the attempts by émigré Americans such as James, Pound and T.S. Eliot to take commanding positions as the great critical arbiters of English literary tradition, and with the concurrent attempts by the Irish Revivalist-period writers such as Yeats, Synge and Joyce to fashion a whole new English literary idiom altogether, changes were under way that would mean that English writers would never again be able to assume the globalized authority or the attendant sense of totalizing vision of the great English Victorians. This did not at all mean that the way was now magically cleared for a new golden age for the Irish novel (the twentieth-century Irish successes in the form have been quite intermittent and patchy, to say the least). But at least the obstacles now to be cleared were quite different to those that loomed when a more magisterial Britannia ruled the subscription library shelves.

6

The dominant forms of English literary history have constructed an evolutionary grand narrative of the novel, which, as William Warner comments,

> tells the story of the novel's 'rise' in the eighteenth century (with Defoe, Richardson and Fielding), of its achievement of classical solidity of form in the nineteenth century (with Austen, Dickens, Thackeray, Eliot, the early James and Conrad), and of its culmination in a modernist experimentation and self-reflection (with the later

James, Woolf, Joyce, and Beckett) that paradoxically fulfills and surpasses 'the novel' in one blow.[47]

Marxist and feminist literary historians have disputed and complicated many elements of this grand narrative, but have not, for the most part, critically challenged the nationalized frame and the developmentalist teleology that secure the overarching narrative itself. That the development of the English novel could appear so autotelic a process is partly a function of the imperial aloofness and insularity of nineteenth-century British culture, and partly of the narrowly nationalised disciplinary boundaries that have typically defined literary studies in the English-based university system in modern times. Irish literary historians have tended too often to borrow their basic models and methods from English literary history, and have taken the English 'Progress of the Novel' narrative as the norm by which Irish deviance, deficiency, and native achievement can then be gauged.

The argument here is not with comparative evaluation as such. However, the development of a properly postcolonial literary history would require a form of comparativist analysis that scrapped the idea that the development of the English novel is somehow normative and universal, that moved beyond the narrowly Anglocentric frame of reference that has (ironically but predictably) dominated attempts to construct Irish nationalist counter-histories, and that would instead situate the nineteenth-century Irish novel in a much broader globalized frame.

Like colonial economies, colonial cultures tend to be more dependent, more open to external interference and influence, more immediately subject to external intellectual pressures, than powerful metropolitan cultures. They differ, too, in that colonialism by definition entails the subordination of one culture to another. The dialectics of cultural development in colonial contexts are thus clearly different in some fundamental ways to those in metropolitan centres, which, because of their economic-military-technological might, naturally represent themselves as cultural leaders, as 'universal' societies, and not as dependencies, regional redoubts, or cultural importers. Moreover, writers and intellectuals in the colonies and peripheries of the world system have no choice but to refer to intellectual and cultural trends in the metropolis; writers and intellectuals in the centre normally feel no compunction to reciprocate. Any worthwhile postcolonial theory or literary history attentive to the importance of such exchange must also attend to the asymmetries that condition that exchange.

This is not to say, though, that colonial and peripheral cultures are consequently always more provincial or backward or indeed any less energetic or creative than metropolitan cultures. If colonial cultures are more dependent than metropolitan ones, they may sometimes be compelled for the same reason to be more innovative and experimental, less insular and more receptive to developments elsewhere. And just as advanced imperial societies always risk losing their hegemony since the technological advances that secured their dominance at one moment in history may actually retard their later development in a changed global environment, so too colonial economies that lagged behind in 'backwardness' at one historical moment may overleap or skip some metropolitan stages of development and move directly on to others. Cultural processes do not operate in the same way as economic or technological processes, but certainly where cultural forms and genres are concerned, a similar calculus of combined and uneven development may be an appropriate interpretive model.

Peripheral cultures, in sum, have to wrestle with different constraints, handicaps and dilemmas than metropolitan cultures do, but this can be a spur and stimulus, as well as an obstacle, to cultural and intellectual creativity. What this means is that the organicist, insular and narrowly nationalized models of social and cultural history usually favoured both by imperialist and anti-imperial nationalist historiography are particularly disabling and misplaced in colonial and peripheral societies. The purpose of a new postcolonial history of the nineteenth-century Irish novel would not be to recover or manufacture after the fact the estimable canon, the want of which both writers at the time and critics since have lamented. Nor would it be to demonstrate how a distressed realism was transmuted by modernist alchemy into international cultural gold. Rather, its object would be to establish both the achievements of the colonial peripheries and the negative consequences that invariably attend such situations. A history of this kind would also work to make connections between different colonial societies, the better to investigate how they negotiated their predicaments. The novel need not always be the hero of its own history; literary history need not always be the *Bildungsroman* of the form. The great metropolitan canons, and the magisterial literary histories they generated, need not be models in colonial or postcolonial situations. But by working to diagnose the complex dynamics of political and cultural power, as they operate nationally and transnationally, postcolonial scholarship may yet illuminate matters more important than either the glories of the nation or the genius of the form.

Capital and Culture in Twentieth-Century Ireland: Changing Configurations

Most accounts of contemporary Irish culture tend to be largely affirmative, even Whiggish, in cast. The contemporary cultural moment is recurrently described as one of renaissance, experiment and iconoclasm, a moment vitalized by the emergence of radical new voices, styles, media, forms, and energies. This upbeat view is clearly underpinned by a broader socio-historical narrative, also of a decidedly Whiggish temper, in which contemporary Irish society is construed as one engaged over recent decades in an often laborious, but on the whole overwhelmingly successful, overcoming of a more repressive, provincial, censorious past. As Irish society leaves behind that past to become more liberal and secular, more multicultural and confidently European in its outlook, contemporary Irish culture — the account runs — gives imaginative expression to this emergent new reality.

The very concept of 'the contemporary cultural moment' presupposes some kind of watershed or break that allows us to distinguish between 'the way things are now' and 'the way they were before'. However, in most of the surveys that document the achievements of the present it is precisely the *absence* of any serious attempt to establish what (if indeed anything) is decisively new about the cultural physiognomy of the present moment that is most conspicuous. Every decade will obviously produce its own cultural novelties (one recalls Walter Benjamin's remark that 'fashion is the eternal recurrence of the new'), but if novelty in this restricted sense is the only measure of change, then no decade can be considered qualitatively very different to any other. Yet when commentators discuss the changing landscape of contemporary Irish culture they generally appear to make some stronger or more excited claim for the present than the mere fact of novelty in this basic sense. The general impression typically conveyed in such surveys is that the emergence of new women writers, of the new urban writing, of more popular literary forms and genres such as 'chick lit' or Irish detective fiction, together with the domestic and international successes of the Irish film and music industries, collectively amount to some sort of sea change more significant than the perennial turnover of personnel and seasonal fashion.[1]

All of this is to say that unless cultural critics can identify some sort of meaningful break with, or mutation within, the cultural system that preceded it, and unless they can diagnose how and why such a rupture might have occurred, then the term 'the contemporary moment' becomes pretty meaningless. The term presupposes some kind of literary periodization, some implicit model of cultural history, but surveys of contemporary Irish culture have tended to evade explicit theoretical engagement with such tasks — the accumulation of lists of new writers, artists, genres, awards and achievements, real or imagined, creating an impression of new things afoot, but without any capacity to identify the nature, significance or direction of change as such. It might even be argued that the five-volume Field Day Anthology of Irish Writing has furnished Irish studies with something like a viable canon of Irish literature (one that is, to be sure, like all canons, gapped, tendentious, and contested), but that Irish studies still lacks serious materialist attempts to historicize Irish literary and cultural production. Marxist critics have always had a special commitment to the historical analysis of culture; the ambitious models of cultural history developed by Georg Lukács and Fredric Jameson are some of the more influential examples in modern times.

The difficulty with the historical schemas developed by Lukács and Jameson is that they cannot easily be transposed onto the Irish situation. Whatever their differences otherwise, these Marxist cultural histories are elaborated with a metropolitan European or Euro-American capitalist history in mind. Lukács's work takes its bearings primarily from French and German (and to a lesser extent English and Russian) literary history; Jameson's addresses itself to a Western European (England–France–Germany) and United States context (though his later work tries to extend the frame). However, from well before the modern period, Irish history had evolved in ways that did not conform in some decisive respects to developments in the metropolitan cultures that inform Lukács's or Jameson's works. To begin with, unlike most of Western Europe, Ireland had escaped the conquest of Roman imperialism, and was, in Brendan Bradshaw's words, 'no more than superficially touched by the cultural and institutional cargo' which that empire brought with it.[2] It was out of that institutional cargo that medieval European feudalism emerged when the Roman Empire collapsed, but, with the exception of areas controlled by the Anglo-Norman invaders in the south and east, the feudal system never substantially penetrated Ireland. Later, from the early modern period, when other

1   For an example of the kind of survey discussed here, see P. J. Mathews, 'In Praise of "Hibernocentrism": Republicanism, Globalisation and Irish Culture', The Republic: A Journal of Contemporary and Historical Debate, 4 (2005), 7–14.

2   Brendan Bradshaw, 'Irish Nationalism: An Historical Perspective', Bullán: An Irish Studies Journal, 5, 1 (2000), 5

Western European countries such as Portugal, Spain, the Netherlands, England, France, Belgium and eventually Germany became, each for a time at least, successive centres of capitalist and imperial expansion, Ireland was the only country in that geographical area to be subjected to a sustained, thoroughgoing and culturally traumatic experience of colonization. For its nearest European neighbours, then, modernity was synonymous with the assumption of key structural positions in the emerging capitalist world system, and with the accumulation of wealth, the monopolization of the means of violence, and that sense of national aggrandisement and cultural distinction that attended the rupture with the pre-modern.

For Ireland, in contrast, modernity meant dispossession, subordination and the loss of sovereignty, the collapse of its indigenous social order, the gradual disintegration of its Gaelic cultural system, and successive waves of politically or economically enforced emigration. Capitalist modernity in Ireland, in other words, advanced within a colonial régime under which the country remained the most chronically unstable and rebellious location within the British archipelago from the early modern period until the late twentieth century. Whereas other Western European economies were dramatically transformed in the nineteenth and early twentieth centuries by the first and second industrial revolutions, most of Ireland remained non-industrialized and its economy continued to be, until very recently, unusually dependent for a Western European region on export-oriented agricultural production. The colonial legacies of economic subordination and dependency, technological underdevelopment, massive emigration to the industrial centres of Britain and the United States, and sectarian violence inscribed in a postcolonial partitionist state order have conditioned much of the shape and texture of twentieth-century Irish history.

Because Marxist models of European history have always assumed as normative the transition from feudalism via absolutism to mercantile and later industrial capitalism, or a series of structural modulations within capitalism of the kind described by Ernest Mandel, Irish history has always proved quite recalcitrant to conventional Marxist emplotment.[3] To take a particularly vivid example, when mid-nineteenth-century English capitalist development issued in the Industrial Revolution that made Great Britain 'the workshop of the world', Ireland was devastated by the social catastrophe of the Great Famine. While the one society, in other words, was being transmogrified by developments that would make it the nineteenth century's greatest superpower, the other was being transmogrified in very different ways by what might be termed an early Victorian holocaust.[4] Nevertheless, while this massive discrepancy in national experience speaks for itself, the real challenge posed by these concurrent developments is to conceive of them not as two altogether alien and disjunctive histories but rather

3   Ernest Mandel, *Late Capitalism* (London, 1975)
4   The term alludes to Mike Davis's remarkable book *Late Victorian Holocausts: El Niño Famines and the Making of the Third World* (London, 2001), which suggests that the Irish Famine might be viewed, in wider global terms, in this way.

as two divergent vectors of the same capitalist modernization process. The particular theoretical challenge of the Irish situation is to be able to deal with the ways in which the country has developed by capitalist modernizing processes quite different to those in the major metropolitan European and American states, while simultaneously allowing for the fact that its distinct development has always been shaped and conditioned by capitalist developments, proximate or distant, in these core metropolitan zones. The challenge, in other words, is to steer a course between a Scylla that would simply stress the country's sameness to the metropolitan states, thereby effacing difference to shoehorn Ireland into a standard metropolitan template, and a Charybdis that would stress only its fundamental alterity (its exceptional or anomalous or aberrant elements) to the metropolitan centres.

   In this light, the object of this chapter is to take a long view of twentieth-century Irish literary and cultural history, locating that history in terms of a wider metropolitan European and Euro-American transition from modernism to postmodernism of the kind theorized by Marxist critics such as Fredric Jameson and Perry Anderson. Though Jameson's work on modernism and postmodernism is the better known, Anderson's will also be considered here because it has usefully 'rewritten' Jameson in ways that attempt to reinsert social and political levels that the latter's work, focused overwhelmingly as it is on connecting cultural developments to changes in the economic base, generally overlooks. The basic assumption will be that Ireland does not exist entirely 'outside' of the histories of capital and culture theorized by these Marxist cultural historians. The history of Euro-American capital and culture is certainly not the universal history many Marxists have taken it to be, but that history has nonetheless impressed itself on developments in most parts of the world, and more heavily on Ireland, perhaps because of its location, than on many other colonized regions.

2

In Mandel's *Late Capitalism*, modern capitalism is deemed to have passed through three successive long economic cycles and systemic mutations, each characterized by its own distinct technologies, labour régimes, and sectoral dominants.[5] Jameson's work rests on the idea that these three phases can be correlated to three major aesthetic dominants or macrostructures that he terms realism, modernism, and postmodernism. The idea of an aesthetic 'dominant' here refers to a cultural ascendancy that will never exhaust the entire phase in question, but that designates, rather, the most novel and salient aesthetic forms of any period. The dominant aesthetic mode of a particular period, therefore, always coexists with residual, contrapuntal and emergent modes as well, though the cultural dominant, as Michael Walsh puts it, occupies 'the hegemonic high ground

5   Mandel, *Late Capitalism*, ch. 4, and *passim*

within a given society at a historical moment'.[6] Radical breaks between one period and
the next are not conceived as involving complete changes of content, but rather as the
structural reconfiguration of a certain number of already given elements: features that
in an earlier period or system were subordinate or peripheral within the larger system
now become central and dominant, and features that had been dominant again become
secondary.[7]

The function of any decisive cultural transformation, Jameson contends, 'will be to
invent the life habits of the new social world', to 'de-program' subjects trained in an older
formation, and to provide imaginary resolutions to the contradictions and antinomies
that constitute specific social orders. Viewed thus, nineteenth-century 'realism' was not
simply a descriptive or mimetic copy of nineteenth-century society; its praxis, rather,
was to deprogramme the older providential and sacred narratives of the pre-capitalist
period, and to provide new cultural paradigms of the subject's relations 'to what now
comes to be thought of as reality'.[8] To understand realism, therefore, we must grasp
it as a component of the vaster historical project of the bourgeois cultural revolution
in which the whole economico-psychic structure of feudalism was dismantled and
a new bourgeois economico-psychic subjectivity installed in its place. For Jameson,
the essential tasks of the realist novel are twofold: on the one hand, to critique and
disaggregate the sacred narratives of the older medieval world; on the other, to produce
the new secular and disenchanted object world of the commodity system, the world of
which it will then claim to be the 'realistic' reflection.[9]

Modernism, as Jameson construes it, is a cultural mode that emerges at a later
moment when capitalism dramatically extends its global reach (via imperialism), but
when, nonetheless, 'the technologically (or socially) modern was still little more than
an enclave; in which the country still coexists with the city and still largely outweighs
it'.[10] As Harry Harootunian puts it, glossing Jameson, the spectacle of lived unevenness
across the political, economic, and socio-cultural domains allowed modernism to
develop, and it was that lived experience of 'simultaneous non-simultaneity' (Ernst
Bloch) that modernism took as its predicate and problematic.[11] Modernism, in sum, is
a term that designates the matrix of possible aesthetic responses to a condition defined
by this clash between the pre-industrial and the advanced-industrial at a juncture when
the latter was still only emergent; it corresponds to the lived experience of the uneven

6   Michael Walsh, 'Jameson and "Global Aesthetics"', in David Bordwell and Noël Carroll, eds., *Post-Theory:
    Reconstructing Film Studies* (Madison, 1996), 481–500, 482
7   Fredric Jameson, 'Postmodernism and Consumer Society', in Peter Brooker, ed., *Modernism/Postmodernism*
    (London and New York, 1992), 163–79, 177
8   Fredric Jameson, *Signatures of the Visible* (London and New York, 1990), 164–66
9   Fredric Jameson, *The Political Unconscious* (Ithaca, 1981), 152
10 Cited in Santiago Colas, 'The Third World in Jameson's *Postmodernism or the Cultural Logic of Late Capitalism*',
    Social Text, 10 (1992), 258–70, 261
11 Harry D. Harootunian, *Overcome by Modernity: History, Culture and Community in Interwar Japan* (Princeton,
    2000), xxii–xxiii

temporalities of 'simultaneous non-simultaneity' produced by the violent collision of these two very different lifeworlds. In his earlier writings, Jameson stresses that both modernism and mass culture must be conceived as dialectical counterparts. Whereas mass culture succumbs to the logic of the commodity (though not without retaining some muted capacity to express dissatisfied desires and utopian longings), the formally difficult experiments of modernism represent a desperate attempt to outflank the commodification process — though the price for this was that modernism took on an esoteric character and that it lost touch with the wider publics to which the great realists still had access.[12]

In Jameson's schema, the postmodern is 'what you have when the capitalist modernization process is complete'.[13] This moment arrives when capitalism has finally attained global reach, having abolished all remaining pre-capitalist modes of production or having subsumed them within its compass. By then it has also penetrated the unconscious and hence become normalized to the extent that we find it increasingly difficult to imagine either pre- or post-capitalist forms of existence. Jameson accepts that there is considerable formal, stylistic and even thematic continuity between modernist and postmodernist artistic forms and cultural practice. But he insists that, despite such similarities, what matters is that cultural production functions differently in the modernist and postmodernist periods, since, with the extension of the commodity logic, the older distinctions between high and mass culture have now largely collapsed. In postmodernity, the disintegration of the older forms of bourgeois subjectivity, already symptomatically beginning to come apart in modernism, is now complete. This disappearance of the older modes of bourgeois psychic economy has taken place concurrently with the disarticulation of any unified class subject as well; hence political dissent in the late twentieth century tends increasingly to be elaborated not so much in terms of some singular agent of historical change (the working class, women), but in more fragmented, localized, and identitarian forms. Jameson does allow for some remaining pockets of resistance within the postmodern moment — identified with the underclass ghettos of the advanced capitalist world and with peripheral 'Third World' formations or anti-systemic movements — but these are not seriously or systematically integrated into his larger theory.

Jameson does not conceive of the relationship between the economic and cultural sphere in terms of base-superstructure reflection; culture serves, rather, as a means of transcoding the dominant mode of production, so that the mediations between the two spheres become a central issue in his work. Nevertheless, even if Jameson allows for what Michael Walsh calls 'the complex semiautonomy of the cultural', because it is premised on tracking the relationship between cultural production and very large scale economic

12 Fredric Jameson, 'Reification and Utopia in Mass Culture', in *Signatures of the Visible*, 9–34
13 Fredric Jameson, *Postmodernism; or, The Cultural Logic of Late Capitalism* (Durham, 1990), ix

changes, the absent intermediate level in his work tends to be the political.[14] In this respect, at least, Anderson's attempts to theorize modernism and postmodernism in terms of a complex conjuncture or intersection of diverse socio-politcal and economic forces represents a useful supplement to Jameson's model. One of Anderson's key concepts is that of the 'conjuncture': a term that denotes the exact balance or configuration of forces, and the overdetermination of the contradictions that obtain within that balance, that can be said to constitute a particular historical moment.

For Anderson, it is significant that the most extensive European modernist movements emerged in the early twentieth century not in the most industrially advanced or most 'modern' country of the time — England — but rather in locations where complex conjunctures allowed for 'the intersection of different historical temporalities'.[15] Modernism, he argues, emerged in continental Europe within a cultural force field comprised of and triangulated by three co-ordinates. The first was the codification of a highly formalized academicism in the visual and other arts that drilled students in the major styles and models of the classical or neo-classical past. These academies were the cultural gatekeepers to societies still massively dominated by aristocratic or landowning classes, which, though in relative decline economically, continued to set the political and cultural tone in Europe for many years after World War I. The second co-ordinate was the incipient, hence essentially novel, emergence within these still largely pre-industrial societies of the key technologies or inventions of the second industrial revolution: the chemical and synthetic industries, electric power, the internal combustion engine, telephone, radio, cinema, aircraft, the skyscraper and the hydro-electric dam. Mass consumption industries, Anderson contends, were not yet implanted anywhere in Europe, however. A third decisive co-ordinate was the imaginative proximity of social revolution. In no European country at the start of the twentieth century was bourgeois democracy completed in the sense that adult suffrage was extended to all (women and many workers did not have the vote), and the insurgent labour movement still remained largely outside of the parliamentary system and had not been co-opted as a political force. The extent of hope for, or apprehension about, revolution varied widely across Europe, but it was everywhere 'in the air' during the belle époque and especially after the Russian Revolution. Across Europe, then, the old order still clung on tenaciously in both the political and cultural spheres, but it was everywhere shadowed by the convulsions triggered by the second industrial revolution and by the spectre of political revolution — a sense that the future was radically open-ended pervaded the moment.

What was the specific contribution of each co-ordinate to the wider force field defining modernism? For Anderson, the persistence of the anciens régimes and the concomitant academicism of the state cultural institutions provided an established set of cultural

14 Walsh, 'Jameson and "Global Aesthetics"', 484
15 Perry Anderson, 'Modernity and Revolution', in Cary Nelson and Lawrence Grossberg, eds., Marxism and the Interpretation of Culture (Houndmills, 1988), 317–38, 324

values against which the otherwise very heterogeneous modernist movements could define themselves. Without this common adversary, the divergent new modernist movements and artistic practices had little unity: it was their shared hostility to the consecrated romantic and realist canons and to the cultural mortmain of the *ancien régime* academies and conservatories that constituted their collective identity as such. But if they rejected a staid official academicism, many different modernist movements also rejected the commodity market as the alternative organizing principle of culture and society. If nothing else, the old order offered a conception of art as a higher vocation (dedicated to conceptions of value at odds with capitalist culture) that was still available to the modernist artist. Finally, the wave of technological advances that defined the second industrial revolution and the prospect of political revolution lent the period an electric atmosphere — oscillating between apocalyptic anxiety and utopian hope — in which it was possible to imagine a wholly transformed social order qualitatively different to that which currently existed.

For both Jameson and Anderson, the gradual disintegration of the co-ordinates that had sustained the modernist cultural field prepared the ground for the contemporary (post-1970s) ascendance of postmodernism. As Anderson conceives it, modernism continued as a defining cultural force until World War II, which delivered the final death blow to the old agrarian and aristocratic élites and their way of life all across Europe. These classes had already been mortally maimed by World War I, but their traditional rival, the haute bourgeoisie, struggled to maintain the distinctive social and cultural universe of the old order for another twenty years, until it too began to dissolve as a class. The suggestion is not that class divisions have diminished since World War II or that overall levels of class mobility have significantly increased. What has changed is that the strong sense of belonging to a distinct and well-defined class that characterized the old élites has evaporated in the new conditions of mass consumerism that developed in Western Europe, especially from the 1970s onwards. In this historically novel situation, the old split between high and popular culture that had rested on the separation between well-educated élites and illiterate or semi-literate majorities began to lose its force. The expansion of higher education and the ubiquity of mass culture made possible by new media have restructured the wider cultural landscape. High culture is now a niche interest cultivated by fractions of the intelligentsia and university-educated middle classes, while the majority of all classes, rich and poor, is attached to the mass entertainment of the culture industry.[16] For long, Anderson argues, sociologists have debated the embourgeoisement of the European working classes, but in 'a monetary world that knows no social fixities or stable identities' it was the *encanaillement* of the possessing classes that represented the more significant phenomenon.[17] In a context

16 On this topic, see Néstor Garcia Canclini, 'Latin American Contradictions: Modernism without Modernization?', in *Hybrid Cultures: Strategies for Entering and Leaving Modernity* (Minneapolis, 1995), 41–65, 58.

17 Perry Anderson, *The Origins of Postmodernity* (London and New York, 1998), 85, 86

where the old academicist establishments and the more rigidly codified bourgeois value-systems against which it rebelled have both become effectively obsolete, modernism has lost the coherence and shock value that depended on the sense of having a well-defined adversary culture, and hence it can no longer maintain the oppositional stance it had once claimed.[18]

Second, whereas modernism in the first half of the twentieth century had thrived on the excitements of the technological advances of the second industrial revolution, technological innovation acquired a more baleful cast by the second half of the century with the invention of the atom bomb and the inauguration of the Cold War: in this climate, the malevolent spectre of technological apocalypse largely eclipsed the technological utopianism of the early twentieth century. The most decisive technological advance of the postwar era, Anderson contends, was television, and especially colour television, which only became generally available in the 1970s. Television and the extraordinary wave of new computer and communications technologies that have followed it, he suggests, following Jameson, are essentially technologies of reproduction rather than production. Where art is concerned, the crucial difference between the wave of technological innovations released by the second industrial revolution and those of the late twentieth century 'information revolution', is that whereas the earlier innovations were themselves silent and were thus available to be represented by the arts since they could not represent themselves, the new computer-and-media-driven, discourse-and-image-producing technical environment of the postmodern moment is such that all the arts are now increasingly engorged into and reprocessed via these new modes of communication.[19]

Of the conditions that had enabled modernism, the last to disappear was the spectre of revolution. This did not vanish overnight; it continued to haunt the post-World War II period and in the late sixties the conjuncture of student and worker strikes across Western Europe, decolonization movements in the 'Third World', the hopes for a revitalized Communism after Stalin, together with the sexual revolution, created a radical ferment of an intensity not seen since the twenties. But this conjuncture proved a mere Indian summer and by the seventies the right resumed control with Thatcher and Reagan. By the end of the eighties, Soviet Communism had collapsed, the 'Third World' postcolonial revolutions had failed to deliver economic emancipation, the welfare state created by postwar social democracy in Western Europe was downsized, and the triumph of neo-liberalism seemed assured.

It is, Anderson argues, in this altered conjuncture that the new postmodernist field emerges into view: 'postmodernism emerged from the constellation of a *déclassé* ruling order, a mediatized technology, and a monochrome politics.'[20] Capitalism itself, he

18 *Origins of Postmodernity*, 86
19 *Origins of Postmodernity*, 87–89
20 *Origins of Postmodernity*, 92

adds, entered a new phase after the postwar boom ended, characterized by the assault on organized industrial labour in the capitalist cores; by outsourcing to the peripheries of the world system; by the dramatic rise of finance capital and exchange speculation relative to manufacturing; and by the vulgar nouveau riche consumerism and hedonism that dominated the eighties and nineties:

> The departure of aristocracy, the evanescence of the bourgeoisie, the erosion of working-class confidence and identity, have altered the supports and targets of artistic practice in fundamental ways. It is not that alternative addressees have simply disappeared. New poles of oppositional identification have emerged in the postmodern period: gender, race, ecology, sexual orientation, regional or continental diversity. But these have to date constituted a weaker set of antagonisms.[21]

In this new conjuncture, the political field no longer lends itself to organization in right–left terms as it once did, and the absence of any clear global alternative to capitalism narrows the spectrum of political choice; this diminished sense of alternative to late capitalism vitiating artistic culture as well. The postmodern cultural moment, for Anderson, lacks both the towering individual geniuses or the intransigent collective vanguard movements of the modernist period. Where new avant-gardes do appear, they are incorporated into the commodity market with unprecedented rapidity. Whereas the modernists had tended, broadly speaking, to ally themselves either with the *élan* of the old aristocracy or with the egalitarian dreams of a still emergent, still radical labour movement, or even in some instances with both, in the altered conditions that constitute the postmodern the possibilities of imaginative investment in either the upper atmosphere of titled leisure or the lower dreams of manual labour have receded.

While the new postmodern conjuncture is no longer organized by the co-ordinates that structured its modernist predecessor, Anderson does sketch what he identifies as a constitutive tension within the postmodernist cultural field between its *citra* and *ultra* tendencies. The *citra* includes all those tendencies that dispense with the more difficult and inassimilable parts of modernism to make it more accessible; the *ultra* refers to those tendencies that have attempted to radicalize modernism's negation of immediate gratification or sensuous intelligibility. The one attempts to adjust art to the ubiquity of commodification and the spectacle; the other, still to elude this fate. But, in the postmodernist moment, the weight of the *ultra* to *citra* tendencies is clearly the inverse to that of the earlier modernist epoch — the seesaw has tilted to the other end.[22] While it is certainly the case that much of the 'Third World' has far lower degrees of consumption and much less advanced levels of technological development than those associated with Western postmodernism, the development of global communications

---

21 *Origins of Postmodernity*, 104
22 *Origins of Postmodernity*, 105–06

systems — especially television — has ensured, Anderson suggests, 'an incomparably greater degree of cultural penetration of the former Second and Third Worlds' than had been the case even as late as the sixties. In these conditions, the influence of postmodern forms makes itself felt well beyond the core Western metropolitan regions, so that today there is little reason to doubt that even 'the damned of the earth too have entered the kingdom of the spectacle'.[23]

3

How helpful is this conception of things for any diagnosis or periodization of twentieth-century Irish cultural development? If, as Anderson suggests, modernist cultural currents were strongest, not where industrialization and the new corporate capitalism were already at their most advanced, but in situations of combined and uneven development, where relatively small industrial enclaves were hatched within an older aristocratic or predominantly agrarian and pre-industrial order, then Ireland accords with this profile well enough. Late nineteenth-century Ireland possessed an unusually modernized state structure (itself a product of colonial rule), strong basic literacy levels in comparative European terms, and Belfast was then the world's fifth largest industrial city. This notwithstanding, across the island as a whole, the economy and workforce were still overwhelmingly rural, artisan, and pre-industrial. For many, a direct link can be traced between this retarded industrial and technological development and the supposed conservatism of Irish cultural production in the Revival period. In his essay 'The Archaic Avant-Garde', for instance, Terry Eagleton argues that Ireland in this period was as much a capitalist formation as its British counterpart, but that the Irish variety 'was a woefully inert brand of rural capitalism, an old-fashioned form of modernity'. Moreover, he contends, the prime mover of modernization in Ireland was 'the rural middle class', which he deems 'one of the most conservative formations in Western Europe' since it 'lacked the challenge of an industrial middle class to spur it into life'. 'There could be,' he concludes, 'no exhilarating encounter between art and technology in such an industrially backward nation.'[24]

Here, Eagleton seems to assume too reflex and unmediated a connection between economic base and culture. It is as though a largely rural society and rural middle class must inevitably produce a reactionary ruralist culture. Yet, as Anderson points out, it was precisely in the least industrially advanced European societies — most strikingly, Italy and Russia — that the most militantly anti-traditionalist modernist movements emerged, as exemplified by the Italian Futurists and the Russian Constructivists. But

---

23 *Origins of* Postmodernity, 122
24 Terry Eagleton, *Heathcliff and the Great Hunger: Studies in Irish Culture* (London and New York, 1995), 277, 299

if these overwhelmingly rural and backward countries produced militant avant-garde movements that hymned technology and industrial transformation, this begs the question why something of this kind did not also occur in Ireland where the industrial north-east might have functioned as crucible and stimulus in a manner not unlike, say, the industrialized north in agrarian Italy?

The answer surely has to do not just with a rural middle class *per se* but with the vagaries of Ireland's colonial history. By the late nineteenth century that history had simultaneously transferred most of the Irish Catholic working classes abroad (in the 1860s New York already had a larger Irish population than Dublin) and rendered the industrial north-east the most determinedly counter-revolutionary region in the entire island. Because of their fierce antipathy to Irish nationalism, and indeed to its supposed liberal allies in England, the northern Protestant industrial bourgeoisie and working classes had embraced the most conservative and chauvinistically imperialist versions of British identity and ideology.[25] The Belfast-centred industrial north, moreover, was integrally tied to the British economy and, while Britain had been the heartland of the first industrial revolution, its global pre-eminence was threatened by the second, in which rivals such as Germany and the United States began to emerge as new superpowers on the international scene. Hence, as they began to catch up with Britain, and with each other, the second industrial revolution generated a heady welter of excitement in what were once industrially backward places such as Germany, Russia or Italy. But in Britain itself the same developments augured a sense of imperial crisis and impending national decline.

Thus, in an early twentieth-century context, when Britain was still the world's leading industrial superpower, the Belfast shipyards could produce the mighty ocean liners that were then considered the brash new icons of twentieth-century technological daring and ambition. But the sinking of the Titanic, the slaughter of the Ulster regiments at the Somme in 1916, and the shrinkage of the Union due to Irish nationalist separatism, collectively helped to ensure that in unionist northern Ireland, as in Britain more generally, early twentieth-century modernity was culturally conceived in terms of catastrophe, collapse and decline — in terms of the sense of an ending — rather than in rhapsodic or euphoric terms. In other words, in the industrialized north-east of Ireland the advent of the twentieth century gave rise to a cultural posture of defensive siege, to a sense of the need to hold on to the glories of the nineteenth-century past: in short, to a reactionary cultural mentality largely inhospitable to the development of modernist art forms.

In Ireland, therefore, the most industrialized enclave and the most substantial industrial working class were peculiarly aligned with the forces of British imperial tradition and counter-revolution, and hence could not be conductor or lightning rod for a modernist cultural efflorescence of the kind that issued from other European

---

25 See Gillian McIntosh, *The Force of Culture: Unionist Identities in Twentieth-Century Ireland* (Cork, 1999) for a discussion of Northern unionist attachments to the conservative elements of British state high culture.

industrial enclaves also encased within largely agrarian societies. It is also true, of course, that the technological advances of the second industrial revolution only lightly affected the island of Ireland as a whole. Nevertheless, it is arguable that in the Irish situation the discombobulating force that Anderson ascribes to this technological revolution had already been effected in a very different manner: that is, by the extraordinary devastation of the Great Famine. The effect of the second industrial revolution in Europe was to corrode the old social order, dissolving its pre-capitalist elements, imploding traditional forms of everyday life and installing in their place new work practices, new modes of transport and communication, new kinds of social space, new gender relations, and so on. Decades before the second industrial revolution and the Great War effected this transformation in England or continental Europe, the Irish Famine had produced a convulsion of this magnitude, devastating the subaltern classes, accelerating the exodus from the land to the core industrial centres of England and America, compelling a shift to very different new property régimes at home, and, not least, dealing a final death blow to Gaelic culture. In 1849, William Wilde, father of Oscar, wrote that the Famine represented a

> great convulsion which society here of all grades has experienced, the failure of the potato crop, pestilence, famine, and a most unparalleled extent of emigration, together with bankrupt landlords, pauperizing poor-laws, grinding officials, and decimating workhouses, have broken up the very foundations of social discourse … In some places, all the domestic usages of life have been outraged; the tenderest bonds of kindred have been severed, some of the noblest and holiest feelings of human nature have been blotted from the heart, and many of the finest, yet firmest links which united the various classes in the community have been rudely burst asunder.[26]

In Wilde's account, as in the famous 'all that is solid melts into air' passage penned just a year earlier by Marx and Engels in *The Communist Manifesto*, we find the same shocked sense of a society bowled by a stunning force with terrific velocity into modernity. The obvious difference is that in the core metropolitan states the convulsions of industrial transformation stirred a combination of excitement and terror, dread and assurance; in a society swept into modernity on the scythe-edge of famine, however, the sense of terror and dread was bound to be in the ascendant. An estimated four million people left post-Famine Ireland between 1855 and 1914; this 'headlong exodus' has been described by one contemporary revisionist historian as 'the instinctive reaction of a panic-stricken people to the spectacle of their traditional way of life breaking into pieces before their very eyes'.[27]

26 William Robert Wilde, *Irish Popular Superstitions* (Dublin, 1853), 9–11, cited in George Denis Zimmerman, *The Irish Storyteller* (Dublin, 2001 [1966]), 208
27 F. S. L. Lyons, *Ireland Since the Famine* (London, 1985), 44

For very good reason, then, the cultural dynamics of that convulsion would play itself out differently in Ireland than similar watershed episodes were to do in other peripheral European societies. For the Italian Futurists and Russian Constructivists, the new technology of the second industrial revolution incited a sense of radical right- or left-wing fervour because it promised to dynamite a pathway to the future for societies that felt themselves smothered under the sheer excess of ossified *ancien régime* tradition. In post-Famine Ireland, in stark contrast, the decisive preoccupation was not with how to discard the excess baggage of a once splendid past so as to move more fleetly into the modern, but rather with the need to salvage something from the wholesale shattering of tradition. Whereas for the Futurists, modern Italy had to blast its way out from under the opulent rubble of imperial Rome and the Renaissance to enter modernity, in Ireland the impetus was not to shake off a once-glorious-now-moribund past, but to recover or to invent an indigenous culture almost totally obliterated by centuries of colonialism, anglicization, and famine. To put it very simply, the Futurists might feel that Italy was smothering under the excessive encumbrance of its once glorious past and heritage, but the real dilemma for the Irish was that so much of the native heritage had already been obliterated. At the distance of but a single generation from the lived trauma of the Great Hunger, a collective drive was under way to salvage something from the last great devastation of Gaelic culture in order to create a modern Ireland in terms that would not simply be British. The establishment of the Gaelic Athletic Association (1884), the National Literary Society (1892), the Gaelic League (1893), the co-operative movement (1894), and the Irish Literary Theatre (1899) all belong, in discrepant and often fiercely antagonistic ways, to this wider institution-building drive; indeed, so too does the campaign for a Catholic university and the massive building programme undertaken by the Catholic Church in the late nineteenth century. The Revival, therefore, is best seen not as a singular phenomenon, but as a matrix of efforts to create hegemonic national institutions and a national public. It was both out of, and also in reaction to, the cultural ferment created by the intersection of these broad popular movements that the modernist strands of the Revival would emerge.[28]

For many Irish scholars — whether liberal or leftist, republican or revisionist — the most embarrassing aspect of the Revival is its folkish idiom and its nationalist tones, both of which seem to put Irish cultural production of this period completely out of step with contemporary European modernism, usually viewed as the brashly iconoclastic and cosmopolitan or internationalist literature of new times, new cityscapes, new materials, new technologies. In other words, if we take the 'shock of the new' as the defining signature of modernism, then the Revivalist neo-Romantic celebration of Celtic saga, the western peasantry, the Big House, and so on, all seem to be distinctly at odds with

---

28 For some pioneering attempts to connect the Revival to the Famine, see Luke Gibbons, 'Montage, Modernism and the City', in his *Transformations in Irish Culture* (Cork, 1996), 165–69, and Kevin Whelan, 'The Memories of "The Dead"', *Yale Journal of Criticism*, 15, 1 (2002), 59–97.

the more forward-looking modernist currents of the times.

But here again one has to assess the Revival in terms of the available cultural resources and longer cultural history out of which it emerged. European *ancien régime* high culture had its origins in the court cultures of the Renaissance, and thrived thereafter under the patronage of the Churches, and especially under that of the big and small absolutist states. The ballet, the opera, architecture and sculpture, the visual and performing arts had all developed in Europe within the carapace of the great continental absolutist courts — Bourbon, Habsburg, Hohenzollern, Romanov — and a host of minor central European courts such as, most famously, Weimar or Bayreuth. Ireland was geographically on the periphery of this continent: it had no indigenous feudal or court culture of its own, and from early modern times it was under the colonial rule of the one major European country (England) that had the shortest-lived absolutist state, a constitutional monarchy with little power, and hence perhaps a court culture that was, by continental standards, undistinguished. England never matched the achievements of its European counterparts in classical music, ballet, opera, the visual or fine arts. The country's major field of cultural achievement in the nineteenth century was in literature, and especially the novel; in nearly all of the other high arts (and the novel before its high modernist elevation was itself a popular rather than high art form) it trailed in the wake of its continental rivals. After the Union, Anglo-Irish Dublin survived only as a declining satellite of this culturally unspectacular centre, while Ireland's indigenous high Gaelic culture had long since been arrested in its development by the successive waves of colonization that had demolished the Gaelic-speaking aristocracy and lead to the suppression of the majority Catholic Church, the only alternative source of cultural patronage, until the nineteenth century. Without major institutions of aristocratic or ecclesiastic patronage to support it, a high Gaelic intelligentsia or culture could not thrive, and over the centuries all aspects of that indigenous culture were subsequently reduced, as is common in colonial situations, to the status of a folk culture: a culture valued more for its ethnographic interest, and the access it supposedly afforded to the charms or peculiarities of a vanishing past, than for its capacity to speak to the present or to function as a resource for the future. Since this meant that the Irish Revivalists, unlike the European modernists, had only a very thin stock of indigenous or vernacular post-Renaissance high culture of their own with, or against, which to work, it was scarcely surprising that they turned to folk and peasant materials, or to the pre-modern saga and epic literature of the pre-Christian past to make good the deficit.

Nor was this turn to the rural world and the indigenous pagan or 'deep' past for inspiration as utterly alien to other early European modernisms as some rather hackneyed conceptions of modernism would suggest. In France, for instance, the Impressionists conducted one of the earliest modernist rebellions against moribund academic conventions, but Impressionist canvases were largely taken with the world of peasants and autumnal harvests or parks and public gardens rather than with the great machinery of modern city and industry. When they did paint cityscapes, the Impressionists recorded artisanal markets and the boulevard cafés and leisure worlds of the Parisian petite bourgeoisie rather than the turbulent ultra-modern landscape of the second industrial revolution. Even for the much more 'modern' Cubists, African and Pacific sculpture were important sources of inspiration for the break with mimetic representation or inherited classical shape and form. In Germany, Wagner's *Ring Cycle* (1876) broke with nineteenth-century German operatic convention and paved the way for the emergence of modernist music, but the Wagnerian *Gesamtkunstwerk* looked to the world of pagan epic, medieval chivalry, and heroic emotion, rather than to the contemporary industrial world for inspiration. In ballet, Stravinsky's *L'Oiseau de Feu* (1910) and *Le Sacre du Printemps* (1913), produced for Diaghilev's Ballets Russes, represented a shocking break with established conventions, but these works were deeply influenced by Russia's concurrent revival of folk culture rather than by the new world of the factory, technology or metropolis. Even in advanced industrial England, some of the most modernist writers — Joseph Conrad, D. H. Lawrence, T. E. Lawrence — drew more heavily for inspiration on the exotic and 'primitive' outposts of empire rather than on the modern metropolis. In the colonial world too, as in Latin America for instance, the first phase of modernism tried to reconcile the experimental advances of European vanguards with indigenous Aztec, Mayan and peasant iconography.

In a variety of ways, then, a fascination with primitive or peasant cultures serves as a fundamental modernist stimulus (as the classics were to the Renaissance) to assault the perceived enervation and automation of the modern world.[29] For present purposes, the point to be underlined is that the late nineteenth-/early twentieth-century turn by Standish O'Grady, W. B. Yeats, Augusta Gregory, J. M. Synge, Patrick Pearse, Douglas Hyde and the other Revivalists to what they took to be the pre-modern world was not by any means entirely at variance with other contemporary forms of early modernism. This turn to pre-capitalist aristocrat and peasant cultures, in Ireland as elsewhere, was often shot through with a reactionary or radical Tory worldview, but a militantly experimental modernism that embraced technology, the machine and the city was no guarantee of a progressive art or politics either. Italian Futurism, to cite only the most obvious example, embraced the brave new world of the twentieth-century with radical missionary zeal, but while the Futurists attacked the monarchy and the Vatican, they also denigrated parliament and socialism and trusted extreme Italian nationalism, imperialism and war to blast the way to the future, whatever the human cost. In other words, the embrace in modernist hands of the archaic pre-modern worlds of aristocracy, epic past and rural countryside or that of the metropolitan city and technology can be equally reactionary. From a political standpoint, what is decisive is not whether a modernist writer embraces the archaic or the modern elements, the country or the city, on this spectrum, but rather how the dialectic between the two is actually elaborated.

29 See Marianna Torgovnick, *Gone Primitive: Savage Intellects, Modern Lives* (Chicago, 1990) and David Richards, *Masks of Difference: Cultural Representations in Literature, Anthropology and Art* (Cambridge, 1994).

When Eagleton concludes that 'what is striking about Irish modernism is its overwhelmingly conservative tenor', the problem is not so much that this verdict is too harshly negative, but that the judgement rests on a whole series of suppositions that are not critically tested.[30] Working within a social formation that was neither continental European nor Anglo-American in character, and thus lacking both the stimulus or common adversarial pole of the extensive *ancien régime* high cultures of the former fully as much as the economico-technological dynamism of the latter, Ireland produced several great modernist writers — first Synge and Yeats, then Joyce, later O'Casey, Flann O'Brien, Ó Cadhain and Beckett — who managed between them to span three successive phases or generations of European literary modernism. In Synge and Yeats, the dialectic between the archaic (or the non-modern) and the modern tended to be weighted towards the archaic, which was associated with value, and to denigrate the modern, equated with degeneration and the loss of value. This was in keeping with a great deal of early or pre-World War I European modernism when a strong sense of aristocratic disdain for the new society emerging out of the collapse of the old order was still decisive. In Joyce's *Ulysses* a tension between the archaic and the modern remains fundamental, but it is no longer calibrated in terms of a tragic collision between pre-modern and modern cultural value-systems, as in Yeats or Synge. Instead, it is reconfigured in terms of the tension between the essentially comic, picaresque and post-heroic mundane formlessness of modern urban experience and the Homeric epic structure that confers on that shapeless lifeworld some ironic sense of order and totalization. The wholly urban Irish milieu of Joyce's work shifts things decisively toward the 'modern' rather than the 'archaic' end of the spectrum, marking a decisive break with earlier literary modernisms. If some kind of elevated hauteur towards the modern remains, then surely it is a kind of intellectual rather than an aristocratic hauteur, one manifest in the tension in his work between a naturalistic immersion in the sordid everyday world of the modern city and the dazzlingly erudite parade of high and low, classical and avant-garde, literary styles through which that experience is registered.

In the post-World War II work of Beckett, defined partly by his attempt to go beyond Joyce, as Joyce had wanted to press beyond Yeats, the teeming plenitude of city and word in turn is abandoned for a null or featureless, devastated, shell-shocked, post-apocalyptic, post-historical landscape in which the whole project of modernity has already proleptically played itself out to its catastrophic dénouement, and in which the detritus of the modern has consequently itself become archaic. Eagleton concludes that what unites these works is their common mandarinism and hence conservatism (there is, after all, no *engagé* such as Brecht on the Irish scene; though in this assumption, Eagleton, like everyone else, overlooks Máirtín Ó Cadhain, surely the most politically committed of the Irish modernist writers, but one whose work is regularly bypassed because he wrote in Irish rather in English). But what seems much more remarkable

---

30 Eagleton, *Heathcliff and the Great Hunger*, 299

is the intellectual radicalism that drives the successive bearers of Irish modernism to make their way, with the relentlessness of a computer virus, through all of the major variations and permutations that the dialectic of the modern and the archaic (a dialectic constitutive of modernism *tout court*) will yield. In the works of the Irish modernists that dialectic will continuously be worked over until, between them, the whole repertoire of 'solutions' it will yield is exhausted or exploded.

If individual Irish writers produced several of the most challenging modernist masterpieces in the English language in this period, it remains the case, nonetheless, that Ireland still produced no extended modernist culture that would decisively change the local social and cultural landscape. This was not so much because Ireland was a pre-modern or traditional rural backwater, too isolated from the rapids of early twentieth-century modernity to do so, but because it was in a complex socio-historical sense too modern, since it had been, via colonialism, catapulted directly into modernity without ever having passed through the feudal stage and hence had so little vernacular high culture that many of its European neighbours had to work on. While in Europe it would take two world wars decisively to liquidate the hoary but obdurate old universe of the *ancien régime*, in Ireland the late nineteenth-century Land Acts (that issued from the class struggles of the Land Wars) had consigned the local aristocracy to their doom decades earlier than their counterparts in England and much of Europe. There could be no extended clash between modernism and the aristocratic and academy-defined high culture of a continental European kind, nor any serious confrontation between innovators and the consolidated culture worlds of the 'haute bourgeoisie', since there was so little of the latter to begin with. The attainment of nationalist independence in what is now the Republic brought to power a lower middle class without any such heritage to defend or attack; it also took most of the island out of the titanic wars of self-destruction that earthquaked the rest of continental Europe until the 1950s. A less isolationist and more internationally engaged twentieth-century history might have yielded the social convulsions that could possibly have stimulated a more extended modernist culture, but stability at least allowed for the preservation of democracy and secured shelter from Europe's successive plunges into self-destruction.

In the end, what distinguishes Irish modernism above all else from its European counterparts was that its literary modernism began so early and still managed to extend itself across several successive stages of modernist literary development, yet without ever reaching much beyond literature.[31] Except for a very modest modernism in painting — like literature, a small scale, individual and artisanal art form — there were no substantive or extended modernist movements in Irish architecture, music, dance, sculpture or municipal design. The experimental thrust of Irish modernism — in Wilde, Synge, Yeats, O'Casey, Joyce, Beckett and Ó Cadhain — was essentially linguistic and it

---

31 See J. C. C. Mays's Introduction, in Poems and Exiles by James Joyce (Harmondsworth and New York, 1992), xl–xli.

was in the carnival of language that the more utopian aspirations of the Revival and of the national struggle found sanctuary. The fact that Irish modernism was so concentrated in literature may be explained partly as a response to a sense of linguistic alienation in English aggravated by the loss of Gaelic Irish culture and partly due to the fact that literature is less immediately dependent on other large scale political and economic institutional supports and constraints than other art forms, such as architecture, sculpture or cinema, for example. But if its more artisan mode of production was one of the things that may have allowed Irish literary modernism to flourish, this also inevitably brought restrictions as well, since literature cannot so immediately or spectacularly translate its visions into the everyday lifeworld of the masses as these other, more public media do. Because it was so confined to high literature, Irish modernism was inevitably, at a time when the bulk of the population had access only to primary education, largely a modernism of the intelligentsia and, as such, destined to remain rather detached from the everyday lives of the broader Irish public. A modernism in music, architecture, public design or the performing arts might have engaged public consciousness in more immediate ways than rarefied works such as *Ulysses* or Yeats's late poetry or *Endgame* could ever expect to do. Ireland, in sum, had an exuberant literary modernism that survived across several generations, but already by the late 1920s, when the Irish revolution had petered out in a conservative partitionist state order on the island, that modernism was increasingly achieved not only in the geographical distance of European self-exile, but also at an increasing emotional distance from the transformative social movements and stimuli that had provided its initial momentum in the first instance.

4

To what extent is it helpful to conceptualize late twentieth-century Ireland in terms of the cultural physiognomy of postmodernism, and in what directions did Irish literary and cultural production develop in this period? Since 1958, when the Irish political élite finally abandoned economic autarky, the southern Irish state's single major project has been to integrate the country into the European Union and global capitalism. The same period witnessed the introduction of new communications technologies, especially television, which brought the country into closer contact with the wider international political scene and, more importantly, into contact with British and North-American consumer society. Initially at least, much of the ruling establishment seems to have believed that economic modernization could be achieved in ways that would leave the conservative Catholic social order consolidated after independence more or less intact. Confronted since the 1970s on a series of fronts — by the women's movement, the very different value-system retailed in mass culture, and the top-down liberalization required by EU membership — the Catholic Church initially rallied its forces to defeat successive attempts to loosen the connections between Church and state and to liberalize sexual mores. After important initial victories fought and won over two decades, that reactionary rally proved to have little political stamina and had largely petered out by the 1990s. The litany of clerical sex and child abuse scandals during that decade has massively dented the Catholic Church's already eroding moral authority. What has emerged in the wake of the old Catholic-nationalist order is best understood perhaps not simply as 'secularization' but, more comprehensively, as a wholesale reconstruction of Irish middle-class subjectivity, now decreasingly defined in terms of participatory citizenship or of adherence to communal Church practices, and articulated instead in terms of individual capacity to participate in various modes of consumer lifestyle. The period since the 1960s, in short, has witnessed a transformation in the technology of subject production as dramatic and far-reaching as that inaugurated in the nineteenth-century Devotional Revolution consolidated after the Famine.

The mediatization of Irish culture has also proceeded apace. While colonial Ireland was only lightly touched by the first and second industrial revolutions, and while independent Ireland's neutrality allowed it to circumvent the nuclear dimensions of what Mandel has called the third technological revolution, by the 1990s the country had become a significant supply centre for what we might call, extending Mandel, the fourth (computer) technological revolution. This has allowed the Irish Republic to overcome many of the handicaps of peripherality it had suffered in earlier phases of capitalism, and to emerge as a strategic nodal point in the global software industry. The Republic is now the second largest exporter of software in the world after the United States (60 per cent of PC-based software in Europe originates in Ireland), and by the end of the twentieth century it was being regularly lauded by neo-liberal economists as one of the most fully 'open' or globalized economies in the world.[32]

The third signature co-ordinate of the postmodernist conjuncture, as defined by Anderson, is the exorcism of the spectre of revolution and a corresponding narrowing of the political spectrum and a diminution of any sense of alternative futures. In the late 1960s, Northern Ireland did experience a surge of revolutionary upheaval in the form of the civil rights campaign that challenged unionist domination of the North. The British decision to take on the forces for change, and to reform the old unionist establishment only very timorously, created the conditions for a long 'dirty war' that unfolded against the backdrop of the grim international horizon of the 'oil crisis', international economic recession, and the further deterioration of East-West relations after the Soviet invasion of Afghanistan. The viciously conducted struggle in the six counties mobilized the northern Catholic working and lower middle classes and has impelled substantive reform of the northern state. In the end, however, republican insurgence was unable either to end partition or to overcome the divisions between the Protestant and Catholic

---

32 Michael Cronin, 'Speed Limits: Ireland, Globalisation and the War Against Time', in Peadar Kirby, Luke Gibbons and Michael Cronin, eds., *Reinventing Ireland: Culture, Society and the Global Economy* (London, 2002), 54–66, 56

working classes, which remain at least as deep today as in 1969 when the current phase of conflict began.

The period since the 1970s, then, has witnessed major socio-cultural change and massive economic transformation in the southern state and substantive administrative reform in the northern one. However, in both states, these positive transformations have been accompanied by an increasing subordination of society on the island as a whole to the cultural norms of a neo-liberal economic order that has actually hollowed out democracy, aggravated social inequality, and led to the normalization of an individualistic consumerist ethos. A wide variety of organizations have worked hard to temper the worst excesses of the newly consolidated economic order. But in Ireland, as elsewhere, the constellation of forces that constitutes the left has found itself compelled to assume a completely defensive posture, its energies almost entirely devoted to conserving social democracy and public provision from further neo-liberal assault. The whole issue of constructing any kind of post-capitalist order scarcely ever became the subject of either theoretical speculation or practical endeavour.

Because Ireland, like much of Southern or Eastern Europe and the 'Third World', had lagged so far behind metropolitan Europe and the United States in economic productivity and consumption levels, the closing decades of the twentieth century were marked — despite the long recession and the northern conflict — by a very strong sense of 'uplift' and 'catch up', and this has created, since the 1990s at least, a public mood of optimism and release that would be very difficult to square with Anderson's dyspeptic conception of the post-1960s period as one characterized solely by an unbroken litany of defeats and a recession of more utopian aspirations. The increased levels of gender equality and sexual liberalism secured by the women's movement across the island; the growing assurance of the new Catholic lower-middle- and working-class constituency spearheaded by Sinn Féin, and the slowly-changing balance of power between the Catholic and Protestant blocs in the North; the new wealth generated and distributed, however unevenly, by a stronger southern economy — these are far from negligible gains. But none of this changes the fact that in Ireland as elsewhere these social gains have actually gone hand in hand with a drastic narrowing of the parameters within which contemporary politics are articulated.

Nevertheless, while the co-ordinates of postmodernism delineated by Anderson and Jameson inventory the wider conditions and constraints within which contemporary Irish cultural change can usefully be analysed, the specific character of the Irish cultural scene ought not to be effaced. For both Anderson and Jameson, it is the waning of an earlier efflorescence of modernism in the arts that has set the scene for a new postmodernism. However, while Ireland produced a magnificently ambitious literary modernism, the country, as has been noted, was in no position to support an extended modernist culture much beyond the literary field. In fact, even in the literary field the real cultural dominant in Ireland during the decades between independence and the end of the twentieth century was not modernism at all but rather naturalism. The Revivalist literature that came into its ascendancy in the period between the Land Wars and the establishment of the Free State was grounded in conceptions of a putatively archaic Irish culture heroically resistant to the defilements of metropolitan modernity. Irish naturalism developed alongside the other Revivalist literary currents, but became an aesthetic dominant in Irish culture only in the ebb tide of the national revolution, negating the idealism of the Revival by insisting on the dreary provincial squalor that was (for naturalism) the defining reality of Irish life. In the theatre, this disillusioned naturalism was already installed as the dominant house style in the Abbey by mid-century: the reigning genres were political farces, peasant comedies, rural and kitchen dramas. Naturalism's ascendancy in poetry was marked by Patrick Kavanagh's *The Great Hunger* (1942); it was Kavanagh, not Yeats, who became the dominant model for Irish poets during the second half of the twentieth century. In narrative fiction, it was the early naturalistic Joyce of *Dubliners* and *Portrait of the Artist*, and not *Ulysses*, that exerted by far the most decisive influence on the development of Irish writing in the post-independence period.

In its French inception, the naturalist novel had provoked intense hostility because it imaginatively explored previously uncharted territories of lower-class urban experience and offended official morality and established definitions of novelistic good taste. But Irish naturalism has been concentrated (with important exceptions) overwhelmingly in small-town and rural Ireland: the fictional territory of writers such as Brinsley MacNamara, Liam O'Flaherty, Frank O'Connor, Sean O'Faolain, Edna O'Brien, John Broderick, John McGahern, Tom Murphy and William Trevor. Like its French counterpart, Irish naturalism was also in its inception a dissident and reformist aesthetic: it measured the distance between the official state ideology of Irish Ireland and its tawdry reality. The naturalist writers probed, with an intimate knowledge of the local terrain conspicuously absent in much of the literature of the Revival, the social and sexual traumas that official Irish culture would not acknowledge and, in so doing, many incurred the wrath not only of state censors but of the reading public for scandalizing their own society before an allegedly hostile Anglo-American audience.

But while naturalism was undoubtedly a dissident and socially committed aesthetic, it would be difficult to regard it in retrospect as a radical one. Its defining feature was its protest against the way in which the communal narrowness and authoritarianism of small-town or rural Ireland stifled all sense of individuality. Yet while it diagnosed with clinical intensity the cramped lives this society afforded, naturalism also consistently reduced — in the manner habitual to the mode — that society to the sordid conditions it protested. Though a combatively engaged form, naturalist narratives are nevertheless typically focalized through the consciousness of characters so socially isolated and so temperamentally alienated from their communities, or indeed from any sense of collective agency or solidarity, that any sense of social protest is typically funnelled into individual rebellion against a common philistinism or smothered by a pervading climate of entropy and fatalism. In Irish naturalist fiction, protagonists usually survive their deathly social condition only if they can escape or emigrate; to remain within or committed to the local community is to atrophy with it.

No one can doubt that the social and sexual problems depicted in naturalism were actual and pressing. The issue is not that naturalism invented or even exaggerated the social grimness that would become its trademark topic. But what can be questioned is the inference that the communities thus depicted were so helplessly paralysed, so bereft of internal dissident forces and resources, as naturalism would typically suggest. And in stylistic terms, naturalism's own formal and linguistic conservatism aesthetically reproduced that very sense of monochrome dowdiness and narrowness of vision that naturalism thematically denounced in society at large. Irish modernism might have become increasingly remote from any form of social engagement as it developed, and thus to have displaced its utopian energies into linguistic play and formal inventiveness; naturalism, by contrast, remained admirably socially committed, but its aesthetic conservatism paradoxically replicated the dour social conservatism of Irish society against which naturalism had set itself. It was as if the colourless monotony of the society — as the naturalists conceived of it at least — could only be conveyed in a drab, colourless, monotonous aesthetic. When compared to the altogether more outward-looking and experimental modernists, the naturalists seem to replicate the very condition of backwardness or inward-looking provincialism their own works protest.

It remains today a critical commonplace to contrast Yeats's imaginary romantic Ireland with the tougher-minded realism of a Kavanagh, O'Faolain, or McGahern, but Yeats was no less scornful of the society that emerged after independence than they; indeed, he was perhaps more intransigently critical and unreconciled. The real difference is that while Yeats conceived of this provincial and puritanical new Ireland as only too typical of the bourgeois-industrial modernity he detested, the naturalists were convinced that the ills of post-independence Ireland were to be explained, rather, by its lamentably archaic rural social order, and that their task, therefore, was to release it from the straitjacket of its crippling traditions into the freedoms of modernity. Both were agreed that the new Ireland was a disappointment; where they differed was that while Yeats attributed its shortcomings to its embrace of the modern, the naturalists attributed the same defects to the supposedly archaic character of Irish society that impeded it from fully entering the modern.

Once the economic modernization drive of the 1960s got under way, an extensive academic and journalistic literature emerged in Ireland that sought to identify those cultural factors that were impeding the development of a modern industrial enterprise culture. Fianna Fáil's version of nationalism, the rural traditionalism of the countryside and the inordinate influence of the Catholic Church featured obsessively as mainstays of Irish backwardness in this literature. In this ideological climate, the bleak conception of post-independence Ireland long since consolidated in Irish naturalist literature was now ratified as the 'real Ireland' and naturalist literature was pressed into the service of the wider cultural programme of capitalist modernization. Writers like John McGahern or Edna O'Brien or Tom Murphy, who had all had works censored by the Catholic-nationalist intelligentsia in the 1960s, would soon become heroes of the new self-declared post-nationalist liberal intelligentsia in the 1970s and 1980s. The speed with which these figures made the transition from being outcasts and iconoclasts of the old order to being admired insiders of the new suggests that post-1960s naturalism was not only battering down an old consensus but also comfortably enough riding the new.

Irish modernism, then, might be the most internationally prestigious literary current to emerge in post-independence Ireland, but domestically it was naturalism that almost wholly commanded the cultural world and that consolidated itself as a cultural dominant, especially after World War II when modernism as a force gradually began to wane. Hence, the emergent cultural dominant of the late twentieth-century moment in Ireland might be described not so much as post-modernism as a kind of neo- or post-naturalism. Or, to put things more precisely, in Ireland the literary postmodern has essentially taken the form of an involution or mutation of naturalism. The most salient strand of the literary postmodern in Ireland, therefore, is not to be discovered by searching for works similar to those normally associated with British or American postmodernism, but rather by tracking the ways in which late twentieth-century Irish naturalism has evolved in new, often ludic, directions. Some of the most internationally fêted, commercially successful and critically debated 'new Irish' works of recent decades fall into a category of this sort. Brian Friel's *Dancing at Lughnasa* (1990), Patrick McCabe's *The Butcher Boy* (1992), later filmed by Neil Jordan in 1998, Martin McDonagh's *The Leenane Trilogy* (1996–97), Marina Carr's *By the Bog of Cats* (1998) and *On Raftery's Hill* (2000) can be read as some significant signposts to the emergence and consolidation of this new aesthetic trend. A parallel development may be observed in Northern Ireland, where the more familiar 'northern thriller', romance-across-the-divide and *Bildungsroman* conventions consolidated since the seventies have been superseded in the nineties by more ludic versions of the same genres, a trend exemplified by works such as Neil Jordan's *The Crying Game* (1992), Colin Bateman's *Divorcing Jack* (1995), and Robert McLiam Wilson's *Eureka Street* (1996).[33] In such works, a new viagra of hectic experiment has been applied to the old naturalist worldview to resuscitate it into some new life or half-life.

Of these works, Friel's anomic Ballybeg in *Dancing at Lughnasa* is closest in temperament to the inherited norms of Irish naturalist drama. But it was the all-woman Dionysian dance scene that lent the play that startling burst of manic energy (all the more striking for being so alien to the wistfully sombre and down-at-heel naturalist ambience of the work at large) that disrupted established convention and expectation and, in so doing, mesmerized audiences and critics alike. The woebegone midland settings to be found in Carr's plays also ostensibly recall the old naturalist drama, but her characters are so extravagantly crazy, repressed and demented that what we get is a grand guignol version of naturalism that lends the worlds of John Broderick or John

---

33 See Richard Kirkland's incisive overview of contemporary developments in Northern Irish narrative fiction in his *Identity Parades: Northern Irish Culture and Dissident Subjects* (Liverpool, 2002).

McGahern a virtually Jacobean ambience. McDonagh's *Leenane Trilogy* inhabits a similar territory of the grotesque, but his is a more self-consciously camped-up or simulacral world comprised of recycled collages of the older naturalist conventions, settings and formulas. In fiction, McCabe's *Butcher Boy* also pushes naturalism in the same comic-grotesque direction. In that novel, the conventional realistic depiction of a depressed Irish small town is transformed by filtering the narrative through the deranged Francie's apocalyptic imagination, in which Irish Catholic and British and American forms of pop culture millenarianism promiscuously commingle. By this means, the more familiar naturalistic renditions of the rickety end of 'de Valera's Ireland' — naturalism's usual stock in trade — acquires a more globalized and mass media span of reference. The result is a quirkily eclectic tragicomic vision of disintegration that inserts the national sense of an ending into a wider global frame.

It is difficult at this early stage to diagnose the significance of this emergent aesthetic trend. On the one hand, the new neo-naturalism would seem to signal that one of the fundamental literary paradigms of post-independence culture is now finally breaking up. But if this is so, then the once dominant naturalist aesthetic is not displaced by some entirely new aesthetic agenda: instead, the old naturalism is denaturalized by pushing its content and conventions to violent or kitschy extremes. In other words, the works of Carr, McDonagh, McCabe and (in the different context of the North) Bateman and McLiam Wilson continue to exploit the same basic conception of Irish society charted by the earlier naturalists, but they do so with a kind of manic or hysterical energy, a knowing formal self-consciousness and eclecticism, and a hectic bravura alien to the older forms. Their neo-naturalism might be read positively as an objective correlative of the contemporary condition, one in which a period of exuberant social flux cannot, however hectically it bids to do so, dispel the nightmare of the long past from which it has so recently emerged. Alternatively, it might as plausibly be argued that these works represent an essentially superficial renovation of an old aesthetic: after all, a naturalism on steroids is still naturalism, and how much has really changed if the new formal experiments remain shackled to the same dystopian, entropic worldview that had always been naturalism's defining signature? There was a time, long since past, when the thematic content of the older naturalism was radical and shocking, even if the form itself was conservative. Now, the new neo-naturalism might be said simply to reverse this ratio: the formal experimentation lending the inherited content a spurious appearance of radicalism, a formal makeover, but the fundamental conception of Irish society rehearsed there, all very familiar indeed.

The contemporary Irish literary field, then, is structured by the intersection of a number of distinct aesthetic currents. An established literary naturalism, identified primarily with some of the now senior reputations in Irish fiction, such as McGahern, Edna O'Brien, Tom Murphy, William Trevor and the late Brian Moore, and with a host of lesser figures, remains a dominant, though now seemingly spent force. A newer neo-naturalist narrative aesthetic, associated primarily with a younger generation of writers, has recently emerged to challenge, though also in some ways thematically to sustain, that dominance. The canonical figures of Irish modernism — Wilde, Joyce, Yeats, Synge, Flann O'Brien and Beckett — continue to tower like a literary Mount Rushmore over the contemporary scene. The belated legatees to this older modernism, such as Thomas Kinsella, Derek Mahon or Trevor Joyce, now operating in unseasonable conditions almost wholly inhospitable to modernism, have found themselves largely ignored by a critical establishment more preoccupied with writers whose styles represent late lyrical versions of naturalism — such as Seamus Heaney or Michael Longley — or with those — such as John Banville, Paul Muldoon and Medbh McGuckian — whose works appear more easily accommodated to wider postmodernist international currents. Distinctions between these wan late modernist and more self-consciously postmodernist agendas seem increasingly hazardous, in any event, because in the period since World War II modernism generally has surrendered both its vanguardist faith in the transfigurative power of art and its mandarin commitment to encyclopaedic and autotelic works of art that aspired to become hieratic texts to an entire culture.[34]

Thus, even as the achievements of the major modernists recede in time, and even as their works lose their initial power to shock as they become normalized by the university and packaged and popularized for consumption by corporation and heritage industries, they continue, because of the grand scale of their ambition and scope of their erudition, to overshadow all subsequent achievements. However much contemporary Irish literature may aspire to outflank or leave modernism behind, therefore, it still languishes in modernism's wake. Works of some merit continue to appear in all of the different aesthetic modes that intersect to constitute the current Irish literary field, but truly significant change perhaps will require work charged with ambition sufficient to disturb and reconfigure the whole literary field itself.

It is also important to note that while modernism and naturalism may be at opposite ends of the aesthetic spectrum, if issues of verisimilitude or representational realism are what is emphasized, in others ways they have actually proved highly compatible. In the overarching context of Ireland's integration into Europe and global capital, that is, the social function served by each has proved largely complementary: naturalism has been generally lauded by cultural critics as the necessary gritty and realistic corrective to Revivalist romanticism and idealism; modernism has been championed as the aesthetic that best expresses the country's post-sixties disdain for cultural nativism and receptiveness to international modernity. In other words, both naturalism and modernism have been brigaded in cultural criticism in ways amenable to contemporary state interests: the one supposedly holding a mirror up to the ugly Ireland created by the national revolution; the other supposedly signposting the multicultural, cosmopolitan

34 The major exception is Thomas Kinsella. While a veritable critical industry has emerged around Heaney, Kinsella's work has received much less sustained attention and has even been excluded from some recent anthologies.

European culture Ireland now wishes to become. For any new literature to emerge, a new cultural criticism capable of shattering this congealed critical consensus (the literary critical outrider of modernization theory) will also be indispensable.

5

While the emergence of neo-naturalism is certainly an interesting sign of the times, the most decisive transformation in Irish culture in recent decades cannot be gauged by tracking mutations within the domestic literary field in its own right or by documenting the emergence of this or that new mode of writing. The more significant changes ultimately are those in the wider lifeworld of late capitalism that have reorganized the larger disposition of cultural production and consumption in recent times. Until Irish critics can begin to offer a coherent material analysis of these wider changes, their capacity to conceptualize contemporary Irish culture in any really compelling way must remain very limited.

On the face of things at least, the closing four decades of the twentieth century ought to have offered the very best conditions for the production of literature and art of a high order in Ireland. From the 1960s onwards, and especially after the 1980s, state censorship of the arts was greatly relaxed, with regard to sexual issues at least, and, thanks to the more permissive fare of the new mass media, social attitudes generally also became much less conservative. In the same period, state and non-state support for the arts both increased exponentially. Famously little state support had been expended in the period between independence and World War II, but the interval since then has witnessed the consolidation of a whole network of state institutions, such as the Arts Councils (established in Northern Ireland in 1943, in the Irish Republic in 1951) and Aosdána, as well as a host of specialized boards, institutes and centres dedicated to particular art forms. This complex network of institutions has attempted to link the arts to national development policy generally and to the heritage and tourist industries more particularly.

As Irish society as a whole has become more affluent, non-state support has also increased, and for some time now banks and corporations have become major patrons of and investors in painting and sculpture. In addition, a consistently expanding network of radio and television stations and new regional arts centres have increased not only public access to the arts but also to debates about the arts. Most importantly of all, the dramatic expansion of third-level education since the 1960s ought to have secured the strongest base resource of all for the arts by creating a public with the white collar income and leisure and the education to appreciate higher art forms. And as the university and other arts-related networks have expanded, this has brought with it opportunities for artists who can now find greater scope for academic or para-academic employment in an expanded educational and arts sector, as well as benefiting from income from obligatory student reading lists or from academic bursaries or residencies of diverse sorts. Nor have Irish artists wanted for subject matter in this period. The conflict in the North; the overhaul of southern Irish society as it made the change from being one of the most depressed economies in Western Europe to becoming one of the more dramatic success stories of neo-liberalism; the emergence of new forms of diasporic consciousness — these have all kept artists well-supplied.

Has the general quality of Irish literary and artistic production increased in ways commensurate with these improvements in the domestic support base? Exacting criteria to assess such matters may be difficult to establish, but a great many broad indicators would seem to suggest that the opposite is more nearly the case. Despite the apparently adverse material conditions of the time, Irish artists working in the earlier half of the twentieth century created not only a national literature of recognized distinction but also made an internationally distinguished contribution to the development of literary modernism. By comparison, the Irish contribution to the wider world of arts and letters in the late twentieth century seems rather slender. It is worth noting in this context that nearly all of Ireland's most distinguished twentieth-century writers and artists were born either in the nineteenth century (W. B. Yeats, James Joyce, J. M. Synge, George Bernard Shaw, Sean O'Casey, Elizabeth Bowen, Jack B. Yeats) or in the very early years of the twentieth (Samuel Beckett, Patrick Kavanagh, Máirtín Ó Cadhain, Louis MacNeice, Flann O'Brien). The decisive international figures in this body (Joyce, W. B. Yeats, Jack B. Yeats, Beckett, Synge, Shaw, O'Casey, MacNeice) had all produced their most important works by the end of the 1950s or, even allowing for Beckett's late career, very shortly thereafter. Even taking into account the fact that the long-term significance of contemporary material is always much more difficult to sift and assess, it would be rather difficult to identify contemporary Irish artists (those working between, say, the beginning of the modernization drive in the 1960s and the present) who have contributed as decisively to some of the aesthetic forms now usually associated with international postmodernism as Joyce did to the development of the modernist novel, Yeats to modernist poetry, or Beckett to (late) modernist theatre.

The contemporary Irish literary field is not without luminaries, of course, but have any of these attained a stature in the international world of letters comparable to their Revivalist and modernist predecessors? Of the Irish Nobel recipients, Seamus Heaney is surely (with the possible exception of Shaw) the most middle brow, the most stylistically conventional, the least formally innovative, the least at odds with the dominant political or intellectual values of the moment. Neither as esoteric as that of Joyce or Beckett nor as politically extreme to the right as Yeats or to the left as Shaw or O'Casey, Heaney's achievements have been absorbed into the national and Anglo-American mainstream much faster than were those of most of the earlier major twentieth-century figures. The country's two most distinguished late twentieth-century novelists, John McGahern and John Banville, have produced impressive and well-respected works, but neither seems even nearly as decisive to the wider international history of the novel as Joyce or Beckett or even a lesser figure such as Flann O'Brien were in their day. Brian Friel and Tom Murphy have both produced sustained and distinguished *œuvres* in the world of theatre, but even their greatest admirers would hardly claim that they have made an impact on the wider world of international theatre equal to that of O'Casey or Beckett. In the early twentieth century, the achievements of individual Irish dramatists and of the Abbey Theatre won Irish drama a place of note in the international history of modern theatre, but the collective achievements of Irish dramatists in the period since Beckett's heyday in the 1950s seems decidedly minor by comparison. The best Irish poets continue to be more than able to hold their own against their contemporary British peers, but this at a time when the international stature of British poetry has itself diminished considerably.

The point here is not to idealize the literary past in order to denigrate the literary present. There are many contemporary Irish figures across all of the artistic fields whose works have earned well-deserved international recognition and acclaim, and even a handful perhaps (including Paul Muldoon and Medbh McGuckian, and perhaps Francis Bacon or Sean Scully?) who might claim to have contributed in some reasonably significant way to new postmodernist forms in poetry and the visual arts. It is not at all to disparage or minimize such achievement to insist, however, that a distinction must be drawn between work that is internationally acknowledged to be estimable (in other words, work internationally recognized to be substantive and noteworthy) and work that is internationally acknowledged to be decisively important because it inaugurates real paradigm shifts within its particular discipline or because it somehow seizes hold of the wider imagination of the times. By that latter and stricter criterion, Irish writers would certainly seem to have produced a far more sustained critical mass of genuinely trailblazing work in the period between 1900 and 1950 than in the half-century since then.

If contemporary Irish literary and cultural production is indeed actually a diminished force, the decisive factors, of course, may neither be the calibre of Irish artists nor the character of the domestic arts scene. It might be argued that the Irish case is only a particular instance of a wider cultural phenomenon whereby the higher arts generally may have suffered a certain loss of purpose and direction occasioned by the wake of modernism and the extension of consumer society. The very term 'postmodernism' may even bear this out, suggesting that the later twentieth century was able to define itself only in terms of an aftermath to modernism or, alternatively, as a new moment defined by modes of art that deliberately refused modernism's grander claims to universality and higher authority. If the weight falls on the first of these definitions, then postmodernism may be construed as a kind of belated and de-energized modernist endgame: an art committed, like modernism, to transgression and innovation, but this at a time when innovation and transgression have long since become *de rigueur*, routine, even banal. If, on the other hand, postmodernism denotes a kind of art that repudiates modernism's claims to grand totalizations or its critical sense of commitment to an altogether different future beyond the present, then the postmodern's very success in this respect will almost certainly rebound against it, because such an art, if it is to be consistent, disentitles itself to the kinds of elevated authority that modernist art had sought.

From such perspective, the difference between a Joyce or a Yeats, on one side, and a Banville or a Muldoon, on the other, is that Joyce and Yeats were there first to establish themselves not only as founders of a new national literature but also as innovators of new twentieth-century developments and hence Banville and Muldoon must inevitably appear belated, since they simply do not constitute the start of something decisively new in the same way. The aggressively defamiliarizing quality of modernist literature, which impelled people to see the world in strange or shocking new ways, depended upon the existence of socially ratified moral and artistic conventions that modernism transgressed. But once modernism had successfully unsettled the artistic conventions and mass culture the moral ones, the point must be reached where the overturning of conventions had eventually become the new convention, and in such context postmodernism would inevitably find it difficult to match modernism's transgressive impact. In that context, even were the formal inventiveness of a Banville or Muldoon to be very great indeed, this would still not carry any great social or political weight; something to excite the connoisseurs of technique, perhaps, but not cultural historians.

Those disinclined to view the world in terms of a downward curve from a 'golden age' of modernism to a 'bronze age' of contemporary postmodernism might object that this presents a much too one-sided view of things and point to modernism's less attractive dimensions: to its aristocratic or intellectual mandarinism; to its failure to secure for art some utopian place outside of the market despite its professed contempt for the market; to its overwhelming masculinism or Eurocentrism. From such a perspective, the postmodern can be defended as a welcome recombination of high and popular and of European and non-European forms that makes art more democratically accessible to those not possessed of exceptional levels of education or specialized cultural capital. If the works of postmodern writers, such as Banville or McGuckian or Muldoon, say, seem less millenarian than Yeats, less esoteric or virtuosic than Joyce, less bleakly apocalyptic than Beckett, might not this be viewed as an advance: as a welcome shedding of some of the sententious historical seriousness that had always been a feature of bourgeois aesthetics and which modernist art, for all its anti-bourgeois sentiment, had certainly maintained? In a specifically Irish context, it might be argued that even if it were to be accepted that late twentieth-century Ireland no longer produced great *auteurs* such as Joyce or Yeats or Beckett, this was more than compensated for by a new 'strength in depth': more nationally respected and internationally recognized domestic artists working at home, rather than in permanent exile in London or Paris; achievements distributed more evenly across all the arts and less exclusively concentrated in the field of literature; significant new developments such as the consolidation of a national cinema, the construction of new centres for the plastic and fine arts, and a less Dublin-centred and more fully regionalized theatre and visual arts circuits; the emergence of phenomena such as 'women's writing' or 'gay writing', indicative of a somewhat less overwhelmingly masculinist and heterosexist arts world, and so forth.

Will such claims stand up? Where Ireland is concerned, the area where the strongest case for late twentieth-century achievement could be mounted is in the field of music, especially popular music. If Irish culture was once best known to the wider world for its Revivalist poets and dramatists and for its high modernist literary giants, today the only figures of really comparable stature on both the domestic and international stage are popular music icons such as Bono, Van Morrison, Bob Geldof and Sinéad O'Connor. And, like those of their earlier literary precursors, the achievements of these individual figures must be viewed as part of a much broader collective endeavour in the field. That collective endeavour spans several different modes of music and several decades and can ultimately be traced to a conjuncture of both national and international forces going back to the international folk revival of the 1960s, which created an appreciative new international and domestic audience for Irish traditional and folk music.[35] The 1960s was also the moment when, in Derek Scott's phrase, musical postmodernism 'ousted [modernist] notions of universalism, internationalism and "art for art's sake", and replaced them with concerns for the values of specific cultures and their differences'.[36] Whereas musical modernism had been wedded to a transnational aesthetic that had little time for local or regional particularities, this internationalism has, Scott argues, given way since the 1960s to a new postmodern cultural relativism signalled both by a resurgent interest in ethnic music (and the rise of ethnomusicology) and a new commercialism that would see classical and pop music repertoires increasingly subjected to largely similar marketing forces.

In this fundamentally altered international landscape, Ireland, which had produced no serious musical modernism, could find the scope to develop instead its own indigenous musical resources. These flourished initially in the folk revival, which would then create the momentum for a whole series of Irish individuals and groups practising very diverse musical styles and forms. The early acclaim won in European and American folk circuits by the more traditional and folk groups such as the Clancy Brothers, the Dubliners, Planxty, the Chieftains or the Bothy Band would later pave the way for crossover experiments between folk and rock music that would generate bands such as Thin Lizzy, Horslips, De Danann, Clannad, Moving Hearts, and the Pogues. In the major groups that emerged in the late 1970s and early 1980s, such as the Boomtown Rats, the Undertones, U2, and the Cranberries, the international rock element typically outweighed any indigenous Irish sound or form. Nevertheless, the strength and influence of the folk scene was such that several of the most successful rock artists, including Van Morrison, Sinéad O'Connor and the Pogues, drew on it at some stage in their careers. What is ultimately important here is neither the listing of individual artists and groups nor deciding which form of music

---

35 On the wider shifts at this time in the Irish state's policy towards music, see Marie McCarthy, *Passing It On: The Transmission of Music in Irish Culture* (Cork, 1999), ch. 6.

36 Derek Scott, 'Postmodernism and Music', in Stuart Sim, ed., *The Icon Critical Dictionary of Postmodern Thought* (London and New York, 1998), 134–46, 135

contributed to the success of the other, but the fact that a critical mass of Irish musical talent, working domestically in a sustained manner over several decades, and in a variety of fields from *sean-nós* and traditional through classical to punk, has created a musical culture capable of tapping into wider global circuits without repudiating a distinctive Irish component. In the opening decades of the twentieth century the Abbey Theatre might have been the nerve-centre of a literary revival whose stars claimed the attention of the literary capitals of London and Paris. By the closing decades of the same century, it was now Windmill Lane Recording Studios that commanded the global limelight; the Abbey Theatre surviving mainly as a museum, a site of pilgrimage for literary tourists in a Dublin now much better known to the world for its rock stars than for its writers.

The obvious objection is that this drastically oversimplifies developments. Surely, it is simply that the world of media hype that aggrandizes the achievements of the Irish popular music industry proportionately diminishes the achievements of the Irish high arts, which will never be exposed to the same inflationary glare? A survey such as this must inevitably simplify, and the power of media to hype is similarly not in question. Nevertheless, if today Irish rock stars seem to be more outsized figures than their high cultural counterparts, the magnifying power of the media may not be the only or even the decisive factor. There is also the fact that the rock stars seem to have an appetite to take on major issues of the historical moment in a way that their literary peers rarely do and that they have the capacity to do so, moreover, with a verve that the latter lack. However one evaluates their efforts, Bono and Geldof have at least had the ambition and tenacity to wrestle with questions of famine in Africa or 'Third World' poverty and debt relief. Sinéad O'Connor's public engagements with issues such as abortion, motherhood or priesthood have been the subject of much media derision, but it would be hard to think of any of her literary peers who have taken so many professional risks for their beliefs or who have dared to buck the social consensus in either the old or the new Irelands as flamboyantly as she has done in both. On the domestic scene, figures such as Frank Harte, Christy Moore or the Pogues have dared to be more openly at odds with the revisionist consensus on Irish nationalism than their counterparts in most of the other arts have been. On the opposite side of the political spectrum on such issues, Bob Geldof's revisionism has the virtue of being never less than courageously passionate and unequivocally outspoken. One of Ireland's leading contemporary classical composers, Raymond Deane, has served as president of the Ireland Palestine Solidarity Campaign. Would any literary figure of comparable distinction have dared to do so?

At a time when many of the more talented figures in the literary world seem to think that the grand political issues of their day have no place at all in art or else confine themselves to slaying only the shrivelled dragons of 'de Valera's Ireland', the leading figures in the field of Irish music have shown themselves much less afraid than most to wander beyond the boundaries of the received intellectual consensus. Is this because the inexorable publicity machines demand constant controversy and self-promotion at any cost? Or is it because those who amass vast fortunes in the commercial world of popular music can afford to take less heed of the political sensitivities (real or imagined) of arts councils, state broadcasting services or newspaper industries than artists in less financially lucrative fields could ever hope to do? Whatever the reason, the fact remains that music has been not only one of the most energetic domains of activity in late twentieth-century Ireland, but also one of the most politically lively as well.

This brings us to a concluding paradox. The closing decades of the twentieth century in Ireland have witnessed a shift of gravity from what Pierre Bourdieu calls the field of restricted production, where the accumulation of long-term symbolic capital was prized above short-term economic profit, to the field of large scale cultural production directed towards immediate economic gain. This shift of weight from high culture to mass culture concords well enough with wider international trends within the postmodern moment generally and corresponds to what Anderson has described as the preponderance of *citra* over *ultra* tendencies in late twentieth-century art. The most distinguished Irish artists to emerge from the late nineteenth-century Revival were mainly writers committed to a high modernism that tried to defy the commodifying tendencies of the culture industry. Works such as *Ulysses* or *Waiting for Godot* were steeped in an awareness of contemporary mass culture, but these were nonetheless formally innovative, oblique, vanguardist texts that even the most avant-garde intelligentsias had to struggle to assimilate. In stark contrast, the works produced by the most internationally fêted artists to have emerged from the current Irish musical ferment are aimed instead at precisely the more popular end of the market that literary modernism resisted.[37] Indeed, those individuals and groups, such as U2 most especially, that have attained the most spectacular success have become themselves multinational enterprises complete with their own extended administrative, investment and security staff and public relations and image-development teams.

This capitalization of culture is not new (and it is much more extensive in rock than in the traditional, folk, or classical strands of the current ferment, which are often mediated to the public through quite different circuits), but when cultural production takes corporate form the interplay between capital and culture is patently intensified. The world of popular music may display these tendencies in particularly aggravated forms, but the saturation of the other arts by big money is also evident. In the publishing industry, for example, processes of concentration have generated huge conglomerates that have enormously increased the sums invested in small stables of leading writers, and in the advertising and promotional sectors that market their wares. All of this has inevitably changed the whole milieu in which art is produced and consumed, with ambiguous, and as yet poorly scrutinized, consequences for both writers and their publics.

Thus, as the Irish cultural field has been expanded and reconfigured in the last several decades, so too has its weight undoubtedly shifted toward corporatized forms of cultural production and consumption, the operations and consequences of which Irish cultural

---

37 Bourdieu, 'Market of Symbolic Goods', *Poetics*, 14 (1985), 13–44

critics, mesmerized by the 'great leap forward' of the Celtic Tiger, have mostly ignored. But while this situation clearly calls for something more than the kind of dizzy excitement and self-congratulation that has characterized so much Irish cultural criticism since the economic boom, something more rigorous than bargain-basement-standard Adornean diatribes about commercialization or the culture industry is also required. The most radical literary art that Ireland produced in the twentieth century was a difficult and oblique high-brow modernism, and not, for reasons speculated on earlier, an openly engaged, militantly politicized avant-garde art along continental models. Today, that high modernist seam seems depleted, and the most dramatic new developments have taken place precisely in those areas of popular culture that modernism once shunned. Yet, as we have also seen, the figures working at that more popular end of the market have not proved nearly as apolitical as the more dsytopian conceptions of the postmodern would predict. On the contrary, if the Irish popular music scene can be taken as a litmus test, an argument can be made that artists working in this extremely commodified field have been much more militantly and ambitiously political than their counterparts in more traditional, less fully commodified cultural sectors. Which is to say, twentieth-century Irish culture has been at its most spectacularly successful at the very outer extremes of the high–low, citra–ultra spectrum. The Irish works produced nearer to the centre of that spectrum have generally been much less impressive, and have certainly won much less international attention.

But even if the opposites meet in this respect, a crucial difference remains. At the end of the day, the most fundamental difference between Yeats, Joyce and Beckett and Bono, Geldof and O'Connor is not that the former are high brow and difficult whereas the latter are low brow and easily accessible. To argue as much is merely to reduce everything to a formalism that overlooks the fact that modernist 'difficulty' was never merely difficulty for its own sake; that 'difficulty' was, rather, an index of its refusal to conform to already established norms of language or value. Popular culture by definition can make no such refusal, and if the 'giants' of late twentieth-century Irish popular music are altogether more accessible than were their more modernist precursors this is because they must perforce be content to operate within the constraints of the already established lifeworld of their times. Bono and Geldof may take on famine in Africa and 'Third World' poverty, but, in the absence of any sense of possibility of a dispensation different to capitalism, they nonetheless look to capitalism to solve problems that appear to be structural or constitutive to its own logic. Van Morrison may find inspiration in Yeats, but he does not (openly at least) profess Yeats's lofty aristocratic disdain for the 'filthy modern tide' of democracy, Christianity and capitalism.

Modernism was never able to extricate itself from the world of capital, but it at least supped with a long spoon. Today, the spoons are shorter, the sense of any real alternatives thinner, and it is this that constitutes the decisive constraint within which both high and popular cultural production in the new Ireland now operates. As the conjuncture on which it thrived closes, the current ferment in Irish popular music will inevitably run down as the Revivalist or modernist ferments did before it. Indeed, if Banville and Muldoon represent the de-energized tail end of the hectic Irish modernist literary experiment, do Boyzone and Westlife and their many clones already represent their vastly more degraded corollaries in the popular music field? We must hope not. No cultural moment is ever without either its structural contradictions or utopian resources, and a radical Irish culture critically responsive to the demands of the new global conjuncture must always attend to these to discover its own project.

This Thing of Darkness:
Conjectures on Irish Naturalism

Twentieth-century Irish naturalism, despite its weight and durability as a literary form, has received surprisingly little critical attention. The major international reputations in modern Irish writing are those associated with the Revival and with modernism, and it is these literary movements that have monopolized the attentions of Irish literary critics and cultural historians. From its inception, Irish naturalism was conceived as a counter-blast to Revivalist romanticism, but since it adhered to realist conventions it did not conform to the anti-mimetic and radically experimental practices of modernist writing either, and hence seemed, from a modernist perspective at any rate, to be almost as conventional and outmoded as the romanticism it opposed. Defined in opposition both to the poetic and heroic aesthetic modes associated with the Revival and to the linguistic and formal experimentalism of Irish modernism, Irish naturalism has managed to sustain itself across a century without ever commanding the extended critical attention that other aesthetics have done.

The vicissitudes of international cultural criticism have also had a hand in the comparative critical neglect of naturalism. Though the different modes of realism have obviously continued to flourish across the twentieth century, ever since the 1960s the ascendant modes of French and Anglo-American literary theory have been far more preoccupied with various kinds of avant-garde writing than with realism. In this climate, a great deal of radical cultural theory would almost uncritically assimilate modernist tenets as its own, and realism would thus become an unfashionable, taken-for-granted mode — its aesthetic conventions and strategies frequently dismissed as inherently conservative and incapable of embodying a progressive politics.[1] To compound

1   While the critique of realism obviously has its roots in the literary practice and cultural criticism of the

matters, the distinction between realism and naturalism has never been fully clear, and the two terms are often used interchangeably. For some, naturalism is simply a dour, unvarnished realism; for others, it is a distinct literary mode that originated in France and the Scandinavian countries in the second half of the nineteenth century, and that was later taken up in other parts of the world that have since developed their own indigenous naturalist traditions.

In an Irish situation, where critical debates on realism have rarely extended beyond the question as to why nineteenth-century Ireland did not produce a realist novel tradition comparable to that of the English or French traditions, realism, and by extension, naturalism, have tended to be ignored or even, in extreme cases, dismissed as more or less alien aesthetics, the argument being that the most successful Irish writing has always been anti-empiricist, anti-realist and hence fantastic and proto-modernist or modernist in temper. This is a drastic simplification of actual literary history, since there have been extended, even if not very prestigious, Irish realist traditions in both the nineteenth and twentieth centuries, and it might well be argued in any event that Irish modernism, in the cases of Joyce and Beckett certainly, displays interesting, though still little-studied, affiliations with Irish naturalism. But for a variety of circumstances, domestic and international, we can see that the conditions that might have allowed for an investigation of the development of Irish naturalism have never been particularly propitious.[2]

This chapter will take a closer look at this unacknowledged stepchild of modern Irish fiction as it developed across the twentieth century. The opening section begins with a brief overview of some of the more significant critical debates that have emerged in relation to European novelistic and dramatic naturalism, and attempts to specify the typical problematics that define this particular mode of writing. Subsequent sections conceptualize the history of Irish naturalism in terms of three successive stages of its development in the hundred years extending from the 1880s to the 1980s. In each of these historical stages, naturalism, it will be argued, acquires a specific mass and temperament and serves different functions within the larger field of Irish writing. Some sense of what these functions are can be gauged by assessing naturalism's disposition

---

modernist writers themselves, and in the debates about the respective merits of realism and modernism that emerged in leftist cultural criticism in the 1930s, it is really in the 1960s and 1970s that the tendency to privilege modernist norms becomes absolutely dominant in leftist cultural criticism.

2 The tendency to conceive of English writing as fundamentally empiricist and realist and Irish writing as fundamentally anti-empiricist and tending therefore towards the fantastic and experimental finds its most vigorous contemporary elaboration in the writings of Terry Eagleton. The rather non-dialectical critique of realism, first developed by Eagleton in a stern Althusserian mode, reappears in his later work in terms of a polarized opposition between Irish and English literary traditions. Whatever its merits, one of the problems with this mode of literary history is that it only compounds the tendency, already inherent in established national canons, to dismiss less dominant or 'minor' traditions as insignificant. The argument here, in contrast, is that we need to allow for a variety of different Irish (and English) realisms, of which naturalism is only one current. See Terry Eagleton, 'Running Out of Soil', London Review of Books, 2 Dec. 2004, 28–30.

relative to the rival aesthetics that define the cultural landscape at a particular historical moment.

In contrast to a good deal of cultural criticism, naturalism is not conceived here as a late nineteenth-century period style definitively stamped once and for all by Zola or Ibsen. Instead, naturalism (which can never be fully disengaged from realism, though it is not the same thing as realism either) is viewed as a relatively mobile and mutable aesthetic that can, within limits, be modified over time as it intersects with other aesthetic modes. In other words, like any other aesthetic, naturalism is best viewed not as a static essence but as a literary mode that can be re-invented to considerable degree in various circumstances, and that can serve different social and aesthetic functions at particular historical conjunctures. The object of this study is not, therefore, to produce some reified catalogue of attributes that would allow critics to say that such and such texts are patently naturalist and thus constitute a self-evident or self-conscious naturalist tradition. Naturalism is conceived here as a critical concept referring to clusters of problematics, modes of characterization, and strategies for sequencing narrative and producing closure that can appear in quite different combinations, but which are nonetheless identifiable enough to allow us to detect significant 'family likenesses' between texts that might in other respects seem to have little enough in common with each other.[3]

2

The general history of European naturalism has been well charted. The naturalist novel has its origins in mid-to-late nineteenth-century France; naturalist drama is in its inception a largely contemporaneous Scandinavian and Russian development. Naturalism in both genres initially provoked a welter of vituperation from literary critics because of its supposed vulgarity of content, but from the start the mode was also hugely commercially successful, and it soon took root in many European and American national traditions. Decisive intellectual influences on the wider naturalist movement were Darwin's evolutionary theories of biology (*On the Origin of Species*, 1859); Claude Bernard's studies of human physiology (*L'Introduction à l'étude de la médecine expérimentale*, 1865); Marx's 'scientific' study of capitalist economy (*Das Kapital*, 1867); and — later — Freud's early works on psychology (*On the Psychical Mechanism of Hysterical Phenomena*, with Charcot, 1893, and *The Interpretation of Dreams*, 1900).[4] These works share a common philosophical materialism (what happens in this world is explicable in terms of the mechanical laws of biology, physiology, economy or psychology) and a strongly determinist accent. This

---

3   The conception of naturalism developed here is considerably indebted to June Howard's *Form and History in American Literary Naturalism* (Chapel Hill, 1985).
4   Chistopher Innes, ed., *A Sourcebook on Naturalist Theatre* (London, 2000), 6

intellectual climate helped to mould the naturalist conception of the writer, articulated most famously by Zola in his prefaces and manifestos, as a detached, clinically objective 'scientist' of human nature or society, with a duty, like that of the scientist or doctor, to vivisect the tissue of conventional moral niceties in pursuit of the deeper 'laws' that governed human behaviour. This emphasis on scientific objectivity, and the conception of the novel as a laboratory where experiments concerning individual and social behaviour could be conducted, contributed to the much commented upon determinist sensibility that supposedly characterizes naturalist fiction: its assumption that the laws of heredity and social environment, abetted by the underswell of an ungovernable sexual instinct, allowed for only a very constricted sense of human agency.

In a cogent analysis of the form, Raymond Williams has remarked that the literary term 'naturalism' indicates a movement that aimed to bring the most familiar usage of the word 'naturalist' — meaning an 'accurate' or 'lifelike' reproduction 'from nature' — and the earlier philosophical sense of the word — meaning doctrines that stressed reliance on natural laws and explanations as distinct from 'supernaturalism' to explicate social and moral matters — into an organic, expressive artistic fusion. As Williams remarks, the intellectual basis for the movement is the sense that human action 'is determined or profoundly influenced by its social environment, with the later and more penetrating observation that this social environment is itself historically produced'.[5] The crux of the matter was that these different stresses tended more often than not to stymie each other. In other words, the stress on the degree to which the social, environmental or biological factors preconditioned human behaviour tended to overwhelm the stress on environment as something that was itself socially produced via human action. In high naturalism, Williams observes, the characters' lives have soaked into their environment, the environment into the lives of the characters; the typical action was an attempted extrication from the environment that usually failed.[6]

The difficulty was always how to maintain a dialectical sense of the interaction between character and environment as a dynamic, mutually transformative process. For many of its detractors at least, the naturalist stress on social environment worked to arrest any contrapuntal sense of history. As a consequence, the telltale signature of the naturalist aesthetic is often taken to be a radical reformist impetus almost invariably checked or derailed by a deterministic fatalism. However, instead of simply dismissing naturalism as a doggedly deterministic realism, it would be better to say that the attempt to reconcile deterministic and reformist sensibilities is naturalism's fundamental problematic. If the mode was shaped by a slew of nineteenth-century discourses that stressed the conditioning power of environment, heredity and evolutionary necessity, naturalism was also animated by a campaigning, social reformist thrust that wanted

5 See Raymond Williams, 'Social Environment and Theatrical Environment: The Case of English Naturalism', in his *Problems in Materialism and Culture* (London, 1980), 125–47, 127.
6 Williams, 'Social Environment and Theatrical Environment', 140–41

to assert that these supra-human forces must be understood and controlled in order to improve human conditions.[7]

Summarizing the recurrent formal characteristics of the naturalist novel, David Baguley argues that these include a scientific or sociological theme, developed as the structuring principle of the novel, that turns on a preoccupation with neurotic or pathological states or on the unmasking of the seamier side of life, establishing an intentionality at work that usually controverts the moral assumptions of earlier bourgeois fiction; plots that are almost invariably dysphoric, the action frequently sourced in scandals or debates reported in the popular press, and commonly involving a crime, fraud, scandal or adulterous affair, these conceived in a non-heroic, non-romantic spirit, that discloses the veiled depravities of lower bourgeois or working-class life or the emptiness of human existence; an action commonly located within a meticulously detailed, usually highly researched milieu — a mining village, a provincial town, the ghetto district of a large city, the bohemian quarter. This led to the criticism, expressed by Georg Lukács and others, that the naturalist writers tended to fetishize objects and surface description at the expense of narrative momentum. In the French tradition at least, Baguley contends, naturalist novels tend to conform to two basic plot models or generic species:

First there is what might be called a Goncourtian type, to which certain of Zola's works, notably L'Assommoir, sometimes adhere, that takes up the tragic scheme of the fall of a single character, presenting it as a temporal process of deterioration, one that derives its causality from particular determining factors (hereditary flaws, neurotic dispositions, adverse social conditions) rather than from the transcendent forces of classical tragedy. The second type is more Flaubertian, one in which the determining factor of deterioration is more generalized as the insufficiency of human life itself, trapping the individual in the snare of routine existence and its sordid compromises. In this type of novel, which seems to dispense with any attempt to elaborate a plot, the only dynamic element proves to be the constant disillusionment of the character whose life is frittered away on the path to extinction ... The first [of these two types of naturalist text] is more dynamic; the second, static, circular, or

---

7 Writing on American naturalism, Charles Child Walcutt observes that the naturalist 'has to establish the validity of two assumptions: that the state of man has to be improved, and that human conditions are determined by the operation of material causes which can be traced, recorded, understood, and, finally, controlled. The ... best possible way to illustrate and validate these two assumptions is to write a "naturalistic" tragedy in which a human being is crushed and destroyed by the operation of forces which he has no power to resist or even understand. The more helpless the individual and the more clearly the links in an inexorable chain of causation are defined, the more effectively documented are the two assumptions which underlie the scientists' program of reform, for the destruction of an individual demonstrates the power of heredity and environment over human destinies. And if the victim's lot is sordid, the need for reform is proved.' See Charles Child Walcutt, American Literary Naturalism: A Divided Stream (Westport, 1973), 24–25. For a more extensive discussion, which situates this as the defining naturalist antinomy, see Howard, Form and History, ch. 2.

repetitive. The first produces plots of submission that take the character steadily downhill; the second produces plots of resignation that take the character steadily nowhere.[8]

The social-Darwinist versions of naturalism, Baguley suggests, emphasize the relentless struggle and strife endemic to life; the more Schopenhauerian versions accentuate the futile repetitiveness of it all.[9] This entropic quality has its sources both in a formal dilemma, the danger of narrative drive being capsized by the lengthy descriptions and weighty research and documentation that are the inevitable correlative of the stress on an exact presentation of milieu or environment, and in the thematic drive to disenchant humanist idealism and romanticism that motivates the genre.

Naturalism's capacity to bring new classes and new social problems into the franchise of fiction is widely regarded as one of its decisive achievements. In *Mimesis*, Erich Auerbach remarks that even among the greatest classical realists of the early nineteenth-century, including Balzac, Stendhal and even Flaubert, 'the lower strata of people, and indeed the people as such in general, hardly appear' and 'when it appears, it is seen not on its own premises, within its own life, but from above'.[10] This is only partly correct. Zola would indeed claim in the Preface to *L'Assommoir* that his novel 'was the first about the common people which does not tell lies, but which has the authentic smell of the people', but in fact peasants had been common in British and French fiction since the 1700s and the lives of the urban poor had featured prominently in Eugène Sue's *Les Mystères de Paris* (1842–43) and Victor Hugo's *Les Misérables* (1862), as well as in the works of Dickens, Gaskell and others.[11] What was new about Zola's work was that the narrative depended for its interest on the working class alone. Zola's compositional rule in *L'Assommoir* was to resist the temptation to alleviate the representation of working-class life by filling it with action or by contrasting it to its bourgeois counterpart.[12]

Donald Pizer has suggested that it is in naturalist fiction that sex (as opposed to rituals of courtship and marriage) starts to become the great theme of modern fiction.[13] The establishment of the naturalist drama in the 1880s and 1890s coincides with the rise of the women's movement and its campaigns for legal equality and voting rights. Male writers dominate the naturalist canon, and some leading naturalists, notably Strindberg, were notoriously misogynist. But, generally, the naturalists' challenge to the established literary and theatrical orthodoxies of the time for representing women were broadly

8   David Baguley, 'The Nature of Naturalism', in Brian Nelson, ed., *Naturalism in the European Novel* (New York, 1992), 13–26, 22
9   David Baguley, *Naturalist Fiction: The Entropic Vision* (Cambridge, 1990), 217
10 Erich Auerbach, *Mimesis: The Representation of Reality in Western Literature*, trans. Willard R. Trask (Princeton, 1991 [1946]), 497
11 Zola, cited in Sandry Petry, 'Nature, Society, and the Discourse of Class', in Denis Hollier, ed., *A New History of French Literature* (Cambridge, MA, 2001), 774–80, 774
12 Petry, 'Nature, Society, and the Discourse of Class', 775
13 Donald Pizer, *Twentieth-Century American Literary Naturalism: An Interpretation* (Carbondale, 1966), 6

emancipatory.[14] But the naturalist mode has also provoked a series of critiques of three fundamental types. The first, which might be termed a bourgeois or moral critique, most stridently expressed in the period when naturalism first emerged, is that the naturalist imagination is magnetically compelled to the pathological, to corruption, to degradation and failure. The outraged clamour provoked by naturalism's vulgarity was in many ways merely the sound of the snapping sinews of a late 'Victorian' official consensus concerning codes of social, sexual and literary propriety. But it must be remembered that this was a period that saw the naturalist and the decadence movements and the first wave of modernism rapidly emerge on the heels of each other, and that also witnessed a dramatic expansion in both mass culture and the so-called gutter press. The whole late nineteenth-century literary field, in other words, underwent a series of convulsive shake-ups that saw the formerly more discrete domains of popular obscenity, specialist or mass pornography and high literature now converge in unexpected ways. That many readers found all these changes perturbing is scarcely surprising.

To reduce the attack on the naturalists in this context to a stand-off between radical literary iconoclasts and censorious bourgeois prigs is too simplistic — a more fundamental cultural sea change or structural reconfiguration of the entire literary field (with attendant consequences for the relationship between writer and audience) was working itself out at that moment in a context where the relationship between mass culture and high culture was quite different to what it is today. The modernists, who were clearly indebted in some ways to the naturalists (both cultivated an aesthetics of shock) were for the most part determined to maintain a Chinese wall between a demandingly intellectual and non-commercial high art and commercial mass culture. But the naturalists' relationship to mass culture was considerably more ambivalent. Frequently expressing the same disdain as their modernist counterparts for mass culture, the naturalists nevertheless traded in much the same 'scandalous' and 'muck-raking' matter as the more sensationalist modes of commercial culture (such as the tabloid newspaper, for instance), and did so using literary conventions more populist and commercial and much less oblique and estranging than those cultivated by the modernists.[15] To sum up, the naturalists, unlike the modernists, tried to maintain the connection between 'serious literature' and 'mass entertainment' so as to reach a mass public. Naturalism, therefore, attracted vituperation from all quarters, not just because it offended Victorian

14 The number of key naturalistic works with women in their titles is striking; examples include Flaubert's *Madame Bovary* (1856), the Goncourts' *Germinie Lacerteux* (1864), Zola's *Thérèse Raquin* (1867), and *Nana* (1880), Hardy's *Tess of the d'Urbervilles* (1891) and George Moore's *Esther Waters* (1894) and even more strikingly in the theatre, in works such as Ibsen's *A Doll's House* (1879), Strindberg's *Miss Julie* (1888), Shaw's *Mrs. Warren's Profession* (1898), or Chekhov's *The Three Sisters* (1901). For more on naturalism and the early feminist movement, see Innes, *Sourcebook*, 18–20.

15 Useful socio-cultural studies of the changing literary field in this period include Ian Hunter, David Saunders and Dugald Williams, *On Pornography: Literature, Sexuality and Obscenity Law* (Houndmills, 1993), Paul Delany, *Literature, Money and the Market: From Trollope to Amis* (Houndmills, 2002), and Lawrence Rainey, *Institutions of Modernism: Literary Elites and Public Culture* (New Haven, 1998).

conservatives, but also because it occupied uneasy ground between an older bourgeois realism and new avant-garde literary practises prepared to sever the connection with the bourgeois expectation more decisively than naturalism was prepared to do.

This leads directly to a second widespread critique, one that might be called either formalist or left-modernist, which differs from the previous critique in that it indicts naturalism, not for its unhygienic or nihilistic structures of feeling, but for its formal conservatism. Lukács could trace a direct line (of descent) from naturalism to modernism, but from the vantage point of a consolidated modernism, naturalism would be dismissed, along with realism *tout court*, as a retrograde and inherently conservative aesthetic. From this perspective, the basic conventions of all realist modes (including naturalism) are such that they can provide only a very limited, tendential grasp of the social. Realism, in this view, is dependent upon a naïve conception of language as a neutral or transparent medium of representation and on an empiricism that holds that 'reality equals what we can see, that perception equals cognition'.[16] Hence, those factors that shape social life but which are imperceptible in phenomenal appearances — such as global socio-economic forces, for instance — are effectively occluded. Thus, realist or naturalist narratives may offer immensely gritty depictions of how those dwelling in urban slums may live — we may get a detailed sense of the sights, sounds, and smells of such a milieu and of the typical problems that beset those dwelling there — but it is much more difficult, if not impossible, within realist conventions to demonstrate much beyond the manifest sensory texture of this situation. The best that can be achieved within realist modes — so the argument runs — is that the audience feels a liberal humanist sympathy for the plight of the poor. But the audience's understanding of their situation is fastened on individual situations and individualist solutions; no higher analytical cognition of the social situation is achieved that would indicate how poverty is an effect of the distributive mechanics of capitalism and its socially structured systems of class inequality and uneven development. Thus, Colin MacCabe can argue that 'classic realism' is 'fundamentally inimical to the production of political knowledge'.[17] Whereas modernist works deploy formal and linguistic experiment to defamiliarize received modes of representation and perception, compelling audiences fundamentally to rethink what they take to be 'reality', realist and naturalist modes, however radical in intention, depend on a liberal humanist aesthetic of the 'real' that is more hindrance than help to any thoroughgoing diagnosis of the complex forces that shape our contemporary world.

Though certainly trenchant, this left-modernist critique's indiscriminate dismissal of all forms of realist or representational narrative as conservative, and its assumption of an *a priori* identity between literary works that foreground their own formal experiment and

16 The argument is summarized by Christine Gledhill, 'Recent Developments in Feminist Criticism', *Quarterly Review of Film Studies*, 3, 4 (1978), 464.

17 Colin MacCabe, 'Memory, Phantasy, Identity: Days of Hope and the Politics of the Past', *Edinburgh '77 Magazine*, 2 (1977), 7–13, cited in John Hill, *Sex, Class and Realism: British Cinema 1956–1963* (London, 1995), 60

radical politics, are serious liabilities. Some greater historical and formal discrimination between the different modalities of realism (and indeed the different modalities of modernism) seems possible and desirable. One of the major weaknesses of the left-modernist position indeed is that, while valorizing modernist defamiliarization as radically subversive, it forgets that the various modalities of realism in their own moment of emergence also operated in defamiliarizing ways. In this context, one of the strengths of the Lukácsian critique of naturalism is that it attempts to evaluate the naturalists not simply by pitting them against the modernists, but by situating them within a wider, more discriminating history of narrative realism.

Contrary to the left-modernists, Lukács believes that realist narrative does have a capacity to depict more than simply the surface texture of reality. Indeed, as he sees it, the whole impetus of major realist fiction is precisely to dig beneath the surface of events 'to penetrate the laws governing objective reality and to uncover the deeper, hidden, mediated, not immediately perceptible network of relationships that go to make up society'. But once the intellectual labour of analysis and abstraction is achieved, the realist writer has then, in the second instance, 'to transcend the process of abstraction' by creating dynamic fictions in which character and plot combine to lend the abstractions a new artistically mediated and dynamic immediacy. Hence, the more complex the writer's grasp of the living contradictions of real life, and the greater her or his command of the dialectic of abstraction and sensuous artistic representation, the more profound the realism she or he can attain. At one very simple level, Lukács's critique of the naturalists is that their excessive devotion to a detailed description of milieu actually limits them to a kind of photographic realism that is actually much less comprehensive than that of the earlier classical realists. Thus, he argues that:

> When the surface of life is only experienced immediately, it remains opaque, fragmentary, chaotic and uncomprehended. Since the objective mediations are more or less consciously ignored or passed over, what lies on the surface is frozen and any attempt to see it from a higher intellectual vantage-point has to be abandoned.[18]

For Lukács, in other words, the naturalists are too positivistic, too empiricist in their methods and hence lack the diagnostic capacities of either the earlier classical realists or the later twentieth-century 'critical realists'; this for him is what underlies their incapacity, as he sees it, to attain the object of all major realism: namely, to give the contradictory dynamics of historical movement concrete sensuous artistic expression in plots that coherently integrate character and action.[19]

18 Georg Lukács, 'Realism in the Balance', in Ernst Bloch et al., *Aesthetics and Politics* (London, 1980), 28–59, 38–39
19 Erich Auerbach, another of the great historians of realism, is more critically appreciative than Lukács of the naturalists. Even so, the two largely concur that the late nineteenth century witnesses a diminishment in the scope of the realist novel and a tendency towards a rather static or arrested conception of society.

Lukács's dismissal of naturalism as a kind of photographic realism actually anticipates and converges to some extent with the left-modernist critique of realism as such. However, there is a more complex dimension to Lukács's work in which he does not simply indict the naturalists for their supposed shortcomings but attempts to explain why things might have arrived at such a pass, whatever the authorial intentions of liberal, left-leaning, progressive naturalists such as Zola. For Lukács, the problem begins with the naturalists' overzealous repudiation of what they considered the 'romantic' excesses of Balzac's or Stendhal's methods of composition. So concerned are writers like Flaubert and Zola to avoid what they see as the bomtbast and subjectivism of romanticism that they are impelled instead to a '"scientific" method [which] always seeks the average, and this grey statistical mean, the point at which all internal contradictions are blunted, where the great and the petty, the noble and the base, the beautiful and the ugly are all mediocre "products" together'.[20]

In fine, Zola's repudiation of romantic afflatus impels him logically to a 'flattened' mode of composition in which the stress must be on 'average' characters and 'average' or undistinguished sensibilities and actions, this distracting from the writer's real business, which ought to be to give sensuous expression to historical development in all its fullness and contradictory richness. The knock-on effect of their pursuit of a method of 'scientific' detachment and of their compulsion to people their novels with diminished or 'average' characters with limited critical consciousness or intellectual capacity is that the naturalists diminish the ability of their works to express any complex dialectical sense of the worlds they conjure. In addition, this predilection for low-mimetic characters with only attenuated agency and self-consciousness creates a compact between the narrator and the reader, whose level of understanding is implicitly or explicitly recognized to be much superior to that of the characters depicted. Hence, however much authorial empathy and exactitude they bring to the milieu or subjects they depict, the immanent formal logic of naturalism tends to open up a disabling degree of intellectual distance between narrator and reader, on the one hand, and the diminished characters on the other — this accounts for the sense of anthropological voyeurism or middle-class imaginative 'slumming' associated with a good deal of naturalist writing.

Repudiating romanticism and all its phoney metaphysics and false contrivances, repudiating also its embrace of the irrational (though what the romantics sometimes opposed was not rational activity as such, but the reduction of reason to instrumental

After the 1840s, Auerbach observes, very few of the European realists display the same capacity for 'a serious representation of contemporary everyday social reality against the background of a constant historical movement' of the kind that had distinguished their earlier antecedents. In the German naturalists especially, Auerbach writes, 'the historical background of the events they represent appears completely immobile'. While rating Zola's achievements higher than Lukács does, Auerbach nonetheless notes an overall narrowing of outlook and scope: 'When we compare Stendhal's or even Balzac's world with the world of Flaubert or the two Goncourts, the latter seems strangely narrow and petty despite its wealth of impressions.' Auerbach, Mimesis, 518, 505.

20 Georg Lukács, 'The Zola Centenary', in his Studies in European Realism (London, 1972 [1950]), 85–96, 91

reason) and its confidence in man's capacity for self-making, the naturalists overstress, in reaction, man's thraldom to a mechanical, machinelike world. Flaubert, Lukács complains, believes that 'climaxes' exist only in art and not in life and hence should be eliminated from the writer's plotting or compositional technique, the better to allow him to capture the tedious, humdrum tempo of everyday modern life. This stress on capturing modern tedium, Lukács contends, merely blinds Flaubert to the subterranean struggles and crises that are constantly working away beneath the surface of everyday bourgeois life, and that do not simply occur in dramatic moments of 'catastrophe' or 'revolution'.[21] For Lukács:

> The decisive ideological weakness of the writers of the descriptive method is in their passive capitulation to these consequences, to these phenomena of fully-developed capitalism, and *in their seeing the result but not the struggle of the opposing forces*. And even when they apparently do describe a process — in the novel of disillusion — the final victory of capitalist inhumanity is always anticipated. In the course of the novel they do not recount how a stunted individual had been gradually adjusted to the capitalist order; instead they present a character who [sic] at the very outset reveals traits that should have emerged only as a result of the entire process. That is why the disillusionment developed in the course of the novel appears so feeble and purely subjective. We do not watch a man whom we have come to know and love being spiritually murdered by capitalism in the course of the novel, but follow a corpse in passage through still lives becoming increasingly aware of being dead. The writers' fatalism, their capitulation (even with gnashing teeth) before capitalist inhumanity, is responsible for the absence of development in these 'novels' of development ... A dreary existence without a rich inner life, without the vitality of continuous development is far less revolting and shocking than the daily and hourly unremitting transformation of thousands of human beings with infinite capacities into 'living corpses'.[22]

Marx, Lukács remarks, had indeed stressed the extreme alienation of everyday life in advanced capitalism but had also stressed the contradictory, crisis-prone nature of the system and the many revolts, whether spontaneous or organized, that continuously erupted to protest this alienation. By virtue of its stress on disillusion and disappointment, modern bourgeois literature actually bears witness against bourgeois society. But when modern writers made the expression of the emptiness of modern life the prime function or goal of literature, 'when they do not afford direct experience with the struggles to restore meaning to life', then, Lukács contends, they inevitably conveyed a sense of

21 Georg Lukács, 'Narrate or Describe?', in his *Writer and Critic, and other Essays* (London, 1970), 110–48, 121–22
22 Lukács, 'Narrate or Describe?', 146–47. My emphasis.

history as something static and arrested in a manner quite different to earlier classical realists such as Scott or Balzac or Stendhal.[23]

While Lukács's critique of naturalism (and particularly his diagnosis of its incapacity to represent contradictory historical movement) remains powerful, it suffers from a tendency to insinuate the norms of realism as the natural or normative conventions of narrative *per se*. In this respect, his critique is the left-realist obverse mirror image of left-modernists such as MacCabe who ascribe modernist norms a similar ahistorical privilege. For Lukács, modernism and naturalism both dissolve the connection between individual and society, thus rendering them both equally unintelligible. Whereas modernism for its part, he believes, turns way from the social to privilege the solitary and the subjective (by way of the stream-of-consciousness techniques or its resort to montage), naturalism, in contrast, focuses obsessively on the objective social constraints on individual agency. But, as June Howard has observed, we need not accept Lukács's value-system in its entirety to find many of his distinctions valid and important. Whereas Lukács deprecates naturalism simply as a failed realism, it might be more productive to work from the assumption that modernists and naturalists alike 'are writers for whom the historical opportunity to correlate action and meaning in a single action has closed'.[24]

The inability to attain some satisfying integration of character and action into a satisfying totality of vision has a number of different causes. The late nineteenth-century expansion of capitalism via imperialism onto a more fully global scale may have meant that neither individual nation-states nor even continental Europe as a whole could any longer be properly comprehended as discrete, knowable spaces. Likewise, an increasingly aggravated capitalist compartmentalization of the domestic everyday lifeworld, something which also led to intensified commodification and specialization within the artistic field itself, may have made it more difficult to achieve the kinds of grand totalization achieved earlier. In reality, the global extension of capital via imperialism and its domestic intensification via commodification are two sides of the same coin. Finding it difficult to achieve any sense of totality in such contexts, but still aspiring to achieve it, the modernists and naturalists typically tried to resolve the dilemma in fundamentally different ways. For the modernists, when the self can no longer discern any order in the material world, there is no option but to look to the self-consciousness of the artist as

---

23 Lukács, 'Narrate or Describe?', 147. Raymond Williams essentially concurs with Lukács on this point: 'The tragedy of naturalism is the tragedy of passive suffering, and the suffering is passive because man can only endure and never really change his world. The endurance is given no real moral or religious valuation; it is wholly mechanical, because both man and his world, in what is now understood as rational explanation, are the products of an impersonal and material process which, though it changes through time, has no ends ... But then this development had real causes. It is, essentially, a deliberate arrest of the process of enlightenment at the point of critical involvement. As such it corresponds to the deliberate arrest and subsequent decadence of liberalism, at the point where its universal principles required the transformation of its social programme, and where it could either go on or must go back.' See his *Modern Tragedy* (London, 1979 [1966]), 69–70.

24 Howard, *Form and History*, 145

an ordering, redemptive principle, that can impose a purely formal order on recalcitrant material (Joyce's 'mythic method' is a famous instance) or that can discover in the past some more aboriginal sense of totality in the form of universal archetypes or collective myths (which would explain the modernist fascination with classical anthropology, the primitive, the occult, and religious and/or aristocratic ritual). The naturalists, unlike the modernists, continued to strive after the conventional integrity of realist plot. But they were impelled by their own logic towards a sense of the world as a place of mechanical and indifferent force that frustrates and overwhelms human understanding and agency, thus dissolving any coherence between character and action. Alternatively, they had to abandon any synoptic sense of comprehensive totality and were forced to organize their material in the smaller totalities of specialized milieux or specific social segments. Hence naturalist fiction's propensity to conceive of the social either in terms of quasi-anthropological investigations of discrete social sectors (the coal or meat industries, the urban ghetto, the financial or artistic districts, the world of journalism) or in terms of 'thesis novels' on discrete social problems ('the woman question', 'the peasant question', 'the housing question', 'the alcohol or drug question', and so on).

Conceived thus, we can conceptualize naturalism neither as a failed realism nor as a depressed, bleakly dystopian realism, but rather as a mode haunted by a commitment to the expectations and conventions of classical realism in a more advanced capitalist context, where these expectations have become increasingly difficult to realise. Thus, the naturalist mode is indeed marked by certain recurrent features—documentary strategies; the anatomy of discrete (generally lower-class) milieux; entropic plots of stasis or decline; particular dispositions of character, narrator and reader. But what ultimately gives it coherence is its constitutive problematic: namely, how to conceive of meaningful human agency in a world where action and understanding, comprehension of the forces that shape society and meaningful intervention into society, are always perceived to thwart and compromise each other.

Like any other aesthetic mode, naturalism took shape in specific historical and geographical contexts, and it would be foolish to expect naturalisms that emerged in very different socio-historical contexts simply to replicate each other. The most comprehensively-studied naturalist literatures are the French, the British, the American, and the North European. These are, of course, the naturalisms of the more advanced capitalist economies and most were also predominantly Protestant in their cultural temper. Naturalism in the United States — to take a significant and much-studied example — emerged as a very formidable literary current in a country by then already fast becoming a leading military and industrial global superpower, in which 40 per cent of the population already lived in urban areas by 1900, and which was characterized by a constant influx of immigrants from Europe, Asia and South America.[25]

25 Howard, Form and History, 34

The contrast between the United States and Ireland — a country still struggling to emerge from a long history of colonial subjection, famine and underdevelopment, still overwhelmingly rural and only poorly industrialized, in which emigration and not immigration was the decisive social reality — could hardly be more pronounced. Despite these stark differences, some similarities are also worth noting. In the United States and Ireland, in contrast to England or France, naturalist narrative took root in still-emergent national literatures that did not have a strong, internationally distinguished realist tradition. Indeed, one might say that in the United States and Ireland naturalism is practically foundational to a vernacular social realism, whereas in France or England it constitutes a late mutation within an already well-established realist tradition. And while the intellectual world at large is nowadays much more familiar with the canonical texts of Irish or American modernism than with those of the naturalists of either country, naturalism was crucial to the development of modernism in both countries and to the particular temper it acquired in each.

3

In its formative moment, Irish naturalism would appear to owe more to Ibsen and the naturalist drama than to Zola and the naturalist novel. However, as far as the long-term development of twentieth-century Irish literature is concerned, the most decisive work to issue from Irish naturalism's opening period is surely Joyce's *Dubliners* (1914). Historians of English literature differ on the significance of naturalism for the development of English literature in the late nineteenth- early twentieth-century period. A few contend that all of the important English writers in the era between Hardy and Lawrence were influenced by naturalism, but most argue that its significance was restricted to writers such as George Gissing, Arnold Bennett and John Galsworthy. Whatever about the English situation, it does seem quite interesting to note — though it is almost never commented on — that several Irish writers played a crucial role in acting as mediators between continental European naturalism and English audiences. It is commonly acknowledged that George Moore, 'the English Zola', played a key role in introducing French naturalism to English letters. But when one adds to this that George Bernard Shaw and James Joyce were also among Ibsen's earliest and most vocal champions in Ireland and England, then the collective significance of the Irish in this matter seems a good deal more noteworthy. Shaw's *The Quintessence of Ibsenism* is now regarded as a manifesto that outlines his own emerging sense of theatrical mission, rather than an incisive study of the Norwegian dramatist. But when it was published in 1891, it was one of the first serious studies of Ibsen in the English language. Joyce's youthful lectures and essays on Ibsen, 'Drama and Life' (1900) and 'Ibsen's New Drama' (1900), are slighter works, but for Joyce 'Ibsen was the first among the dramatists of the world', and his admiration for the Norwegian as the exemplary 'modern' artist decisively shaped his own sense of what the artist should be.[26]

Moore was the first of the Irish writers to acquaint himself with French naturalism and the only one with extensive personal connections to the Parisian literary scene and to the Médan circle, when naturalism was still in its earliest and most innovative stage.[27] His early novel *A Mummer's Wife* (1885) was the most self-consciously naturalist work to appear on the English scene in the 1880s. The works of the major French naturalists were slow to be translated into English — the first Zola translation did not appear until 1883; the first Goncourt in 1886; the first Maupassant in 1887; *Madame Bovary* was not translated until 1886 (by Eleanor Marx), *L'Éducation sentimentale* had to wait until 1898. When the translations did come, they came with a vengeance. During the years between 1884 and 1889 Vizetelly published seven novels by Zola in English (all expurgated), with reportedly a million copies in circulation at one time.[28] Moore's naturalist phase and his public campaigns against Mudie's Select Library system occurred in a moment when a wider English public was already coming into direct contact with the French naturalists via Vizetelly's publications. Moore was certainly adept in stirring up controversy about the naturalist movement, but as Zola's self-styled 'ricochet in England', he was ultimately more significant as an early importer of naturalism than as an original, creative innovator in this mode. His enthusiasm for naturalism in any strict sense was fleeting, and after Joris Karl Huysmans's break with naturalism to cultivate the decadent novel in *À Rebours* (1884), Moore too repudiated the Zolaesque novel to experiment in other more self-consciously aestheticized idioms.

Terry Eagleton has remarked that naturalism is 'really just aestheticism flipped inside out' — the naturalist an 'objective', 'scientific' connoisseur of the salacious and the squalid; the aestheticist a subjectivist aficionado of the refined and the rarefied.[29] For Huysmans, the embrace of aestheticism and decadence went hand in hand with a fascination with the rituals and mysteries and 'colour' of French Catholicism, but Irish Catholicism exercised no such spell for Moore. In the latter's work, Catholicism in particular and religion more generally are essentially conceived as a kind of deadening commitment to control that appeals only because it offers refuge from the vicissitudes of life; he once remarked that 'the Roman Catholic Church relies upon its converts, for after two or three generations of Catholicism, the intelligence dies'.[30] Religion certainly preoccupied Moore. Much of his best fiction is structured in terms of a conflict between the gravitational pull of religion (either Protestant or Catholic) and moral scruple, on the

---

26 This phrase appears as part of an extended encomium to Ibsen in Joyce's *Stephen Hero*. For further discussion, see Klaus Reichert, 'The European Background of Joyce's Writing', in Derek Attridge, ed., *The Cambridge Companion to James Joyce* (Cambridge, 1990), 55–82, 62.

27 For a useful account of Moore's contacts with Zola and the Médan circle, see Adrian Frazier, *George Moore, 1852–1933* (New Haven, 2000), 61–65 and 95–116.

28 Baguley, *Naturalist Fiction*, 32

29 Terry Eagleton, *Heathcliff and the Great Hunger: Studies in Irish Culture* (London, 1995), 216

30 The remark from *Hail and Farewell* is cited in Declan Kiberd, 'George Moore's Celtic Lawn Party', in Robert Welch, ed., *The Way Back: George Moore's The Untilled Field and The Lake* (Dublin, 1982), 13–27, 23.

one side, and some version of the artistic or sensual or instinctual life, on the other.

That structuring antithesis may be observed already in *A Mummer's Wife*, in which Kate Ede, a woman brought up in strict evangelical circumstance and living a thankless life of self-sacrifice to an asthmatic husband, runs off with Dick Lennox, an easy-going, morally disengaged actor working in a travelling theatre company. For Kate, Dick and the theatre company represent a world of imagination, sensuality, and emotional freedom that her asphyxiating religion cannot accommodate. To its credit, the novel does not, in Dickensian manner, represent the theatre as the romantic antidote to the hard grind of work and religion. Instead, in a kind of proto-Adornean move, it suggests that religion and the world of mass entertainment are dialectically interdependent. The theatre survives by offering the poor access to cheap forms of sensation that allow them to relax from the rigours of work and the exactions of their self-mortifying religion. But it does nothing to alter the basic conditions that produce such needs in the first instance; it is simply a distraction served to sustain the relentless routine of working-class life. Even though Kate yearns for freedom, she remains — in typical naturalist fashion — prisoner to her early emotional formation. So, after her elopement, she is racked with guilt, takes to drink to ease her conscience, loses her child through neglect, and her career thereafter exemplifies — to recall Baguley — a Goncourtian-type trajectory in which she progresses steadily downhill, eventually to die a sordid death.

Esther Waters (1894), often considered Moore's finest work and a return to naturalism, is in fact a naturalist palinode.[31] Telling the story of a servant girl impregnated and disgraced, the novel rehearses a familiar naturalist pattern of lower class descent into shame and squalor, only to thwart environmental determinism by showing how Esther's innate moral instinct and devotion to her child allow her to survive adversity and eventually to find a modicum of happiness. As in *A Mummer's Wife*, the novel offers its heroine a false choice between two ways of life, each the apparent antithesis of the other but in reality only two sides of the same debased coin. On the one side, there is Fred Parsons, a strict Calvinist whose faith is essentially a glorification of his own powers of discipline and denial, but who nonetheless has enough humanity to struggle against his own bent and to want to take Esther and her child into his home. On the other side, there is William Latch, publican and bookie, a kindly but amoral man who makes a living by exploiting the weakness of the poor for gambling and drinking. Latch takes exploitation to be simply the way of the world and gambling, whether on the stock exchange or at the racecourse, to be ubiquitous. The contrasting male characters are used to highlight each other's limitations and their related strengths: Fred embraces a rigid religion that would eliminate chance and make life secure by predetermining everything; William simply embraces blind chance and has no real creed or alternative system of value at all. Both are false solutions but Esther, who learns to accommodate herself to life's vicissitudes without simply surrendering to them entirely, represents an instinct for something

31 For further discussion of *Esther Waters*, see Baguley, *Naturalist Fiction*, 119.

better than either. Conceived as an anti-*Tess of the d'Urbervilles* (1891), *Esther Waters* deploys all the machinery of naturalism in an attempt to confound the deterministic temper of naturalism that Hardy's novel exemplified and that Moore had come to repudiate. It is as though Moore recognizes in naturalism's adherence to the iron laws of determinism a secular version of English Puritanism and Calvinism. *Esther Waters* struggles to articulate some alternative to both religious creed and secular aesthetic, but ultimately can offer by way of conceptual alternative only Esther's simple moral sensitivity — ironically, an endorsement of the nineteenth-century English novel's liberal humanist faith in the honest individual that Moore had wanted to disturb by resorting to French naturalism in the first instance.[32]

In *The Lake* (1905), a novel he considered one of his finer works, Moore returned to the same problematic, though this time in an Irish Catholic context. Oliver Gogarty, a Catholic priest, had publicly denounced an attractive young schoolteacher Nora Glynn (her name is Rose Leicester in the first edition; the more Irish and Ibsenesque Nora comes later) because she was expecting an illegitimate child. His attack causes her to flee to London. Corresponding with an older, more compassionate priest, Father O'Grady, who has spent his life working with the London poor and who has befriended Nora, Gogarty comes to realize that she has had the courage to develop her own life in exile, whereas he has simply taken refuge from life in religious and social conventions in which he no longer believes. Through his correspondence with O'Grady and later with Nora, Gogarty eventually achieves an honest self-understanding and a saner appreciation of life. At the end of the novel, he feigns suicide, swims across the lake that is a metaphor for the depths of his own instinctual inner life, and leaves Ireland and the priesthood to begin anew in America.[33]

The Lake is a psychological study rather than a naturalist novel. What connects it to the earlier works is the construction of the plot in terms of an agon between religion and conscience versus an aesthetic and instinctual impulse to some more comprehensive sense of existence. In Moore's best English fiction his main protagonists, Kate Ede or Esther Waters, are working class but, when dealing with Ireland, Moore seems generally more comfortable with educated, upper-class types, as in *A Drama in Muslin* (1886), or with middle-class types such as priests and schoolteachers. His control of his Irish materials is sometimes off-balanced by a broadly satirical anti-clericalism; his most empathetically drawn priests are those who have either abandoned their religion (Gogarty in *The Lake* or Peter in 'The Exile') or those who are temperamentally at odds with Church authority (like Father McTurnan, who appears in stories such as 'A Letter to Rome' or 'A Playhouse in the Waste'). It is as though Moore has serviceable English

32 Though one of his most distinguished novels sets out to reverse the naturalist 'revolution' he had once thought to lead in England, much of Moore's best fiction remains nevertheless indebted to his naturalist period.

33 For a suggestive overview of Moore's novels, see Richard Allen Cave, *A Study of the Novels of George Moore* (Gerrards Cross, 1978).

and French traditions to hand that allow him to deal in a comprehensive and empathetic way with his English working-class heroines, but that these will not quite transfer to his handling of the Irish lower classes. When he writes of the Irish peasantry, he cannot altogether rid his writing of the sentimental, the anthropologically whimsical or the condescendingly comic-satiric, traits practically endemic to writing in English about the Irish lower classes.[34]

It is striking how commonly the device of 'exile' resolves Moore's Irish plots. It is as though he simply could not imagine that his protagonists could ever achieve their true potential if they remained in Ireland, or that Irish society could ever be transformed. Some of the fundamental devices that organize his work — the conflict between the sensitive, artistically inclined, isolated individual and the suffocating realities of a clericalist culture; the assumption that Catholicism was a greater impediment to Irish freedom than English rule or the class system; the flight into exile and the concomitant lack of interest in local political attempts to transform Irish society — have remained staples of Irish naturalist fiction throughout the twentieth century. Moore's younger contemporary, James Joyce, was to explore similar matter in a more urban context. But Joseph O'Leary is correct to note that while Moore's Father Gogarty undertakes a journey of self-discovery that will impel him from Ireland 'back to normality', Joyce's Stephen Dedalus aspires instead to a 'creative abnormality'.[35] Moore's protagonists, in other words, must escape Ireland in order to live normally abroad; Joyce's work does not depend on the ideal of some achieved normality elsewhere and asserts a desire to forge the 'uncreated conscience' of the race, this expressing a faith that the country can be transformed. It is not that Joyce was a patriot and that Moore was not. Joyce's diagnosis of the Irish social condition may be indebted to Moore's, but the relationship of art to nation in Joyce is conceived in significantly different terms. Joyce, belonging to a later generation that was more revolutionary in both political and literary matters, believes that art can eventually act to invigorate the torpid national conscience; Moore takes that torpor as a given and envisages only individual redemptions.

Shaw's contacts with continental naturalism were less direct and more filtered through English circles and translations than were Moore's, but his contact with the movement was nonetheless extensive. In 1891 he published *The Quintessence of Ibsenism*, and his first play, *Widowers' Houses* (1892), was written with the collaboration of William Archer, Ibsen's English translator and the most effective promoter of naturalistic drama in England. In 1886 Eleanor Marx conducted a reading of 'Nora', her translation of *A Doll's House*, in which Shaw played the part of Krogstadt, with Edward Aveling as Helmer and Marx herself as Nora. Like Moore's, then, Shaw's ideas were developed in the London-based feminist and left-wing intellectual circles that were then most receptive

34 See various essays in Welch, *The Way Back*, especially those by Welch and Richard Allen Cave, the latter a sympathetic reader of Moore who still acknowledges that Moore's treatment of the Irish lower orders suffers from these weaknesses.
35 Joseph Stephen O'Leary, 'Father Bovary', in Welch, *The Way Back*, 105–18, 107

to European naturalism, but Shaw's commitment to naturalism was to take his work in a very different direction.

In *The Quintessence of Ibsenism* Shaw makes it clear that his conception of Ibsen's theatre is a didactic one and his own early works were all associated with campaigns for specific social reforms. At the same time, Shaw always insisted that Ibsen's drama was anti-idealist: Ibsen constantly interrogated not just corruption in its more conventional senses but also the corrupting power of high ideals that 'like the gods of old, are constantly demanding human sacrifices' — these ideals, Shaw remarks, must constantly be tested to prove they are worth the sacrifices offered in their name.[36] His lecture on Ibsenism, delivered a year before *The Quintessence* was published, specifically used Ibsen to attack the 'idealist Socialism' of the Marxists, whom he accused of being more consumed by a destructively utopian vision of total social transformation than by the prosaic business of actually making socialism work. From the tension between these competing drives — to place his drama in the service of social reform; to interrogate all forms of idealism, including those kinds dedicated to social reform — Shaw was to make some of his best theatre.

Frequently, though, that tension slackens into a kind of complacent gradualist reformism quite consonant with mainstream English liberal and literary traditions. The morality Shaw attacks is nearly always conceived as a popular or 'middle-class' morality that is dismissed as an intellectually lazy, tiresomely philistine obstacle to progress. He seems to think that exposing morality as a vulgar sham clears the way to implementing the desired social reforms. For his admirers, his drive to shock his audiences and his interest in 'a theatre of ideas' anticipate Brecht's anti-naturalist epic theatre. For the sceptics, his naturalistic drive to undermine conventional middle-class morality simply leads him towards a romanticism of the intellect, that so cripples his capacity to deal with emotion that the human body becomes the ultimate embarrassment.[37]

But while Shaw's devotion to an intellectual drama places him at odds with the wider naturalistic currents that were eventually to be variously consolidated in the English and Irish theatres, his tendency to tackle politics in terms of individuated 'questions' does connect him to naturalistic techniques. Just as Zola's novels tend to be defined in terms of specific issues — alcoholism, prostitution, the conditions of miners, the condition of the peasantry — so too Shaw's plays (even when they are not naturalistic in technique) tend to be equally single-issue and thesis-driven. Thus we get a play on rack-renting and municipal corruption in *Widowers' Houses*, on prostitution in *Mrs. Warren's Profession*, on 'the Irish question' in *John Bull's Other Island* (1904), on religion and arms-manufacture in *Major Barbara* (1905), and so on. As noted earlier, this tendency to conceive of the world in terms of specialized 'questions' represents a certain reification of aesthetic vision and

36 George Bernard Shaw, *The Quintessence of Ibsenism* (1891), cited in Innes, *Sourcebook*, 62.
37 For more extended discussions of these divergent estimations of Shaw, see Raymond Williams, *Drama from Ibsen to Brecht* (London, 1987 [1952]), 253, and Innes, *Sourcebook*, 217–18.

a diminishment of the more synoptic or integrative impulse to be found in a Balzac or a George Eliot or in modernists such as Joyce or T. S. Eliot, even if in the latter cases the drive to totality can be maintained only by self-consciously artificial arrangements of a debris of fragments. Shaw seems by disposition unreceptive to the extravagance of vision and the concomitant drive to programmes of aesthetic revolution that typified both right- and left-wing modernism. Hence, for all his sallies against the tyranny of received ideas, his drama continued to remain rather comfortably within the established institutions and conventions of English theatre.

Born three decades later than Moore and Shaw, Joyce began his artistic career at the turn of the century when the French naturalist movement had already been overtaken by the French and Edwardian 'decadence' movements and when Ibsenesque theatrical naturalism had also reached its climax. As a student in Dublin, he had neither Moore's direct personal contact with the French naturalists nor Shaw's familiarity with the freethinking, left-wing and feminist circles in London. Nevertheless, the young Joyce idolized Ibsen so much that he set about learning Dano-Norwegian to read the master in the original and he later studied German in his attempts to read and translate Gerhard Hauptmann, the naturalist playwright he regarded as Ibsen's finest successor. In his essay 'The Day of the Rabblement', Joyce even styles himself Ibsen's 'third minister' whose hour of going forth into the world was now at hand.[38]

Though Joyce may have been further removed from the continental naturalists than his Irish predecessors, his actual contact with the down-at-heel lower-class urban worlds that featured so prominently in French naturalism was altogether more immediate and intimate. Moore and Shaw wrote about this lower-class world from above, in order imaginatively to enter it; Joyce wrote from within it, partly to escape it. When Ibsen displaced Zola as the exemplary naturalist writer towards the end of the nineteenth-century, naturalism had gravitated somewhat up the social ladder towards middle-class drawing rooms and away from the slums or working-class and peasant settings Zola had depicted. In Joyce's naturalism, especially in *Dubliners*, the compass would come to rest somewhere between these two social levels. His short stories, anticipating the later novels, typically concentrate on economically straitened lower-middle-class figures rather than on aristocratic or prosperous middle-class or manual working-class or lumpenproletarian types. The early works, in other words, are populated by figures genteel enough to be constrained by middle-class values but at the same time never so entirely closeted in middle-class security as to be able to remain happily unconscious of the working and underclass worlds that jostle and swirl about them. In addition, as Emer Nolan has pointed out, for Joyce, the depiction of this petite bourgeoisie is not a descent into the underworld to shed light on some strange, marginal sub-world. In Ireland, this class was actually to be the historical motor-force of political change, supplying the

---

38 James Joyce, 'The Day of the Rabblement', in Kevin Barry, ed., *James Joyce: Occasional, Critical, and Political Writing* (Oxford, 2000), 50–52, 52

leadership cadres in the War of Independence and giving its stamp to the cultural and political life of the new state.[39] The social function of the petite bourgeoisie within Irish society was quite different to that of its English counterpart and Joyce's preoccupation with this class, in *Dubliners*, *A Portrait of the Artist as a Young Man* (1916) or *Ulysses* (1922), may be seen as an attempt to diagnose the nature of the emergent nation that it would shape.

While Moore's and Shaw's major naturalist works are situated in England, Joyce's fiction is rooted from start to finish within the city limits of Dublin. Their labours in naturalism were directed at a securely institutionalized conservative English Victorian literary world located in the world's most metropolitan city. Both inclined towards European naturalism in their early careers because it allowed them to be aggressively modern in that conservative English milieu, though their modernity in retrospect looks (to borrow a phrase from Raymond Williams) not much more than a 'very local transition from a Victorian to a post-1918 world'.[40] Joyce's espousal of Ibsen, in contrast, was taken up in the much more volatile context of a city where a declining Anglo-Irish élite, an emergent Catholic strong middle class represented by the Irish Parliamentary Party, and a restless Catholic petite bourgeoisie, which would eventually find its political expression in Sinn Féin, were strenuously vying for political and cultural hegemony within the national movement. Lacking the settled weight of cultural tradition that secured the English literary world, the whole idea of what was to constitute a national culture was up for grabs in early twentieth-century Ireland in a way that it was not in London. Joyce sought in Ibsen some alternative to the literary modes cultivated by the Anglo-Irish literary élite as represented by O'Grady, Yeats, Gregory and Synge and to the more Irish Ireland literary modes associated with the Gaelic League.

In writings such as 'Drama and Life', 'Ibsen's New Drama' or 'The Day of the Rabblement', the young Joyce expounds more warmly on the ways in which Ibsen serves as an exemplary role model for the modern writer than he does on anything else. His commentaries on the actual content and technique of the dramatic works he discusses seem nearly as conventional in their praises as were the rote denunciations of Ibsen by the young middle-class university students he opposed. What Joyce admires in Ibsen are his unswerving discipline and industry ('His output of dramas has been regulated by the utmost order, by a clockwork routine, seldom found in the case of genius') and his capacity to remake an entire artistic medium — the drama — and, in so doing, to recast the intellectual life of an epoch ('It may be questioned whether any man has held so firm an empire over the thinking world in modern times. Not Rousseau; not Emerson; not Carlyle; not any of those giants of whom almost all have passed out of human ken.'). He also admires the Norwegian's knowledge of humanity and of women in particular ('Ibsen's knowledge of humanity is nowhere more obvious than in his portrayal of

39 Emer Nolan, *James Joyce and Nationalism* (London, 1995), 46
40 Williams, *Drama from Ibsen to Brecht*, 244

women') and his magisterial reticence ('Ibsen's power over two generations has been enhanced by his own reticence. Seldom, if at all, has he condescended to join battle with his enemies.').[41]

This image of a loftily aloof Ibsen wholly indifferent to his critics may be as much a stratgeic distortion as Shaw's didactic version; indeed, Joyce's fastidiously detached version of the Ibsenesque artist seems strongly refracted through Flaubert, another admired role model. But whereas Joyce and Shaw agree in seeing Ibsen as a man of genius to be defended against a puritanical public that would condemn him for immorality, the young Joyce depicts Ibsen's career in a rather floridly Christlike idiom of persecution and priestly vocation (the references to ministry and discipleship and hour of revelation) and he admires, above all, the total and unswerving commitment to his art that supposedly allowed the Norwegian to persevere in his long career to revolutionize the whole of European drama. Shaw sees in Ibsen a didactic naturalist that can help him to articulate his own campaign to reform English drama and lend it a greater intellectual seriousness, but Joyce's version of Ibsen is informed by a romantic sense of the artist as aloof and persecuted visionary and by a modernist emphasis on the need to create a whole new dispensation in art. Shaw, in other words, is appropriating Ibsen to wage war on the stultification of an existing English theatre; Joyce admires him as someone who overcame the obstacles of the local to create something entirely novel in art and hence trans-European in its significance. Ibsen may be what we would nowadays call a naturalist, but Joyce's mode of critical appreciation is incipiently modernist from the outset, since it stresses a shattering of the existing forms of art to create something entirely new. That romantic-modernist version seems to owe much to its Irish and Revivalist contexts (where there was also an insistence on the need to create a whole new art), but Ibsen is also being appropriated to help Joyce contest the kinds of art cultivated within that same milieu.

Yeats and (more complicatedly) Synge turned away from a prosaic modern realism or naturalism to the world of heroic saga or peasant primitivism that might supply some sense of the coherent community, linguistic vivacity and pagan vitality that had supposedly been leached from the modern world. The Joycean diagnosis of the modern world is ultimately not entirely different to the Anglo-Irish Revivalists; for him, too, a life-crippling, middle-class religion, a hypocritical morality, and the mechanical routine of alienated labour are the defining conditions of modern existence. The essential difference is that Joyce finds in the heroic, primitivist or exotic literary modes none of the resuscitating powers the Revivalists do; for him, these forms, or even Wilde's dandy aestheticism, are themselves simply the gaudy verso of the dull Victorian sensibility they affect to repudiate. Thus while Yeats or Synge (or in a different way Wilde) will turn away from the wretched soulless prose of modern life in search of some more vital alternative, Joyce, in true naturalist spirit, will insist in Dubliners that the fundamental

41 James Joyce, 'Ibsen's New Drama', in Barry, James Joyce, 30–49, 30, 45

fact of the modern condition is its colourless prosaicness — this, for him, is the Medusa face of the modern that must steadfastly be contemplated. Synge will invent a colourful, virtuoso Hiberno-Elizabethan idiolect to express a sense of vagrant energy that rebukes contemporary degeneration. Yeats will be fascinated by almost any kind of violence and exoticism (fairy, Fenian, pagan, occult, Fascist, apocalyptic) that promises respite from a drab, soulless modernity. But in *Dubliners* all of Joyce's formidable energy is deployed to create the sense of a world 'winnowed of vigour' (to use his own phrase), defined by an unremitting dreariness, decrepitude and stasis.[42]

Like a muffled drumbeat, the word 'grey' is repeatedly semaphored across a whole succession of stories in *Dubliners*. There is 'the heavy grey face of the paralytic' priest in the opening 'The Sisters'; the 'grey light' of dawn that confronts Jimmy Doyle when he has lost his money at cards in 'After the Race'; 'the warm grey evening air of August' that descends upon the city in 'Two Gallants'; the pandered Polly's 'grey' eyes in 'The Boarding House'; the 'grey, gleaming river, winding along towards Dublin' contemplated by Mr. Duffy in 'A Painful Case'; the 'grey-haired' and acne-skinned young Mr. O'Connor in 'Ivy Day in the Committee Room'; 'the grey impalpable world' of the dead into which Gabriel Conroy feels his soul swoon at the end of 'The Dead'.[43] Colourlessness and the want of colour, inertia and the want of purpose, disillusion and the want of spirit: these are the fundamentals that Joyce's stories individually and cumulatively stress.

If naturalist narrative, to recall Baguley, tends to divide between Goncourtian-type plots in which the characters incline steadily downhill and Flaubertian-type plots in which life goes steadily nowhere, then *Dubliners* patently gravitates towards the second, more static model. That sense of paralysis or stasis or arrested time that Joyce famously ascribes to Dublin in this collection is, in other words, an inevitable consequence of pushing a Flaubertian-inflected naturalism to its logical extreme. Repeatedly in *Dubliners* the stories oscillate in Bovaryesque manner between the unrelieved oppressiveness of the provincial everyday and some sort of 'romantic' fantasy of transcendence or escape — the sacred or secular transcendences of religion or of art; the exoticisms of the Orient, Argentina, the Wild West or the Irish West; the cultural cosmopolitanism of London or Paris; the inebriated sociability of the Irish public house. As in *Madame Bovary*, the idioms of realism and romanticism leach through one another to produce a sense of inexorable stalemate: when the characters — Eveline, in the story of that name, is an exemplary instance — succumb to 'the real' they doom themselves to provincial paralysis and monotony; when they take flight into romantic consciousness, like the infatuated young narrator who sets off after the wonders of the bazaar in 'Araby', they may merely be snaring themselves in vain, deluded fantasy. Hopes of transcendence or escape invariably disclose themselves in *Dubliners* to be only desperate chimeras to assuage the monotonous awfulness of the actual. In so far as there is any significant

42 James Joyce, 'Two Gallants', *Dubliners* (Harmondsworth, 1976), 50
43 Joyce, *Dubliners*, 11, 48, 49, 62, 117, 118, 223

event in these eventless tales, it is always located in that subjective instant when the deluded fantasy that had allowed someone imaginatively to evade and so to sustain the quotidian grimness of the everyday is shredded. Everything turns on that climactic, or more accurately, anti-climactic moment when the protective-smothering veil of self-delusion is ripped and the disabused character suddenly comes face to face with the warty, unvarnished 'real'. Any number of such moments can be cited. They include the doggedly chirpy Marie in 'Clay' putting her hand in the 'soft, wet' saucer of earth that intimates her imminent death; a still hung-over Jimmy Doyle dimly realizing he has been had in 'After the Race'; the ageing, put-upon Farrington in 'Counterparts' losing the arm wrestling contest to the English youth and taking out his loser's spleen on his own son; Little Chandler discovering 'he was a prisoner for life' in 'A Little Cloud' and shouting in fury at his child when he does so; Mr. Doran grasping that he has been carefully set up by mother and daughter in 'The Boarding House'; the puncturing of Gabriel's satisfied conception of himself and of his marriage in the chill, grey dawn of the hotel room in 'The Dead'.

However, it is not the grey, dilapidated landscapes or interiors, the unusually constricted agency of the characters, or even the recurrent plots of disenchantment that will warrant a conception of *Dubliners* as a naturalist masterpiece. These are all standard features of the naturalist mode certainly. But several other standard elements of the mode are conspicuously absent. We will find in *Dubliners* none of the panicky sense of post-Darwinian crisis that is so stark a feature of early American naturalism (especially in Sherwood Anderson, Frank Norris or Jack London), little of the obsession with the issues of hereditary degeneration common to French, Scandinavian and American naturalism, and nothing of the anthropological voyaging into the underworlds of destitutes, criminals and freaks common to the more lurid versions of the mode. Neither the muck-raking nor the politically charged investigative features of naturalism, in other words, have any appeal for Joyce — they do not serve his aesthetic of 'scrupulous meanness', which requires an understated stylistic economy.

Hence, those who would contend that *Dubliners* is a masterpiece of realism will object, and not without reason, that the term 'naturalism' is totally misapplied here. Nevertheless, there is strong reason to maintain the term, since these stories are always configured so that the narrator and the reader are invited into a compact that implicitly imputes to them a level of shared understanding superior to that of the characters whose fates they contemplate. The characters in *Dubliners* — whether in the early stories organized around bewildered child protagonists or in the later ones in which the protagonists are largely gulled or self-gulled, uncomprehending adults — never achieve a level of consciousness capable of illuminating the murky worlds in which they are confined. Their understanding of their situation is never equal to the understanding of the narrator or reader, who can penetrate more fully into the opaque mystery of things. The grey, crepuscular world of *Dubliners* is more than simply atmospheric; that greyness is the correlative of large forces only dimly understood, a function of the conceptual murk or incomprehension that confounds the actual characters, and that the stories attempt to penetrate.

Perhaps the most obvious example of the way in which narrative irony is managed in *Dubliners* to signify the gap that separates the inferior consciousness of the characters and the superior compact of narrator and reader is 'Ivy Day in the Committee Room'. That story famously comes to conclusion with Joe Hynes's recitation of 'The Death of Parnell', the performance of which wins Hynes a round of applause from his comrades. The story ends, flatly, with the line: 'Mr. Crofton said that it was a very fine piece of writing'.[44] The whole sense of the ending here depends on the reader knowing that Hynes's recitation is a sorry piece of doggerel and appreciating that nothing so fully confirms the sorry state of post-Parnellite Irish nationalist politics as the inability of any of the nationalist characters to call a spade a spade and dismiss the piece for what it is. There may perhaps be a few in the company who do realize that the elegy is indeed tosh (there is, after all, an awkward moment of suspended silence when the piece concludes), but they are too cowed or deferential to the maudlin spirit of collective bonhomie to say so. The conservative-unionist Crofton, who utters the praise, may be only being agreeably polite or even slyly condescending. But whatever his real thoughts, he chooses not to breach the communal camaraderie established by the eventual arrival of the overdue drinks; it was the delay in serving these that had triggered the acrimony Hynes's song smoothes over. The only actual dissenters to the verdict offered on Hynes's elegy, then, are the narrator and the reader; it is their greater understanding that sets them outside the cosy but crippling consensus of the 'gratefully oppressed' that subtends what passes for community and conviviality in Dublin.

In 'A Painful Case', the story that immediately precedes 'Ivy Day in the Committee Room' in the volume, this sense of the superior and isolated individual standing in elevated judgement over the inferior collective might appear to be more severely tested. In this story, the would-be Nietzschean Mr. Duffy explains to the woman with whom he establishes a brief but failed affair that he had been compelled to abandon his earlier socialism, since:

The workmen's discussions ... were too timorous; the interest they took in the question of wages was inordinate. He felt that they were hard-featured realists and that they resented an exactitude which was the product of a leisure not within their reach. No social revolution, he told her, would be likely to strike Dublin for some centuries.[45]

The narrative irony of the piece undercuts Duffy's sense of his own class and intellectual superiority to the working men with whom he once used to associate, and betrays the

44 Joyce, 'Ivy Day in the Committee Room', *Dubliners*, 135
45 Joyce, 'A Painful Case', *Dubliners*, 111

pseudo-*Übermensch* self-regard that makes him such an unattractive misanthropic prig. As such, his sententious assessment of the low level of revolutionary consciousness of the Dublin lower classes sits uncomfortably alongside the subsequent 'Ivy Day' story, since the latter actually seems to invite a verdict scarcely less damning than Duffy's. The side-by-side placement of the two tales in the volume might appear to function as a critical warning to the reader about the dangers of adopting a Duffy-like posture of pseudo-intellectual condescension towards the collective mentality of the lower orders.

The apparent tension between the two stories — the first of which ironizes a middle-class ex-revolutionary's dismissal of working-class radicalism; the second of which seems to confirm the assumption that the typical level of political consciousness in Dublin is indeed abysmal — dissolves itself if we take the target of Joyce's irony in the second story to be, not the working classes, but the conservative middle-class Parnellite nationalists who gather in the committee room. But this reading, however attractive, does not fully convince either, because if we take the volume as a whole as our measure, it is clear that a lack of any real intellectual understanding of their situation is something that unites all characters in *Dubliners*, whatever their station, gender or class. The young boy who puzzles over the unfinished sentences of the adults discussing the dead priest in 'Clay', the inebriated Jimmy Doyle who knows he is cheated but is too stupefied to know how he has been taken in or by how much, and many other self-deluding characters, such as Mr. Duffy or Maria or Gabriel Conroy or Lily — all fail to make sense of their situations. To live in a 'grey' fog of confusion is their common lot.

Whether the central protagonists in the stories invite our sympathy or our contempt, the structure of the relationship remains essentially the same: the narrator/reader always retains a sense of intellectual superiority to the characters whose limited grasp of their own situation the narrator challenges the reader to make good. Within this structure, the characters are destined always to remain intellectually compromised captives to their condition (without understanding they cannot act effectively), and the reader is destined always to adopt the stance of a superior but detached observer. The detachment persists however much even the more sympathetic characters may move us because the deficient understanding of the characters precludes any real sense of reciprocity — we do not engage with them as intellectual equals, but essentially as inferiors. The reader may be kept on his critical toes and be put through his mental paces by the narrator's finely filamented ironies. He may even feel that he too lives an existence nearly as humdrum or alienated as the characters do. But by supplying the critical acumen the characters lack, he enters, nonetheless, into a higher intellectual or analytical fellowship with the narrator.

In *Dubliners*, the characters repeatedly resort to the sentimental fellowship of religion or the public house to sublimate their individual miseries and dissolve social tensions; the reader is expected to recognize these collective acts as compensatory gestures. But if this leaves the reader stranded on the lonely perimeter of the convivial circles of the collective from which he has been exiled by his higher critical intelligence ('an outcast from life's feast', as Mr. Duffy puts it), he is compensated at least by the intellectual compact with the ironic narrator.[46] The structure of feeling that animates the volume may well be critically acute and socially reformist; it is also fundamentally paternalist. The reader is challenged to reach some rigorous appreciation of the Dubliners' predicament, but the Dubliners, individually or collectively, have nothing positive to teach the reader, since they themselves seem never to be able to learn anything from, and only to be subdued by, their own experience of life.

In *Dubliners*, action and understanding seem destined to remain forever severed. The fictional characters act, but always in ways that are either extremely constrained or that only compound their capitulation to the tyranny of their circumstances. The narrator and the reader, on the other hand, understand more deeply than the characters do, but their function is to evaluate the sorry general human condition from their more elevated vantage; they are not constrained to enter into a complex terrain of choices and consequences. The superior intellect reserved for the narrator, and which the attentive reader can also acquire by exercising due diligence, is never ascribed to any of the limited characters in the stories themselves.[47]

This antinomy returns in Joyce's later fiction in different configurations. In *A Portrait of the Artist as a Young Man* the detached 'objectivism' of *Dubliners* is exchanged for the detached 'subjectivism' of Stephen Dedalus, the artist-hero who flees into a permanent exile, yet attempts to rescue through his high art the very people whom he has escaped. In *Ulysses*, both poles of the antinomy are personalized. On the one side, we have Bloom, *l'homme moyen sensuel*, grounded, as one critic puts it, 'to a comically extravagant degree in the world of the body'; on the other, Stephen Dedalus, the 'theorist-intellectual who longs for a world disembarrassed of the physical and the sexual, where the self can achieve a purity of origin that radically distinguishes it from the common or dominant forms of sociality'.[48] The Bloom–Stephen dichotomy certainly seems to exemplify Lukács's conception of naturalism as an aesthetic striving for a spuriously conceived objectivity and modernism as one that surrenders to extremes of subjectivity; the latter both outgrowth and verso of the former. Yet far from being vulnerable to Lukács's critique, *Ulysses* seems all too cognizant of the sense of lost totality that he diagnoses as the defining condition of modern fiction. Joyce's novel, that is to say, knows quite well that the antinomy between subjective and objective worlds cannot be healed — it self-consciously resorts to the artifice of myth and the play of styles to integrate what will not otherwise cohere.

46 Joyce, 'A Painful Case', 117
47 For different readings of the function of naturalism in *Dubliners*, see Emer Nolan, *James Joyce and Nationalism*, 28–36, and Luke Gibbons, '"Have you no homes to go to?": James Joyce and the Politics of Paralysis', in Derek Attridge and Marjorie Howes, eds., *Semicolonial Joyce* (Cambridge, 2000), 150–71.
48 Seamus Deane, 'Dead Ends: Joyce's Finest Moments', in Attridge and Howes, *Semicolonial Joyce*, 21–36, 33

What, then, can be concluded of Irish naturalism in its formative stages? It was, first of all, patently an aesthetic cultivated by writers sceptical of the more archaizing, exoticizing and heroicizing thrust of the Irish Revival, and in Joyce's hands it produced at least one international masterpiece that would also become an enduring touchstone of twentieth-century Irish literature. It was also, broadly speaking, an aesthetic of the left. It was left-wing parties like the Irish Socialist Republican Party and left-wing or populist nationalist activists (such as Fred Ryan, Andrew Patrick Wilson, Terence MacSwiney, Daniel Corkery or St. John Ervine) that were most interested in exploiting the possibilities of naturalism, while it was the aristocratic-minded Yeats that favoured more poetic dramatic modes.[49] Nevertheless, while Moore, Shaw and Joyce all shared a largely sceptical view of the Revival, they were united only by that negative dissent and they themselves had no positive common cause or alternative. The Revivalists had a programme, one that would eventually issue in institutions such as the Gaelic League, the Abbey Theatre, the Cuala Press, An Taibhdhearc, and the Irish Academy of Letters. The work of Joyce, Moore, Shaw (or of more minor figures such as Corkery or St. John Ervine) was conscripted into no such common agenda at the time — though by the 1930s cultural critics, such as Corkery and Sean O'Faolain, were still trying to fashion different rationales for an Irish realism that would represent a viable alternative to Revivalist aesthetics, and to some extent that project continues to this day.[50]

Still, the works of Moore and Joyce established moulds or templates for a great deal of twentieth-century Irish fiction, though it is arguable that those templates would ultimately prove as constrictive as they were initially enabling. In the French or United States national traditions that emerged in roughly the same formative period, naturalism would acquire epic ambition, as in Zola's massive Rougon-Macquart cycle, Theodore Dreiser's *Trilogy of Desire* or Frank Norris's projected trilogy *The Epic of the Wheat*. The Irish tradition, by contrast, found its decisive opening achievement in the mini-world of the short story, and in some sense Irish naturalism has always been most impressive when it remains in that nether region between the short story and the quasi-autobiographical first novel. The form does not seem to be capable of sustaining some more capacious ambition. If Joyce was the most talented of the early Irish naturalists, he would forsake the mode in his artistic maturity, developing instead complex modernist 'epics' in *Ulysses* and *Finnegans Wake* that would relegate the whole naturalist tradition to the shade.

That said, the suggestion that there is some absolute new departure between the naturalist Joyce of *Dubliners* and the modernist Joyce of *Ulysses* may be overstated. Many

49 For a more extended account of these other writers, see Ben Levitas, 'Plumbing the Depths: Irish Realism and the Working Class from Shaw to O'Casey', *Irish University Review*, 33, 1 (2003), 133–49.
50 Attempts to develop some sort of coherent social agenda for Irish realism would include Daniel Corkery, *Synge and Anglo-Irish Literature* (Cork, 1931); Sean O'Faolain's many essays in *The Bell* and elsewhere (discussed later in this essay); the Raven Arts Press project that supported the 'Northside realism' associated with Dermot Bolger and Roddy Doyle. Critical works championing the 'lost' moment of Irish realism in the Revival include John Wilson Foster, *Fictions of the Irish Literary Revival: A Changling Art* (Syracuse, 1987) and, more ambivalently, Richard Kearney, *Transitions: Narratives in Modern Irish Culture* (Manchester, 1988).

of the cardinal features of naturalism shape the texture of *Ulysses* and conditioned its vituperative early reception. These features include the forensically descriptive interest in the mundane and banal routines of modern life; the candid treatment of sexual and lower bodily functions; the sense of provincial immiseration and stasis; the interest in 'unorthodox' female sexuality; even Joyce's boasts about the meticulousness of his research and the scrupulous fidelity of his descriptions of Dublin's streetscapes. To this extent at least, there is as much continuity as rupture with the naturalist mode of *Dubliners*.

The decisive difference is that in *Ulysses* the sense of torpor that is sustained only in the compressed temporality of the short story in *Dubliners* is now sustained over the very lengthy temporality of the epic novel. Maintaining a sense of stasis and entropy in a short story is one thing; maintaining it over the marathon distance of a long novel can be managed only by reducing everything that happens to a scrupulously detailed unfolding of a single day. This eventlessness of *Ulysses* — the absence of socially transformative event, or dramatic plot twists, or the acquisition of a fundamentally new wisdom conventional to novel or epic plot — rendered the novel unutterably tedious to many of its initial readers, who were of course still untrained in modernist art. But Joyce was no Beckett and where history will not yield any grand novelty or revolutionary event and where the passage of time does not enrich understanding, a virtuoso style steps in at least to fill the vacuum. In *Ulysses*, therefore, the bleached 'scrupulous meanness' of *Dubliners* is abandoned for a much more opulent aesthetic carnival in which historical momentum asserts itself at least in the negative form of a succession of collapsing styles.

As such, though he may have started his career as an anti-Revivalist naturalist, Joyce seems implicitly to have conceded considerable ground to the Revivalists, who had long since complained that the dour, colourless limits of naturalism would prove drastically constricting for any artist of ambition. Thus, *Ulysses* is really a curious Irish confection in which naturalism and Revivalism copulate to create a work that surpasses anything that either one or other managed to produce separately. The merger of Revivalism and naturalism is not exactly a repudiation of naturalism as such, since *Ulysses* still offers a fundamentally disenchanted (even if comic) vision of the modern city — one in which the city is redeemed or transformed not by the collective action of its citizens (the story is famously set well before the Irish 'revolution', though the novel was written during it), but by the extraordinary aesthetic virtuosity of the artist-creator. The denizens of Dublin that populate the novel remain as incarcerated as ever in their paralysis. But in *Ulysses*, if not in *Dubliners* or *Portrait*, their immobile world at least is redeemed for an extravagantly sinuous art.

4

Irish naturalism's 'second' phase extended from the 1920s to the 1950s. Its decisive early expression was Sean O'Casey's Abbey trilogy (1923–26); the fiction of Liam O'Flaherty, Frank O'Connor and Sean O'Faolain consolidated the mode; its culminating achievement was Patrick Kavanagh's *The Great Hunger* (1942). A number of key factors distinguish this second stage from the earlier one. First, the naturalist writers in this phase, unlike those in the first, made the big events of Irish politics their immediate subject. Unlike Joyce's or Moore's works, which described a world either void of politics or where politics was merely a sorry sham, O'Casey's deals directly with the traumatic upheavals of Easter 1916, the War of Independence, and the Civil War. Like O'Casey, O'Flaherty, O'Connor and O'Faolain had all been active in the national struggle, and all tried to make some retrospective reckoning with that experience in their fiction. Second, the works in this second phase were written mainly by writers working largely within rather than outside Ireland, and the mode attained, especially under O'Faolain's critical tutelage, a more programmatically or self-consciously anti-Revivalist edge.

Finally, when Moore, Shaw or Joyce had developed their versions of naturalism, the Irish Revival and naturalism were each more protean phenomena than either the one or the other would be by the 1930s. The Revival in that earlier stage was still an activist, institution-building, reasonably broad-based counter-hegemonic cultural movement affiliated to an insurgent Irish nationalism.[51] But by the mid-1920s, the post-partition state system was already *in situ* and key Revivalist organizations (such as the Gaelic League or the Abbey Theatre) were already being assimilated into the institutional cortex of the new Free State. In the late nineteenth-century, naturalism was still a controversial literary mode, but by the 1930s the various continental avant-garde movements were stirring new debates about the role of cultural institutions such as museums, galleries and theatres in mediating the relationship of art to its public. From this vantage point, naturalism could seem only a late nineteenth-century surface radicalization of the content of the novel or drama — not a mode that addressed the more radical issues the avant-gardes wished to press. The contest between Revivalist and naturalist aesthetics in this second stage became more acute, then, at a time when both had acquired more definite shape and consistency, but when neither was as close to the cutting edge of literary experiment as had earlier been the case.

Any assessment of the role of naturalism in this phase must take account of both national and international cultural developments. Domestically, the key element is a sense of post-revolutionary, post-Civil War bitterness and disillusion that settled in over several decades as first the Cumann na nGaedheal and then the Fianna Fáil régimes failed

51 On the Revival period, see P. J. Mathews, *Revival: The Abbey Theatre, Sinn Féin, the Gaelic League and the Co-operative Movement* (Cork, 2003).

to deliver the radical social renovation of Irish society that Sinn Féin had promised.[52] As was to happen in many postcolonial societies, when the great expectations of the national struggle were not realized, there followed a period of post-revolutionary disappointment marked by a literature of satire or disenchantment. Internationally, this was a period of global capitalist crisis, some of the starker manifestations of which were the Great Depression and the rise of European Fascism. By the mid-1930s, both the Soviet and the Fascist régimes in Europe had officially denounced modernist art forms as a symptom of bourgeois decadence, and in the Soviet Union socialist realism was imposed as the official aesthetic of the new Communist order. Modernism was not yet established as the institutionally endorsed art of liberal capitalism, as it would increasingly become in the Cold War, so in some quarters it seemed a much less compromised aesthetic than realism. The 1920s and 1930s, therefore, was a volatile period when the relative political values attached to realism and modernism were still not settled in radical intellectual circles. On the one hand, the dire exigencies of the global crisis seemed to many on the left, most famously Lukács, to require a tough new critical realism capable of diagnosing the historical tendencies of the times. On the other hand, the adoption of socialist realism as the official aesthetic of Stalinism and the fact that neither Communist, Fascist nor liberal capitalist societies seemed able to assimilate modernism made it seem the more genuinely radical aesthetic.

These continental European and American debates about realism and modernism may seem greatly removed from Irish society. But without some sense of the wider international cultural configuration of the times, it is impossible to gauge what the consolidation of naturalism as the major domestic counter-Revivalist aesthetic might actually mean at this juncture. In contrast to much of Western Europe between 1930 and 1950, Ireland remained, relatively speaking at least, remarkably becalmed politically. These were essentially decades of extended state consolidation in both the North and the South. In other countries, such as Germany, France, Italy or the United States, the Depression sharpened conflicts between right and left, but in Ireland it seems only to have aggravated emigration and smothered socially transformative vision, and thus to have cooled down rather than heated up social conflict. In such a context, Irish realism and naturalism were to emerge, neither as an official state-endorsed aesthetic nor yet as an aesthetic associated with some sort of radical or internationalist revolutionary campaign for an alternative to the existing order (naturalism in the United States in the 1930s, for example, was very much associated with the Communist left). Naturalism after the Irish Civil War may have proved one of the most vigorous strands of domestic literary social critique, but it is also a mode of writing inflected with a strong sense of post-revolutionary disenchantment and commitment to 'realism', with all of that word's connotations of shedding extravagant delusions and adjusting sights to what

---

52 On this aspect of the Counter-Revival, see Terence Brown's fine essay 'The Counter-Revival: Provincialism and Censorship', in Seamus Deane, ed., The Field Day Anthology of Irish Writing, vol. 3 (Derry, 1991), 89–93.

was feasible. The peculiarity of Irish naturalism in this second stage, then, was that it was to become a literature of domestic dissent and social critique, but these were elaborated essentially in terms of a desire for normalization, not radical transformation. For Sean O'Faolain, who did much to articulate the critical vocabulary for a new counter-Revivalist literature, Ireland had had a surfeit of 'romantic' revolutionary dreaming. That revolutionary moment now over, it was high time for Irish society to wake from its fantasies and face its impoverished reality. This was the new grammar of literary enterprise and cultural critique.

On its surface, Sean O'Casey's Dublin trilogy might seem distant indeed from literary naturalism. Its colourful verbal razzle-dazzle and bursts of comic high spirits are much closer to Synge and Revivalist romanticism than to the listless, grey, achromic world of Joyce's *Dubliners*; its heterogeneous mix of popular dramatic genres very different to the restrained decorum of Ibsen's or Chekhov's well-made plays. Nevertheless, O'Casey's trilogy is fundamentally naturalistic in ways that are conceptual and not merely to do with its slum settings or bleak endings. In the trilogy, as in the naturalistic drama generally, the stage area where the plot unfolds is always a closed domestic interior. This organization of space dictates that historical action always takes place offstage and appears therefore as something remote and alien from 'the street', which eventually breaches the stage enclosure to shatter the vulnerable domestic world it contains. For all their tempests of colourful talk, O'Casey's slum-dwellers are essentially spectators to, and not makers of, historical action. The Dublin they inhabit is much more historically eventful than Joyce's, but since O'Casey's characters are victims rather than agents of change, their world is actually just as historically paralysed and immobile as Joyce's. History tests and usually worsts O'Casey's characters, but it is not conceived, as in Brechtian theatre, as something the people themselves actively create.

O'Casey's admirers typically counter such critiques by arguing that this is the whole point of the trilogy. If O'Casey's slum-dwellers are essentially acted upon by history, this accurately reflects the fact that the Irish nationalist 'revolution' was a bourgeois and essentially superstructural affair, the violence of which brought added hardship to the Dublin poor without improving their fundamental situation. O'Casey is still popularly viewed as a working-class socialist critic of Irish nationalism, but this is hard to reconcile with the socialist figures in the trilogy being as prone to bombast and fantasy as their nationalist counterparts. Socialism is indeed used to critique and embarrass nationalism. But since the socialists themselves replicate the nationalists' defects, socialism is ascribed no value that exceeds this limited end and its deployment is fundamentally opportunistic. O'Casey's overt targets are Pearse's militant nationalism and Connolly's republican socialism, both convicted and found wanting in the court of an affective humanism that will not itself — as even the trilogy itself seems tacitly to acknowledge in places — withstand much critical scrutiny either.[53]

53 The most decisive critique of O'Casey along these lines remains Seamus Deane's 'O'Casey and Yeats:

In an astute reading that contests the idea that the trilogy espouses the liberal humanism that O'Casey's admirers or detractors typically ascribe it, Ronan McDonald comments that the debunking of Irish nationalism and socialist republicanism in these plays acts as a decoy that allows O'Casey to suppress a despairing conviction that the world is governed by nihilistic forces ultimately not susceptible (despite the playwright's own Communist commitments) to any kind of rational human control. In other words, when the trilogy suggests that the tragic follies of recent Irish history are essentially the product of the nationalist or republican socialist ideologies they lampoon, it clings at least to the idea that these tragedies were man-made and avoidable and thus might yet be corrected were some saner, more 'realistic' politics to emerge. McDonald contends, however, that this overt critique of the Irish revolution conceals a more fundamental, but subterranean and semi-disavowed, nihilism that holds that human suffering has its ultimate roots not simply in bad politics but in an inherently perverse universe where human desire will always be thwarted. In this reading, the Dublin trilogy is not informed by the conventional humanism it seems to espouse as an alternative to the debased cant of politics (a rather sentimental humanism that indicts the political 'stupidity o' men' as the cause of all our woes), but rather by a bleakly disintegrative vision in which the 'whole worl's in a terrible state of chassis' — an essentially Schopenhauerian worldview on which the consolations of humanism too are withered.[54]

McDonald's reading of the trilogy makes for a more interestingly self-contradictory O'Casey than either his enthusiasts or critics have allowed. But it also returns us to the antinomy between a commitment to social reform and an aesthetics of disenchantment inherent to the naturalist mode. Forged in a post-Darwinian era when the belief in a divinely and benignly ordered and essentially progressive universe was beginning to be replaced by a belief in one that was either simply chaotic (without any principle of order) or subject to remorselessly mechanical laws of adaptivity ultimately indifferent to human value (rigidly determinist or survivalist), the naturalist movement had always been torn between, on the one hand, its commitment in the name of social reform to disenchant or demythologize the complacent 'romantic' pieties of the bourgeoisie — their confidence in progress, their complacent morality, their sentimental desire for happy endings — and, on the other hand, a countervailing sense that in a post-Darwinian world the drive to reform itself lacked any strong philosophical basis or grounding.

O'Casey's trilogy offers a classic example of this naturalist antinomy. Were it to make that antinomy its overt subject matter, the trilogy would be a much more ambitious work than it is. But even if founded on this antinomy, O'Casey's trilogy has no intention whatever of seriously addressing the issues involved. The dramatic tension between the drive to political critique and the nihilism that McDonald discovers indeed charges the

Exemplary Dramatists', in *Celtic Revivals: Essays in Modern Irish Literature 1880–1980* (London, 1985), 108–22.

54 Ronan McDonald, *Tragedy and Irish Literature: Synge, O'Casey and Beckett* (Houndmills, 2002), 85–126

cycle, but it finds expression only in the interstices of O'Casey's plots; that tension is not intellectually worked through. There are no characters from one end of the cycle to the other who are allowed the mental capacity to wrestle with such issues. None is ever shown to be capable of making a strong, articulate case either for a Schopenhauerian view of things or for the positive value of revolution or reform. Instead, the onstage tenement-dwellers are left to their fine blather and sorry circumstances and to their uncomprehended tragedy, while the middle-class audience or intellectuals are left to take up the more philosophical issues if they choose. But this dramatic structure only reconfirms the fundamental divide between the passive wretchedness of the poor (whose sufferings are put on display, but who cannot articulate any sense of coherent alternative to the way things are) and the passive contemplation of the middle class (a drama where political intervention seems conducive only to cant and folly will hardly encourage anyone to act) that any more energetically socialist drama would want to disturb.

The influence of the Dublin trilogy on the works of other disillusioned republican writers in the 1920s and 1930s is palpable, though the nature of that influence differs from one to another and none was to produce an artistic vision of the epoch of national insurgency as fully realised or enduringly influential as O'Casey's. Liam O'Flaherty's *The Informer* (1925) owes much to *Shadow of a Gunman*, but eschews the comedy of O'Casey for a more conventionally grim naturalism in which a hapless, instinct-driven protagonist, Gypo Nolan, is harried to death by the puritanical left-republican movement, 'the Organisation', that he has betrayed. The novel is strong on oppressive atmosphere and a sense of dumb victimhood. Nolan is an almost animal-like creature trapped in an action beyond his very limited comprehension: hence the work's diagnostic ambitions on any socio-historical level are nugatory. O'Flaherty's version of naturalism owes more to the American than the French tradition and, like Jack London's, is shot through with a contradictory mix of socialistic critique of the existing bourgeois capitalist order and proto-Fascistic feeling for an elemental world of primitive force altogether anterior to civilization. There is a strong element of hard primitivism in O'Flaherty's work, in which all the usual forms and conventions of society are deemed suspect and what is valued most are the raw elemental energies that sustain creaturely survival in an indifferent universe. Maybe this is why his spare short stories about animals and birds are nowadays often taken to be his finest literary achievements, whereas the early novels such as *The Informer*, *Mr Gilhooley* (1926), *The Assassin* (1928) or *The Puritan* (1931) seem of historical interest only.

Sean O'Faolain described O'Flaherty as an 'inverted romantic', but the epithet could be applied to the entire field of counter-Revivalist realism in this period, including not only that of O'Flaherty but also of O'Faolain himself and of Frank O'Connor. In the famous title story of his first short-story collection *Guests of the Nation* (1931), O'Connor produced an enduring touchstone of post-revolutionary Irish literature. Set during the War of Independence, but narrated from the chilled vantage of disillusioned retrospect, the story tells how two young Irish volunteers befriend two English hostages, Hawkins and

Belcher, whom they are later compelled to execute in retaliation for the British army's shooting of IRA prisoners. The intimacy that develops between captors and captives and the wrenching of that human bond when events dictate that the Englishmen must be executed are superbly rendered. The story's conceptual indebtedness to O'Casey is manifest in the way in which Hawkins's Communism is used to embarrass Noble's rather sentimental Irish Catholic nationalism; then these delicately caricatured antagonists are both undercut in their turn by the politically noncommittal, virtually wordless stoicism of the bigger of the two Englishman, Belcher. In other words, O'Connor plays off English Communism against Irish nationalism just enough to discomfit the latter, but also plays Hawkins's rote credo of working-class solidarity against Belcher's resigned and agnostic humanism in a way that shows the latter as the less self-deluding sensibility. In this way, and in a manner that recalls O'Casey's work, Belcher's stoic humanism is allowed to trump all systemic political creeds.

An O'Caseyite note is also evident in the way that the story closes with a long-shot fade-out in which the action is seen by the traumatized narrator as though from a vast, alienating distance:

> with me it was the other way, as though the patch of bog where the two Englishmen were was a million miles away from me, and even Noble mumbling just behind me and the old woman and the birds and the bloody stars were all far away, and I was somehow very small and very lonely. And anything that ever happened me after I never felt the same about again.[55]

Here, as in Captain Boyle's speech about the stars at the close of *Juno and the Paycock*, the work's ostensible humanism wobbles before a philosophically starker sense of an alien universe so vast and mechanically indifferent as to mock all human endeavour. The word 'chums' (not counting variants such as 'pals' or 'good lads' or 'decent chaps') is repeated twenty-two times across this succinct tale. That tattoo pleads the preciousness of the small quotidian bonds that connect man to man, though in the end that preciousness can be registered only by demonstrating its pathetic fragility and even inadequacy, rather than through some more affirmative action. The rosary of 'chums' and 'pals' suggests that human compassion and commitment to a political cause cannot be reconciled. The notion that genuine human compassion might actually dictate rigid commitment to a political ideal or cause is never allowed to check the sense that the two must always be at odds. Its sense of flummoxed disillusion and numbed helplessness before the vast anonymity of historical and natural forces (the IRA volunteers and their British army captives are both merely cogs in larger military-bureaucratic machines that are mirror images of each other; the universe itself a non-human immensity that reduces action to insignificance) makes 'Guests of the Nation' one of the more accomplished works of

---

55 Frank O'Connor, 'Guests of the Nation', *Selected Stories* (Dublin, 1946), 19

naturalism in this historical phase. Like O'Casey's trilogy, the story would acquire an unexpected second life many decades later by becoming a template for late twentieth-century fiction on the northern conflict.

It is as a cultural critic rather than as a literary writer that Sean O'Faolain is most crucial to any survey of naturalism. By his own account and that of a wider critical consensus, O'Faolain is now chiefly remembered as a frustrated novelist whose best work was (like that of so many of the counter-Revival realists of this period) accomplished in the short-story form. There is no reason to dispute this critical commonplace, but the stress on 'failed novelist' typically obscures the degree to which O'Faolain, as cultural critic, managed to establish a very durable way of conceptualizing the development of modern Irish literature, the operative grammar of which is itself typically naturalist.

A conflict between romance and realism — also constitutive to the naturalist texts already examined here — conceptually organizes O'Faolain's literary criticism on Ireland across the span of his career. As he construes it, modern Gaelic literature, until its collapse under the pressures of colonialism, and the literature of the Anglo-Irish Literary Revival were both fundamentally aristocratic literatures, and hence heroic and romantic in their basic sentiments. The nineteenth-century Young Irelanders had, to their credit, encouraged Irish writers to turn to national materials, since without this 'prolonged voyage of discovery ... into the common reality of Irish life' Irish writers would have remained merely provincial colonial imitators of English literary models. But the Young Irelanders' great defect was to make art subservient to political propaganda, thus producing a literature 'as high-minded and high-hearted as the songs and essays of early Garibaldians' but too crudely local and polemical to generate a realist novel in the manner of a Balzac or a Stendhal.[56] Their most enduring contribution, therefore, was to prepare the ground for Yeats and the Irish Revival, which had finally produced a great literature, though one marked by the 'absence of a deep-cutting critical objectivity'.[57]

For O'Faolain, Yeats's aesthetic and that of Synge and the Revival generally was romantic:

> In the most creative fifty-years of Anglo-Irish literature then (from about 1890 to about 1940) the Irish writers saw life, in the main, romantically. It was as a poetic people that they first introduced themselves to the world, and it is as a poetic people that we are still mainly known abroad.[58]

After the establishment of the Free State, the Revival began — he argues — quite quickly to wane, the peasant folk-world that had charged the romantic imagination

---

56 For the full account, see the chapter 'The Writers' in Sean O'Faolain, *The Irish* (Harmondsworth, 1969 [1947]), 122–44, 129.

57 Sean O'Faolain, 'Fifty Years of Irish Writing', in David Pierce, ed., *Irish Writing in the Twentieth Century: A Reader* (Cork, 2003), 740–47, 740. The essay was first published in *Studies* in 1962.

58 *The Irish*, 142–43

disappearing and romance degenerating thereafter into the sentimental state kitsch of the tourist industry. By the early 1920s, therefore, the realism of O'Casey and, above all, Joyce emerges to challenge the romance of Synge and Yeats. For O'Faolain, Joyce was the exemplary realist and the tutelary figure for all later twentieth-century Irish writing, which finds its whole *raison d'être* in the need 'to explore Irish life with an objectivity never hitherto applied to it'.[59] Where Yeats's work is characterized by the heroic impulse, by imagination, by a typically romantic inclination towards the transcendent, Joyce was, in contrast, 'a realist with his feet planted on the ground, or, if one wishes to say so, in the gutter ... The vital difference between the two is one of emphasis, the poet reaching for the transcendent element, the novelist insisting on the human.'[60]

The inflections may vary from one piece to the next, but in O'Faolain's many surveys on modern Irish literature this basic agon between romance and realism remains an absolute constant, as are the predictable sets of dichotomies that it generates. Thus Ireland has moved, or is now tardily moving, from an aristocratic world to a middle-class democratic one. As it does, it passes, or must pass, from an art that is essentially poetic and idealistic to one that is essentially prosaic and de-idealizing. Hence the movement from Revival to counter-Revival, from the romance of Yeats, always searching out a loftiness of vision, to the realism of Joyce, the novelist with his feet in the gutter insisting on the grossly human. Where Yeatsian romance, like all romance, is a 'princesse lointaine', Joycean realism depends on the ruthless close-up. Yeats is not interested in capturing the actuality of things; he 'did not have an observing eye. He could evoke like a magician; he could not draw a picture.'[61] Romance, in sum, is visionary but uninterested in exact detail or clinical observation; realism, by contrast, is the art of scrupulous observation and intimate detail, its task to supply 'the deep-cutting critical objectivity' that the whole Revival period had lacked.

In the restricted economy of O'Faolain's cultural criticism, the term 'naturalism' is itself a negative one, denoting, conventionally enough, a diminished, doggedly descriptive realism. But the terminology and the essential conception of the function of art here are still inherently naturalistic. Like Lukács, his great contemporary, O'Faolain's criticism evinces a wistful hankering for the classical realist novel, but O'Faolain's whole conception of realism, of literature generally, is actually (his poor regard for Zola notwithstanding) Zolaesque. This is so because in the agon between romance and realism, realism will invariably be for O'Faolain the privileged term. In his credo, Ireland has had a surfeit of romance; it urgently needs a realist art to correct its extravagant self-delusions; in any event, realism is the only art appropriate to the contemporary post-heroic global condition. Yet though the case for realism is repeatedly urged, it is never really matched by any sense that it is actually being achieved. The majesty of Yeats's

59 O'Faolain, 'Fifty Years of Irish Writing', 744
60 *The Irish*, 139
61 *The Irish*, 138

romantic art is always allowed, the realism of Joyce is always registered as the necessary alternative, but again and again O'Faolain will conclude in dispirited vein with what he sees as the post-Revivalist generation's failure to produce the great realist art that the country requires. Even as late as the 1960s O'Faolain is still lamenting the fact that twentieth-century Ireland has produced scarcely a handful of great novels. The short story is adjudged 'probably the best product of our period', but this is clearly considered only a secondary achievement or consolation prize.[62]

O'Faolain's explanations for the relative failure of the Irish realist novel vary: Ireland remains a peasant and intellectually conservative nation hostile to cities and to art; Irish society lacks the complexity necessary for the novel to thrive; the Irish realists may have nominally championed Joyce, but it was with Yeats that they remained besotted and only Yeats had been truly assimilated; the post-Revival generation had come to read Joyce's *Ulysses* properly only very late in the day and by then 'we were already set. Too old to be influenced by him.' But whatever the reason or combination of reasons adduced, the final verdict is always the same and always negative: 'However they might think of themselves, and many thought themselves tough realists, ruthless satirists, or even (Heaven help us!) keen intellectuals, Irish writers remain *au fond* incurably local and romantic.'[63] In O'Faolain's view, a generation determined to leave behind Yeats to create a sterner new realism had yielded only 'inverted romantics' or else only a non-intellectual realism that is in effect 'a merely descriptive local naturalism'.[64]

Despite his tone of self-chastizing, rueful self-deprecating honesty, O'Faolain never stops to consider whether the real problem here might not be so much the thinness of Irish society as the narrowness of his own critical programme. His many surveys of Irish writing never pause to contemplate whether the terms 'romance' or 'realism' are at all adequate to compass the development of Irish literature over a span of two centuries. Nor do they invite us to enquire whether Yeats's work will be contained by the term 'romance' any more than the term 'realism' will accommodate Joyce's. We will look in vain in his criticism in these decades for any trace of the wider contemporary international debates about realism or modernism or about the ways in which bourgeois cultural institutions mediate art to the public. In sum, despite its continual urging of the need for an oppositional art to replace the now-exhausted Revival, O'Faolain's criticism displays a seriously limited, indeed quite conservative, conception of what might constitute a radical or oppositional art in the circumstances. Nor does O'Faolain ever really consider that 'a merely descriptive local naturalism' might actually be the logical outcome for any artistic programme that defines its oppositional vocation exclusively in terms of an obligation to debunk or disenchant 'romance'.

O'Faolain's critical surveys of twentieth-century Irish writing describe the same

62 O'Faolain, 'Fifty Years of Irish Writing', 745
63 *The Irish*, 141
64 *The Irish*, 130

arc or parabola as the fiction of his contemporaries. Essays that begin with a robust combativeness, asserting the need to move beyond romance, end on a deflated note concluding that the possibilities for any kind of sophisticated realism in Ireland is very limited. As we have seen, O'Casey's trilogy starts out in the same way to disenchant the deluded political romance of Irish nationalism or republican socialism, only eventually to modulate into a sense of disillusion so generalized as to call into question the value of politics as such. Reiterating this pattern, O'Faolain's surveys start out by urging the need to move beyond Yeatsian romance to plot a whole new course for Irish literature, but typically finish by asking despondently whether Irish society can support a genuinely realist literature at all. For both playwright and novelist-critic, what begins as a socially reformist drive to disenchant some specific political or artistic object (the romance of nationalism, the romance of the Revival) veers eventually towards a negation of the possibility of politics or of the novel altogether — though at this point in both instances the nihilistic conclusion is held in check by a rather wan humanism. (It will take Beckett to pursue this logic more sternly to its end.)

Given O'Faolain's abiding anxieties about the Irish novel, perhaps it is fitting that Irish naturalism in this second phase should find its decisive apotheosis neither in novel nor drama but in poetry. Yeats died in 1939; *The Great Hunger*, Patrick Kavanagh's definitive and only truly major work appeared three years later to signal the end of an era in Irish poetry, and to set the template for a new one. Of all of the counter-Revivalist luminaries, Kavanagh had the slightest involvement in the independence and Civil War struggles, and the least developed interest in politics. For these very reasons, perhaps, he was also the least systematically committed to any counter-Revivalist agenda, though *The Great Hunger* was written early in his career when he was still most under O'Connor's and O'Faolain's tutelage. Kavanagh's great strength would appear to have been his maverick instinct; coming from a small tillage-farmer background, he was able to position himself as the literary voice of the Irish 'peasant' — that totemic figure around whom so much Revivalist and counter-Revivalist skirmishing had always been conducted.

But is *The Great Hunger* a naturalist work? Since naturalism generally equates lyric poetry *per se* with romance and the transcendent, the very idea of a naturalist poetry might seem a contradiction in terms. Poetry is certainly the literary mode in which the tensions inherent to the naturalist aesthetic can be expected to be most acute, but it was no doubt precisely because the Revival had always been so closely associated with poetry (with the presiding genius of Yeats, with the poetic drama of Synge) that the creation of a naturalist masterpiece in verse would constitute so decisive a breakthrough. In other words, it would require a naturalist poetry to break the Revival's monopoly on poetry; but once that monopoly had been disaggregated and some new template established, naturalism could finally consolidate itself as the dominant post-Revivalist aesthetic.

The naturalist dimensions of *The Great Hunger* are evident enough. The fictional characters that populate the poem are remorselessly determined by natural and socio-economic laws. There is no sense whatever in Kavanagh's poem that socio-economic laws might work themselves out in contradictory ways, generating class and other struggles, and thus some small scope for historical manoeuvre and movement. The *Great Hunger* demands to be read as a political poem, but in the world of Paddy Maguire the peasants lack any political consciousness. Those who rush to celebrate the anti-Revivalist realism of the poem might pause to remember that, however beaten down the Irish small farmers, peasants or agricultural labourers might have been in the 1940s, these classes had never lacked a capacity for political consciousness or self-assertion. In the drumlin country that commanded Kavanagh's imagination, from the Defenders through to O'Connellism, from the Land Wars to the various republican mobilizations, they had displayed, in many ways, remarkable capacity for political organization in the most adverse circumstances. After a decade of global economic depression and in the stalled economy of the Free State, they had perhaps lost their resilience. Yet, nationally, it was these same class fractions that would throw their weight behind Clann na Poblachta or Clann na Talmhan in the 1940s in one last desperate heave to break the middle-class arm-lock of the southern political system. Kavanagh's *Great Hunger* is not to be castigated for not including this long history of rural restiveness. But the total absence of any conception of subaltern rural agency is fundamental to the vision of this epic of failure.[65]

The *Great Hunger* depicts a world of mechanical automatons — 'the potato-gatherers like mechanised scarecrows move / Along the side-fall of the hill' — whose only strongly marked human qualities are a ruthless dedication to small-scale accumulation, crushed sexual instinct, and a capacity to feel pain without any capacity to resist or intellectually to comprehend it.[66] We have not in this poem escaped the spell of the aesthetic to discover at last the tawdry 'real Ireland' that Yeatsian or de Valerian romance or pastoral had wizarded away. We have substituted, rather, a pastoral for a naturalist aesthetic, and, ironically, history remains just as static and immobile in the naturalist mode as it had ever done in the pastoral. The human figures in the poem are so dumbly acquiescent to their fates that they are never really capable of expressing anything other than a momentary brute, inchoate rage to punctuate an otherwise meek compliance with their lot.

Since the rural folk themselves suffer their lot with dumb brutishness, such sense of protest as there is in the poem is reserved exclusively for the narrator and addressed to a spectator ('If we watch them an hour is there anything we can prove / Of life as it is broken-backed over the Book / Of Death'[67]). That spectator, invited into the compact of that opening 'we' with the narrator is clearly deemed the intellectual superior to those on display; he or she is obviously someone whose mental life is not restricted, as theirs is, to '*Reynolds News* or the *Sunday Dispatch*, / With sometimes an old almanac brought down

---

65 The economically depressed 1930s stimulated various forms of rural protest movements such as the no-rates policy of the Irish Farmers' Federation (established in 1937), the political party Clann na Talmhan (established in 1938), and Clann na Poblachta (established in 1946).

66 Patrick Kavanagh, *The Great Hunger*, in *The Complete Poems* (Newbridge, 1972), 79–104, 79

67 *The Great Hunger*, 80

from the ceiling / Or a school reader brown with the droppings of thatch'.[68] Usually celebrated as a blistering riposte to ignorant middle-class idealizations of the peasant, whether of Yeatsian or Gaelic League (read Protestant or Catholic) variety, The Great Hunger is itself addressed, nonetheless, to an audience that is clearly imagined as middle class. However angrily the poem excoriates the middle-class's fatuous ignorance of the realities of the rural world it loves to idealize, it is still the implied middle-class reader that is engaged in intellectual dialogue, over the heads of Maguire and his kind, by the narrator. The Great Hunger, that is to say, displays, however unconsciously, a strong sense of anthropological condescension: the middle-class reader is invited into the poem by the narrator, who acts as a kind of well-educated native informant to the miserable world to be investigated, and such sense as may be made of that broken-backed world will have to come from these two — the rural lower orders are themselves clearly not expected to have anything to contribute except a passive dumbshow of their miseries.

The world of Paddy Maguire in The Great Hunger is a world chained to the seasonal cycle, man's tragedy being that while his biological instincts viscerally quicken to that cycle, he lacks nature's capacity for annual self-renewal and grows only ever older. This inescapable biological tragedy is aggravated by a social system in which the associated dictates of petty accumulation and Catholicism enjoin on the rural poor a degree of toil, caution and self-abnegation so drastic as to utterly mutilate and mangle them. In later, more comic works such as Tarry Flynn, which is informed by an aesthetic idiom quite different to the naturalism of The Great Hunger, the wanton sexualized extravagance of nature acts as a comic rebuke to the miserly self-denial humans inflict on themselves. However, in The Great Hunger nature is not at all bounteous, but stingy, flinty, mean and unyielding — hence that lumpish, wet clay; that stony, grey soil — and the Paddy Maguires must therefore perpetually wrestle with the miserly earth if they are to subsist. The effect of this conception of nature as essentially hard is, peculiarly enough, to blunt the edge of social critique, since a skinflint nature seems logically to require from humans a relentlessly tough, ascetic, self-denying mentality if they are successfully to accommodate themselves to their penurious environment.

But if Kavanagh excoriates the sentimental pieties of soft primitivism or peasant pastoral — 'There is the source from which all cultures rise, / And all religions, / There is the pool in which the poet dips / And the musician' — he is equally keen to defuse any sturdy heroics of hard primitivism — 'To the fields once again / Where eunuchs can be men / And life is more lousy than savage'.[69] If Yeats's or Synge's flamboyant peasants romanticize too much in one direction, the hard primitive machismo of Liam O'Flaherty's Skerritt (1932) or Robert Flaherty's Man of Aran (1934) does so in another. In this poem, Kavanagh will have neither the idealized peasant at one with a benevolent nature nor the muscular heroics of the peasant at war with an intractably hostile one: hence, the

68 The Great Hunger, 93
69 The Great Hunger, 100, 83

logical alternative is to stress a reduced humanity with scarcely any agency. Thus, the poem's time is essentially an arrested time; it stresses the hopelessly extended cyclical routine of lives so frustratingly uneventful and unproductive as to make death a release. The sexual tortures of ageing celibacy are unsparingly delivered. Maguire masturbates 'an impotent worm' into a dying fire. His 'straddle-legged' sister is described as having 'One leg in hell and the other in heaven / And between the purgatory of middle-aged virginity' — surely a wonderfully vicious if typically sexist burlesque of Peig's (1936) 'cos liom san uaigh agus an chos eile ar a bruach'. These become the controlling metaphors to suggest a timorous, onanistic Ireland so abjectly unable to imagine a way beyond its lousy, condition that it can only wank itself to death.[70]

The disenchanted depiction of 'the ignorant peasant deep in dung' offered here is undoubtedly powerful and purgative. But as far as its diagnostic capacities go, The Great Hunger is scarcely more than a scabrously versified Arensberg and Kimball. (Conrad Arensberg's The Irish Countryman had been published in 1937; Arensberg and Solon Kimball's Family and Community in Ireland in 1940.) What forces have brought the country-folk to this sorry pass? Why are they so meekly submissive to their life-denying Church, and so dumbly resigned to such narrow lives? Have they no desire to rebel against their condition? These questions cannot be answered because The Great Hunger has no interest in asking them. What lifts the work above versified documentary is that it has absorbed not only the idealizing Revivalist and Irish Ireland aesthetics it assaults, but a variety of other modes of writing about rural Ireland as well (Man of Aran; the Blasket biographies, the anthropological treatise, the tourist brochure), and hence it is able to energize itself on their idiomatic energies even as it satirises the whole shebang as a farrago of ignorant nonsense.[71] And while O'Faolain is surely correct when he adjudges in the late 1940s that neither he nor his novel-writing contemporaries had properly absorbed Ulysses, it is clear that Kavanagh had to his credit assimilated the great masterpiece of English modernist poetry — The Waste Land. The Great Hunger is patently a lesser work, but, in both technical (the incantatory repetitions, the slack-line endings, the off-rhymes, the abrupt direct turns to the reader, the apocalyptic or faux-apocalyptic ending) and idiomatic ways (the use of cliché, the abrupt epigrammatic line, swift swerves from the sacred to the grotesque), it has many traces of Eliot. Indeed, one of Kavanagh's real achievements is to map The Waste Land onto a rural Irish landscape, to find a form to express for the

70 The Great Hunger, 83, 94

71 The Great Hunger is generally perceived as, in Terence Brown's words, 'an eloquently bleak riposte from the heart of the rural world to all those polemicists, writers and demagogues who in de Valera's Ireland sought to venerate the countryman's life from the study or political platform'. Terence Brown, Ireland: A Social and Cultural History, 1922–1985 (London, 1985), 187. Whereas this posits a simple antithesis between de Valeran pastoral and Kavanagh's anti-pastoral, the proposal here is that Kavanagh's work inserts itself into a wide array of contesting discourses of rural life, of which some key examples are Tomás Ó Criomhthain, An tOileánach (1929), Daniel Corkery, Synge and Anglo-Irish Literature (1931), Robert Flaherty, Man of Aran (1934), Peig Sayers, Peig (1936), Conrad Arensberg, The Irish Countryman (1937), Flann O'Brien, An Béal Bocht (1941), and the Abbey Theatre 'peasant play'.

domestic Irish context that sense of civilizational failure and run-down that Eliot had already associated with the modern metropolis. For decades, Ireland had liked to think itself a wholesome rural alternative to the spiritually desiccated modern urban wasteland, but by hibernicizing and ruralizing the idiom of The Waste Land, Kavanagh suggested this was a delusion. Associated by the Revival with primitive pagan vitality and by Irish Ireland with deep Christian spirituality, rural Ireland now became the exemplary site to express the quintessence of Irish social backwardness and spiritual bankruptcy. In Kavanagh's early work, rural Ireland was deconsecrated for Irish poetry; in his later career, suburban Ireland was quietly invested as its redemptive alternative.[72]

In his later work, Eliot had moved steadily towards a more religious verse; Kavanagh's later career follows a similar trajectory. The road from the scurrilous satirical vehemence of The Great Hunger leads around a few choleric bends to the sanguine, reconciled buddha of suburbia. With Seamus Deane's verdict that 'Kavanagh managed in that quarter century [the span of his writing career] to lift the burden of Irish and world history from the stooping shoulders of the Irish poet' there can be little dispute.[73] Like the works of O'Casey and O'Flaherty, O'Connor and O'Faolain, Kavanagh's work sets its face against the afflatus of the Revival, insisting instead on the need to recognize the unimpressive local reality that mocked the grand vision. This cumulative naturalist assault on the pretence of the new Ireland was undoubtedly warranted. But the extent to which that assault was issuing a radical challenge to the new post-revolutionary nationalist establishment should not be overstated, since naturalism's mockery of idealized vision comported quite well in many respects with the regnant ideology of a state that was now, in any event, trimming its old revolutionary rhetoric of transformation and stressing — in religious and political terms — the need for a 'realistic' accommodation to the actual.

His capacity to detonate Yeats's and de Valera's ossified arcadias has earned Kavanagh deserved reputation, but the patchiness of his œuvre as compared to Yeats's much more sustained one is possibly testimony to the ways in which the naturalist aesthetic tended to stymie all of the counter-Revivalists, whether novelist, dramatist or poet. Like the novelists, Kavanagh can scarcely ever sustain a longer dramatic narrative form and just as they find in the short story the métier most serviceable to their abilities (if not most satisfying to their ambitions), so too Kavanagh will ultimately settle for the short lyric in his late period. O'Faolain continues across the decades to fret that the assault on the romance of the Revival will yield not much more than the short story. By comparison,

---

72 The term 'suburban' here must not be taken literally to mean the new residential tracts on the outer perimeter of the city, but rather a domesticated neutralized landscape where the country and the city are merged and mutually divested of both their more 'negative' (wilderness/urban jungle) or 'redemptive/ utopian' (pastoral garden/heroic metropolis) qualities. Kavanagh's Baggot Street and Grand Canal landscapes are suburban in this second sense, and pave the way for a great deal of postmodernist poetry invested in landscapes of this order.

73 Seamus Deane, A Short History of Irish Literature (London, 1986), 234

Kavanagh seems altogether less fretful with the short lyric, supplementing a naturalist attention to homely detail in the later work with spiritual grace notes that urge the salvific qualities of the quotidian. His late poetry is that of a world that has abandoned not only the heroic, romantic, visionary impulses of the Revival, but also the critical sting of naturalism and the difficulties of modernism. To such a downsized, quietest art, so well accommodated to the accustomed, neither de Valera nor Lemass, neither Archbishop John Charles McQuaid nor the post-Vatican II Church, were likely to have many objections.

5

The second generation naturalist writers nearly all attempted works of epic historical sweep. O'Casey's 1920s plays encompass the Easter Rising, the War of Independence, the Civil War and World War I. O'Flaherty produced three historical novels — *Famine* (1937), *Land* (1946), *Insurrection* (1950) — that attempted an even longer march through nineteenth- and twentieth-century Irish history. O'Faolain essayed a roughly similar novel cycle stretching from Fenianism to state formation in *A Nest of Simple Folk* (1933), *Bird Alone* (1936) and *Come Back to Erin* (1940). Kavanagh worked in the opposite direction, but *The Great Hunger* invoked the greatest trauma in modern Irish history. Even O'Connor, the writer most content with the short-story form, wrote an historical biography, *The Big Fellow* (1937), and O'Faolain wrote several biographical works, including studies of de Valera (1933, rev. edn. 1939), Markievicz (1934), Tone (1937), O'Connell (1938) and O'Neill (1940). The longer arc of modern Irish history was of concern to all these writers (Kavanagh least so), therefore, and whether their inability to achieve works to match such ambition stemmed from the problem of reconciling it with the naturalist aesthetic they espoused or whether European writers generally were confronted with similar difficulties in the dark climate of the 1930s, which troubled any progressive sense of history, is an interesting question. For present purposes, it suffices to note that the second generation naturalists continued to be interested in realizing some sort of sustained national epic, even though they were seldom able to give that interest satisfying artistic expression.

The recession of this interest is one of the features that distinguishes the third from the second generation of naturalists. Brian Moore, Edna O'Brien, John McGahern and Tom Murphy have all worked in their later careers with forms at some remove from naturalism, but they share in common the fact that they all established their 'Irish' reputations after World War II with bleakly naturalist works: Moore's *The Lonely Passion of Judith Hearne* (1956), O'Brien's *The Country Girls* trilogy (1960–63), Murphy's *A Whistle in the Dark* (1961), and McGahern's *The Barracks* (1963) and *The Dark* (1965). Other notable naturalist works to appear in this period, but which cannot be examined here, include John Broderick's novels, *The Pilgrimage* (1961) and *The Waking of Willie Ryan* (1964), Eugene McCabe's *King of the Castle* (1964), and William Trevor's short-story collection *The Ballroom of Romance*

(1972). Unlike the counter-Revivalists, this subsequent generation of naturalists had not been involved to any degree in the national revolution, and it is distinguished from its predecessor by a lack of overt political engagement or affiliation.

As the role of 'the writer' becomes more narrowly specialized in the post-World War II period, a sense of historical time seems somehow to have diminished or atrophied. This is all the more curious since the period between the 1960s and the end of the twentieth century was undoubtedly dramatic: this was, after all, an epoch that witnessed a massive wave of decolonization across the 'Third World', the sexual revolution, the Cold War, the construction of the European Union, and, at home, the traumatic return of the Troubles in the North. The imprint of these events clearly marks the fictional worlds of the third generation of Irish naturalists, but the lack of direct engagement with these wider events is still quite remarkable. In the writings of this generation of naturalists, Irish society is repeatedly indicted as an oppressively insular and provincial backwater. But in some respects that provincialism is at least as true of the writers as of the society they depict. Generally speaking, we will find in this 1960s generation's works neither an interest in Irish political history of the kind that yielded works such as O'Casey's trilogy or O'Flaherty's and O'Faolain's historical cycles, nor the interest in the longer span of Irish and European literary history that issued in studies such as O'Connor's *The Lonely Voice* (1962) or *The Backward Look* (1967) and O'Faolain's *The Short Story* (1948) or *The Vanishing Hero* (1956).[74] In this and other ways, the 1960s naturalists are very much Kavanagh's successors.

In a wider global-political sense, World War II is what separates this third stage of naturalist writing from the second. Culturally, however, the decisive figure that stands between the two generations is Samuel Beckett, now increasingly recognized as a pivotal figure in a wider international transition from a modernist to a postmodernist conjuncture. Beckett is often viewed as the least 'Irish' of the Irish modernists, yet in many respects his work's temperamental affinities seem to lie with a vein of scabrously comic Irish naturalism that begins in 1941 with Flann O'Brien's *An Béal Bocht*, and that

74 Belfast-born Brian Moore, the most senior by a decade of the writers considered in this section, is an obvious exception here since his later works display a strong interest in international politics conspicuously lacking in that of southern contemporaries. Although Edna O'Brien, John McGahern, Tom Murphy or William Trevor can all obviously be read 'politically', none has made politics the explicit subject of their work in the way either the earlier generation of southern naturalists from O'Casey to O'Connor or contemporary northern naturalists, such as Moore, have done. McGahern's work is always obliquely shadowed by the northern conflict, and O'Brien does address the northern situation late in her career, in *A House of Splendid Isolation*, but for the most part there is little attempt to develop either history or politics as an overt subject matter in Irish writing (and especially southern Irish writing) since the sixties. The other major Irish writers of the same generation who have made Irish history and politics into an overt theme have generally either done so through other aesthetic modes such as the historical novel or drama (Thomas Kilroy's *The Big Chapel*, Brian Friel's *Making History* or *Translations*), the drama of ideas (Kilroy's *Double Cross*), or in 'late modernist' styles (the poetry of Thomas Kinsella). Edna O'Brien has produced a short critical study of James Joyce, but in general the 1960s naturalists have produced remarkably little cultural criticism.

comes to the fore in the 1950s with Máirtín Ó Cadhain's *Cré na Cille* (1949), J. P. Donleavy's *The Ginger Man* (1955) and Brendan Behan's *Borstal Boy* (1958). All these works display the disenchanted, anti-romantic thrust common to Irish naturalism. The crucial difference, however, is that their temperament is no longer tragic, as was the case even in O'Casey, but has become instead comically grotesque and satirical — the object is no longer to deliver a savage critique of society so much as to parody the conventions of romance and of naturalism alike by pushing them to absurd or zany extremes.

One way to read Beckett's major works in both novel and drama, then, would be to say that they achieve their distinct identity by pushing naturalist conventions to the point where that mode begins to capsize on itself. If naturalists' plots typically go either steadily downhill or steadily nowhere, then why not make the very idea of plot itself an object of ridicule such that stasis, lassitude, dejection and mechanical repetitiveness become the very essence of things? Beckett's characters possess the extremely attenuated human agency common to naturalism generally, but his work is permeated by an altogether more thoroughgoing scepticism about the capacity of anything whatever to meliorate, redeem or reform this utterly fallen, hopelessly thwarted condition. In contrast to any of the conventional kinds of naturalism that set out to debunk some humanistic romance, in Beckett's work there is no romance to begin with and hence none that requires to be disenchanted. Instead, we inhabit a world always-already so thoroughly fumigated of any expectation that it might be improved that the very notion of redemption seems either a gratuitously added torture or merely a wan absurdity. In Beckett, in sum, we have an art in which naturalism's preoccupation with a sordid, disenchanted world is taken to its ultimate extremes and conceived as a subject for wry philosophical speculation rather than as an historical or social problem to be solved — at which point his work ceases to be troubled by the antimony of disenchantment and social reform that generally motivates naturalism. It thus ceases to be naturalism and becomes something else.

However, while this was happening, a naturalism of a more conventional kind was emerging in postwar Britain in the form of a gritty literary and cinematic 'working-class realism'. 'Social problem' novels and films in this period engaged with specific social issues such as youth culture, juvenile delinquency, tensions between the claims of authority and self-expression, marital frustration and infidelity, and the stigmas of homosexuality or race. Working-class realist works were very similar in form, but dealt with the decline of traditional working-class community and the emergence of a modern consumer society, and with the dilemmas of working-class or lower-middle-class characters coming into lived contact with an upper-class milieu for the first time.[75] The efflorescence of the Irish naturalist novel and drama in the late 1950s and 1960s is partly an extension of a longer tradition of Irish naturalism and partly a regional variant of this

---

75 On English literary realism and naturalism in the post-World War II period, see Williams, 'Social Environment and Theatrical Environment', 125–47. On cinematic versions, see John Hill, *Sex, Class and Realism: British Cinema, 1956–1963* (London, 1986).

wider British current. In works such as Moore's *The Feast of Lupercal* (1957), Murphy's *A Whistle in the Dark*, O'Brien's *The Country Girls* or McGahern's *The Dark*, issues such as the class structure of the education system or the travails of the talented, upwardly mobile but deracinated 'scholarship' boy or girl, which feature so prominently in English working-class realism in this era, also appear. Likewise, there are similar concerns in both countries with the erosion of inherited communities, typically northern industrial working-class communities in the English case, more commonly rural versions in the Irish.

But if naturalism enjoyed a strong resurgence in both Irish and English fiction in this period, the crucial difference is that it modified their respective national literary fields in fundamentally different ways. English working-class realism and social problem fiction in the post-World War II period developed in the context of a more-or-less continuous realist tradition that was always very prestigious in the English literary canon. The first and second generation Irish naturalists had, in contrast, laboured either in the domestic shadow of the Irish Revival or in the international shadow of Irish modernism. However, the waning of the Revival and of European modernism generally meant that the third generation naturalists no longer suffered so much in comparison with Irish contemporaries working in non-naturalist modes. In academic and critical circles, the long-standing cachet of the Revival and the enormously escalated prestige which Irish modernism enjoyed within the Euro-American academy after World War II may well have eclipsed the extent of this actual shift. But the degree to which the modernist impulse begins to run down in Irish culture from the 1960s onwards is nonetheless dramatic, leaving the way clear for naturalism to command the late twentieth-century Irish cultural landscape more completely than had ever been the case before.[76]

Of the débutante works to be discussed here, Moore's *The Lonely Passion of Judith Hearne* is the most formulaically naturalist. Its subject — the sexual frustration, spiritual distress and collapse into alcoholism of a genteel but impoverished middle-aged spinster — recalls the Goncourts' *Germinie Lacerteux* (1864), a seminal novel of French naturalism. Moore himself has described how his subject was essentially his own loss of faith in Catholicism, but to avoid comparison with Joyce's *Portrait*, he 'decided to write not about an intellectual's loss of faith, but the loss of faith in someone devout, the

---

76 A brief word on the geography of this cultural development may be in order here. According to the national census, 1966 was the year in which the urban population of the Republic exceeded the rural (which includes settlements with less than 1,500 people) for the first time. To simplify a little, then, we can say that for most of the twentieth century Ireland was mainly a rural society whose leading writers came from Dublin, but that after the 1960s it became a largely urban island, dominated by Dublin, most of the leading writers of which have come, however, from what is commonly considered rural Ireland. There is some reason to think, therefore, that post-sixties Irish naturalism is really an aesthetic that expresses the moment when the old rural Ireland dies and disappears but when the new urban Ireland (including an urbanized and industrialized countryside) has not yet found any other identity except the negative one of repudiating the rural world it has displaced. The thematic preoccupation with adolescence and coming-of-age in these novels might thus be read as a symptom of this wider societal transition.

sort of woman my mother would have known, a "sodality lady"'.[77] The author's decision
to depersonalizse his own immediate experience may have been well advised. But by
focalizing the novel through a character of only limited discernment, Moore also opted
intellectually to simplify the whole treatment of religion, and instead of attempting
something more ambitious than what had already been accomplished by a youthful Joyce,
he produces a novel in which a strong sense of disdain for the religious narrowness of
Belfast society overwhelms all else.

Stephen Dedalus in *Portrait* is only a cocky adolescent, but he has at least a reasonably
well-developed comprehension of Catholic theology and of Irish national history as well
as some idiosyncratic theories of art. By situating his young hero in a university milieu,
Joyce also creates some sense in the novel of a society where ideas about religion, national
identity and art are matters of wider social concern or controversy. In contrast to Joyce's
Stephen, Moore's Judith Hearne has only a smattering of education, no independence
of mind, and a very slender grasp of Catholic doctrine. Her faith, like that of every other
character in the novel, is a wholly uneducated, emotional, indeed neurotic, condition.
The story of her decline is essentially a catalogue of episodes of shame and degradation,
each successive episode intensifying her mortification without ever generating any real
conflict of value at the level of plot. The reader may be voyeuristically compelled by
the extended spectacle of Judith's mortification, but since her faith is shown from the
start to be utterly without value, its collapse can hardly be felt to be in any way tragic
or constitutive of a genuine crisis of value. Moore's technique, therefore, is essentially
melodramatic: the plot is sustained not by any contention of values or ideas, but only
by a serial process of humiliation and degradation that is not without misogynistic
overtones.

Judith Hearne's pathetic fate is acted out in a Belfast boarding house peopled by a
uniformly unattractive cast of characters. That boarding-house milieu seems to have
come directly northwards from *Dubliners*, but even sympathetic critics accept that
Moore's descriptions of sordidness of person or milieu are always much more laboured
and extended than Joyce's.[78] Madden is a bully and rapist; Miss Friel a puritan bigot;
Lenehan a nationalist bigot; Mrs Henry Rice a skinflint; her son, Bernard, a tubby, amoral
Machiavel with absurd poetic pretensions; Mary, the servant, a helpless victim bent solely
on survival. Moore's Judith Hearne never commands the same level of empathy from the
reader that Joyce's spinster, Maria, does in 'Clay', and Mary is, by the same token, less
engaging than Joyce's man-troubled servant, Lily, in 'The Dead'. It may be the case that
when Moore extends to novelistic length the character cameos sketched in a few deft
sentences in *Dubliners* this will inevitably create figures so diminished that they elicit
disgusted condescension rather than any genuine understanding. Hence the reader

---

77 Denis Sampson, *Brian Moore: The Chameleon Novelist* (Dublin and Toronto, 1998), 88
78 For a comparison of Joyce's and Moore's use of description, see Jo O'Donoghue, *Brian Moore: A Critical
Study* (Montreal and London, 1991), 26–35.

comes away from the novel with a strong sense of the deathly and bigoted atmosphere of the North, but without any comprehension of how or why things have come to this pass or whether this sordid situation is peculiar to Belfast or simply the way of the world in general. *The Lonely Passion of Judith Hearne* convicts Belfast of masking a complete lack of human feeling behind a Pharisaical religiosity. That critique is implicitly issued in the name of a more tolerant, empathetic secular humanism, but the novel exudes such an indiscriminate sense of disdain for the entire society it depicts that its own humanism seems ultimately just as intolerant as the religiosity it condemns.

The titles of his novels *The Barracks* and *The Dark* convey that impression of defensive enclosure and abiding gloom that was to become the decisive signature of John McGahern's early work. *The Barracks*, organized around the consciousness of Elizabeth Reegan, a woman married to a querulous and brutally selfish husband, and dying of cancer in lonely isolation at the age of thirty-nine, disclosed the fundamental structure of feeling that shapes McGahern's imaginative world: a traumatized sense that death is always the ultimate and most visceral reality, and that an emotionally assimilated acceptance of one's own transience, and that of others, will afford the only decent response to this condition. The later novels will rework this conception of things in new directions, but the fundamental worldview remains remarkably constant across McGahern's career.

The second novel, *The Dark*, shifts the fulcrum of narrative consciousness to a male adolescent character, and takes up the issues of masculine sexuality that dominate McGahern's middle career. The opening chapter, which describes a child-beating episode that reappears in later works with the shattering force of a primal scene that demands continuously to be revisited, is by far the most completely realized thing in the entire novel. The scene begins with the father's explosion of rage when his son utters a swear word. The child is first compelled to repeat the expletive 'F-U-C-K' and then to strip naked to be leathered for this offence. The sickening feeling of terror and degradation visited on the son by his helpless subjection to his father's outraged will is terrifically rendered. His father's insistence that the punishment be enacted in 'the girl's room' and that the boy's undressing and flogging be witnessed by 'the house' as a whole aggravates and sexualizes the disgrace inflicted on the child.[79] However, when he metes out the flogging, the father never actually allows the strap to touch his son, striking only the leather armrests of the chair on which the child is prostrated. The father's carefully calibrated exertion of his will is pushed to a point where the child loses physical control and wets himself, but the fact that he is not literally beaten fixes the emphasis on the mental humiliation and shame rather than on the physical brutality involved. McGahern's skill and restraint is such that the father, despite his cantankerous cruelty, is never dehumanized: his appalling violence and emotional manipulativeness are expertly conveyed, but so too is a sense of the thwarted neediness and the social and

79 John McGahern, *The Dark* (London, 1977 [1965]), 7

existential frustration and rage that torment him. In fact, despite their antagonism, the boy and the father are shown to be trapped in a curious compact: the boy is shamed by the fact he can be stripped of all self-possession by the brute exertion of his father's will, but the father himself is so helplessly at the mercy of his own petulant self-pity and sudden eruptions of anger that he too is pathetically lacking in self-possession or control. Control, in the dual sense of being subjected to a negative external constraint or pressure and as a positive state of inner self-command to be achieved, is the enigmatic condition or value that motivates McGahern's work. At both its thematic and stylistic levels, control is what the novel is about.

The control that both the father and the child lack and seek in their respective ways has its social dimensions. Both are keenly aware that they are from a low social class in a society controlled by others, and both know that success in this society requires a kind of violence: "'Dog eat dog, who'll eat and who'll be eaten, and what'll the eaters and the eaten do" there was at least grim laughter. "'Go on aten, and being et," Mahoney said.'[80] But the routine indignations and frustrations that issue from a sense of having one's life controlled by forces beyond one's reach is not the whole story; there is an existential dimension too to the sense that one is at the mercy of things. Thus, the father's anger stems in large part from his frustrated incapacity to make peace with the passing of time; it issues from an intuition that his life, like all life perhaps, is lived without anything that would confer on it discernible reason or meaningful purpose: "'This is my life, and this kitchen in the townland of Cloone is my stage, and I am playing my life out here on," and he stood, the eyes wild, as if grappling for his lines. "And nobody sees me except a crowd of childer."'[81] The sense of control that the father is unable to secure, either socially or existentially, is precisely what the son will seek in the novel. But in the end the search for any kind of control in the social domain will prove to be barren; only the existential quest for some sort of inner command of the self is ratified in the novel.

There is a tension in The Dark, as in all of McGahern, as to whether the terrible sense of frustration and deprivation that the characters feel have their source in social causes — such as the tyranny of the father, the inherited trauma of Irish history, the repressiveness of Irish society — or whether they are ultimately an inevitability of human existence. The Dark is really an exclusively father–son affair: it is a bewildered, blighted Bildungsroman in which the generic impulse to development is stymied by a sense that while the enclosure of the family maims and brutalizes, the world beyond its confines is a Sahara of indifference and alienation. The world that the novel's young protagonist inhabits is an extraordinarily masculine one: the boy's sisters are mere background shadows (only one is even named) and the other male authority figures that he moves between (Father Gerald, Brother Benedict, the physics lecturer, the Dean of Studies) are all versions of the father, sometimes kinder and more worldly than he, but so remote and lacking in

80 The Dark, 108
81 The Dark, 95

any credible authority as to be each only narrative dead ends. The father's compound of bullying despotism and wheedling neediness is detested, but he nonetheless has a charismatic and an enigmatic quality that diminishes all the other competing male figures by comparison.

Young Mahoney's struggles with whether or not he has a vocation for the priesthood are somewhat plodding and inertly rendered since there is no real religious feeling anywhere in the novel; the long dispiriting slog of the leaving certificate examinations are meticulously documented; so too the sense of shame and self-disgust that attend his adolescent masturbations. The boy desperately longs for some fuller sense of life. But the enormous self-discipline required to rise out of the lower orders and to get on in the world is shown to be so exhausting, and the ends to be achieved by such struggle so dubious in any case (the priesthood carries no conviction, the university students are all obsessed with good jobs and security) as to call into question whether the gruelling slog required for 'success' could ever be worth it. When young Mahoney decides to leave the university shortly after arriving there to take up a soul-destroying office job, he knows immediately that this is to accept defeat before his life even begins. But the sense of murderous rage at having to settle for such diminished expectations is remarkably transient, since one option is ultimately deemed as good or bad as the other in the end:

It was hard to walk quiet out of the University at Mahoney's side and see the goalposts luminous in the grey light of the rain and not give savage expression to one murderous feeling of defeat.

Though not even that lasted for long, the rage and futility gradually subsiding as you walked through the streets of that wet day. What right had anybody or anything to defeat you and what right had you to feel defeated, who was to define its name?

One day, one day, you'd come perhaps to more real authority than all this, an authority that had need of neither vast buildings nor professorial chairs nor robes nor solemn organ tones, an authority that was simply a state of mind, a calmness even in the face of the turmoil of your own passing.

You could go to the E.S.B. If it was no use you could leave again, and it didn't matter, you could begin again and again all your life, nobody's life was more than a direction.[82]

What ultimately matters most at the end of *The Dark* is not any kind of social authority — all forms of which seem here equally fake, dependent as they are on the theatrical props of 'vast buildings', 'professorial chairs', or 'solemn organ tones' — but the subjective inner authority that comes from 'a calmness even in the face of the turmoil of your own passing'. What is validated in effect is an essentially existential form of authority that depends on coming to terms with one's inevitable transience, and this, peculiarly

82 *The Dark*, 139

enough, is what brings father and son as close to each other as they ever can be.

When *The Dark* was first published, some critics complained that the mood shift from defeat to defiance registered in the above passage was unearned, and that the son's occasional capacity to reconcile with the father was likewise unconvincing.[83] However, the major moment of *rapprochement* between the two occurs when the father redeems a botched day out with a feeble joke passing a graveyard — 'No matters what happens it winds up there. And you wouldn't mind only there's people dying to get into it' — which prompts the son's momentary outburst of approval in which he can exclaim to himself, 'You are marvellous, my father.'[84] It is no accident that this moment of filial acknowledgement of the father occurs at an instant when the latter recognizes death as the supreme and overarching reality, the final end that puts all the dog-eat-dog viciousness of human struggle (for escape, advancement, knowledge, security, emancipation) into its properly comic or absurd perspective.

While mid-career novels, such as *The Leavetaking* (1974) or *The Pornographer* (1979), are set in Dublin and offer rather disenchanted examinations of sexuality as a means of self-emancipation, McGahern turns resolutely back in his later career to the rural mid-west of the opening novels. These later novels, *Amongst Women* (1990) and *That They May Face the Rising Sun* (2002), are commonly agreed to display an 'autumnal' serenity that distinguishes them from the grimness of *The Barracks* or *The Dark*, and that shift in tone is usually attributed to the notion that Irish society had managed in the interim to leave behind the punitively conservative Catholic order that the early novels depicted. In addition, these two later novels seem to move away from the more individualized register of the early fiction and to become more expansively national in their ambitions. The Faber paperback edition of *Amongst Women* carried on its cover an image of an Irish tricolour, inviting a reading of its family saga as national allegory. *That They May Face the Rising Sun* represented in its turn a new departure for McGahern, since the narrative was no longer organized in terms of the claustrophobic family dramas that shaped the earlier works from *The Barracks* to *Amongst Women*; now the scope of the tale was widened to encompass a broader sense of rural community. The late fiction seems, in other words, to discover not only a serenity lacking in the grey early novels, but also to convey the impression that this serenity has a collective, national dimension.

These later novels do represent a significant shift. *Amongst Women* is effectively a reworking of *The Barracks* and *The Dark*. The daughters who had existed merely as anonymous shadows in the background of the earlier work are brought to robust individual life in the later one. The caring but dying mother figure of *The Barracks* is partly restored in *Amongst Women* as the kindly, pragmatic Rose; the world of this later novel is not nearly so exclusively masculine as that of *The Dark* therefore. The emotionally numbed

83 See John Cronin, 'The Dark is not Light Enough: The Fiction of John McGahern', *Studies*, 58, 232 (1969), 427–32.

84 *The Dark*, 119

young Mahoney of *The Dark* reappears as Luke in *Amongst Women*, but he is displaced now from the centre of narrative consciousness and removed to exile in London. Since such an emotionally stunted character could hardly work as the focalizing consciousness for any kind of affirmative plot, his relegation to the margins of things, as a figure of irreconcilable withdrawal and unrecoverable loss, is a very effective device; Luke haunts the family from the remove of London much more effectively than he could ever have done so long as he remained the novel's centre of consciousness. The tyrannical father distinctly reprises the Mahoney of *The Dark*; he remains a tormented figure, still capable of unpredictable domestic atrocity, still agonized by his incapacity to command himself or the world he inhabits. But the difference is that *Amongst Women* is his story and not the elder son's, and it is the extended depiction of the father's waning power and his painful coming to terms with his own mortality that monopolizes much of the reader's attention.

Narrative consciousness is more widely and democratically dispersed in *Amongst Women* than in the earlier novels, but the father, far from having receded into the background with the passage of time, as might have been expected, is actually more than ever the charismatic centre of things. His contrary energy and tormented emotions are the dynamic generator of plot, the active element to which all the other characters merely respond; the enigma of his angry, thwarted personality is what sustains suspense. In short, what has happened here is that the individualized adolescent struggle and strife of the young male *Bildungsroman* that had structured and motivated the novels of the early career have now, in *Amongst Women*, been dispersed to include the children generally. But the story of their maturation has to share equal space with the extended narrative of the father's decline. To put it another way, *Amongst Women* combines two contrapuntal narrative temporalities: the forward-moving *Bildungsroman* temporality of the children's development is run up against the more elegiac narrative of the father's demise. Time moves forward for the young as they acquire new experience; time recedes for the father as he anxiously tries in his decline to make something of his already completed experience. But though this is to some degree a story of how the children weather out the death of the father, the novel itself can never, or chooses never to take us beyond the time of the father. What compels the reader's interest is how each of the children learns to cope with the world Daddy dominates till the very end; what happens to them afterwards is not of the slightest concern to the novel. In this sense, the novel is structured in such a way that everything is subordinate to the time and world of the father. Though that world and that time may be coming to an end, there is no substantive sense of any alternative time. What ultimately matters is the running down of Daddy's world, not whatever succeeds it.

Coming more than a decade later, *That They May Face the Rising Sun* moves even more determinedly back into this disappearing rural world, displaying even less interest than its predecessor in what will take its place. This time, the narrative is restricted to a cast of rural characters all beyond middle age; the charismatic/dread centre of the father and the whole younger coming-of-age generation that had structured McGahern's earlier novels are both dispensed with here. What we are left with, in their absence, is a virtually static world freed now from forward movement or impulsion of almost any kind. The dynamic of generational struggle, the axle on which so much of McGahern's fiction had always turned, is cast aside, and instead we have a group of people already well beyond the meridian of life: seasoned characters for whom the major hurly-burly of life is already over, and for whom what remains is essentially to make sense of what it all might mean. In other words, the coming-to-terms-with-death theme is no longer singular or confined to the parent, as it was in The Barracks or Amongst Women; instead, it is democratized now — the sense of an ending, or perhaps the struggle to make some sense of an ending, has now become collective or communal.

But if That They May Face the Rising Sun is more relaxed and serene than the earlier novels, this is not (as readers seem commonly to imagine) because we have entered some brave new Ireland, but only because all the agitations and false expectations of life have now been so thoroughly exorcized as no longer to be relevant. The characters that have attained stoic acceptance are sympathetically drawn in this work; those that are still agitated by restless, ungovernable passions, most obviously the horrifically violent and sex-obsessed John Quinn, appear more grotesquely ludicrous than anything else.

That They May Face the Rising Sun is, therefore, a novel with almost no interest in action or event. Hence its widely remarked chapter-less, plot-less, action-less, climax-less shape. There is no worldly quest to pursue; no external conflict to be resolved; no dramatic end or strong conclusion to be reached; only the individual day to be lived as well as one can, the closing season of life to be decently weathered out. McGahern's fiction would seem to acquire its 'late serenity', therefore, not from any sense that after a desperately traumatic struggle a repressive national order had finally given way to some new and more humane world, but rather from the idea that happiness is to be found not in the vain struggles of life at all, but only in making one's peace with one's inevitable transience. The search for 'a calmness even in the face of the turmoil of your own passing' that had shaped McGahern's imagination from the very outset — taken up thematically in the dying figure of Elizabeth Reegan in The Barracks; announced as the only basis for 'a real authority' in The Dark — eventually finds the authority or resolution of its own expressive form, its own distinct structure of feeling, in That They May Face the Rising Sun.

However, commendable as the attainment of 'a calmness even in the face of the turmoil of your own passing' might be as an individual ethic, it would seem to translate into a fatalistic quiescence or helplessness of a rather dubious nature if extended into the social realm. There seems to be a significant mismatch or disconnect between the types of readings McGahern's novels have typically depended upon for their critical validation. On the one hand, McGahern's reputation rests on a perception of him as a courageous social critic of Irish society, as someone who has dared to excavate the traumas (of family violence, sexual abuse, clerical repression, patriarchal authoritarianism) that a particular social dispensation (rural Catholic Ireland) managed too often to suppress. This drive to dig beneath the surface of things in order to expose the more sordid reality beneath is a fundamental feature of naturalism, and McGahern's deserved authority as a writer rests in no small measure on his capacity to deliver such exposure in an unusually restrained and reflective manner. At the same time, the logical corollary of the drive to expose the hidden vices of a society would seem to be a commitment to social reform and hence some interest in how some alternate or more humane form of society — one that would not be so disfigured by such vices — might be brought about. However, in McGahern's fiction there is no corresponding impulse of this kind whatever. On the contrary, the whole impetus of his fiction is, as already suggested, in the opposite direction: it is to evict history altogether and to discover a narrative form adequate to an essentially existentialist philosophy premised on the futility of worldly struggle and on the need to discover some inner authority and calm in the face of life's evanescence. In short, McGahern the socially engaged investigator of the secrets and lies of Irish rural life and McGahern the detached philosophical existentialist do not cohere in any satisfying way, and yet McGahern's admirers have never fully attempted to resolve this dilemma or even to acknowledge it.

To a large degree, what we get in McGahern is ultimately a secular humanist version of the more religiously-inflected reconciliation with the quotidian that animates the late Kavanagh. In Kavanagh, the naturalist drive to expose, to excoriate and to reform is to the fore in *The Great Hunger*; the reconciliatory impulse comes to the fore only at the end of his career in the late lyric poetry. In McGahern, these two drives (to expose the hidden traumas; to celebrate the small rituals of the quotidian) uneasily coexist in his fiction from the beginning. Kavanagh and McGahern may well be remembered for their critical exposures of rural Catholic Ireland. But the serenity that each displays towards the end of his career has nothing whatever to do with the discovery of some new confidence in the course or direction of Irish history; it stems, rather, from the repudiation of history and all its false hopes and empty promises altogether. Paradoxically, their serene late works may be even more pessimistic than their ostensibly darker early ones. Whereas the grim early works intimate some conviction that the disfigured Irelands they depicted demanded to be reformed, the serene later ones are premised on a kind of fatalism and a withdrawal from the social in favour of a coming to terms with life's essential transience.

Edna O'Brien's early novels seem in some ways the least naturalistic of the 1960s works discussed here. We will find in those works the shabby and chill interiors and the dysfunctional families tyrannized by the abusive fathers conventional to Irish naturalism. The difference is that O'Brien's young heroines negotiate these familiar obstacles with more spirited defiance than do their male counterparts in Moore or McGahern. Diarmuid Devine in Moore's *The Feast of Lupercal* is cowed and beaten by the Catholic school authorities for which he works, and McGahern's young Mahoney is worn down by the educational system in *The Dark*. In contrast, O'Brien's young women manage to have themselves expelled from their convent boarding school and set off for 'the neon fairyland of Dublin' in a spirit of high excitement quite different to the mood of the already world-weary young Mahoney who leaves for that city at the end of The Dark.[85] O'Brien's narrative technique differs also. The narrative consciousness of Moore's and McGahern's early novels are focalized by solitary young males, but O'Brien's trilogy is organized around two protagonists, Caithleen and Baba. This device of the paired protagonists means that the two heroines are never so completely marooned into their own isolation as Moore's or McGahern's companionless young men are, and the contrasting temperaments of the two girls allows O'Brien to counterpoint alternative modes of response to the types of situations they confront.

Though the early works of McGahern and O'Brien deal with remarkably similar types of experience, they handle that experience differently in other ways also. In both The Country Girls and The Dark, the young protagonists have to deal with the traumatic death of a mother, the brutality of an inadequate father, the trials of a punitive Catholic secondary education, and the adolescent anguish of sex and sin. However, the father figure in O'Brien's fiction is always kept at a much greater narrative remove and is ascribed neither the magnetic charisma nor the enigmatic mystery that even the most brutal fathers in McGahern's works always possess. Even in the opening novel, The Country Girls (1960), Baba makes fun of Caithleen's father and cuts him down to size. Since he is a much less compelling figure, Caithleen breaks free of him with much less emotional cost than McGahern's young Mahoney or Luke are able to do. When he and his cronies come in the second novel, The Lonely Girl (1962), to 'rescue' Caithleen from the immoral clutches of her seducer, her father is depicted as more ridiculous than terrifying. The scene is narrated from the perspective of Caithleen suffocating under the bed where she hides (reciting prayers, Latin nouns, Macbeth, and multiplication tables to keep from sneezing) and the fracas between father and lover is ended when the doughty house servant Anna enters to break it up by firing a shotgun. The power of the father, indeed male power generally, always has its farcical side in O'Brien, then, and an Anna or a Baba can often puncture its terrors with abrupt aplomb.

As remarked earlier, the distribution of narrative consciousness between Caithleen and Baba distinguishes O'Brien's early work from that of her male contemporaries. This formal device is key to any analysis of O'Brien's work because it is the vehicle through which the habitual naturalist tension between romance and anti-romance is negotiated in the trilogy — Caithleen representing the quest for romance, the more worldly, cynical Baba consistently debunking that quest. As O'Brien herself has remarked: 'Kate was looking for love. Baba was looking for money. Kate was timid, yearning and elegiac. Baba took up the cudgel against life and married an Irish builder who was as likely to clout her as anything else.'[86] Caithleen's voice is typically lyrical and poetic, somewhat

85 Edna O'Brien, The Country Girls, in The Country Girls Trilogy (New York, 1986 [1960]), 131
86 Edna O'Brien, 'Why Irish Heroines Don't Have to be Good Anymore', New York Times Book Review, 11 May 1968, quoted in James Cahalan, The Irish Novel: A Critical History (Dublin, 1989), 287–88

mordant, unworldly and searching; Baba's, in contrast, is bawdy, slangy, tough, bored, humorous, materialistic and pragmatic.

Given the different values they each represent, it is significant that at the end of the trilogy Baba survives; Caithleen (her name by the second novel anglicized to Kate) does not. The first two novels in the trilogy are narrated in Caithleen's voice; in the third, the narrative voice is taken over by Baba, who becomes witness to and commentator on the story of Kate's tragic end. Exhausted by a succession of disappointed romances, a broken marriage, and the loss of her son, *Girls in Their Married Bliss* (1963) comes to a close with Kate who, having had herself sterilized, is now too numbed by life even to be racked any longer by Catholic guilt. In the 'Epilogue', narrated by Baba, we learn that Kate has committed suicide by drowning. That act brings the trilogy to a grim cyclical end, recalling the sorry death of the drowned mother, an opening event in the first novel that had represented for Kate 'the last day of her childhood' and the beginning of her own story.[87]

It is not its litany of defeats compounded by that circular ending that makes *The Country Girls* trilogy a naturalist work. Because her central characters seem so often doomed to masochistic repetition and failure, O'Brien has sometimes been accused of dwelling excessively on women as victims. But had the women in the trilogy been depicted as more successful, O'Brien might equally have been charged with complacency, since so many things in Ireland then impeded women's self-realization. The charge of defeatism can be countered in any event with the argument that the trilogy releases disruptive energies that are never entirely contained by its deflated endings. However, it is certainly striking, nonetheless, that the fine balance between romance and anti-romance sustained for so long in these novels should in the end be settled so decisively in favour of anti-romance and, also, just how constrictively female romance is conceived. The final verdict of the trilogy is that a Kate cannot survive, only a Baba can. Romance, for Caithleen, is essentially personal or sexual romance, the only grail she ever quests is that of a satisfying emotional relationship. But though it debunks Caithleen's constant seeking after such individualized fulfilment (this quest dismissed eventually as the will-o'-the-wisp 'De Luxe Love Affair' that never happens), the trilogy as a whole displays little or no genuine interest in any kind of female romance beyond the privatized and emotional.[88] The more public or collectivized 'romances' of work or politics are obviously no more immune to disillusion than the personalized romance of self-realization, but it can reasonably be argued that the trilogy wins its sense of worldly disenchantment a little too easily, never having put any alternatives even to the test.

The single most crucial 'discovery' of the trilogy is that while the whole baggage of traditional romance (of marriage, motherhood, the perfect affair) can be a snare for women, any conception of sex thoroughly demystified or stripped of romance is also

87 *Country Girls Trilogy*, 45
88 *Country Girls Trilogy*, 501

equally unsatisfying. Baba's attitude to sex and self-fulfilment is always more toughly materialistic than Kate's is, but while Baba survives Kate, the trilogy itself does not. In other words, while she requires a Baba to bring Caithleen's disenchanted narrative to a close, O'Brien will always find it difficult to make a thoroughly modern 'material girl' like Baba the beginning of a satisfying new narrative. The anti-romantic Baba is always-already too impoverished of expectation, too reconciled to the limits of the actual, too little capable of dreaming, to carry an O'Brien narrative. Baba, therefore, is essentially a narrative cul-de-sac, a survivor but not the bearer of some new social values superior to those buried with Kate.

The romance of sexual emancipation is sustained as an ideal across O'Brien's trilogy only to be disclosed the more decisively in the end as a delusion. Like the national or republican socialist revolutions in O'Casey's trilogy, the sexual revolution in O'Brien is unable to live up to its own rhetoric; it is a romance that cannot be realized. That said, O'Brien does not repudiate romance as mere cant; the more dismissive satirical thrust of an O'Casey is foreign to her work. Hence the reader is not invited at the close of the trilogy to scorn Kate's dreamy romance nor to endorse Baba's values instead. Still, in a typical naturalist fashion, when the romantic values of a Kate can no longer be sustained, nothing else much remains. In O'Brien, as in Irish naturalism generally, anti-romance is deployed to negate romance, but since anti-romance is not actually a carrier of substantive alternative value in its own right, all that remains when romance has finally been cancelled out is a kind of void. Anti-romance, in other words, depends parasitically on the romance that it destroys, and thus the negation of romance inevitably produces a kind of pyrrhic ending that suggests less a clearing space for the emergence of new values than an absence of value altogether.

In the naturalist narratives of the 1960s, migration, either from the country to the city or from Ireland to England (sometimes America), recurrently functions as a device that enables plot closure. Thus the move from the rural and putatively provincial to the urban and putatively modern, or eastwards from Ireland to England, is as conventional to Irish naturalist narrative as the reverse journey 'into the West' was in the nineteenth-century national tale or in Revivalist fiction.[89] Telling the story of the Carneys, a tough working-class family from Mayo now living in emigration in Coventry, Tom Murphy's *A Whistle in the Dark* brings the mythicized national landscapes of rural western Ireland and industrial England into direct collision with each other, and suggests that to be working

---

89 In the national tale, characters tend to travel westwards from England to Ireland, occasionally stopping briefly in Dublin and then travelling on to some westerly region of Ireland. In the naturalist novel, the plot trajectory is typically in the opposite direction, beginning in the West, mid-west or midlands (in places like O'Brien's Clare, John Broderick's Athlone, McGahern's Leitrim, Murphy's Mayo), moving initially to Dublin, then on to 'exile' in England or North America. In the former, the Irish West is valorized in romantic terms as an exotic and therapeutic alternative to an enervated England; in the latter, in contrast, England allows for a certain escape from an asphyxiating Ireland, though there is little enough sense in McGahern, O'Brien or Murhpy that England can ever fully live up to its promise as an authentic source of escape.

class in one of these iconic national locations is every bit as brutalizing and oppressive as the other. A Whistle in the Dark can be viewed in this sense as a naturalist work that aims to disenchant not so much the romances of Irish nationalism or the Irish Revival as the inverted romance of emigration and modernity latent to Irish naturalism itself. In other words, if Irish naturalism is typically constituted in terms of an implicit antithesis between Ireland (construed as a site of repression and dysfunction) and emigration to some more modern place beyond Ireland (construed as a site of potential freedom and new beginnings), then Murphy's play serves to disenchant the inverted romance of escape into metropolitan modernity that is part of Irish naturalist narrative's symbolic logic. This is accomplished in A Whistle in the Dark not by re-enchanting Ireland, but by disenchanting the residual utopian associations of both western Ireland and metropolitan England alike. Yet although A Whistle in the Dark struggles more than other texts of the period to think its way through the assumptions that define Irish naturalism, the work remains nonetheless completely trapped within the logical binds it strives to overcome.

As A Whistle in the Dark construes matters, the dilemmas of the working classes and the dilemmas of Irish nationalism in a period of postwar economic liberalization are remarkably symmetrical. For both the proletarian classes in their own right and for economically 'proletarian' nations like Ireland, the new era of postwar liberal democratic modernization essentially offers two choices: either a stubbornly recalcitrant and defiant adherence to inherited class or national cultures or else an assimilationist embrace of new gentrified cultures and identities. However, the crux of the matter is that while the only available inherited cultures are deeply dysfunctional, the more respectable new ones simply rehabilitate older hierarchies and injustices in different guises. Where class is concerned, expanded state education systems appear to be a vehicle of meritocratic egalitarianism and as such to offer the working classes a welcome opportunity for self-advancement. Michael, the eldest of the Carney brothers, enthusiastically embraces education as a means to escape not only the poverty of opportunity in Ireland but also the combination of violence and shame that — within the imagination of the play at least — defines what it means to belong to a lumpen working-class culture. However, the other Carney brothers, especially Harry, dismiss the educational system as a sham, intuitively recognizing that this so-called meritocratic apparatus can operate only by dividing the world into 'clever blokes' and 'thick lads', thus actually legitimizing the hierarchical social structures education pretends to want to undo. Feeling only contempt for Michael's aspirations to better himself, the brothers dismiss his attachment to education as a deluded romance (pointing out, correctly, that for all his education Michael has progressed scarcely further up the social hierarchy than they) and heap scorn on the kind of changes it actually brings about (namely, Michael's timorous deference to superiors, his sense of superiority to his 'thick' brothers, and what they see as his emasculated distaste for physical violence). Refusing to take his lead, Harry and the others defiantly embrace the lumpen culture Michael repudiates, and are determined to assert themselves by brute force against all rivals (English, Irish, Muslim, black) in

Coventry's underworld, hoping some day to win by such means the wealth and status that Michael's individualist pursuit of self-improvement has not brought him.

What lends *A Whistle in the Dark* its bleak power is its premise that the only options on offer to the working classes are extremely limited and equally depressing. People in that class can embrace the promise of the new education system and work their way out of their inherited class cultures by means of individual self-improvement or, by refusing this route, they can hang on to their inherited culture, which, though tribal and brutal, sustains some sense of hardy self-reliance. The educational option will yield only modest returns at the collective level, and even on an individual level Michael has not ceased to be working class but merely become respectable working class. In addition, the individual who chooses advancement through education must detach himself from his natal milieu and act as a privatized subject, in effect cutting himself off from the collective. Thus, despite his desire for social mobility, even Michael vacillates and is reluctant to detach himself entirely from the larger family, and it is never quite clear in Murphy's play whether it is the rigidity of the social system or Michael's own residual attachment to his utterly dysfunctional kin that ultimately destroys him. On the other hand, if the lumpen working class takes the second option and rejects education, it can act out this refusal only by wilfully embracing stereotypes of loutishness, thus committing itself to a brutalized and brutalizing ethos shown to be deeply nihilistic.

The Hobson's choice that confronts the Carneys at the level of class repeats itself at the level of national identity. Coventry is attractive to the Carney brothers not just because it affords better economic opportunity than Mayo, but also because emigration to England allows them to escape the sense of stigma that attends their low social status in their own homeland. When they remain at home, Irishness is a disabling identity for people like the Carneys because although they are ostensibly included within the fraternal embrace of the imagined community or family of the nation, in fact they are deeply despised as only second-class members of that family. In the racially mixed society of metropolitan England, where people are racially defined as English, Paddys, Muslims or 'darkies', they can at least manipulate Irishness as a kind of tribal rallying cry to compete with other subaltern groups. However, to become fully integrated into 'normal' English society, the Carneys would have to shed not only their working-class culture but their Irishness as well, this represented in the play by the fact that Michael has married an Englishwoman, whereas Harry and the other 'hard men' embrace the identity of the drunken, brawling Paddy. If it is interpreted not just as a social problem play about class or emigration but also as a national allegory, *A Whistle in the Dark* seems to suggest that for a modernizing Ireland under Lemass, as for the working class, the choice is one between either Harry or Michael: the country can continue in bitter and resentful defiance of the world to perform a deeply dysfunctional 'heroic' and macho version of the indomitable Irish or accede to a kind of gentrification that will secure a modest respectability even though it will not change the fundamentally unequal structure of a racially defined international labour system at all.

Having set out the restricted choices available to the Carneys — whether as class or national subjects — *A Whistle in the Dark* works these up to a crisis that it cannot, however, resolve or work through. This sense of eventual impasse is clearly evident at the level of the plot, which suddenly stops in its tracks in an inconclusive manner. Throughout the play, Michael and Harry compete to persuade Des, the youngest of the Carneys, and the one with options still open, to choose between the different kinds of life they each exemplify. The death of Des at the end of the play — he is accidentally killed by Michael when the latter is hectored into a family fight by Dada, the windbag paterfamilias — symbolically represents the fact that the play cannot imagine any future beyond the imagined impasse it elaborates. When Des is killed, any sense of open-ended future dies with him. The death is very dramatic of course, but it is also something of a cop-out, since it means that the playwright does not have to make any choices between the two unhappy options he sets forth. In effect, then, the death is gratuitous: an accident intended by no one but determined by the whole violent milieu, it effectively substitutes shock or sensation for understanding since it does not help in any way to illuminate or to advance the Carneys' predicament.

Deservedly hailed as a classic of modern Irish theatre, *A Whistle in the Dark* nevertheless offers a textbook illustration of the ways in which Irish naturalism typically works up a tragic predicament that must then be aborted or smothered, since the demands of verisimilitude dictate that the predicament in question can never become the subject of serious intellectual deliberation. It is as though, on the one hand, these works look to the suffering of some subaltern section of society as the authentic stuff of tragedy while assuming, on the other hand, that if the subalterns in question are to be authentically or realistically depicted, then they cannot be shown to be capable of articulate cognition. One of the basic compositional antinomies of *A Whistle in the Dark* is that Harry is supposed to be the voice of the 'thick' group of Carney brothers, and Michael and Des the actual or potential 'bright' boys of the pack, but in fact the plot logically requires that Harry must actually be much the more decisively intelligent. If, after all, an audience is to be persuaded that Michael's optimistic confidence in the possibilities of education as an avenue to social mobility is rather naïve, then this can only be managed if Harry is somehow sharp enough to cut through Michael's deluded optimism with some conviction. Should Harry fail to unmask Michael's faith in the system, an audience can only conclude that Harry's resentment against the school system is only a mask for his own inadequacies and, by extension, that stupidity and a whiny blaming-the-system attitude are indeed the only real impediment to working-class mobility.

As it happens, the play does tilt things Harry's way by suggesting that Michael is a well-meaning but rather unimpressive individual and that Harry's brutalist worldview is in many respects less self-deluded than Michael's. But since Harry must simultaneously deconstruct the optimism of Michael while still representing the thick lads — those always doomed to be the rejects of the meritocratic education system — the logic of verisimilitude seems to demand that he can never be allowed to develop his worldview in any genuinely articulate way. After all, if the thick Harry's critique was suddenly to become verbally sophisticated, then the whole conceptual architecture of the play would suddenly buckle in on itself. There is a very telling moment just before the climactic showdown when Des is killed, when Harry, his confidence and sense of personal authority in full flush after a viciously-won victory over a rival gang, seems to be about to slice through the garrulous self-deceptions of Michael, Des and Dada (all three bright boys) only suddenly to discover that he has exhausted his vocabulary:

> HARRY: I could admire he saying he's no money. It's the other — the — the other things — the — the
> DADA: Implications, Henry.
> HARRY: Things! He doesn't think we can think straight. The things that's behind him. The things — where does he stand? Getting fed two sides, like. The sort of — the — the —
> DADA: Implications.
> HARRY: Things! (He kicks a chair)[90]

The difficulty here, clearly, is that if Harry was intellectually to expose the condescension that the supposedly intelligent habitually display towards those deemed thick and stupid, then he could not be all that stupid to begin with. As so often in naturalism, the audience is invited to identify with the tragic dilemmas of the lowly, but since realism seems to require that the lowly and oppressed must not themselves be capable of coming to any truly articulate intellectual self-consciousness of their situation, then that labour of interpretation has to remain outside the structure of the work itself. In other words, since the subaltern characters cannot provide an intellectual interpretation of their own situation, this task must be left to the supposedly superior intellect of the audience, which must feel itself competent to complete the gaps and to finish the sentences that Harry himself cannot. A Whistle in the Dark is sufficiently self-conscious of this dilemma to have an abrasively defiant character like Harry recognize the condescension at work here: he snarls at Dada, Michael and Des: 'Things are clear enough to me. There's been so many good intelligent blokes for so long explaining things to thick lads.'[91] But even if he is sharp enough to resent the intelligent blokes who presume to speak for thick lads like him, the logic of the play still requires him to remain one of the thick lads, and this in turn seems to dictate that his resentment can only emerge as an inchoate primal force — some terrifyingly violent, elemental force welling up from the dark, but that cannot illuminate it.

Like many naturalist works, A Whistle in the Dark sets out to shock its middle-class audience by confronting it with some horrifically violent underworld. But in order to do

90 Thomas Murphy, A Whistle in the Dark (Dublin, 1970), 68
91 A Whistle in the Dark, 69

this 'realistically', it seems to accept that it must show the creatures of this underworld to be struggling inarticulately against appalling odds, and hence it is left to the audience to try to make sense of things in a way that the victims themselves supposedly cannot. Were an Irish audience to approach this work not as a social problem play but as a national allegory, and were it therefore to identify with the Carneys not so much as working-class subjects but as fellow Irish nationals, then things obviously become more complex. In such circumstances, the impasse that the play identifies — choosing between a submissive modernizing gentrification and a defiant but nihilistic mode of recalcitrant Irishness — has to be recognized as one that confronts not only the lowly emigrant but Irish society as a whole. However, even if Murphy's play is to be taken as a national allegory, the fact that the tragic impasse is elaborated only then to be aborted by the non-resolution of Des's death seems to suggest a considerable helplessness at this level of meaning also. If neither the characters nor the action can illuminate that tragic impasse, then the audience may well conclude that if the only choice is between Harry and Michael, then there is really no choice at all.

The third generation naturalist works discussed here all represent different 'solutions' to a common problematic. For all these narratives, Ireland is the place both of affect (often inscribed in the form of a dead or suffering or abused mother) and of atrocity (recurrently identified with a brutal, authoritarian, disastrously inadequate father). England, America or the city may offer exits of a kind from Irish atrocity, but they typically prove to be emotionally sterile places that allow for no re-enchantment of the world, no decisive recovery of new purpose and destiny. Thus Moore's Ireland-repudiating early novels are set in an asphyxiated Belfast, but his later ones unfold in a cold, affectless North America. McGahern's young men are crushed in the country, but the city offers them no rejuvenation, and the countryside remains the magnetic pole to which the later novels will always return. O'Brien's young heroines set off in high excitement to discover 'neon fairylands' in Dublin or London only to suffer there newer versions of the unsatisfying relationships they leave behind. The Carneys exchange the crushing class system of Mayo for the lethal racial hatreds of Coventry. In naturalist narrative, in other words, Ireland may be the site of atrocity, but as such it will at least afford a plot of suffering and endurance, of coming through and leave-taking. Exile, on the other hand, may offer an exit from such atrocity, but it seems to work better as a device to mark an end to the old national romance rather than as one that signifies the opening up of some authentic new departure, since the world beyond Ireland is typically conceived as a place where one simply exchanges a narrative of endurance and escape for a loss of narrative momentum altogether.

In the second stage of Irish naturalism, the repressive reality of the 'real' Ireland is exposed in order to show the hollowness of the national romances of the Irish Revival. For the third generation of naturalists, these Revivalist romances of nationalist or socialist or cultural revolution are no longer even at issue. When these historically archaic romances survive at all in 1960s narratives, they do so only as the deadweight of history incarnated in the form of tyrannical War-of-Independence-surviving fathers that must now be escaped if the protagonists are to have any chance to live. Since for this third generation, then, Ireland is always-already almost entirely bereft of romance and become virtually synonymous with a monochrome grey repression, the romances of sexual emancipation or of modernity acquire a powerful allure because they offer a way out of this Stygian Hibernian gloom. The naturalist fictions of the 1960s trade heavily on the attraction of these new romances: the ideals of escaping Catholic repression into sexual self-discovery or of leaving behind rural parochialism and philistinism to become modern and cosmopolitan are what motivate the protagonists in their adolescent pilgrimages out of the Irish dark. But given the constitutive logic of naturalism, a resolutely negative mode committed by reflex to the slaughter of romantic ideals, it is scarcely surprising that sexual emancipation or modernity should transpire in their turn also to be romances that seduce only to delude and betray.

The shattered family romance of Ireland will never be restored in these 1960s narratives, but the romances of sexual revolution or of modernity eventually survive, when they survive at all, only when they in their turn have shed their initial lustre and are downsized to more modest proportions. Hence, the typical narrative disposition in these works is one in which it is accepted that that journey into global capitalist modernity must indeed be made, but that it must be travelled without grand illusions or great expectations. For all that they try to shock their implicitly middle-class audiences out of their supposed complacency, these forms thus disclose in the end a structure of feeling that corresponds quite closely, in curious ways, to the 'there is no alternative' mentality of the Irish state élites that have managed Ireland's long Lemassian voyage into the global capitalist order ever since the old romance of national self-reliance was discarded.

It may well be the case that historically there was actually no alternative and that Irish society did indeed have few substantial options to choose between. Ireland's postcolonial accommodation to global free-market capitalism has after all patently proved the rule rather than the exception, and the line of states that emerged from twentieth-century nationalist or socialist revolutions, hoping to create some new society, only sooner or later to find themselves submitting to the neo-liberal version of modernization is now a lengthy one. Even so, one of the functions of any strongly radical art is not to ratify the apparently inexorable order of things, but to imagine how life might possibly be otherwise, to wrest some sense of alternative from the meshes of the actual. All too often, when all other romances have been negated in these naturalist narratives, the romance of their own radicalism is the only one that remains intact.

6

What general conclusions will an historical survey of this kind afford? First, it must be stated that any literary mode that includes texts such as *Dubliners*, the O'Casey trilogy,

The Great Hunger, The Country Girls trilogy, *A Whistle in the Dark, The Dark* or *Amongst Women* demands acknowledgement and respect. Naturalism has clearly been one of the more significant and fertile aesthetic modes in twentieth-century Irish literature, and it makes no sense to deprecate such works — in literary critical terms that take modernist norms as their starting point — as archaic or regressive simply because they are not experimental in a modernist or postmodernist sense. The most accomplished works of Irish naturalism suffer a little when compared to the most accomplished works of the Irish Revival or Irish modernism, but Irish naturalism has managed nonetheless to sustain and renew itself more than either of the Revivalist or modernist aesthetic modes have done. In the closing decade of the last century, the 1960s naturalism of the kind associated with Brian Moore, John McGahern, Tom Murphy or Edna O'Brien seems to have been superseded by a new neo-naturalism exemplified by writers such as Martin McDonagh, Robert McLiam Wilson or Patrick McCabe. In this neo-naturalism, the older tropes and conventions of naturalism are recycled in a more knowing and self-conscious and often deliberately exaggerated and ludic or parodic manner. The emergence of this neo-naturalism may signal that well-established naturalist conventions have finally become exhausted through overuse and overfamiliarity, and can function now only when they are deployed with a self-reflexive tongue-in-cheek irony. Yet comic versions of naturalism are not exactly new either; they were also quite pronounced in the 1950s. It may well be the case, therefore, that the current spate of neo-naturalist works may signal only the exhaustion of that particular stand of naturalism that had become dominant since the 1960s, and not of naturalism *per se*. Whatever the truth of the matter, naturalism has certainly had a long innings in Irish literature and this is something that calls for historical explanation rather than deprecation.

Second, as this chapter has shown, many of the criticisms conventionally levelled at naturalism generally, and at Irish naturalism more specifically, tend to be reductive. The tendency to dismiss naturalism *tout court* simply as a morbidly pessimistic or defeatist determinism is an instance in point. After all, it can easily be argued that Beckett's modernism is much more intransigently pessimistic than any Irish naturalist work and yet it would normally be considered rather philistine to berate Beckett on that account. To depict the oppressive and miserable side of human existence is not in itself necessarily to be a pessimist; a keen sense of the wretchedness of existence has always been essential to any strong tragic vision or to the development of any genuinely politically committed art or indeed to most forms of comic art. Pessimism and optimism are best conceived not as reified temperaments but as dialectically interconnected conditions. The pessimism with which someone like Adorno, for example, surveys the 'fallen' world of modern mass culture and the 'administered society' is logically the verso of his virtually utopian conception of the freedom that humankind had the potential to achieve, even if it had failed to do so. Conversely, someone who had never expected much of humankind in the first instance, someone convinced that the kinds of freedom Adorno aspired to were absurdly impossible, would have much less reason for pessimism than Adorno, for where aspiration is limited, the capacity for disappointment must be also.

What this chapter has shown, hopefully, is that what distinguishes naturalism is neither its determinism nor its pessimism as such, but, rather the tension inherent to the mode between the drive, on the one hand, to break through the veneer of civilization in order to disclose its underlying brutality, this drive motivated by an interest in social reform, and, on the other hand, an innate scepticism towards all forms of idealism or utopianism, the latter distrusted as extravagant romantic fantasies that only diminish our capacity to confront the full awfulness of the actual. If the naturalist mode has an innate weakness it is not, then, that it is too gloomy or too grim, but that it is so frequently unable to bring its socially reformist impulse and its drive to demystify, to disenchant and to debunk into any kind of productive dialectical relationship. It is always easier to create narratives that expose to view the more corrupt and brutal dimensions of a society than it is to offer narratives capable of expressing both an intellectually strenuous and a concretely sensuous historical sense of why that society should ever have become as it is, or to offer any imaginative vision as to how it might ever become otherwise. If there is a case to be made against the depiction of Irish society in naturalist fiction, it is not that naturalism is too hard on Irish society, but rather that the mode does not press its own informing criteria of evaluation and assessment hard enough.

Third, from a specifically leftist standpoint, the thing that discomfits most about the naturalist mode in an Irish context is that it should at once be the most socially engaged and overtly political literature that the country has produced and that its conception of the historical and the political should at the same time be so drastically narrow. One of the most striking features of the naturalist mode, from Moore to the early Joyce, from O'Casey to Kavanagh, from McGahern to O'Brien, is that despite the recurrent indictments of the social conditions in Ireland, there is so little substantive interest in Irish politics or in Irish political struggle as such. Naturalism may be modern Ireland's most overtly politicized literary mode, but it is nevertheless a mode that tends to treat politics as such remarkably reductively. O'Casey's drama is the worse as drama (let alone the more limited politically) because it reduces Pearse and the 1916 rebels to cartoonish versions of themselves. For O'Connor and O'Faolain, literature is conceived as an instrument capable of changing society, yet the mechanics of social change seem scarcely ever to be an object of serious reflection in their own fiction. In the works of the generations of naturalists that come after Kavanagh, it is as though the country had no political life worth the writer's attention at all; no feminists or socialists or republicans or liberal Catholics or Protestants committed to change; no community groups, no rural or urban co-operatives, no student organizations or trade unions or grassroots associations agitating for improvement. While all of these writers have offered eloquent indictments of the oppressiveness of Irish society, one will search their works in vain for any equally compelling or memorable depiction of the many who have collectively struggled with the resources to hand to transform that society or at the very least to mitigate its ills. One contemporary Irish writer has remarked that the scene in John McGahern's *Amongst*

Women that impresses him most is that in which two local politicians attend the burial of Moran, each vying with the other to be noticed by the assembled mourners, then falling back 'in amiable conspiratorial camaraderie, sometimes turning their heads to look back to the crowd gathered about the grave in undisguised contempt'.[92] Politicians do indeed behave something like this at funerals but, even so, this passage may still be more indicative of McGahern's weakness than of his strengths as a writer. Might it not be argued, after all, that in cameos such as this McGahern settles for an all-too-easy dismissal of politics as mere gombeenism and, in so doing, actually betrays an inability to integrate the political dimensions of Irish society into his fiction in some more forceful and compelling fashion. A depreciative comic sketch such as this is all very well but it is easily accomplished, and where it substitutes for an articulated political vision it may be considered a defect rather than a strength.

Commenting on naturalism in the United States, Malcolm Cowley has observed that:

> Many naturalistic works are valuable historical documents, but the authors in general have little sense of history. They present each historical situation as if it had no historical antecedents, and their characters might be men and women created yesterday morning, so few signs do they show of having roots in the past.[93]

Something rather similar might be observed of Irish naturalism. There can be no strongly historicized structure of feeling where there is not some acute sense that the organizational structures of society in the past were different to those that obtain now and that those that obtain now might well be subject in their turn to some kind of radical transformation in the future. For all its indictment of Irish society, Irish naturalism possesses very little sensibility of this kind. The condition of paralysis that Joyce attributed to Dublin is actually a defining condition of the naturalist worldview, and hence that sense of stasis returns again and again in the works of O'Casey, Kavanagh, McGahern, Murphy and the rest, even though these works themselves are, oddly enough, typically conscripted into a literary criticism that stresses how they contributed to a changing, modernizing, maturing Ireland. One might speculate that the sense of paralysis that so preoccupies Irish naturalism is not only native to the aesthetic, as Lukács complained, but also an effect of the country's historically peripheral and subordinate inscription within the global capitalist order — the by-product of an historical condition that has allowed Irish society (like other peripheral societies of its kind) only extremely limited scope for historical manoeuvre and only a very limited sense that it could ever command its own future. To argue this would be to suggest that

---

92 John McGahern, *Amongst Women* (London, 1990), 183. For the appreciative commentary on the funeral scene, see Joseph O'Connor, 'John McGahern', in Anthony Roche, ed., *The UCD Aesthetic* (Dublin, 2005) 183–89, 188

93 Malcolm Cowley, 'A Natural History of American Naturalism', in George Becker, ed., *Documents of Modern Literary Realism* (Princeton, 1963), 429–51, 446

Ireland's historically underdeveloped economy and the development of Irish naturalism are connected in ways more complex than this chapter has been able to disclose. But even were this shown to be the case, naturalism would still remain more interesting as an aesthetic *symptom* of a national condition, rather than as a sophisticated aesthetic *diagnostic* of that condition.

Whatever the merits of this or that naturalist work, one of the most limiting aspects of naturalism as a distinct literary mode, therefore, is its conception of what constitutes a political art. The naturalist tendency to want to shock its middle-class audience by exhibiting to its view some brutalized subaltern segment of society, while simultaneously appealing to the middle class to socially concern itself with the fate of those it has apparently brutalised has already been discussed here. Naturalism of this sort seems continually to want to indict the middle class for crimes that class would apparently prefer to ignore, while at the same time recognizing the middle class as the only real court of social appeal. However much it sets out to *épater les bourgeois*, the bourgeoisie always remains naturalism's fundamental addressee. In naturalist writing, oppressed and exploited subaltern constituencies are objects worthy of representation, but scarcely ever subjects to be addressed in their own right. One could almost say, therefore, that naturalism is the name we can give to one kind of aesthetic impasse that recurrently emerges when a dissident literary reformism directed at the middle classes runs up against its own constitutive limits.

This would strongly suggest that the thing most urgently needed to develop a post-naturalist political art in Ireland is not some more optimistic or upbeat outlook, but rather a conception of art less tied to the idea of simultaneously attacking and appealing to the sensitivities of the middle classes. The creation of such an art would require, first, the development of a more intellectually rigorous appreciation of the antinomies of naturalism, and, second, the development of a far greater level of interest (on the part of both writers and cultural critics) in the whole complex of institutions — schools, universities, theatre houses, academies, publishing corporations, advertisement industries — that structure cultural production and consumption in our times. There is considerable evidence that over the last decade or more there are many Irish writers who have wanted to develop new aesthetic practices that are simultaneously both post-modernist and post-naturalist. Unfortunately, there is little evidence to suggest that many of the writers in question have any greatly developed sense of just what might be required to do this. A radical art cannot be voluntarily willed into existence and a chasing after more up-to-date literary fashions elsewhere is not likely to be of much help either. Some forms of contemporary magical realist and postmodernist art, for example, have much greater technical versatility and a more capacious worldview than is common in Irish naturalism. It is quite possible to imagine that elements of these forms could be grafted onto what would nonetheless remain a fundamentally naturalist conception of the world, such graftings effecting an appearance of change that would serve to disguise only a fundamental continuity.

In the cultural field, as in any other, substantive change usually requires two different but complementary types of labour: an energetic and open-minded commitment to literary experiment (much of which can be expected to fail, but which ought not to be dismissed entirely on that account), and a painstaking commitment to diagnosing the historical and structural conditions of operation of the field itself. Without a commitment to experiment and intellectual labour of these kinds, Irish cultural production in the early twenty-first century seems more likely to repeat the shortcomings of naturalism than to develop in new and more radical directions.

Into which West?
Modernity, Moving Images and the Maternal Supernatural

Cinema in Ireland is usually said to have begun in Dublin on 20 April 1896 with the first public screenings of films in Dan Lowrey's Star of Erin Theatre of Varieties (now the Olympia). However, moments of origin are always a slippery business and it might be argued that cinematography had already made a controversial appearance in Ireland some seventeen years earlier, not in Dublin but in the small rural village of Knock, County Mayo on the night of 21 August 1879, where fifteen people claimed to have witnessed an apparition of the Blessed Virgin against the outside gable wall of the local parish church. For those sceptical about the authenticity of this apparition, the hypothesis of cinematographic projection was one way to rationalize the inexplicable, to demystify the apparently supernatural. The sceptics argued that even if the fraudulent collusion of the witnesses was ruled out, the apparition could still be explained by rational means. Those who viewed the apparaition, it was suggested, were themselves the victims of an ocular delusion achieved either by the projecton of an image of the Blessed Virgin onto the gable wall of the church by some sort of magic lantern or, alternatively, by the painting of the figure onto the wall of the church with a phosphorescent substance which might later have been illuminated with a magnesium lamp.

The hypothesis that the Marian apparition was really the work of a hidden projectionist deceiving credulous villagers is one that would seem to place cinematography in this instance firmly on the side of a secular materialist rationalism. Cinematography, that is to say, figures as yet another instrument in the arsenal of what Max Weber described as the rationalist 'disenchantment' of the world. Yet things are not altogether so clear-cut as this suggests. After all, the idea that the supposed apparition might naturally be accounted for as an ocular delusion, produced by a hidden projectionist, was first advanced not by some anti-clerical rationalist, but rather by a Dr. Francis Lennon, a member of the Catholic clergy and Professor of Physics at St. Patrick's College, Maynooth. Dr. Lennon advanced this theory in his report to Archbishop Cavanagh, who had asked him to investigate the circumstances of the apparition shortly after it had occurred. It would be all too simple to reduce the events at Knock and the subsequent struggle to make sense of them to a straightforward opposition between religious irrationalism or supernaturalism and materialist or Enlightenment rationalism. As Cavanagh's appointment of a clerical professor of physics to investigate a supposed manifestation of the supernatural would suggest, what we have is a considerably more complex affair, in which the late nineteenth-century Catholic Church found itself in the awkward position of having to negotiate between the evidentiary standards of a modern scientific secular worldview and a belief in the possibility of the miraculous, inherent in its own doctrines.

The notion that the apparition might well have been only a 'trick' of the camera is one that comes freighted in any event with the inference that cinematography itself belongs intrinsically to the category of the fraudulent: cinematography is construed, in other words, not as an instrument of rational demystification, but rather as a technology of mystification or perhaps re-enchantment — one capable of simulating its own 'false' version of the experience of the miraculous. From its inception, and in ways that speculation about a hidden projectionist being the material source of the apparition at Knock seems curiously to anticipate, there is a suggestion that cinema itself has a capacity to function for the masses in the way religion had also done. It too was conceived as a technology of wonder and rapture, an instrument of mass delusion, an elaborate apparatus of dubious consolation in an alienated world. As the technologies of cinema and mass media generally began to extend their sway over modern society, they were accompanied by strong currents of twentieth-century cultural critique that charged them with many of the negative functions once attributed to religion: both religion and mass media tended to be understood essentially as 'opiates' called into existence by the supposed unhappiness of the masses, their function to assuage that unhappiness in ways compatible with the preservation of the existing social order.[1]

1   In his analysis of the early years of cinema in Europe, Noël Burch contends that the Catholic Church was conscious from the start that cinema was a dangerous rival. See Burch, *Life to those Shadows* (London, 1990), 77–78 n.13. The association of the cinema with a kind of mindless rapture continues to be insinuated in a work such as Guy Debord's *The Society of the Spectacle* (Paris, 1967), with its famous cover image of a cinema audience transfixed before the screen in a pose that might recall that of worshippers before an apparition. One might also think in this context of Theodor Adorno's essays on the occult and mass culture collected in Stephen Crook, ed., *Adorno: The Stars Down to Earth and Other Essays on the Irrational in Culture* (London, 1994). However, Burch stresses that the various churches did not simply fulminate against the cinema; they were also among the first to try to deploy the new technology to their own ends in things such as temperance campaigns or to propagate church doctrine. To date, Irish film studies has tended to pose the question of the relationship between church and cinema in Ireland almost exclusively in terms of censorship. The issue of censorship is certainly crucial, but it has tended to pit the churches and cinema as polarized antagonists and hence to deflect interest from some of the more complex ways in which the various churches and cinema compete with or indeed co-operate with each other. For pioneering works

For the sociologist or anthropologist of religion, the wave of Marian apparitions in nineteenth-century Europe — at least nine major apparitions occurred in the period between 1830 and 1933; five in France, two in Belgium, one each in Portugal and Ireland — is generally interpreted as part of a wider struggle between an advancing Enlightenment and a religious conception of the world now in retreat.[2] At a time in Europe when a secular rationalist outlook was increasingly becoming the intellectual dominant, popular Catholic acceptance of the Marian apparitions argued a recalcitrant belief in the supernatural that remained stubbornly defiant of the prevailing secularizing trends. The establishment of supernaturalist doctrines as dogmas of Catholicism, such as that of the Immaculate Conception in 1854, can be seen as gestures on the part of the Church authorities that gave ecclesiastical lead or sanction to this defiance.[3]

However, in the latter half of nineteenth century, Roman Catholicism was not the only intellectual system for which the figure of what might loosely be termed the 'Great Mother' would become an issue of considerable importance. In 1861 Johann Jakob Bachofen, a Swiss-German student of philosophy and ancient law, published his work Das Mutterrecht, the first scientific study of the family, which challenged existing conceptions of patriarchy as the originary social form by arguing that it was in fact only a late evolutionary development that had emerged after the overthrow of an earlier matriarchal stage of human history when women had dominated social and cultural institutions. Positing not only the historical priority of matrilineality over patrilineality, Bachofen also construed the matriarchal stage of human history as a condition of harmony with nature and as a lost epoch of human happiness before a male revolt led to the establishment of a more alienated, dominative, masculine-oriented modern civilization. Bachofen's work was a product of nineteenth-century romantic idealism, but the 'travelling theory' of the matriarchate was to have a considerable impact on the development of nineteenth-century sociology, and on thinkers as various as Simmel, Freud and Nietzsche. It would

that venture in new directions, see Lance Pettitt, *Screening Ireland* (Manchester, 1999), 82–85, and Sunniva O'Flynn, 'Black and White and Collar Films: Exploring the Irish Film Archive Collections of Clerical Films', in Ruth Barton and Harvey O'Brien, eds., *Keeping It Real: Irish Film and Television* (London, 2004), 39–51.

2 See, for instance, Victor Turner, *Image and Pilgrimage in Christian Culture* (Oxford, 1978). Turner observes that the period after 1830 saw a marked increase in Marian apparitions in Europe, and that these were increasingly associated with warnings of dire calamities to be visited on mankind if it did not repent and mend its ways, thus constituting 'a kind of Catholic millenarianism' (149). He notes that the nineteenth century and the first half of the twentieth century have constituted what has been called, in Catholic circles, the Age of Mary, but other commentators have argued that there was no sustained decline in Marian devotion in the latter half of the twentieth century. While post-Vatican II reformers may have emphasized the importance of Christ and Scripture and de-emphasized the role of Mary proportionately, the ascension of Pope John Paul II in 1978, with his motto 'Totus Tuus sum, Maria', and his many subsequent pilgrimages to Marian shrines, which received huge media coverage, is said to have dramatically rekindled devotion to Mary in the twentieth-century *fin de siècle*. The controversial but soon highly attended Marian apparitions beginning in June 1981 in Medjugorje in Yugoslavia and the 'moving statues' episode in Ireland in 1985 must be situated in this wider context.

3 See Marina Warner, *Alone of All Her Sex* (London, 1985), 236–37.

eventually find its way into socialist thought by way of Friedrich Engels's *The Origin of the Family, Private Property and the State* (1884). Although critical of what he held to be Bachofen's idealist treatment of mother-right, and leaning more heavily on the work of the American Lewis Henry Morgan, whom he believed to have put the topic onto a more solidly materialist footing, Engels accepted the notion of the matriarchate as a general phase in human history, one which was only superseded with the development of private property and the formation of class society. Twentieth-century Euro-American anthropology would generally come to reject the idea of the matriarchate and relegate it to the status of a curiosity in the history of the discipline, but the concept retained a certain currency both in Soviet anthropology and in Western popular culture long afterwards. In certain forms of radical feminism, in some strands of the ecological movement, and in many New Age subcultures in the West, the idea of the matriarchate would even enjoy something of a resurgence in the late twentieth century.[4]

What is of interest here is the way in which the figure of the 'Great Mother' seems to acquire a certain prominence from the nineteenth century in a whole variety of discourses — religious, romantic, sociological, anthropological, socialistic, feminist, ecological, and so forth — that are clearly doctrinally diverse, indeed often fundamentally at odds with one another. The meaning and function of the Great Mother patently varies from one to the other, but what they all appear to share in common is a certain dissatisfaction with some or other element of the project of modernity. In each case, the deployment of the figure of the Great Mother would seem to be pivotal to the expression of this dissatisfaction. Whether it takes the secular form of some matriarchal epoch before the advent of capitalism and private property, or the religious form of Marian apparitions mourning or admonishing the sins and excesses of modernity (with secularism generally and socialism or Communism more specifically commonly held to be the chief of these), or radical feminist attempts to recover some sense of the significance of women written out of memory by millennia of patriarchy, the figure of the Great Mother operates in all of these different modalities as a nebulous but powerful signifier of a utopian desire for some alternative to the world as it presently exists.[5]

Viewed against this wider historical and intellectual context, the events in Knock in

4 For a discussion of the modern genealogy of the matriarchate, see Carolyn Fluehr-Lobban, 'A Marxist Reappraisal of the Matriarchate', *Current Anthropology*, 20, 2 (1979), 341–48. Fluehr-Lobban suggests that in none of Marx's writings on primitive communist societies is there any suggestion that he accepted the historical priority of the matriarchate and that Marx's reservation on the subject is consistent with his generally more tentative attitude to the whole notion of primitive communism. See also on Bachofen, Elizabeth Fee, 'The Sexual Politics of Victorian Social Anthropology', in Mary Hartman and Lois W. Banner, eds., *Clio's Consciousness Raised: New Perspectives on the History of Women* (New York, 1974) and Rita Felski, 'On Nostalgia: The Prehistoric Woman', in *The Gender of Modernity* (Cambridge, MA, 1995), 35–60. See also Walter Benjamin's discussion of Bachofen in *The Arcades Project*, trans. Howard Eiland and Kevin McLaughlin (Cambridge, MA, and London, 1999), 361 [Convolute J75a].

5 It should be clear that the reference here is *not* to all forms of socialist or feminist or ecologist thought, but only to strands within each.

1879 begin to seem less provincial, less a manifestation of Irish exceptionalism, than they are sometimes assumed to be. Moreover, the issues provoked by those events have more than a merely historical interest, since they have continued to resonate in various ways in the late twentieth century as well. In 1985, for example, Ireland was to experience a series of Marian apparitions right across the countryside, in places such as Ballinspittle in County Cork and Carns in west Sligo. The fact that thousands of people gathered to witness these apparitions was widely held at the time to be a sign of some deep malaise in Irish society, though opinions differed widely as to how to interpret that malaise.[6] Were this late twentieth-century Irish fascination with the figure of the Great Mother restricted to the 'moving statue' apparitions, it would be easy to conceive of the phenomenon as an exclusively rural Irish Catholic affair and to dismiss it as a symptom of morbidity, as the 'last gasp' of a collapsing rural dispensation, and hence as something essentially marginal to the preoccupations of an increasingly secular and urbanized Ireland. There is some reason to query this supposition, however, since in the secularized world of Irish mass culture the haunting figure of the Great Mother continued to make its presence felt as well. For instance, in 1991 Dermot Bolger's play *One Last White Horse*, performed in the Peacock Theatre, told the story of a Dublin heroin addict, Eddie, who experienced recurrent hallucinations of a white horse, which transpired to be the spirit of his mother who is in turn linked in the play to Mary, the suffering mother of Christ.[7] Drawing on a similar set of images and associations, the 1992 film *Into the West*, scripted by Jim Sheridan and directed by Mike Newell, also revolved around the figure of a spirit-mother who returned in the form of a white horse to rescue her family from a condition of material and psychic distress in Dublin's Ballymun towers.[8] In the same decade, Sinéad O'Connor,

6   The 'moving statues' episode in the summer of 1985 emerged against a complex and conflicted national and international context. As noted above, the period after Vatican II (1962–65) was widely perceived as one in which many customary forms of devotion to Mary were being downgraded by liberal reformists in the Catholic Church, but this also had the effect of mobilizing more traditionalist Catholics, who mounted strong resistance to such developments. Pope John Paul II went to the Marian shrine in Knock during his visit to Ireland in 1979; the Medjugorje apparitions in Yugoslavia in 1981 were much publicized in Ireland in the early 1980s and helped to renew already established forms of Marianism such as the strongly anti-Communist and catastrophist Fatima cult; and domestically a whole series of conservative Irish Catholic movements, often overlapping with or enlisting Marian organizations, were campaigning in favour of inserting a 'pro-life' (anti-abortion) amendment to the Constitution of the Irish Republic in 1983 and against the removal of the ban on divorce in 1986. The passing in 1985 of a Family Planning Bill by the Fine Gael–Labour coalition led by Garret FitzGerald (a move strongly opposed by Fianna Fáil), which liberalized the sale of contraceptives, was viewed at the time as a major reverse for conservative Catholicism. For a recent survey of Anglophone Marianism in modern Ireland, see James S. Donnelly, Jr., 'Opposing the "Modern World": The Cult of the Virgin Mary in Ireland, 1965-85', *Éire-Ireland*, 39, 1–2 (2004), 183–245.
7   Dermot Bolger, *One Last White Horse*, in *A Dublin Quartet* (Harmondsworth, 1992)
8   *Into the West* was Jim Sheridan's first film script, and was originally to have been directed by Robert Dornhelm, but was eventually directed by the English director, Mike Newell. The film shares many preoccupations that recur in later Sheridan films, and will be referred to here in shorthand, and in order to avoid the cumbersome Newell–Sheridan locution, as a Jim Sheridan work. For Sheridan's comments on the film, see Ruth Barton, 'Interview with Jim Sheridan', in her *Jim Sheridan: Framing the Nation* (Dublin, 2002), 139–54, 154.

Ireland's most controversial female singer, was writing about what she described as 'Ireland's massive loss of contact with any kind of spirituality'. In an interview in the *Irish Times* in 1995, O'Connor argued that this loss of spirituality was part of an Irish cultural trauma brought about as a result of English conquest, the Famine, the loss of the Gaelic language, and an attendant loss of cultural memory. The widespread problems of alcoholism and drug addiction in modern Irish society, she contended, were symptoms of a general emptiness in that society, a manifestation of a spiritual desolation that could best be overcome by renewing contact with a God whom she preferred to think of as a woman. The unconditional love and compassion of God, O'Connor suggested, are best thought of in maternal terms since: 'A mother is connected to a baby by an umbilical cord; a man is never connected to a baby in that way. God is something that's connected to me no matter what I do.'[9] Her 1994 album, *Universal Mother*, O'Connor remarked in the same interview, represented her attempt to work through her own personal version of the collective cultural traumas to which she referred.

However much they might differ otherwise, the moving statues episode, Bolger's play, Sheridan's film, and Sinéad O'Connor's conception of Irish history all rehearse strangely cognate constructions of contemporary Irish reality. In each case, a lack or hollowness is posited at the heart of Irish modernity, and it is this lack that then generates an appeal to the figure of the Great Mother, who serves somehow both to register and to assuage the suffering involved. It would be tempting to conclude that this simply represents the reduction of a complex history to a regressive late twentieth-century pop psychology, but the fact that this gendered narrativization of things has a complex intellectual history that stretches back into the nineteenth century, and a currency sinuous enough to stretch from popular Catholicism into the very different world of mass culture, suggests that the cargo of anxieties expressed in these narratives of the Great Mother is real and heavy. In this chapter, therefore, I want to tease out some of the implications of this construction of things in late twentieth-century Irish popular culture, primarily by way of an analysis of Jim Sheridan's *Into the West*. In Sheridan's film, I argue, a cluster of social anxieties, about everything from the historical direction of Irish society to the atomization and alienation of modern life to the role of religion or cinema in all of this, converge around the figure of the spirit-mother, and do so in ways that can ultimately be shown to be symptomatic not only of contemporary Irish society but of the wider historical moment as well.

2

Given that Ireland had made a very distinctive contribution to the development of nineteenth-century gothic literature — the names of Maturin, Le Fanu, Stoker and Wilde being only the most noteworthy in this regard — it seems somewhat odd that cinematic

9   John Waters, 'Sinéad The Keener', *Irish Times*, 28 Jan. 1995

narratives of the supernatural in Ireland appear largely to have bypassed this rich literary inheritance and to have turned more commonly for inspiration to the more marvellous mode of the fairy tale and the folk tale. The 'supernatural Ireland' of the big screen has tended, at any rate, to be a world more readily associated with fairies and leprechauns than with vampires and ghouls and haunted aristocratic houses or the terrors and ecstasies of religious mania. In the feudalized ambience of the gothic mode, the sense of the supernatural characteristically attaches itself to the claustrophobic interiors and dark declivities of the Big House or it emanates from sites of historical atrocity, carrying with it a distinct whiff of corruption and degeneration. In the quite different world of the fairy or folk tale, however, stemming perhaps from the pre-capitalist origins of these forms, the supernatural more commonly clings to or infuses the out-of-door spaces of the landscape itself; a sense of magic or the marvellous is linked to woods and mountains or to liminal sites of some sort where human and other-worlds converge.[10]

While it is conventional enough to depreciate the kitschy banality of cinematic constructions of this mode, a more materialist criticism might probably wish to explain why cinema should generally have preferred to take its cues from the Ireland of folk or fairy tale rather than to plunder the archive of the more sinister, sadistic world of the gothic novel. Part of the answer undoubtedly has to do with the fact that in cinema generally, and in American cinema especially perhaps, 'Ireland' has tended very commonly to stand as a veritable signifier of the positively or benignly pre-modern, its landscape 'magical' precisely to the degree that the country can be made to appear a pleasingly archaic one that stands outside of the world of advanced capitalism altogether. In films such as *Finian's Rainbow* or *Darby O'Gill and the Little People*, Ireland becomes a magical landscape suffused with a strong Anglo-American nostalgia for a lost world of the pre-industrial past, a place not yet disenchanted by capitalism and its modern technologies, but not part of the darkly feudal world of the gothic aesthetic either. At the risk of stretching things a bit, it might even be argued that this cinematic construction of a fantastic fairy-tale Ireland — its landscape still numinous with wonder, its narratives free of the constraints of realism — represents some kind of low-brow version of those forms of magic realism (*real maravilloso*) nowadays associated with Latin American and some other 'Third World' cinemas — narrative forms and styles that are, as Fredric Jameson has suggested, constitutively dependent on a content that betrays the overlap or coexistence of pre-capitalist and nascent capitalist modes of production.

The difference, for Jameson, between the American nostalgia movie and 'Third World' magic realism is that the former is organized in terms of the temporality of the generation and has as its object the recapture of the sensorium of some relatively recent earlier decade such as 'the twenties' or 'the sixties', whereas the latter is articulated instead in terms of

10 I am thinking here of the importance of films such as *Darby O'Gill and the Little People* or *Finian's Rainbow* to the representation of Irishness in the United States, but it is interesting that Ireland's two leading contemporary film-makers, Neil Jordan and Jim Sheridan, should both have experimented in their early careers with the fairy-tale mode in *The Company of Wolves* and *Into the West* respectively.

the temporality of a mode of production still locked in conflict with traces of some older one. The magical realist narrative, therefore, achieves its distinctive stylistic effect by its capacity to combine whole layers of the past (pre-colonial and colonial eras, the war of independence era, the period of post-independence American domination, and so forth) within the warped but capacious temporality of the present, not by meticulously re-creating the 'feel' of this or that decade as the nostalgia movie does.[11] The supernatural Ireland conventional to the cinema screen may lack this rich magical realist dimension, but neither is its temporality and style that of the nostalgia film, for the object of the Irish films is scarcely ever the faithful recapture of some particularized moment from the past. What is curious at any rate is that cinema — one of the few major art forms to emerge within the world of industrial capitalism — should have provided one of the most hospitable mediums within which versions of a folk- and fairy-tale Ireland have managed to sustain themselves across the twentieth century. In *Celtic Revivals*, Seamus Deane suggests that the dour reality of post-Treaty Ireland effectively put an end to the aggrandizing and self-exoticizing myths of Ireland developed by the Literary Revival.[12] This may be largely accurate where domestic literature is concerned, but some facets of the fairy and whimsy of the Revival did not so much evaporate as migrate: evicted from the poetry and drama of post-independence Irish literature, they found refuge instead in the more visual lifeworld of cinema, where they have since enjoyed an extended residency.

Jim Sheridan's *Into the West* is, in its basic form, a cinematic fairy tale, and one that would seem to display a postmodern self-consciousness of its indebtedness to these literary and cinematic traditions. The film tells the story of how two young Traveller brothers, who are unhappily settled with their drunken father in Dublin's decrepit Ballymun towers, make their escape out of the city and into the rural West of Ireland on a mysterious white horse. The Dublin of the film is very much the degraded urban landscape of romantic convention. It is a damp and dilapidated, graffiti-scrawled, waste-strewn dystopia where Papa Riley (Gabriel Byrne), a former 'King of the Travellers', has abandoned the old nomadic ways of his people for the sedentary life of the city. Papa's rejection of the traditional life of the Travellers seems to be motivated by the fact that he blames the 'old ways' and 'superstitions' of his people for the death of his wife, Mary, a death with which he has clearly failed to come to terms and which he has refused to mourn in accordance with the traditional Traveller rituals. Although Papa is anxious that his sons, Tito (Ruaidhri Conroy) and Ossie (Ciarán Fitzgerald), should learn to read and write in order to equip themselves for the modern world, his own sense of abjection and continual drunkenness makes it clear that the transition from the 'old ways' to the new is far from being a successful or emancipatory one. When their maternal grandfather (David Kelly) arrives in the city on return from the West of Ireland accompanied by the

11 See Fredric Jameson, 'On Magic Realism in Film', in *Signatures of the Visible* (London, 1990), 128–52, 138.
12 Seamus Deane, *Celtic Revivals* (London, 1985), 33

white horse, the younger of the two Riley boys, Ossie, strikes up an intuitive relationship with the animal that suggests that the pull of the old nomadic life continues to exert an instinctive force even in the alien environment of the city. Intrigued by Grandpa Ward's stories of Oisín's voyage to the fairy-world of Tír na nÓg on the back of a magical white horse, Ossie and Tito take possession of their own white horse, only to discover that the modern world of city and state has no place for such creatures or can only accommodate them if they can be commodified. After a series of misadventures, in which the horse is seized and impounded by corrupt policemen and sold illegally to a wealthy County Meath businessman and landowner, who names the animal National Security and is determined to put it to lucrative use in the horse-jumping circuit, the two boys finally recapture the beast and set off westwards across Ireland with aggrieved businessman and police force in hot pursuit.[13]

As the narrative progresses, it is made increasingly clear to the audience that it is the white horse that is directing this journey 'into the West' and that the horse is in fact the returned spirit of the boys' dead mother, a mother whom Ossie had never known, as she had died when giving birth to him. As this spirit-horse carries the two boys further and further westwards, Papa, now searching for his lost sons with the help of some other Travellers who have refused to succumb to the settled life, realizes that the horse is leading him back to the landscape of his own and his wife's past. The narrative reaches its climax when the horse eventually reaches the Atlantic coast and, harried on all sides by its pursuers, carries Ossie out to sea, where both boy and horse are submerged beneath the waves. Just when it seems certain that he must surely drown, Ossie eventually resurfaces and is carried to shore in the arms of his father, though not before being granted a vision of the mother he had never seen. Father and children are taken back into the embrace of the 'unfallen' travelling community, and Papa promises his sons that there will be no returning to their previous life in the city: the phrase 'I'll never take ye back to the towers, I swear, I swear' is twice repeated in the closing moments of the film, though where or how exactly the Rileys will live in the future remains opaque.

The contrary meanings and values associated with the word 'West' in an Irish context, and a consequent sense of uncertainty and ultimately unresolved anxiety as to what exactly a journey 'into the West' might mean in our late capitalist moment, are what give this narrative its defining structure and resonance, and its peculiarly thwarted temporality. In one obvious sense, the 'West' referred to here is clearly that much-

---

13 Into the West taps into, for an Irish audience at least, diverse strands of populist anti-state and anti-establishment feeling that include not just the moving statues phenomenon but also the dissident subculture whereby Dublin underclass youth tried to keep large numbers of horses within urban ghettos in the eighties and nineties (much to the annoyance of the city authorities who eventually stepped in to end this practice), and to events such as the Shergar kidnapping. The film also refers to the ongoing drugs crisis in Dublin and the visual landscape of the city shown in the film is everywhere scrawled with pro-IRA graffiti. The film was extremely popular with Irish and American audiences and is ranked as the seventh highest-earning Irish film of the decade in Lance Pettitt's Table for Box Office Figures for Irish Films in the 1990s. See Pettitt, *Screening Ireland*, 286.

mythicized landscape that has dominated literary representations of the Celtic regions in Europe since at least the nineteenth century, though, as the references to Tír na nÓg suggest, the film alludes, too, to a pre-Christian Gaelic literature that had its own version of a wondrous western world. This West of Ireland landscape is the magical 'Celtic West' made famous by Sydney Owenson's national tales, by Arnold and Renan, by Synge and Yeats; it is a version of the West as the place of the romantic sublime stretching with remarkable structural consistency from the Celtic exoticism of Ossian and Scott to the Irish Literary Revival and beyond that into the cinematic world of Robert Flaherty's *Man of Aran* (1934) or John Ford's *The Quiet Man* (1952). As Joep Leerssen has argued, whether the relationship be that between Brittany and France or Wales and England or between the western and eastern regions of Ireland, this Celtic West is always constructed in terms of an imaginary geography which sets off a materialist, modern and mundane 'east' against a dreamy, mystical and timeless 'west'. According to Leerssen: 'The most striking point which such representations have in common is their strongly vectorial bias. They describe not a place, but a direction, a penetration or an approach, a movement from the east to the west, into or towards an unknown Celtic world.'[14] For Leerssen, this discourse of the West describes not so much an arrival as a constant deferral, a quest for some absent Other Place that always lies somewhere further to the west beyond the horizon.

The complication here is that, in another less geo-literary and more geo-political register, 'the West' can also connote precisely the opposite of all this. After all, 'the West' is also shorthand for the advanced capitalist economies of the modern industrial world; the term is virtually synonymous with the late capitalist lifestyles of the United States and Western Europe. This is the advanced capitalist Euro-American 'West' into which Ireland as a small, vulnerable and dependent economy has become increasingly integrated across the twentieth century, and especially since the 1960s.[15] Though widely hailed as initiating an era of increased national prosperity and social liberalization, the lived experience of that integration has nonetheless been an extremely anxious one for at least two reasons: first, because its price seems to be increasing political and economic subordination to state and corporate agencies headquartered outside Irish society itself; second, because the process of modernization has threatened the abolition of the non-industrialized rural Ireland that secured the exoticism of the other Celtic West, which had always furnished the Irish state with its own distinct cultural mythology and with its

14 Joep Leerssen, 'Outward Bound: The Locale and Ontology of Cultural Stereotype in the Case of Celtic Exoticism', in Roger Bauer et al., eds., *Proceedings of the XIIth Congress of The International Comparative Literature Association*, 4 (Munchen, 1990), 212–16, 212. On the aesthetics of 'the West' in Irish culture, see also Joep Leerssen, 'The Burden of the Past: Romantic Ireland and Prose Fiction', in his *Remembrance and Imagination: Patterns in the Historical and Literary Representation of Ireland in the Nineteenth Century* (Cork, 1996) and Luke Gibbons, 'Synge, Country and Western: The Myth of the West in Irish and American Culture', in his *Transformations in Irish Culture* (Cork, 1996).
15 For a useful historical survey of Western and non-Western ideas of the West, see Alistair Bonnett, *The Idea of the West: Culture, Politics and History* (Houndmills, 2004).

most idealized and utopian fantasies of itself.

As constructed in Sheridan's film, this political 'West' is represented by the visually drab, spiritually desiccated Dublin, where the Travellers have traded in their earlier ruggedly nomadic independence for a sedentary dependency on the state. We see this helpless dependency first in the form of the Murphys ('the most common name in all Ireland') gathering together their teeming children for the inspection of the social welfare officer who controls the state dole on which they rely. The dominant figure in this landscape is Papa whose habitual drunkenness and loss of purpose colour the landscape of the city as a whole. This 'Dublin', in other words, is clearly no more a 'real' place than is the Celtic West into which Ossie and Tito will eventually flee. It functions in the film, rather, as a visual metaphor for a pre-Celtic Tiger Ireland's problematic position as a chronically dependent and dysfunctional economy being increasingly subsumed into a soulless late capitalist 'West' on which it abjectly relies for its very survival.

However, there is also a third 'West' in the film, one which complicates the conventional literary binarism already described for us by Leerssen. This is the American 'Wild West' of Hollywood legend: the mythic celluloid world into which Tito and Ossie like to imagine they are fleeing. It is also the sign within the text whereby the film demonstrates to its audience that it knows itself *as film* and signals its capacity to self-reflexively locate itself within the familiar canons and conventions of the Irish and American 'Wests' that structure its plot. In contrast to the Celtic West that has its origins in the realm of national oral and literary culture, this Wild West is a product of mass culture, and, for the barely literate Ossie and Tito, raised in the era of cinema and television, it is this celluloid West that most vividly structures their fantasy worlds. This cinematic West does not then simply coexist alongside or run parallel to the other two Wests described earlier; it is actually the archetypal frame that subsumes or contains both. As the boys flee Dublin and journey across Ireland towards the western coast, which for them is an escape into the Wild West of cinematic fantasy, the audience is compelled to recognize that authentic flight away from the urbanized world of advanced capitalism into some legendary other Ireland is no longer really an option at all, if only because this flight is mediated by cinema, and cinema itself is both product and instrument of the advanced capitalism that is apparently being left behind. It may well be possible physically to leave the city behind, but the repeated references to the Wild West remind us that this journey is nevertheless only the stuff of cinema. The audience is nudged every now and then to recall that the colonization of the subconscious by Hollywood and the commodification of the Irish landscape by cinema mean that the West of advanced capitalism is always one step ahead no matter how hard one might wish to escape that reality. Acknowledging the impossibility of any genuine leaving behind of the modern urban world, the film gestures to its audience that we are in the domain of the spectacle and the simulacrum here, not in any world of 'the real'. If Ireland is worryingly dependent on or subordinate to the West in economic terms, so too is Irish cinema, not just in a crassly financial sense but because the whole narrative grammar of popular cinema is essentially American.

Hence, only if Irish material can be accommodated to the mythemes of Hollywood will it become at all legible to a contemporary mass public.

For an Irish film-maker, this sense that modernization is also Americanization is necessarily uncomfortable for what it implies both for the future of Irish culture, which must be translated into an American idiom if it is to make the cut in the present order of things, and for Ireland's capacity to continue to function as a source of raw materials for cinematic romance. The Hollywood Western, like the literary imperial romance that is clearly a precursor, has always divided the world into a civilized but humdrum zone of relative order, security and secularity, which is reassuringly safe but hostile to adventure and hence to action or plot, and a non-modern zone of adventure, magic and disorder, which is threatening and needs to be tamed but which is nonetheless rich in the materials of adventure and plot in a way that the civilized zone is not. As John McClure has argued, romance is designed to satisfy collective longings for adventure and the exotic, but it cannot manufacture its wondrous dreams from thin air: it depends for their production on our capacity to imagine regions 'beyond' the pale of civilization, regions rich in what McClure calls the 'raw materials' of adventure, magic and mystery — regions and populations as yet unconquered and untransformed by the forces of secularization and rationalization. However, as advanced capitalist culture saturated the entire globe toward the latter part of the twentieth century, and as the last elsewhere threatened to be eliminated by this process, romance itself inevitably experienced a crisis of the 'raw materials' of magic and mystery that it had always depended upon for its existence.[16]

The crisis that underlies Into the West, then, is to some extent a crisis in the production of romance itself (or a crisis in the production of romantic Ireland at least), since Ireland's journey into one West (that of advanced capitalism, the world of which cinema itself is part) effectively threatens to obliterate the other West (the non-modern rural Ireland that subtended the Celtic exoticism on which so much Irish cinema has always traded) and, in so doing, to deprive Irish cinema of its conventional raw materials. To the extent that it is capable of bringing this contradiction to self-consciousness, Sheridan's film can be said to be a kind of thwarted meta-romance, and the journey 'into the west' can thus be conceived as a desperate quest to seek out the conditions that make romance possible in a world that seems continually to extend the conditions that make it impossible. Conflating as it does the flight into the Celtic West and Wild West, Sheridan's film implicitly acknowledges the impossibility of any real or authentic escape from the fallen modernity of the city; in the world of advanced capitalism the simulacrum of escape, which is all that cinema itself actually offers, is the only 'escape' that remains.

The two intertextual references to other films in Into the West tend to confirm this suggestion. Early on in the narrative, before they even set out on their own journey, Tito and Ossie furtively watch a screening of Butch Cassidy and the Sundance Kid, a classic closing-of-the-American-frontier movie that tries desperately to resuscitate the run-

16 For a more extended discussion, see John McClure, Late Imperial Romance (London, 1996).

down romance of the Wild West by taking the final stages of its narrative off to 'Third World' Bolivia, once the North American Wild West has itself been tamed and overtaken by the forces of modernity. Later, when they have made their way halfway across Ireland, the boys spend a rainy night in a local cinema where they watch *Back to the Future III*, an exemplary postmodern nostalgia film (as described by Jameson) that can find a place for exotic old-style adventure only by venturing back into an inert and remaindered past it knows solely through stocks of celluloid image. Within *Into the West*, in other words, the narrative trajectory takes us from a classic closing-of-the-American-frontier text to a popular postmodern work (itself endlessly recyclable, since it is *Back to the Future* for the third time) in which the past has become entirely toothless and depthless, a set of images to be consumed now in their own right as images rather than as representations of something else. Ireland (like many other non-modern 'Third World' spaces) has existed for Hollywood primarily as a place to feed its insatiable hunger for primitivist romances of pre-modern or non-modern otherness. But where is Irish cinema, itself an instrument of modernization in an increasingly modernizing Ireland, to find the resources to maintain that sense of non-modern primitive otherness in a late capitalist moment when the non-modern retains only the most vestigial and precarious of existences, when it is always threatened with abolition or with survival only as kitsch?

Sheridan's film, therefore, demonstrates a considerable degree of anxiety about the implications of advanced capitalism both in terms of what it means for Ireland generally and, more specifically, for the destruction of the raw materials of romance. Given its acute discomfort with the journey Ireland is making into this political West (that of advanced capitalism), which is also a journey into the future, the film has only one direction to go: into the other Celtic West, which is also a journey into the past. At the level of plot at least, this journey into the past would appear to be, as mentioned earlier, a wholly therapeutic one. It forces Papa to confront and work through his hitherto unresolved grief and melancholia; Ossie is granted a restorative vision of the mother he has never known; and the story concludes with the family's apparent reintegration into the larger communal family of the unfallen Travellers. In terms that recall Freud's famous essay, 'Mourning and Melancholia', the drama acted out here is one which connects Papa's melancholia with an inability to undertake the 'work of mourning' generated by some trauma in the past — a trauma obviously associated in Sheridan's narrative with the loss of the mother. Read socially, the inference of the narrative is that Ireland's joyless modernity (the shabbily down-at-heel modernity represented in the film by an abject, chronically dependent Dublin) has something to do with its persistent refusal or inability to confront and come to terms with the traumas of its past — traumas somehow therapeutically worked through in the narrative by means of the journey into the rural West.

It is important to note, though, that this apparently restorative journey into the West is by no means without its own deep anxieties: indeed this turning back to the world that Papa had wanted to leave behind him cannot avoid fretful suggestions of both psychic and political regression. The stress marks of this particular anxiety manifest themselves at several tense moments in the narrative. One such moment occurs when Ossie and Tito eventually tire of the hardships of living outdoors and decide to return to the comforts of the city only to discover that the white horse has a will of its own and refuses to allow them to do so. Once embarked upon, the journey into the West appears not to permit of any turning back and, though it eventually does prove regenerative, the film concludes thus only after it has first proposed another altogether more disastrous or tragic ending during those long suspenseful moments in the ocean waters when Ossie disappears beneath the waves and it seems that he must certainly drown. The sense of near tragedy is so vividly etched here that this alternative ending cannot entirely be expunged; it releases anxieties that linger on in the mind after the film has closed and that unsettle the happy ending with which the narrative actually concludes.

There is, in addition, the fact that the upshot of the voyage should ultimately remain so curiously elusive. On the one hand, everything seems to suggest that the journey on which the boys have been conducted by the spirit-mother has been a wholly regenerative one: it culminates with the rehabilitation of the father, the re-integration of the family, and with a 'proper' ritualistic mourning for the lost mother. The film then ends with the funereal burning of the caravan of the dead mother, this registered as a gesture of obeisance to Traveller custom and as a letting go of the past that Papa had earlier refused to enact. Thus, there is an apparently decisive rejection of the city and its alienated mode of existence. On the other hand, since the whole point of the journey back to the West seems to be that this can finally create the conditions that allow for a healthy letting go (of grief for the mother, of the sullen melancholia that binds one to the past), the film seems to assert that the point of returning to the past is not to remain there but quite the opposite: to grieve and let go and then to move healthily forward in a way that meets the demands for a perfectly therapeutic Hollywood closure. But forward to where or to what? Since the city is repudiated ('I'll never take ye back to the towers, I swear, I swear') and so too is the idea of a return to the old ways (to keep on going west in that direction is eventually to drown in the maternal ocean), the film seems to be able to suggest only the need for some kind of utterly abstract 'moving on', to which it can give no social or political definition at all. Unable affirmatively to embrace a modernity associated with trading in one's independence or to repudiate it in the name of a return to a lost source, it is the irresolution of *Into the West*'s resolution that seems finally its most striking and significant feature.[17]

It would be wrong to imagine that the anxieties referred to in the previous paragraphs

---

17 My reading of *Into the West* differs to that of Martin McLoone, who contends that the narrative simply rejects the city and offers an unambiguous reaffirmation of a return to Traveller roots in the recuperative embrace of the West of Ireland. McLoone's reading misses the extent to which the film vacillates about the meaning of the voyage 'into the West' and reads the ending of the narrative as far more unambiguously affirmative than it actually is. See Martin McLoone, *Irish Film: The Emergence of a Contemporary Cinema* (London, 2000), 211.

are frontally engaged in the film. They are not and instead *Into the West* oscillates throughout between a disenchanted romanticism, for which capitalism is seen as an irreversible and inexorable even if not very appealing destiny, and a past-oriented romanticism, which holds that a return to some civilizational stage before capitalism might indeed be desirable.[18] Though at one level the film is suffused with a desire to get away from the city and the degraded capitalist modernity it represents, on another level it seems ultimately unable to extricate itself from a disenchanted structure of feeling that dismisses this as the stuff of impossible fantasy, of fairy tale. Trussed in the coils of its own irresolutions, lacking the will to engage its contradictory impulses in some more vigorously intellectual manner, the anxieties referred to earlier appear in the film only as points of stress in the narrative or as moments of hesitation or confusion. For the most part, though, the film proves quite adept in managing its misgivings, displacing them in all sorts of interesting ways.

One of the ways in which Sheridan's film manages to contain whatever misgivings it might have about the regressive implications of the flight from the city into the rural West is its construction of a third space — one which is properly neither modern 'east' nor redemptive pre-modern 'west' — onto which these misgivings can be projected: that third space in the film is 'the midlands'. When Ossie and Tito first escape the city, they feel a rush of exhilaration and release. Later, as they make their way across the countryside, they experience hunger, cold and loneliness, and Dublin begins to appear more attractive. In moments such as this, the world beyond the city loses its numinous 'soft primitivist' aura of pre-capitalist enchantment and appears instead as a 'hard primitivist' place of privation, scarcity and want.[19] This obviously registers the anxiety that a return to the state of nature might actually be a return to a condition of hardship rather than to an unalienated world of natural plenitude; and the socially regressive possibilities that such a voyage might entail also suddenly erupt in the episode where Papa and his companions are met with naked and ugly anti-Traveller prejudice in a small midlands town. The space beyond the city is subdivided into two locales then: a sour, provincial midlands, which gathers into itself all of the more unattractive implications of a return to the rural past, and an almost completely unpeopled West, free of any such negative associations. The midlands here, it would appear, functions as a kind of purgative zone, where the film's more generally suppressed anxieties about the regressive nature of the journey into the past can find narrative and verbal expression. The midlands serves, that is, as a place where *Into the West* can articulate its misgivings and divest itself of its 'bad conscience' before setting these aside and moving on into the

---

18 For an incisive study of the differences between various forms of romantic conceptions of the past, see Michael Löwy, 'Marxism and Revolutionary Romanticism', *Telos*, 49 (1981), 83–95.

19 For an extremely influential discussion on 'soft' and 'hard' primitivist aesthetics in Irish cinema, see Luke Gibbons, 'Romanticism, Realism, and Irish Cinema', in Kevin Rockett, Luke Gibbons and John Hill, *Cinema and Ireland* (London, 1987), 194–257. Sheridan's *The Field* offers a much more 'hard primitivist' version of the Irish West than does *Into the West*.

West proper. By affixing onto the midlands all of the more negative things that might accrue to a journey into the past — hunger and want, crude sexism and racism — the film manages to retain the fantasy of some more sublime and pristine further-west, free of any such regressiveness.

Since *Into the West* belongs to the category of romance and fairy tale and not to that of social realism, it is important to recognize that the Travellers in the film demand to be read allegorically and not in any social realist or documentary mode. Essentially, they function as fantasy figures through which the film can express a desire for a kind of communal collectivity that seems to be imaginable (if at all) only in some time-space anterior to the present fallen world of property relations and capitalist value. Commenting on the tremendous popularity of the *Godfather* movies, Fredric Jameson has observed that what differentiates these movies from earlier paradigms of the outlaw or gangster film is their tremendous emphasis on the 'archaic' collectivity of the criminal world they depict. Whereas the gangster movies of the film noir period constructed the gangster as a solitary but existentially defiant individual living and dying on the edges of society, the *Godfather* films took the form of a family or ethnic saga, a morphology Jameson deems key to their attraction for a modern audience. Subaltern ethnic minorities in the United States, Jameson suggests, are not only the object of prejudice and loathing but also of an intense, if unacknowledged, envy:

> The dominant white middle-class groups — already given over to *anomie* and social fragmentation and atomization — find in the ethnic and racial groups which are the object of their social repression and status contempt at one and the same time the image of some older collective ghetto or ethnic neighborhood solidarity; they feel the envy and *ressentiment* of the *Gesellschaft* [corporative society] for the older *Gemeinschaft* [organic community] which it is simultaneously exploiting and liquidating.[20]

This, it seems to me, describes exactly the function of the more recalcitrant or still non-settled Travellers in *Into the West*: nomads attached neither to the city nor to the country, they represent a precarious utopian desire for some sort of primitive social order embodying a lost happiness that might once have existed in some prelapsarian time before the individuation and alienation of modern subjectivity associated with private property, the bourgeois nuclear family and capitalist modernization.

Even though the Travellers fulfil a structural function in Sheridan's work similar to that which Jameson ascribes to the Italian Mafia-family in the *Godfather* films, they clearly represent, nonetheless, a utopian fantasy of a rather different order. Whereas the Mafia of the *Godfather* movies is a complex composite of the ruthless value-worlds of American advanced capitalism and Sicilian feudalism, the Travellers in Sheridan's work rehearse

20 Fredric Jameson, 'Reification and Utopia in Mass Culture', in *Signatures of the Visible* (London, 1990), 9–54, 32–33

a fantasy of a much more idyllic pre-capitalist community. Sheridan's Travellers are nomadic wanderers who seem to exist outside of the sedentary world of fixed property relations altogether; vestiges of a primeval animism and pagan magic cling to them. Tito tells Ossie ruefully at one point that the Travellers of old could 'tell fortunes, make things out of tin, do magic'. In the *Godfather* films, American capitalist modernity and Sicilian pre-modernity are both fantastically violent: one must kill in order to live in the essentially hard primitivist, survivalist landscape of both the Old and New Worlds alike. In *Into the West*, by contrast, the fantasy of the pre-modern is much less harsh and sinister, much more soft primitivist, and closely linked to a kind of artisan self-reliance and to some sort of contact with both nature and supernatural forces.

This soft primitivist conception of the pre-modern is secured in no small measure by the fact that that world is gendered in *Into the West* as maternal and construed as (largely) redemptive. Whereas the Mafia-family in the hard primitivist world of the *Godfather* movies suggests a nostalgia for a tightly-integrated family or kinship unit presided over by the terrifying yet charismatic authority of a god-father figure, Sheridan's pre-capitalist Traveller community is presided over by a spirit-mother. The matriarchal connotations of the journey westwards, and the return to the old ways with which the journey is associated, are underlined by the fact that it is the returned spirit of the dead mother that lures her fallen family out of the city, drawing it back into the embrace of the larger community of their still-nomadic kin. Though the non-settled Travellers seem nominally to be ruled over by a male, Tracker (Johnny Murphy), real authority is ultimately vested in his sister, Kathleen (Ellen Barkin), whose screen presence dominates and glamorizes this world. It is Kathleen, and not Tracker, moreover, who takes on the task of helping Papa to track his boys and in her capacity as sympathetic guide on this journey into the West she effectively becomes a kind of surrogate figure for the spirit-mother who presides over things.

The fact that the journey westwards comes to its climax in the ocean — where an underwater shot set to a soundtrack of sentimental harp music shows the motherless boy-child Ossie in an expression of rapture as he experiences some sort of near-death vision and is then guided to the surface by an elegantly-beckoning female hand — obviously invites a psychoanalytic reading that would interpret the yearning for the lost mother as a longing for the psychic plenitude of a pre-Oedipal condition. The maternal body for which the child yearns, in other words, is associated with a fullness of presence and with an originary harmony that is contrasted to an adult consciousness of alienation and lack. (Ossie, haunted by the legendary fate of Oisín who ages horribly when he returns to Ireland after his sojourn in the land of eternal youth, had earlier expressed his own terror of growing up.) Although this psychic register is certainly relevant, it would be wrong to read the narrative in exclusively psychoanalytic terms, since the quest for the redemptive vision of the mother is linked, inter alia, to the rejection of the city (with its suggestion of a degraded, atomized, demoralized existence); to a return to the old ways (with its connotations of self-reliance, non-dependence on the state, and a preference for communal or extended modes of kinship rather than the nuclear family unit); and to a recognition of the value of customary rites of mourning (the voyage brings the family back to the mother's grave, and then to the burning of her caravan in the manner prescribed by tradition). In *Into the West*, in other words, the figure of the lost mother is positioned as a very powerful object of nostalgic desire, but the nature of the desire that attaches to her is amorphous and polyvalent, capable of suggesting a whole assortment of wants and lacks within a modernity conceptualized as masculine and which is also perceived to be, despite its deficiencies, an inexorable destiny.

The conceptual underpinnings of Sheridan's narrative have their sources, then, in a longer history of post-Enlightenment discourses that are not simply reactionary but range right across the spectrum, from the conservative to radical feminist and Marxist, and that share in common with each other only the fact that they all construe femininity and modernity as existing in antithetical relationship to each other. Within these discourses, as Rita Felski comments,

> Woman was identified with a primitive or preindustrial era in the same way as she was linked through her maternal function to the unselfconscious being-in-the-world of the not yet socialized infant ... Within this tradition, nostalgia and the feminine come together in the representation of a mythic plenitude, against which is etched an overarching narrative of masculine development as self-division and existential loss.[21]

It is no doubt the conception of the journey into the West as a return to a more maternal world that dictates that the mother can appear in the film only in supernatural form. The association of the Celtic West with the lost plenitude of the mother and all that that connotes could never be depicted, in other words, within a naturalistic or social realist mode (these are the modes reserved in the film for the depiction of the city and the midlands, the worlds to be escaped) and can only achieve figuration (to the extent that it can be figured at all) in the register of the marvellous and the supernatural. Were Ossie's mother to be presented as living Traveller woman and wife, it would obviously be very difficult to represent the journey back into the past as a voyage into a more 'feminine' landscape, given the deeply patriarchal bent of Traveller society, as indeed of Irish society generally. In the same way, Kathleen is also, necessarily, a highly implausible figure: represented in a manner that indiscriminately hybridizes her as an idealized Native American female tracker, a Celtic mystic and a New Age free spirit, she too belongs to the world of fantasy or wish-fulfilment rather than to 'the real'. Thus, the feminized Celtic West of *Into the West* can be sustained only by continually keeping in check all of the darker suggestions that a voyage into a the premodern past might connote for women. However, it is characteristic of the general ambivalence and irresolution of the

21 Felski, 'On Nostalgia', 39, 38

film that, even as it attempts to transcend social realism and work in the medium of the supra-real (or supernatural), it can never altogether dispel the social realist anxiety that in some ways the past might have been darker than the present. After all, Mary, the spirit-mother in the film, had died in childbirth, and Papa blames her death on Traveller superstition and a concomitant refusal to come to terms with modern medicine.

In sum, Into the West is a film pressured by a strong vein of anti-modern sentiment, a profound ambivalence with regards to the supposed benefits and values of both the modern and the pre-modern or non-modern, and a powerfully registered, though amorphously represented, yearning for some more 'maternal' alternative to the present order of things. Since its view of capitalist modernity is an overwhelmingly negative one, the film is unable to locate any seeds of resistance to the present condition of things within the city itself; hence the narrative turns its back on this world and looks for a redemptive alternative in an idealized version of the pre-modern, pre-capitalist past that it always-already knows to exist, however, only as the stuff of legend or fantasy. The return to this latter zone is constructed as a return to a condition of pre-Oedipal oneness with the archaic mother, a condition that the child experiences as an undifferentiated unity where all its needs are provided for. But the utopian desire that impels the quest into the West can find no material actualization or figuration within the narrative itself and exists, therefore, only as a kind of magical 'wish' that motivates the fairy-tale quest; the film as a whole displays a considerable burden of anxiety as to whether the wish that motivates its fantasy is actually a positive or a regressive one.[22]

The narrative trajectory of the film superimposes three parallel quests upon each other — a quest for the lost maternal world of early childhood (Ossie's search for the lost mother he cannot remember); a quest for the historical childhood of humankind (Papa's abandonment of the city and return to the old ways when the Travellers were still nomadic and not so dependent on the state); and the film's own need to imagine a space not yet disenchanted by the forces of rationalization and progress, a space where the raw materials of romance might still be found. But though these quests collectively exude a strong sense of longing for a kind of social order very different to that represented by the dependent, fallen modernity of the city, Into the West lacks belief in its own utopian impulse and ultimately does not know to which West, if any, its real loyalties lie. Suffused with a vague utopian longing, unable to give any real social content or transformative impetus to it, overwhelmed by nervous anxieties about its dangers, Into the West is in many ways an exemplary postmodern narrative. That is to say, it is a narrative of a late modern condition in which the longing for some alternative world retains a powerful

22 The anxiety that the journey into the Celtic West is a regressive one is quite explicitly registered a number of times in the film. At one stage, Papa asks Grandfather Ward, 'Is it a good horse or a bad?' Grandfather Ward shakes his head, unable to tell apparently whether the spirit-horse/spirit-mother is a benign or malign force. Later, when Ossie seems certain to drown, Grandfather Ward, who had earlier been a strong critic of the city and of settled travellers and a very confident voice for a return to the old ways, utters the repentant cry, 'Me an' my stupid stories'.

subterranean charge, but in which any conviction of how to realize that alternative world, or what we might even want it to be like, has become extremely wizened.[23]

3

It will be clear by now that we have left neither the nineteenth-century world of Knock nor the late twentieth-century world of moving statues behind. Though Sheridan's film is by no means a religious one, the spirit-mother in Into the West performs a role within that narrative structurally analogous to that of the Madonna in Marian apparitions. What Sheridan's film offers its audience is an essentially dejected and melancholic vision of a fallen modernity, a world where life has run down and lost its sense of direction but is then revitalized and given a renewed sense of purpose by the supernatural intervention of the spirit-mother. In Into the West, as in the Marian apparition at Knock or the moving statues episodes of the mid-eighties, the spirit-mother functions both as a silent figure of admonition (the apparent effect of her intervention in the film is to lead Papa to return to the old ways of the tribe) and as a figure of enormous consolation (reassuring Ossie that he has not, after all, been abandoned in a cold and heartless world), but in both instances the longing for some more maternal world cannot get beyond a kind of gestural wistfulness. If there is a difference between the apparitions and the film, it may be that in the structure of feeling that subtends the latter there is a stronger (and more conventionally cinematic and late capitalist) sense in the closing frames of the need to grieve and let go: while the spirit-mother in the film presides over the self-renewing pilgrimage into the West and apparently succeeds in re-integrating her family and restoring their morale by way of a revitalizing contact with the old ways, the funereal scene of the burning caravan that brings the narrative to a close would seem to suggest that, having finally and fully grieved her loss, the family is now at last ready to move on.

From the perspective of a triumphalist narrative of modernization, the more modern a society becomes the more secular it will also inevitably become — secularization here meaning: an increasingly structural differentiation of social spaces resulting in the separation of religion, politics, economy, science, culture, and so on, into their own distinct spheres; the privatization of religious experience; and the declining social significance of religious belief.[24] For many contemporary observers, the continuing,

---

23 Although Into the West draws suggestively on Irish and American literary and cinematic heritages, the deeper concerns registered in the film belong not to any specific country but rather to an historical moment. Into the West should be seen, therefore, as an Irish variant on a much broader corpus of late twentieth-century films that display a strong nostalgic-utopian primitivist and quasi-religious fascination with pre-industrial minority cultures deemed to be on the verge of extinction. Some of the more striking mass culture exemplars of this mode would include Kevin Costner's Dances with Wolves (1990) and Lee Tamahori's Once Were Warriors (1994).

24 This definition of secularism is taken from José Casanova, Public Religions in the Modern World (Chicago, 1994). For a thoughtful analysis of the topic of secularism and religion in the modern period, see also Talal Asad, Formations of the Secular: Christianity, Islam, Modernity (Stanford, 2003).

possibly even increasing, vitality of politicized religion almost everywhere across the world has cast considerable doubt over this triumphalist narrative. Nor can it plausibly be argued that the 'return' of religion to the global political scene is simply evidence of a passionate rejection of capitalist modernity. While there are indeed many examples of politicized religion that support the notion of a late twentieth-century backlash of this order, there are as many instances where highly politicized religious movements have proved themselves to be extremely serviceable to late capitalist modernizing agendas: examples might include the role played by the Catholic and other Churches in toppling the authoritarian Communist régimes and restoring capitalism in Eastern Europe, the role of evangelical Protestantism in the articulation of a neo-conservative 'new world order' in the United States, or that of Hindutva in legitimizing the aggressively neo-liberal economic politics of the New Right in India. Acting sometimes as a force to galvanize support against authoritarian régimes and to rebuild civic society (as in Poland), sometimes as a focal point for debates around civil rights or liberal values (as in the case of the role of several US Churches in the campaign for African-American civil rights or the contemporary Anglican Church's wrestling with the issue of homosexuality), sometimes associated with anti-imperialists or communitarian-leftist projects (as in the case of several versions of political Islam or Catholic 'liberation theology' in South America), the relationship between religion and modernity is, it would appear, considerably more complex and variegated than many liberal and leftist commentators will usually allow. The tendency in such quarters to conceptualize the relationship between religion and our contemporary late capitalist moment simply in terms of a uni-directional contest between 'tradition' and 'modernity' seems inadequate to the complex dynamics of the world in which we live.

But it is not simply the continued vitality of politicised religion in the present moment that gives check to the triumphalist narratives of modernization and secularization. There is also the fact that, as this chapter has been suggesting, we can detect within many of the key discourses of the modern itself (the discourses of progress, of development, of sociology, anthropology, feminism, Marxism, and many others) modes of thought and structures of feeling that owe more than a little to the older religious templates they generally reject. More commonly than not, continuities of this sort are acknowledged only in the form of a traducing of political opponents: as, for example, when right-wingers or liberals dismiss nationalism or socialism as only a thinly secularized or bastardized versions of religion, or when leftists argue that capitalists are prepared to contemplate the desacralization of everything save the sanctity of private property or the moral omnipotence of the state. The ascription of hidden continuities between religion and its apparent others also extends beyond the domain of politics, and shows its face in the frequently remarked suggestions that one or other of the domains of modern mass culture now fulfils the role formerly performed by religion: hence the commonplace that sport or shopping or sex or television and cinema, or whatever, now constitute the 'new' or 'real' religions of our times. However crude these commonplaces, however much they glide over all sorts of essential distinctions between religion and late capitalist mass culture, they nonetheless index the fact that the socially integrative, ritualistic and the utopian/nostalgic/consolatory functions served by religion continue to demand fulfilment in some way or other, in what are often considered to be 'post-religious' consumerist secular societies.

In the circumstances, there is little reason to assume that the apparition at Knock in the late nineteenth century or the more recent moving-statue episodes, are simply the freakish last gasp of some 'anachronistic' or 'traditional' or 'residual' formation within Irish society, destined soon to be swept away by the inevitable march of modernization and secularization. On the contrary, there is much greater reason to assume that capitalist modernity, committed as it is to unceasing revolution in the forces of production and to the constant social upheaval that this requires, generates, as its automatic reflex, an ongoing demand for some sort of ontological security and stability that economic prosperity as such (even in that very small number of societies where it exists) cannot completely satisfy. As many commentators have pointed out, capitalist modernity generates, not simply the constant agitations and excitements of 'the shock of the new', but also a concomitant nostalgic longing for some putatively non-alienated pre-modern world. Nostalgic longings are constitutive to the modern capitalist order itself, not simply the traces of some pre-modern residue captured within the meshes of the modern but stubbornly recalcitrant to its logic.

Nor indeed is there any reason to assume that all forms of nostalgia are equivalent or that all are inherently reactionary. Some thinkers have tried to distinguish between restorative forms, designed simply to dissolve the anxieties of the modern by recovering the supposed certainties of tradition, and more radical and reflective varieties that do not shy away from a critical examination of the contradictions of modernity and that try to retrieve from the past its unfulfilled utopian dimensions.[25] Much as they might disagree on other things, contemporary Marxists and poststructuralists (including of course feminist-Marxists and feminist-poststructuralists) have, as Felski notes, tended to find common consensus in a shared deprecation of nostalgia: the latter want to read any appeal to an originary unity as symptomatic of a reactionary metaphysics; the former to interpret it as a sign of conservative backsliding or passive daydreaming. It is not clear, though, as Felski also remarks, why idealizations of the past should necessarily or automatically be any more suspect than idealizations of the present or future; it is ultimately the social content rather than the temporal location of the object of desire that really matters. It is certainly the case that a desire for an idealized past has helped in modern times to fuel extremely reactionary fundamentalist and conservative campaigns

25 See Felski, 'On Nostalgia', 58. For further reflections on nostalgia and utopian thought developed within the Marxian tradition, see Löwy, 'Marxism and Revolutionary Romanticism', and Ernst Bloch, The Utopian Function of Art and Literature (Cambridge, MA, 1996). For an interesting post-Marxist study that attempts to distinguish between restorative and reflective versions, see Svetlana Boym, The Future of Nostalgia (New York, 2001).

for a 'return to basics' and to inspire the struggles of some quite radical feminist, ecological and anti-imperialist movements as well.[26]

As this chapter has argued, the whole politics of nostalgia is complicated in any event by the fact that a femininely gendered conception of a non-alienated nature has never simply been the preserve of religious or romantic conservatives. Such motifs recur in fact within certain lineages of both feminist and non-feminist thought and across the political spectrum from right to left. To avoid either an uncritical embrace of an avant-gardist discourse of modernization as unambiguous progress (a 'tough-minded' and 'unsentimental' approach that may well blind itself to the contradictions of the modern no less than restorative versions of nostalgia), or the equally passive embrace of the pre-modern (which amounts only to a kind of romantic anti-capitalism and a melancholic politics shorn of transformative impetus), socialists and feminists need constantly to keep in mind the complex dialectics that underpin the relationship between modernization, nostalgia and utopia, and to remember as well their own indebtedness to the intellectual histories they want to build upon or move beyond.

The hesitancies and the sense of directional impasse that are the most striking features of *Into the West* may have their immediate origins in the uncertain social climate that issued from a desperately struggling capitalism in the late eighties in Ireland, but these are the telltale symptoms of the wider post-Cold War global moment as well. It would be foolish to think that the anxieties to which the film gives narrative (if wholly un-intellectualized) expression have simply been dissolved by the economic prosperity that Irish society has enjoyed in the interval since the film first appeared. In the context of the wider global crises of late capitalism, and given the ominous ways in which these crises have already begun to manifest themselves at the start of the new millennium, our sense of what it means, for Ireland, as indeed for the world at large, to journey 'into the West', however construed, in the twenty-first century may well have become more rather than less acute over that interval. If this be the case, then the real weakness of *Into the West* may well be not so much that it rejects capitalist modernity for some nostalgic or utopian alternative, but rather that the utopian or nostalgic impulse of this irresolute postmodern fairy tale should ultimately prove so invertebrate, so lacking in determinate content.

26 Felski, 'On Nostalgia', 58–59

Modernization and Aesthetic Ideology

In Cathal Black's *Korea* (1996), a darkly lit and moody film set in rural Ireland in the summer of 1952, there is a scene in which the inhabitants of a small village assemble by lamplight for a ceremony to mark the turning on of the recently installed electricity. On a platform, surrounded by a knot of local notables sitting under a banner inscribed 'Rural Electrification', an elderly parish priest presides over the ceremony, scattering holy water and intoning a passage from Genesis about the creation of light 'which shines in the darkness and the darkness has not overcome it'. However, when the priest pulls the lever that is supposed to light up the village for the first time, nothing happens and the bemused villagers break into fatalistic laughter: 'Nothing works in this town,' one guffaws; 'The electricity, how are yah!' another mocks. A moment later, though, there is a burst of illumination when the new streetlights suddenly flicker on, and the villagers erupt into excited applause. 'Rural electrification,' a local dignitary proudly declaims, 'is more than an amenity. It is a revolution that will sweep away the inferiority complexes.' In the crowd, a disgruntled republican veteran of the War of Independence watching his Free State rival bask in satisfaction at this latest sign of the state's progress into modernity, grudgingly remarks: 'It wasn't for street lamps we fought.' By now, however, the villagers are belting out the national anthem, and the scene concludes with a shot of a magnificent summer moon evenly sliced between darkness and light.[1]

For the political or constitutional historian, 1948 represents a landmark in modern Irish history, the moment when the Irish Free State severed its residual links with Britain

---

1 Cathal Black co-wrote and directed *Korea*, which is based on a John McGahern short story of the same title in his collection *Nightlines* (London, 1973). Set in the 1950s, published as a short story in the 1970s, and re-presented for the cinema in the mid-1990s, the narrative is indicative of the way Irish culture continued over the last quarter of the twentieth century to rehearse the breakdown of 'de Valera's Ireland' as the decisive transitional moment in recent Irish history.

to become a fully independent and sovereign republic. For the economic historian, 1958 — the moment when Sean Lemass and T. K. Whittaker launched the First Programme for Economic Expansion that abandoned the protectionist policies of the previous generation and opened the country to foreign investment and multinational capital — will seem the more decisive watershed. But it is the actual conjunction of the two events that is most suggestive, since the declaration of political sovereignty was to be followed so soon by an acknowledgement that any kind of economic sovereignty or self-reliance was more or less a lost cause, thus indicating the difficulty of co-ordinating the ideals of economic and political self-control generally deemed the fundamental *raison d'être* of any state. Though anti-partitionists did not concur, the declaration of the Republic was hailed at the time as a moment when the long struggle for Irish sovereignty finally attained its goal or end-point. A mere ten years later, a sceptic might argue, that vaunted sovereignty had indeed reached its end — not as fulfilment, but as terminus — when the strategy of autarkic development was jettisoned and the state embarked on an alternative strategy of dependent development that would see Ireland increasingly integrated into the global capitalist economy and into the European Economic Community (EEC), a process that would entail a steady erosion of the national sovereignty that had supposedly reached its apotheosis only a decade earlier in 1948. Hence, one of the lessons of twentieth-century Irish history would seem to be that political autonomy could be had but only at the cost of economic poverty; economic prosperity could be had but only at the expense of a considerable diminution of the state's political autonomy; to maximize the two simultaneously seemed practically impossible. In Ireland, no less than anywhere else, the difficulty was that its citizenry, schooled in the political ideals of national sovereignty and self-determination that fared rather poorly in an increasingly globalized corporate order, was disposed to expect that national political autonomy and national economic prosperity ought to be compatible, indeed complementary. But they found themselves living a reality that suggested otherwise.

Though the strategy of dependent development pursued over the last four decades of the twentieth century in Ireland is nowadays generally considered much more successful than its autarkic predecessor, in reality both have been characterized by recurrent, sometimes very severe, crises. During the period of autarkic development, the state's official policy was to build up domestic industry behind a protective wall of tariff barriers designed to encourage import-substitution, to stimulate indigenous economic self-sufficiency, and to reduce an inherited dependence on British markets. Frequently caricatured nowadays as a kind of sulkily puritanical retreat from the world, the Listean ideal of national political and economic self-sufficiency was a perfectly orthodox one in the period between the world wars. Attempts to realize different versions of that ideal were made in many places in the last century from the United States to the Soviet Union, as well as in many emergent postcolonial states such as India. But by the end of the 1940s, economic stagnation, continued dependence on Britain, and very high levels of emigration all seemed to confirm the ignominious failure of this particular modernization project in Ireland. When the alternative strategy of dependent development was inaugurated in the late 1950s, import restrictions were removed and a variety of fiscal incentives were gradually put in place to court multinational capital to supply the drive to economic development that domestic efforts had failed to generate.

Yet from the 1970s until the 1990s, southern society suffered a severe and protracted recession, begging the question whether dependent development would prove any more successful than the abandoned autarky. Throughout this period Irish society struggled under a massive burden of international debt, continually escalating unemployment levels (in 1991 this exceeded the 20 per cent mark), and rates of emigration that had, by the late-1980s, reached levels not witnessed since the 1950s. When the Institute for Public Administration came in the early 1980s to assess the Republic's achievement's since the late 1950s, it inventoried the many severe problems then facing southern Irish society, commented anxiously on the rising sense of despondency that seemed to be sapping the morale necessary to tackle those problems, and concluded dourly that: 'It is difficult to avoid recalling the grim fifties, the last severe economic depression.'[2] The spectre of the failures of the past, the report acknowledged, continued to agitate the present. If the 1980s were the 'new fifties', then a quarter of a century of dependent development seemed only to have delivered the country back to the traumatic historical moment from which it was supposed to have redeemed it.

The episode of rural electrification dramatized in Black's *Korea* can be read as a nicely compressed allegory of this wider history. The scene registers not only the sense of heightened expectation, but also the many false starts and attendant social tensions and misgivings that have characterized the course of Irish modernization in the latter half of this century. In several of the great continental-size countries of the modern world, including the United States, Russia and India, one of the quintessential icons of modernization is the railway (symbol of the industrial conquest of time and space and of a new-found capacity to bind the hitherto far-flung locales of the national territory into a single unit). But in Ireland rural electrification has always been the favoured icon of this process — as though modernity was taken to be in this instance less a matter of industrialization or state aggrandizement than a kind of quasi-religious redemption from an inchoate primeval darkness. The centrality of the motif, in other words, suggests that in the Irish context there is a particularly acute stress on modernization, not simply as a matter of technological or industrial development, but as a project that is expected to deliver cultural and psychological release from the purgatorial nightmare of Irish colonial history as well; to serve as a kind of therapeutic 'revolution that will sweep away the inferiority complexes', as the dignitary in Black's film grandly declares. The shift from autarky to dependent development is commonly understood in precisely these terms; as a transition from the 'dark age' of de Valera to the liberal light of Lemass, from

---

2   See Frank Litton, Preface, *Unequal Achievement: The Irish Experience 1957–1982* (Dublin, 1982), cited in Terence Brown, *Ireland: A Social and Cultural History, 1922–2002*, rev. edn. (London, 2004 [1981]), 319.

the insecurity and oppressive dolefulness of a benighted rural Ireland into a brave new world that would finally embrace the urban, the European and the American excitements and refinements of modernity. The transition from the putatively introverted, rural and religious Ireland of the past into the putatively extroverted, urban and liberal secular Ireland of the present is commonly framed, in other words, in mythic terms, themselves freighted with quasi-religious resonance.

While Black's film deploys this quasi-religious, quasi-Enlightenment language of light and darkness, of murk and redemption, the awkwardly suspenseful moment when the switch is tripped and the expected illumination fails to materialize suggests that the transition from primeval darkness to technological enlightenment is neither smooth nor assured. When a particular modernization strategy falters — as happened in the 1940s and 1950s, or again in the 1970s and 1980s — doubts quicken and cynics readily step forward to assert that political and economic failure constitute the only predictable pattern of Irish history. In *Korea*, however, the electricity, despite embarrassing glitch and anxious delay, does come on in the end and the darkness does not overcome it. To this extent, the film expresses a distinctively 1990s sense of confidence in the course of Irish modernization, the travails of the previous quarter century notwithstanding.

On the other hand, there is also the voice of the disgruntled republican on the edges of the excited throng who protests, amid the general chorus of approval, that 'we didn't fight for street lamps'. In Black's film that voice, with its apparently begrudging and outmoded idealism, is inflected with a sense of *ressentiment* that undoubtedly undercuts its authority. Nonetheless, that voice still strikes a discordant note, one that registers the anxiety that the path of contemporary Irish modernization might actually represent the dissolution rather than the fulfilment of the Irish sovereignty for which so much struggle and sacrifice had been expended. The curious title of the film, moreover, naming as it does a small Asian country partitioned during the Cold War, the southern state becoming a beacon of capitalist modernization but only at the cost of a deeply controversial subordination to American international interests, the northern one remaining autarkic but becoming atrociously dysfunctional, can scarcely avoid awakening anxieties about the nature of Irish modernization — though these are voiced in the actual narrative only by the disgruntled republican. Muting these issues, but not closing them down either, and concluding with that striking shot of the moon evenly segmented between light and darkness, the opening episode of *Korea* seems in the end to hesitate between confidence and doubt, to suggest a sense of tentativeness about the course of Irish social development that will not easily resolve itself.

2

The political and intellectual conception of modernization that has prevailed in Irish society for some time now is a restricted and impoverished one. When the Republic entered the EEC in 1972, the Labour Party led the campaign against integration but in the period since then it reversed its position and became one of the standard-bearers for increased integration. Though some of the smaller political parties, such as Sinn Féin and the Green Party, are more Euro-sceptical and more concerned about the democratic implications of a single-state Europe than are their larger counterparts, there has been very little organized party political opposition to European integration, and hence only limited scope or capacity within the public sphere to give coherent articulation to any sense of sustainable alternative. Since the late 1980s, when the Communist states across Eastern Europe collapsed and those few states that still remained outside of the neo-liberal capitalist order increasingly sought to accommodate themselves to it, the sense of any viable alternative to the neo-liberal economic orthodoxies of the post-Cold War system has weakened further. In this conjuncture, nearly every form of opposition to the prevailing system is easily dismissed as merely a regressive or restorationist attempt to reinstate nationalist or socialist strategies that had already historically failed. In this climate, the capitalist entrepreneurial classes have been boldly able to reclaim their role as the radically internationalist or cosmopolitan avant-garde of history, breaking down via corporate globalization the Chinese walls of 'tradition' and benighted nationalist isolation, and thus forcing their opponents — of whatever political hue — on to a defensive terrain, whereby their essential function seems to be to *defend* and *conserve* the status quo (in campaigns to maintain workers' rights to unionization, to defend nationalized enterprises or the welfare state or to protect the environment), rather than to break the established moulds of society to create radical new futures. In a situation where the avant-gardist and transgressivist rhetorics and mentalities that the left had long thought its own have been dramatically reappropriated and refunctioned to new ends by a resurgently triumphalist right, the whole language of modernization — always deeply problematical in any event — has been emptied of value, reduced to a currency designed to secure the economic and social adaptation of states to the supposedly iron constraints of a fully globalized market.[3]

None of this is to suggest that an entirely supine consensus is the only order of the day. Dissent both to European integration and to capitalist globalization (and support for the former should not be conflated with support for the latter) continues to exist in Irish society, and to come from both the left and the right wings of the political spectrum. The two political wings sometimes even come into mutually uncomfortable alliances, as in 2001, when they combined to win a national referendum against the Nice Treaty. Though the major political parties soon rallied to reverse the verdict of that referendum, the episode served to register the surprising fragility of consent with regard to the direction of Irish society and to demonstrate the existence of unreconciled constituencies of dissent within the body politic. The main weakness of these constituencies was their

3 For a more extended discussion, see Joe Cleary, 'Introduction: Ireland and Modernity', in Joe Cleary and Claire Connolly, eds., *The Cambridge Companion to Modern Irish Culture* (Cambridge, 2005), 1–21.

own incohesion and their incapacity to articulate any strongly developed sense of an alternative. In all sorts of other ways, genuine antipathy to the status quo was and remains noticeable. Sometimes taking carnivalesque or deeply nihilistic forms (as in youth binge-drinking and drug-taking), sometimes more political expression (as in the rise of youth and working-class votes for Sinn Féin in the supposedly securely post-nationalist South or in the strong levels of support for campaigns against capitalist globalization), sometimes existing in other forms too (as in ecological or international debt-relief campaigns), these subcultures of dissent might be very difficult either to quantify or to channel to coherent strategic ends. But they demonstrate, nonetheless, that the dominant tendencies in any society also summon up complex patterns of resistance that constitute sets of potentials for an alternative order, even when those involved are unable to give anything like a co-ordinated or programmatic sense of definition to what that alternative might be.

Given the nature of the domestic and international conjuncture that has prevailed since at least the late 1980s, perhaps the real surprise of the 1990s was that the political establishment was not able to cement more support for its neo-liberalist policies of dependent development. After the tremendous anxieties and agitations of the 1980s, the extraordinary economic success of the Celtic Tiger boom that took off in the 1990s would inevitably be interpreted as a hard-earned and much-deserved, even if drastically delayed, vindication of the strategy of dependent development. After the 1980s it could no longer be doubted that all attempts to exit the capitalist state system — whether radical leftist of a Soviet or a Nicaraguan kind or religious-fundamentalist of the Iranian kind — had failed. For those disposed to see the essential conflict in Irish society as one between the backward forces of 'tradition' and the progressive forces of 'modernization', the essential compatibility of economic and social progress seemed also to be confirmed by events, as economic liberalization and social liberalization marched hand in hand. The introduction of divorce in 1996 represented a significant victory for the forces of liberal secularism over those of Catholic conservatism. There is no doubt that, as the Irish Republic became more economically prosperous in the 1990s, it also became more sexually tolerant and permissive as well — even if some of the forms that this tolerance took were hardly of the kind that feminist or gay rights activists of earlier decades had envisaged. When the long war of attrition between Catholic conservatives and liberals over social legislation was decisively settled in the latter's favour in the mid-1990s, and when this was then followed in 1998 by the overwhelming public endorsement of the Good Friday Agreement, the southern state's capacity to function as a 'normal' and prosperous liberal European capitalist democracy, unthreatened by either conservative backlash from its own rural badlands or by war on its northern borderlands, seemed finally more assured. The 1980s had been haunted by an uncanny sense of the 1950s revisited, but the 1990s seemed to have inaugurated a genuine new departure that set the scene for a decisively new dispensation.

If the Republic of Ireland economically and socially re-invented itself in the 1990s, then culturally it might have been expected to do the same. While some upbeat accounts suggest that this is precisely what did happen, in actual fact a survey of the cultural production of the decade — especially if by that term we mean the literary and cinematic production of that time — indicates something remarkably different. Far from suggesting a climate of radical innovation or dramatic new departures, nearly all the most critically lauded and commercially successful Irish works of that decade continued to be very strikingly invested in 'the dark ages' of the mid-twentieth-century rural Ireland that the country had supposedly left behind. In the worlds of the theatre and the novel, this was the decade of Brian Friel's *Dancing at Lughnasa* (1990), John McGahern's *Amongst Women* (1990), Patrick McCabe's *The Butcher Boy* (1992), Dermot Healy's *A Goat's Song* (1994), Seamus Deane's *Reading in the Dark* (1996), and Martin McDonagh's *The Beauty Queen of Leenane* (1996) or *The Cripple of Inishmaan* (1996). In the cinema, it was the decade of Jim Sheridan's *The Field* (1990), Thaddeus O'Sullivan's *December Bride* (1990), Cathal Black's *Korea* (1996), Neil Jordan's *The Butcher Boy* (1998), Pat O'Connor's *Dancing at Lughnasa* (1998), and many other films that were also set in a version of pre-sixties, pre-industrial Ireland. The same decade also saw several highly successful Irish memoirs and autobiographies, most notably Frank McCourt's Pulitzer Prize-winning *Angela's Ashes* (1996) — the publishing sensation of the decade, and very quickly to be converted onto the screen in Alan Parker's film version of the same title in 1999 — and Nuala O'Faolain's *Are You Somebody?* (1996), both of these works also dealing with the business of growing up in de Valera's Ireland. In 1998, RTÉ screened major national television adaptations of John McGahern's *Amongst Women* and Deirdre Purcell's *Falling for a Dancer*, both of which also explored the same era. The Celtic Tiger of the 1990s may have been attempting to get as far away as fast as it possibly could from de Valera's Ireland, but in the literary, dramatic and cinematic worlds that Ireland continued to be the biggest business in town.[4]

There is no reason to suppose that socio-economic and cultural developments should march in temporal lockstep with each other; time lags of a certain kind between the various levels of society are the norm rather than the exception. Nevertheless, the fact that so many of the major writers, dramatists and film-makers in Irish society, even

4 Perhaps the only major narrative work produced in the South to achieve anything like the popular success and critical recognition attained by the works mentioned above was Roddy Doyle's urban novel *Paddy Clarke Ha Ha Ha*, which won the Booker Prize in 1993. Doyle's success, building on earlier achievements such as *The Commitments* (1988), *The Snapper* (1990) and *The Van* (1991), was widely celebrated as a major new departure in Irish writing, his work (rather naïvely) credited in some circles as giving successful literary voice to an Irish urban world that could find no place for itself until then in a national imagination committed to a heavily ruralist sense of the national community. But in Doyle's *Paddy Clarke*, and in his earlier novels, which were located in a rather hermetically sealed and economically blighted, down-at-heel Dublin ghetto milieu, the action is almost completely severed from the wider currents of middle- or upper-class Dublin life. Hence, the imaginative world of Doyle's novels remained almost as distant from the social world of financial services centres, computer industries, comfortable middle-class suburbs and golf clubs, designer boutiques, congested motorways or city-centre gay saunas, gyms or sex shops, as were Friel's *Dancing at Lughnasa* or McCourt's *Angela's Ashes*.

in the swinging 1990s, were to remain so thoroughly fixated on the decades of Irish autarkic development does raise questions of some interest. How do we explain the fact that, at that very moment when Ireland was so successfully marketing itself as a vibrant and brashly modern (or postmodern) 'Tiger' economy, as a bullishly high-tech, post-industrial silicon society strategically traversing the global crossroads between Boston and Berlin, so many of its most distinguished artists in a variety of media should have concerned themselves with a largely pre-industrial rural Ireland that had long since become virtually synonymous with failure? Why was it that, at the very moment when the country was being widely hailed as the youngest and most 'open' or 'globalized' economy in Europe, it was the old and supposedly closed and arthritic, autarkic Ireland of the mid-century that so compelled the cultural imagination?

A number of answers suggest themselves. Literary and cinematic works, it might be argued, usually take considerable time to gestate, and those that appeared in the 1990s, therefore, were imaginatively conditioned, not by the temper of the decade in which they actually appeared, but by the altogether darker and more uncertain climate of the preceding decade. Imaginatively hatched in a decade of extended crisis that had so commonly summoned up the spectre of the dreadful fifties, these works, even though apparently set in the past, expressed concerns and anxieties that were actually those of the present. In an ancillary mode, it could be argued that it is the very nature of historical trauma that it should take a long time to disclose itself. The pain and suffering endured by one generation in one set of historical conditions is often doomed to remain silent and inarticulate, sometimes awaiting the radically altered historical conditions of a later generation before it can find terms and conditions propitious to its expression. From this perspective, the obsessive return to the age of de Valera in the 1990s suggests a sense of Irish history as trauma; it discloses a need to revisit a disturbing turning point in Irish history that could not be fully assimilated at the time of its occurrence, and which had therefore been belatedly repossessed. It required the convulsive, deck-clearing social clashes between the Catholic right and the liberalizing forces of the 1980s, and the eventual ascendancy of the latter, to create the conditions for a full settling of accounts with de Valera's Ireland, and for a full venting of all its long pent-up silences and griefs. Viewed thus, the works of the 1990s represent an unavoidably belated, but perhaps decisive and even 'final' reckoning with an earlier historical moment; a return to the past in order to confront it and also a letting go that would have to be accomplished before the nation was ready to redefine itself and to take full possession of its new future.[5]

5 For an argument that attributes a solidly critical function to the kinds of texts discussed here, see Luke Gibbons, 'The Global Cure? History, Therapy and the Celtic Tiger', in Peadar Kirby, Luke Gibbons and Michael Cronin, eds., Reinventing Ireland: Culture, Society and the Global Economy (London, 2002), 89–106. For Gibbons, the 1990s texts set in the mid-century are radical because they remain focused on the social ills of Irish society, thus refusing the official euphoria of the Celtic Tiger and the notion that economic prosperity will automatically assuage the hurts of history. Gibbons argues that the Irish fictions of de Valera's Ireland serve like Toni Morrison's work, for example, to retrieve hitherto silenced voices to bespeak a deeply traumatic history of suffering and oppression. But this downplays the differences between Morrison's

There is much to recommend these arguments, but they do tend to suggest that the literary and cinematic works in question share a strongly critical function; to argue along these lines is to assume that these works compelled audiences because they challenged them to face up both to the dark side of their historical past and to the uncomfortable continuities between that past and the present. But do the works in question really operate in this strongly critical manner? Might it not as well be argued that they actually served to affirm and validate the present rather than to unsettle it? In many ways, the recurrent return in the 1990s to the dark age of de Valera's Ireland acted as a backhanded validation of the present, which was clearly understood as a lucky escape 'from all that earlier business'. Far from asking hard questions about either past or present, the texts in question reassure their audiences that the major social ills that trouble contemporary Ireland are only the residues of an older order, the hangovers of de Valera's Ireland that continue to linger on into the present.

It might also be possible, of course, that the anxieties that charge these works may have to do neither with the past nor the present, but rather with the future. After all, in the post-Cold War neo-liberal order of the 1990s that was widely touted as ushering in 'the end of history', the real question confronting Irish and other societies might be whether there was any new future at all left to imagine. After the end of history, as Fredric Jameson has wryly remarked, no future beginnings being foreseen, our own time can only be imagined as the end of something else.[6] It might plausibly be argued that in this situation one of the things that impelled Irish writers back to the fifties, back to the dark ages of de Valera, was a nostalgia for a time where there were still battles to be fought, still alternative futures (or the appearance of such at least) to be struggled for. But this is not nostalgia as it is commonly understood — not some sentimental search for a time of greater innocence — but a peculiarly post-modern, post-revolutionary nostalgia for a lost time of meaningful historical conflict when the nation could imagine that it still had (or seemed to have) weighty, decisive historical choices left to make.

The works that discussed in this chapter — Jim Sheridan's *The Field*, John McGahern's *Amongst Women* and Brian Friel's *Dancing at Lughnasa* — offer an index of the possibilities that the various reconstructions of de Valera's Ireland in this decade made available. The contradictions, antinomies and anxieties of Irish modernization are the emotional raw materials that go into the making of these works; these are the grit or grist of 'the real' with which they all wrestle. In all of them, we can detect both critical and affirmative impetuses at work, but in none does anything like a strong or intellectually radical critique of the late twentieth-century social order emerge.[7]

---

formally adventurous historical novels, which typically overlay past and present within a national history, and the more naturalistic Irish fictions that operate within more compressed time frames and that deal with a foreshortened historical past.

6   Fredric Jameson, 'The End of Temporality', *Critical Inquiry*, 29 (2003), 695–718, 695. See also Fredric Jameson, *A Singular Modernity: Essay on the Ontology of the Present* (London, 2002).

7   The temporal setting of any of these texts cannot be taken as an a priori indicator of its politics. A strong argument could be made, for example, that in Northern Irish fiction especially, the tendency by

3

In *All that is Solid Melts into Air*, Marshall Berman argues that the works of some of the major writers of the nineteenth century are distinguished by their capacity to grasp both sides of the contradictions of capitalist development. 'Our nineteenth-century thinkers,' Berman writes, 'were simultaneously enthusiasts and enemies of modern life, wrestling inexhaustibly with its ambiguities and contradictions; their self-ironies and inner tensions were a primary source of their creative power.' But their twentieth-century successors, Berman argues, 'have lurched far more toward rigid polarities and flat totalizations. Modernity is either embraced with a blind and uncritical enthusiasm, or else condemned with a neo-Olympian remoteness and contempt; in either case it is conceived as a closed monolith, incapable of being shaped or changed by modern men.'[8] For Berman, this drastic polarization in modern thought is exemplified by the rhapsodic modernolatory of Marinetti and the Italian Futurists, Le Corbusier and Marshall McLuhan, on the one side, and, on the other, by the visions of modernity as catastrophe in Weber, Spengler, Eliot, Kafka, Leavis and Adorno. Berman's work rests on an untenable distinction between a nineteenth-century intelligentsia receptive to the dialectics of modernity and a twentieth-century one that is invariably much less so. Yet the importance of his overall argument prevails — that blind and uncritical enthusiasms or outright condemnations of modernity represent no substitute for an attempt to experience it whole, to see it dialectically as a world where 'everything is pregnant with its contrary'.[9]

The more romantic and heroic strains in the literature of the Irish Revival shared the anti-realist, anti-mimetic thrust and a good deal of the anti-bourgeois sentiment that characterized all the main currents of European modernism. On the whole, however, that literature tends very definitely, to borrow Berman's terms, towards the critical rather than the celebratory conception of modernity and modernization. But while the more realist and naturalistic modes of writing that were first developed within the Revival by George Moore, Brinsley MacNamara, James Joyce and others rejected the romantic view of ancient pre-colonial or pre-Christian Ireland or of the peasantry or of the West, the conception of the modern that emerged in this oppositional current was just as bleak and negative. Joyce or Moore or MacNamara repudiated the backward look commonly associated with Ascendancy versions of the Revival, but they did not embrace

certain authors in the 1990s to imaginatively locate their works in some period earlier than the 1970s was potentially a liberating move: one that allowed writers to free the imagination from the tyranny of the immediate present that mutilates so much 'Troubles' fiction, thus at least preparing the conditions for a new type of fiction temperamentally more inclined to elaborate some longer historical view of the Northern conflict.

8   Marshall Berman, *All that is Solid Melts into Air: The Experience of Modernity* (Harmondsworth, 1988 [1982]), 24

9   Karl Marx, cited in Berman, *All that is Solid Melts into Air*, 35, 36

or affirm the world of modern, urban capitalism either; the vision of small-town Ireland that emerges in MacNamara's *The Valley of the Squinting Windows* (1918) or of the capital city in Joyce's *Dubliners* (1914) are both ruthlessly disenchanted. In the period after the establishment of the Irish Free State, this naturalistic aesthetic tended generally to insist on the social meanness, the cultural narrowness, and the general suffocation or torpor of spirit in post-independence Ireland. The vision that emerged was one in which the romanticism or primitivism of the Revival was sandblasted, but all that remains is either a sense of wearied and generalized disenchantment with politics as such or a sense of diminished expectation or embittered resignation.

The Irish Revival repudiated the world of bourgeois capitalist modernity and quested after the energies of some more vital pre-modern alternative; Irish naturalism cultivated a disenchanted social vision in which the pre-modern was leached of all value and the world of bourgeois capitalism was construed as an inexorable if generally unlovely destiny. The net effect was a literature that always kept its distance from the affirmative or heroic or rhapsodic versions of the modern. In sum, in practically all of its more robust twentieth-century narrative lineages — Revivalist, naturalist, modernist, Big House — Irish literature has inclined far less towards a positive conception of modernity as dreamworld than towards one of modernity as some kind of catastrophe.[10] The production of narrative in late twentieth-century Ireland draws on the wider repertoire of literary modes described here, especially on the naturalist one.

Where cultural historians were once disposed simply to equate modernist art with the great metropoli of Western modernity — to see it simply as the art of London, Paris, Vienna, New York, Berlin or Moscow — it is now more persuasively argued that modernism can better be understood as a culture of incomplete modernization. However, by the latter half of the twentieth century this modernist conjuncture begins to break up (in the Euro-American world at least) and to disappear. When the grip of the pre-modern vanishes — as the world of the aristocracy and the peasantry is subsumed into industrialized agriculture, a suburbanized countryside, and a vastly expanded tourist and leisure sector — and when the new mass consumerist culture of late modernity is triumphantly installed everywhere across the Western world, then any sense of alternative pre-modern or non-modern temporality disappears or recedes with it as well. With it goes that sense of 'deep time' (to use Fredric Jameson's phrase) that the early modernists had incorporated into their art.[11] At the same historical moment, any strong sense of utopian futurity also began to evaporate as the Communist world stagnated after World War II and failed to keep pace with the consumerist and welfarist societies of the West. Following on from this wholesale liquidation of the 'deep time' of the pre-modern, on the one side, and the 'utopian time' of futurity, on the other, there remains

10 The terms are derived from Susan Buck-Morss, *Dreamworld and Catastrophe: The Passing of Mass Utopia in East and West* (Cambridge, MA, 2000).
11 Jameson, 'The End of Temporality', 699

only the reduction to an eternal present that constitutes the dominant temporality of the triumphantly consumer capitalist postmodern conjuncture.

There was a remarkable renaissance of late modernist and utopian energies in the 1960s. However, the resurgence of the right and the extraordinary capitalist boom in the last quarter of the twentieth century largely put an end to this, and dramatically lowered political expectations of any substantial change to the wider international order. In Ireland, the local waves of radical dissent that issued in this period in the nationalist–republican assault on the state in the North and the largely feminist-driven challenge to the conservative Catholic state in the South seems not to have generated much by way of a late modernist or utopian resurgence in the cultural or aesthetic fields. But they did certainly inject new life into Irish literary naturalism. For the dissidents, especially those in the South, the conception of Ireland as a deeply oppressive society was predicated on the idea that the country was too rural, too Catholic, too nationalist, and that it badly needed to modernize to become urban, secular and post-nationalist. The available body of literature that was most serviceable to this particular view of things was Irish naturalism. The view from the nationalist North might look quite different, but British unionism and Irish revisionism combined so successfully to interpret the republican upsurge there as a restoration (of some romantic 'old Ireland'), rather than rebellion, that most southern intellectuals could scarcely differentiate between the working-class driven insurgency of the North and the middle-class conservative Catholic backlash in the South — conflating both as evidence of a concerted nationalist recoil against modernity and as evidence that the nightmare of de Valera's Ireland was still alive and well.

But if the assault on the conservatism of the southern state was initiated by Irish feminism in the sixties, it was ultimately completed by a resurgent neo-liberalism gathering pace, not only domestically, but across the globe in the last quarter of the century. The neo-liberals might hold in contempt the radical utopianism of the sixties (whether of the republican, socialist or feminist variety), but the consumer capitalism they championed had even less sentiment to spare for the old Catholic nationalist dispensation — with its antique anti-consumerist puritanism and quaint ideals of a frugal or modest materialism — than those at the opposite end of the political spectrum. No less impatient for change than those on the left, therefore, the neo-liberal modernizers could also find in naturalism's disenchanted vision of Ireland a literature that largely confirmed their own negative conception of post-independence history. In this climate, a renovated naturalism could be adapted reasonably well to meet some of the fundamental needs of both the left and the right as they each struggled to free themselves from de Valera's Ireland. Or, to put it another way, in a *fin de siècle* social climate where there was a strong sense of an ending but little sense of futurity, naturalism might well seem a rather old-fashioned literary aesthetic, but it still answered well enough to the needs of the moment to allow it another literary season.

4

Like so many Irish narratives of the 1990s, The Field, Amongst Women and Dancing at Lughnasa all depict, in a largely naturalist idiom, a crepuscular rural world about to be pulverized by the imminent arrival of industrial modernity. Attitudes to the arrival of the new order vary from one narrative to another. The most common response, as in Pat O'Connor's The Ballroom of Romance (1982), a screen version of William Trevor's much-lauded short story of the same title, is to see the arrival of the new order as a welcome redemption from the pervading social darkness of the old dispensation. In O'Connor's film, rural Ireland of the 1950s is depicted as a boorish world cursed with problems of social and sexual deprivation, emigration and male tyranny. One of the recurrent topics of conversation between the characters is that 'The factory is coming to town' — an event that seems to promise a welcome end to the arthritic social order depicted in the film. Brian Friel's Dancing at Lughnasa is set at the close of the 1930s, but here again we are dealing with an order at the end of its days. The play tells the story of the Mundy sisters living in straitened circumstances in a small Donegal townsland at a moment when, as the narrator in the play tells the audience, 'The Industrial Revolution had finally caught up with Ballybeg.'[12] For Friel, the belated arrival of this 'industrial revolution' carries none of the sense of the redemption that it does in The Ballroom of Romance. Instead, it triggers the dissolution of the Mundy family, making two of the sisters, who earn their living by hand-knitting, redundant, and thus accelerating a narrative of decline already in evidence from the start.

McGahern's Amongst Women depicts once again a narrow and oppressive social order on the brink of its ultimate demise. Set sometime in the middle decades of the twentieth century, the central part of the novel consists of an extended retrospect that tells the story of Moran, a small farmer and ex-guerrilla fighter in the War of Independence, and of how his second wife, Rose, and his five children cope with his tormented and oppressive rule over the world of Great Meadow. This central narrative is framed by a brief opening sequence, which describes the closing stages of Moran's life, and by a concluding one that deals with his death and funeral. At the end of the opening sequence, Rose smuggles into the house the brown Franciscan habit in which her husband will be buried. Since the repressive world at the centre of the narrative proper is framed by its own demise, the narrative strategy at work here is one that serves to enhance a sense of the pastness of Moran's world, to place it at a remove from the temporality of the reader. A similar narrative device operates in Friel's Dancing at Lughnsa, in which an adult narrator interrupts the narrative flow to comment on the action that occurs at a time when he himself was still a small boy. In each case, the device establishes a sense of distance between narrative and audience that may well encourage a sense of critical detachment, but which also runs the risk of simply making the audience, to borrow a

12 Brian Friel, Dancing at Lughnasa (London, 1990), 59

phrase from Roger Bromley, 'tourists in other people's reality'.[13]

Though generally more linear in shape than the McGahern or Friel narratives, Jim Sheridan's The Field re-creates a very similar temporality. John B. Keane's play The Field (1965), which Sheridan film adapts to its own ends, was actually produced and set in the 1960s but Sheridan moves events back to 1939, thus locating the action in a sensuously altogether less modern and much more primitivist landscape than the original. In Keane's play, for example, there are references to motorbikes, bingo halls, hairdressing salons and telephones, and it is a contemporary 1960s boom in land prices that precipitates the crisis on which the narrative turns. In the Sheridan version, all of this paraphernalia of modern mass culture is stripped away, and what we see on the screen instead is a still ruggedly peasant society depicted via a hard primitivist aesthetic that suggests a grimly relentless struggle with an unyielding natural world. The characters and the action, too, take on strongly mythopoeic and would-be epic qualities that suggest an effort either to transcend time altogether or to create some sort of distinctly pre-modern or non-modern heroic temporality. Modernization in this instance takes the form of a violent conflict between the Bull McCabe (Richard Harris), a local patriarch whose ambitions for 'the field' are thwarted by the arrival of a Returned Yank (Tom Berenger), a stylized figure clearly representative of American capitalism. The Bull has spent a lifetime of toil trying to improve the field, but the American plans to have it concreted over in order to construct a hydroelectric power station and a lime quarry that he will use to build 'highways all over Ireland'. In Keane's 1960s play, the interloper who competes with Bull for the field is a Galwayman, William Dee, who returns from England and plans to build a factory on the site. By shifting the conflict away from a colonial or postcolonial Irish–English axis and onto an Irish–American one, The Field transmits the sense that late twentieth-century issues about the control of the national territory (for which the field itself is metonym) in a period of American-led capitalist globalization are being negotiated here. But while Sheridan updates Keane's narrative in this direction, the hard primitivist setting established by the visual iconography works to haul history backwards in the opposite direction — establishing, as do Friel's or McGahern's narrative devices, a considerable temporal distance between the narrative and the receiving audience. Once again, the collapse of an old social order — the common theme in all these tales — is something that the audience contemplates from a narratively organized remove, secure in the knowledge that its own present is somewhere safely on the other side of the crisis that occupies its attention.

'The moments we call crises,' Frank Kermode writes in The Sense of an Ending, 'are ends and beginnings.'[14] This may be so, but in the narratives described here it is endings and not beginnings that invariably monopolize attention. It is, in other words, always the death rattle of old dispensations, and not the birth of what is destined to displace

13 Roger Bromley, Lost Narratives: Popular Fictions, Politics and Recent History (London, 1988), 10
14 Frank Kermode, The Sense of an Ending: Studies in the Theory of Fiction (Oxford, 1966), 96

and replace them, that compels narrative scrutiny. Thus in *The Ballroom of Romance* or *Dancing at Lughnasa*, 'the factory' exists only as a topic of conversation, and the whole sensory world associated with factories has no substantive presence in either narrative. In *Amongst Women*, the quarrel between Moran and the more worldly McQuaid, his former lieutenant during the War of Independence and now a cattle-dealer and a master of the commercial arts that elude Moran himself, represents the superseding of an older military ethos by a new pragmatic capitalism in the post-revolutionary period. McQuaid — big-bellied, vulgar, driving a white Mercedes, brashly confident — is a conventional enough icon of the rural bourgeois class that would come to dominate the post-revolutionary southern state; yet McQuaid's milieu, like that of the Dublin and London where Moran's children live their adult lives, has only the sketchiest of existences in the novel as a whole, and the real focus is always the determinedly insular and separate world of Great Meadow. Likewise, in *The Field*, the audience listens to the American describe his plans for quarries, power stations and highways, but the visual landscape of the film itself, as noted earlier, is a primitive one where such things still exist only in the future and can as yet scarcely be imagined. Even if the superseding of an old rural formation by a more modern industrial social order is always inexorably assured at the level of plot, the narratives themselves remain stubbornly rooted in the sensorium of the old order. Though nominally victorious at the narrative level, the emergent order, lacking its own distinctive sensorium, remains curiously ethereal; too willowy and insubstantial, too null in any sensory sense, to command either the strong assent or rejection of the audience.

Of the works mentioned here, the one that strives hardest to work the dilemmas or conundrums of Irish modernization into some sort of decisively epic or tragic contention of opposing forces is *The Field*. In Sheridan's version, the conflict between the Bull McCabe and the American can be read as one in which the programmes and value-systems of Irish autarkic and dependent development come into irresolvable head-on confrontation with each other. It would be reductive to read the film, as many commentators tend to do, simply in terms of an external disturbance of a settled or static traditional social order, since it is clear that the Bull and the American are *both* aggressive modernizers, though of a different kind.[15] The Bull, in Sheridan's version, is no traditionalist conservationist of some immemorial peasant order. At one stage, a

---

15 In an otherwise suggestive reading of Sheridan's *The Field*, Cheryl Herr, for example, contends that 'the Bull is less an individual than a representative patriarch, whose sensibility speaks to deep, changeless traditions'. But the colonial history to which the Bull is so alert was in fact remorselessly destructive of 'deep, changeless traditions', and what the film actually presses into conflict are two different, and equally ruthless, non-conservative and unsentimental modernizing programmes. Herr is correct when she notes that Sheridan's *The Field* was conditioned by 1980s debates about 'the displacement of tradition by modernity', but while it shows some indebtedness to the rather reductive modernization discourses of the period, the film is actually far less indebted to a conception of de Valera's Ireland as simply a bastion of static 'tradition' than are many other works of the period. See Cherly Herr, *The Field* (Cork, 2002), 26, 52.

scene is introduced that shows him replacing his thatched roof with a slated one, and the emotional conviction that underpins his claim to the field rests on the fact that he has expended huge labour to wrest it from hard rock and to turn it into prime agricultural land — it is visually represented on the screen as a lushly verdant pasture that stands in vivid contrast to the hard primitivist landscape all about it. The difference between the Bull and the American, then, is not at all that one represents a static commitment to unchanging custom and the other dynamic modern innovation. It is that the Bull's project is one of fiercely self-reliant agricultural improvement, while his rival's scheme is of a more industrial character that will be financed by American capital.

For the Bull, land may be all about keeping a grip on a means to survival in a harshly competitive economic order, but at the same time that land is not reducible to its cash value. From his perspective, the field is the product of a long history, a non-fungible sign of hard-won victories over nature, famine and British domination, and he feels duty-bound, in the name of the many sacrifices made in its name, to pass on control of it to future generations. In contrast to the Bull's fiercely historicized conception of the land, reinforced by a sense of the labour-value embedded in it, the Widow's and the American's conviction that it is simply an exchangeable commodity, to be purchased on the open market by the highest bidder, seems impersonal and abstract. Nevertheless, while his plans undoubtedly spell ruin for the Bull's dreams for the field, the American's project also has its positive side, since it will, he asserts, bring employment and prosperity to the region and indeed to the country as a whole.

Moreover, while the Bull's claim to the field on the basis of the labour-value invested in it by ancestral struggles are registered with genuine passion and conviction, that claim is neither sentimentalized nor allowed to go critically uncontested in the film. The Bull's almost fanatic devotion to the improvement of his land is secured by his sense of heroic transgenerational struggles, but it also goes hand in hand with a great deal of aggressive machismo and with a contemptuous disdain for all those who have lost their grip on the land (namely, emigrants and Travellers). At one point in the narrative, the Bull recalls that when his own mother had died in the field, he and his father had worked on to ensure that the hay would be saved, and had only stopped to go for the priest when the day's work was completed. The anecdote conveys a sense of hard primitivist heroics but suggests, too, that the struggle required to dominate external nature demands a suppression of one's own emotional nature that is in the end extraordinarily costly and even, in human terms, self-defeating.

While the Bull attempts to secure public support in Carraigthomond by representing the conflict between himself and the American as one between local and foreigner, or between labour-value and exchange-value, the narrative demonstrates a more complex situation. The American is not simply an 'outsider' but the son of an Irish emigrant, and his plans to industrialize the countryside will, he is adamant, provide the employment that will spare others his father's fate. The Bull's mode of self-reliant agricultural modernization, in other words, is a form of protectionist or autarkic development that works only for those who already have land and it has little or nothing to offer those who do not; the American's more industrial model may wrest control of its own affairs away from the locality, but it may also bring economic benefits to a far greater number of people.

Finally, the Bull's passionate commitment to maintaining his family's grip on the land is shadowed from the outset by an undisclosed trauma that has destroyed the bond between himself and his wife and between himself and his son. The emotional climax of the film is reached when the source of that trauma is revealed: driven by the Bull's constant insistence that the family farm could support only one of his two sons, and that the other would have no option but to emigrate, Shamie, the elder son, had taken his own life and had consequently been refused burial by the Church in consecrated ground. What this revelation suggests, in the first instance, is that emigration is the dark side of economic autarky, the disavowed knowledge or bad faith that dogs its whole credo of rootedness in the land and sturdy self-reliance. Moreover, where the film had earlier critiqued, in the voice of the Bull, a dehistoricized and depersonalized conception of the land as fungible abstract commodity, this disclosure works in an opposite direction: it serves to indict both religious and nationalist investments of the land with an inviolable 'sacredness', since these too turn land into a transcendent value as alienating in its own way as the iron laws of commodification. The ascendancy of market value is dehumanizing because it divests the land of all intense human association and labour input by reducing it to an abstract commodity, but religious and/or nationalistic inscriptions of the land with absolute symbolic importance (while acting as a brake on commodification) also prove alienating, because once the land is converted into fetishes of this kind, they too take priority over human needs.

The Field, then, sets in motion a conflict between autarkic modernization (represented here as charismatically independent and bullishly nationalistic, but also as oppressively patriarchal and domineering in spirit) and dependent development (characterized as energetic and enterprising, as quite possibly more broadly beneficial than the Bull's intensely family-oriented programme, but recognizing no values beyond the cash nexus) and tries to lend the clash between the two the aura of a Hegelian tragedy where the fundamental conflict is between two irreconcilable 'goods'. Things are then pushed towards the point where these two value-systems are brought into definitive collision, but the film cannot ultimately sustain its own convictions or commitments: having set out to represent the confrontation between the Bull and the Yank as one that involves a fearsome clash of antithetical positive values where something of value has to be lost, it is as though somewhere along the line the narrative falters and finds itself finally unable to endorse the values associated with either one or the other of the two central parties to that conflict.

For much of the time the audience's sympathies are tilted in favour of the Bull, a larger-than-life character who dwarfs all the others and to whom Richard Harris lends a formidable mesmeric power. But the silence his wife has maintained for years and the disclosure towards the end that his son had committed suicide, suggest that the Bull's project is fatally flawed and self-destructive; the level of human sacrifice demanded in its name is too high and the sense of rugged independence that constitutes its most positive value is compromised by the unacknowledgeable shame of emigration. The American also has his attractive side: he is a visionary dreamer of grand schemes. But the real source of his power is money, and while the film lends him a certain brash glamour, he is essentially a one-dimensional figure, with none of the Bull's fiery human grandeur.

Since the plot builds up the Bull and the American as heroic antagonists only then to distance the audience from each in turn, the clash between the two sides eventually loses much of its force. Thus the narrative cannot produce the consequential 'big finish' that authentic tragic collision would require. Instead, in the emotionally heightened but curiously anti-climactic and rather histrionic murder scene, the American is killed off; but the Bull's victory is a pyrrhic one that does not alter anything in the outer world and that unleashes chaos in his own inner psyche. From the outset, the Returned Yank is a cipher for American capital and foreign investment, and since killing the individual capitalist does nothing to alter the power of that system, the whole episode is rather meaningless. The representative of autarkic modernization is granted a temporary victory over the representative of dependent development, but that victory is an irrelevant sideshow, since the audience knows that, historically, the latter will inevitably prevail.

A fundamental contradiction in Sheridan's film is that while constantly upping the emotional ante to suggest that the struggle to control the field is a matter of genuine importance, it simultaneously suggests that that struggle is really much ado about nothing. From the outset, Tadhg (Sean Bean), the Bull's son, is shown to be incapable of measuring up to his father as a custodian to 'the field,' and in any event his infatuation with the glamorous Tinker Girl (Jenny Conroy) seems to suggest that his real desire is to escape his inheritance. The Travellers here — as in *Into the West* — are a mobile pre-modern community whose 'freedom' is connected to their existence outside the property system. For the Bull, the Travellers are a source of anxiety because they represent the degradation that befalls those who lack the determination or ability to maintain their grip on the land (at one point he tells his son, 'This is what we'd be without the land, boy', and blows a dandelion into the air). Yet when holding on to the land is shown to require so much aggressiveness and repressive self-abnegation, it is scarcely surprising that Tadhg is secretly envious of the Travellers' rootlessness, and that, after the killing of the American, he should decide to elope with the Tinker Girl.

Do the Travellers function in the text as a metaphor for some non-modern and non-nationalized communistic collectivity that emotionally rebukes the fanatic drive to proprietorship exemplified by both the Bull and the American? Or do they insinuate the more de-territorialized diasporic versions of Irish national identity that were emerging in response to the new capitalist globalization of the 1990s? (Redefinitions of nationality along such lines were fashioned during Mary Robinson's presidency at the start of the decade and later on by the Good Friday Agreement.) What is clear is that if the American represents all of the more negative anxieties that attend globalization, the Travellers represent its more utopian dimension.

From a narrative or dramatic point of view, the decisive factor is that the Travellers emerge as a symbolic resolution to the irreconcilable conflict between the Bull and the American, thus in effect serving as a narrative valve that releases pressure from the main conflict and siphons off much of its significance. Thus, a would-be tragedy teeters at the end into histrionics; a would-be epic into a declamatory monumentalism.[16] Having worked hard for much of the plot to persuade the audience that whether the Bull or the American will inherit the field is of real consequence, it is as though it is eventually decided that no field could be worth so much bloody bother. A possible happy ending is momentarily dangled before us (renouncing both Irish Bull and the American Dream, Tadhg abandons the whole wretched business of the field to go off with the Tinker Girl), but then immediately revoked for a sense of all-encompassing tragedy (Tadhg is killed when he is swept over a cliff by the cattle that his father in his madness has stampeded). There is something unsatisfyingly stagey about the conclusion of the The Field, and this is surely connected to the fact that it shuffles so rapidly through a whole deck of all-too-obvious tragic endings (there are echoes of Shakespeare's King Lear and Macbeth, of Yeats's On Baile's Strand, of Synge's Playboy, of O'Casey's Juno and the Paycock). A better way to put this might be to say that The Field works hard to depict post-World War II Irish history — the clash between two modes of national development — as the stuff of national epic or tragedy, but finds itself unable to sustain that tragic vision (which depends on some sense of conviction that the stakes are real and substantive) and offers us instead, therefore, simulations of other tragic endings ransacked from literary and cinematic archives.

In John McGahern's Amongst Women, the drama of Irish modernization is also constructed as that of patriarchy in crisis. Moran, the central protagonist in the novel, is an insecure and cantankerous domestic tyrant who nonetheless commands the loyalty of all but one of his children. Though he is a product of the revolutionary phase of Irish nationalism, the novel is set in a time when that period is long past and neither the values nor the political accomplishments of the national struggle compel much admiration. Moran's daughters attempt to restore their father's declining spirits by reviving Monaghan Day, with its memories of republican militancy during the War of Independence, but that attempt is shown to be miscalculated and futile: 'Monaghan Day had revived nothing but a weak fanciful ghost of what had been.'[17] Moran himself thwarts his daughters' recuperative project by disowning any heroic conception of

16 For an interesting discussion of critical responses to the ending of The Field, see Herr, The Field, 49–50. As Herr notes, several Irish, British and American reviewers commented on the film's failure to realize its epic ambitions, some noting the way Harris's over-the-top performances tended to diminish the other characters too much, others remarking on the way the dialogue frequently collapsed into declamatory bombast.

17 John McGahern, Amongst Women (London, 1990), 7

the revolutionary period, sourly dismissing it as 'a bad business' ('We didn't shoot at women and children like the Tans but we were a bunch of killers') that achieved nothing of any real substance: 'What did we get for it? A country, if you'd believe them. Some of our own johnnies in the top jobs instead of a few Englishmen. More than half my own family work in England. What was it all for? The whole thing was a cod.'[18] This derisive assessment of the post-independence period, which refuses to acknowledge that anything at all positive emerged from the national struggle and that allows the post-independence period no achievements worth the name, is not explicitly endorsed in the novel, and Moran's attitude to the new state is clearly rooted in a sense of *ressentiment* that stems from his failure to retain in the postwar period the social status that he had enjoyed as a guerrilla commander. At the same time, there is no strong repudiation of Moran's assessment of either the national struggle or its outcome in the novel either, and the extended and harrowing depiction of Moran's crass and puritanical despotism over Great Meadow clearly registers an overwhelmingly negative impression of post-independence Irish society.

The different trajectories of the post-revolutionary nationalist generation are represented in the novel by Moran and McQuaid. McQuaid is enterprising and aggressive and makes his way in the post-independence world, but he is depicted as a one-dimensional vulgar philistine. Moran stubbornly insists that his society is a travesty of the grand ideals of the independence struggle, but his own sullenly rejectionist stance is productive of no alternative set of political values except for his desperate cult of the family, which seems in part at least to function as a form of compensation for his loss of authority in the wider public sphere. However, as observed earlier, the structure of the narrative establishes from the start that this post-revolutionary generation has reached the end of its days. What about the next generation then? What will its values be and what kind of Ireland will it represent?

Within the terms given to us by the novel, these are questions to which there can be no real answers. Moran's children are depicted here as survivors of an old order, but not in any sense as the creators of a new one. Mona, Sheila and Maggie all settle in the world beyond Great Meadow, but, as Maria DiBattista observes, the girls 'always return to "Daddy" and the parental home to regain an identity imperilled in the cosmopolitan world of London or Dublin where they are no more than urban debris, "specks of froth"'.[19] Michael and Luke, Moran's sons, both rebel against paternal despotism, but Michael is of easy-going disposition and is soon reconciled with his father, and only Luke remains permanently alienated, the affective bonds that link him to his father and his siblings irreparably shattered by a brutal upbringing he can never forgive or forget. Yet although Luke's is the only outright and sustained rebellion against the values

---

18 *Amongst Women*, 5
19 Maria DiBattista, 'Joyce's Ghost: The Bogey of Realism in John McGahern's *Amongst Women*', in Karen R. Lawrence, ed., *Transcultural Joyce* (Cambridge, 1998), 21–36, 25

represented by Great Meadow, his unforgiving repudiation of Moran, like Moran's of the post-independence Irish state, generates no positive set of values in the novel. In his detachment and isolation in London, Luke seems emotionally crippled or stunted — 'Luke had always been slight of build and he hadn't filled out much with the years.'[20] It is as though the tremendous effort required to break free of Moran's familial nets had emotionally exhausted him, suspending him in a condition of permanent affective arrest that allows neither for reconciliation with the past, nor for strong interaction with the present, nor for future growth and development.

This extraordinary novel is constructed in terms of two refusals, each of which displays a certain adamant integrity, but neither of which can offer any humanly satisfying alternative to the world that is refused. Moran's insistence that independent Ireland is a sorry travesty of the high ideals of the independence struggle is registered sympathetically, but the twisted cult of the family, the only alternative that he himself can offer, empties his rejectionist stance of positive content. Likewise, Luke's unrelenting rejection of his father's domineering cult of the family is depicted as humanly understandable, but Luke's own life is so emotionally sterile that his rejectionist stance is also bleached of positive content. The indictments of the social and political shabbiness of post-independent Ireland, and of the narrow cult of the family that is represented as an introverted response to that wider public shabbiness, are both allowed to stand, but what is clearly absent in the novel is anything that might amount to a positive alternative to those conditions that are indicted. Commemorating the past, as the Moran daughters do when they revive Monaghan Day, is shown to generate 'nothing but a weak fanciful ghost of what had been', but those, like Luke or Moran himself, who fiercely repudiate their pasts remain stunted figures, incapable of forging generous emotional bonds with those about them. *Amongst Women* seems to advocate, and to want to embody, a politics of memory that will avoid both the feel-good nostalgia of Monaghan Day-type commemorations (which whitewash history of its violence and horror) and aggressively or sullenly unforgiving repudiations of the past (which insist only on the violence and horror, and will allow the past no other dimension or value).

In a novel in which the thematics of family and home are central, Great Meadow is a place of shocking trauma and terror, but one from which most of the younger generation nonetheless manage to draw strength, and the world of the city is conceived in contrast as a place of transcendental homelessness. Luke, significantly, studies accountancy in London and 'had become friendly with a Cockney man ... who had been a french polisher and who now sold reproduction furniture to antique shops from a van. He mentioned some plan they had of buying old houses and converting them into flats for sale.' Sheila's house in the Dublin suburbs is described as 'a low, detached bungalow in a new estate of a couple of hundred bungalows exactly the same, the front gardens

20 *Amongst Women*, 147

still raw with concrete'.[21] The descriptions here are spare and noncommittal, but the urban houses are nonetheless sketched in terms that suggest transience, mechanical reproduction and unfinishedness — they are dwellings that somehow fall short of that sense of lived-in attachment that would convert them into homes. It is this failure of the city to provide a satisfying alternative to Great Meadow that seems to explain the Moran sisters' constant return to the country in search of regeneration:

> The closeness [offered by Great Meadow] was as strong as the pull of their own lives; they lost the pain of individuality within its protection. In London or Dublin the girls would look back to the house for healing ... Beneath all differences was the belief that the whole house was essentially one. Together they were one world and could take on the world. Deprived of this sense they were nothing, scattered, individual things.[22]

Here, again, we have the contrast between a turbulent, traumatic, problematical rootedness and a deracinated scatteredness that we have already encountered in The Field. But in McGahern's case scatteredness has none of the utopian connotations it sometimes has in Sheridan.

Instead, the vision of Irish modernity that informs Amongst Women is more or less consistent with the conventional opposition between pre-modern Gemeinschaft and modern Gesellschaft that structures the nineteenth-century sociology of Tönnies, Durkheim and Weber. Great Meadow displays the conventional negative and positive qualities of Gemeinschaft. It is rigidly patriarchal, illiberal and intolerant by modern standards, and governed by seasonal and ritualistic rather than linear-progressive notions of time (the recital of the rosary runs like a refrain across the novel), but its mode of authority, though despotic, is personalized and charismatic, not contractual or bureaucratic. Likewise, the world outside of Great Meadow displays the usual qualities of the Gesellschaft. Sheila and Mona escape Great Meadow not by overt rebellion but through the state education system that takes them into the civil service and the city. In other words, the tight communal world of Great Meadow is superseded by the administrative apparatus of the state, and the younger generation abandons the country for the city, a place associated in the novel with greater personal freedom but also with the dissolution of kinship bonds and with social atomization and alienation. The distinction here is not only between two different kinds of society, and their contrasting impacts on the quality of human experience, but also on two historically successive stages of development within one and the same society; whatever the gains and losses involved in this transition, rural Gemeinschaft inevitably gives way to urban Gesellschaft — which represents the only available future there is.

21 Amongst Women, 67, 151
22 Amongst Women, 85, 145

Whether deployed by sociologist or novelist, an element of nostalgia is perhaps unavoidable in this construction, but McGahern's novel seems quite determined to close off any sentimentalization of the past or regressive desire for its recovery. The world of Great Meadow is too grimly depicted to invite any sense of tragic loss, and restorationist attempts, such as Monaghan Day, are shown, in any case, to be useless. Thus, in both McGahern's novel and Sheridan's film, the dissolution of the period of Irish autarkic development is represented in terms of the demise of a charismatic but unattractively authoritarian patriarch. Whereas Sheridan's film, invested in the heightened mythopoeic tempo of classical Hollywood epic or tragedy, works towards but cannot deliver a decisively apocalyptic showdown between the old and the new, McGahern's novel, conveyed in an altogether more understated style and more stately tempo, represents the demise of the old order incarnated by Moran in terms of the slow and natural passage of time. The one narrative constantly tries to generate some sort of a final showdown between opposing forces (those of the Bull and the American), suggesting a sense of historical transition as something that works its way through society in the form of catastrophic clashes that shatter old formations to their foundation. Amongst Women, on the other hand, slows things down to convey a sense of history as trauma that can nevertheless be worked through incrementally. Within the quietist and more evolutionary sensibility of McGahern's novel, all strong forms of revolt seem somehow psychologically suspect.

Yet despite their differences, the strongest value that Amongst Women and The Field are able to affirm in the end is a pragmatic 'feminine' capacity for survival: a quality associated in Sheridan's film with that concluding shot in which the Bull's wife and the Tinker Girl stand side by side looking down from the cliff-top to survey the wreckage of the old masculinist patriarchal order below, or, in McGahern's case, by the women who surround Moran and who, without ever severing their allegiance to him, still manage eventually to master him, and who walk away from his grave in the closing pages with an assured sense of their own power. These endings may well be read as a timely nod to acknowledge the coming-to-power of Irishwomen that the Robinson presidency at the start of the 1990s was so frequently taken to signal. But there is more than a hint, too, of an O'Caseyite tendency to associate the tumult of Irish history with a destructive maleness and to posit the world of women as one of endurance — endurance representing not so much an alternative value-system in its own right so much as a stoic capacity to weather out the madness and chaos of the old order.

Of the three works discussed here, Friel's Dancing at Lughnasa seems, on first encounter at least, the one most steeped in nostalgia for pre-industrial community and most openly hostile to industrial modernity. The narrative, in which the adult Michael summons to memory a moment from his childhood past, is, at the outset, openly wistful and elegiac in tone. Friel's Ballybeg, moreover, is a softer landscape than Sheridan's or McGahern's, since it is identified not with aggressive patriarchal figures such as McCabe or Moran, but with a struggling community of sisters who, despite tensions and frustrations, are gamely supportive of each other. And when 'the Industrial Revolution' does arrive in

Donegal, it leads not to some grand vision of a vastly different Ireland but only to the redundancy of Aggie and Rose, setting them on the road to a squalid end in England. The tone of wistful reminiscence that frames the main narrative, the ambience of harvest festival, and the melancholy sense that we are reliving the last days of this tight-knit band of sisters just before their world collapses, all work to establish an autumnal atmosphere that inevitably tints the past in sepia and that tends to cast the emergent social order that will displace this little world in humanly destructive rather than redemptive terms. What we are offered in the play is a remembering of a world on the eve of its extinction, a world glowing in the final shafts of its setting sunlight.

Though that initial impression is not altogether misplaced, closer inspection will prove the play to be considerably more complex than this allows. After all, the imagined Ireland of *Dancing at Lughnasa* is not some pristine pre-modern community whose rude health offers some kind of genuine alternative to modernity, but only the incompletely realized modernity of de Valera's Ireland of the late 1930s. Ballybeg is no pre-modern pastoral idyll, but only a claustrophobic and rather mean-minded little village, where the sisters have constantly to run the gauntlet of local gossip, where opportunities for love and fulfilment are few and dwindling fast, and where circumstances generally are straitened and a constant effort is needed to keep disaster at bay. The faltering radio set, which starts into song only soon to stutter silent again throughout the play, is a metaphor for this condition of faltering, vacillating modernization. Friel's Ballybeg is imagined, in other words, as a repressed and essentially fragile society, pressured between two different kinds of Dionysian energy that threaten to overwhelm and shatter it; between pre-modern pagan energies associated with Africa and the local wild people of the back hills and modern (or even 'postmodern') Dionysian energies identified with the mass-culture dance tunes played over the radio. This affinity between the pre-modern and the advanced modern is established in the opening lines of the play when Michael recalls his family's acquisition of 'our first wireless set' and how Maggie 'wanted to call it Lugh after the old Celtic God of the Harvest'.[23] This peculiar complicity is reiterated when Michael recalls the pivotal dance at the centre of the play:

> I remember the kitchen throbbing with the beat of Irish dance music beamed to us all the way from Dublin, and my mother and her sisters suddenly catching hands and dancing a spontaneous step-dance and laughing — screaming! — like excited schoolgirls ... I had witnessed *Marconi's voodoo* derange those kind, sensible women and transform them into shrieking strangers.[24]

Audiences usually perceive this dance, the dramatic and emotional centrepiece of the play, in wholly positive terms as a liberating outburst of repressed energy that expresses

23 *Dancing at Lughnasa*, 1
24 *Dancing at Lughnasa*, 2. My emphasis.

the pent-up protest of the sisters against the narrow constraints of de Valera's Ireland. It is this, obviously, but Friel's script makes it clear that the dance is shot through with both positive and negative qualities; it has a duality that resembles that which Nietzsche associated with Dionysian ecstasy or intoxication.

For Nietzsche, Dionysus might represent the positive instinctual energy associated with 'the approach of spring when the whole of nature is pervaded by lust for life', but in its unalloyed form the same energy could always degenerate into 'that repulsive mixture of sensuality and cruelty which has always struck me as the true "witches' brew"'.[25] In Friel's extended stage directions to the dance scene, both qualities are clearly involved: we are told that 'there is a sense of order being consciously subverted', and the word 'defiant' appears several times, but it is also stressed that there is a sense 'of near-hysteria being induced' and that 'the sound is too loud; and the beat is too fast; and the almost recognizable dance is made *grotesque*'.[26] The dance is an eruption of sensual frenzy, then, but the collective moment of transport is not a wholly transcendent or triumphal one. It is worth remembering in this regard that the play is set against the wider continental collapse of 1936, its action shadowed by the rise of Fascism, the overthrow of the Spanish Republic, and by Europe's imminent descent into World War II.

Friel's play turns on a dialectical opposition between primitive and modern civilization conventional to nineteenth-century romanticism and exoticism, but it de-energizes this opposition as well, hollowing it out, yet conserving it in weakened form. When set against the anomie and sexual repressiveness of Ballybeg, Father Jack's Ryanga appears to possess attractive qualities of primitive communal vitality and sexual tolerance. 'In Ryanga,' Father Jack tells us, 'women are eager to have love-children. The more love-children you have, the more fortunate your household is thought to be.'[27] But while Ryanga may serve as a reminder of some more sexually liberal and tolerant non-modern popular culture that had once existed in Ireland too, a culture that de Valera's Ireland has had to push to the margins to assert its own strait-laced authority, we are also reminded that Ryanga is a run-down leper colony, not some idealized Edenic state. England's more advanced urban modernity, too, has positive qualities when compared to the small parochial world of Ballybeg. Bernie O'Donnell, Maggie's childhood friend, leaves Ireland in disgust when she and her partner are cheated of victory by local judges in a dancing competition in a neighbouring parish. When Bernie returns years later, married to a Swede, glamorous as 'a film star' and with two beautiful children, the evident success of her metropolitan life contrasts painfully with Maggie's homebound stasis and childlessness.[28] Nevertheless, England is not presented either as some salvific alternative to Ballybeg: it also appears in the play as the rather grim place where the homeless Agnes and Rose descend into despair and disaster.

25 Friedrich Nietzsche, *The Birth of Tragedy and Other Writings*, trans. Ronald Speirs (Cambridge, 1999), 17, 20
26 *Dancing at Lughnasa*, 21, 22. My emphasis.
27 *Dancing at Lughnasa*, 41
28 *Dancing at Lughnasa*, 19

The Ireland or Ballybeg of *Dancing at Lughnasa* is essentially conceived as a transient and ephemeral limbo suspended somewhere between the worlds of Ryanga and London and destined to move only in the direction of the latter, since the hour of its industrial revolution is at hand. It is too trapped in its prissy Catholic respectability (a quality exemplified by Kate, the eldest sister, who is identified, like McCabe and Moran, with the national struggle for independence) to be able to respond to either London or Ryanga except in terms of scandalized disbelief. But since neither 'primitive' Africa nor 'advanced modern' industrial England represents any wholly positive pole of value, there is little sense in Friel's work that there are any actual or attractive historical choices open to Ballybeg. If England is where the homeless Aggie and Rose meet their disconsolate end, Father Jack's account of how the sisters might return with him to Ryanga and live as wives to one husband in a small commune is clearly the stuff of comic farce. In *Dancing at Lughnasa*, in other words, the non-modern Ryanga, the as-yet-not-quite-but-soon-to-be-modern Ballybeg, and the more advanced modernity of London all have their attractions, their utopian dimensions even, but all are subverted and disenchanted by recurrent ironies as well. Ballybeg's course into its 'industrial revolution' is taken to be inevitable, but that course is certainly not emancipatory (Michael's tells us that after the factory opened Agnes and Rose departed for England, his mother 'spent the rest of her life in the knitting factory — and hated every day of it', and that after that September 'much of the spirit and fun had gone out of their lives'[29]).

Such nostalgia as there is for the past in *Dancing at Lughnasa* is activated not by a desire to resurrect that world, but only to put into question a modernity to which the past itself patently represents no alternative. Unable to identify substantive historical options, the narrative is essentially static and returns at the end to the still-life tableaux of the sisters that opened the play at the start — now, however, the figures are a little shabbier, indicating that any nostalgic view of their world that Michael or the audience might initially have entertained has not been sustained. History has already volatilized into memory here; the world of the sisters has no actuality beyond Michael's reminiscences of his youth, no existence beyond the stage where it is re-enacted. As the action concludes, the play consigns the sisters to their doom and settles for a kind of wistful bitter-sweet postmodern playfulness (the music of 'Anything Goes' and 'It's Time to Say Goodnight' play out the piece) that issues from a sense of helpless resignation.

As in Friel's earlier *Translations* (1980), a plangent note of cultural loss does issue from this sense of an era ending, but that sense of loss is so completely subordinated to or controlled by a sense of historical fatalism as to carry no political charge or meaning whatever. It is as though Friel can discern no positive value outside of the sphere of art or the formal order of ceremony (one of the key words in this work) and the play concludes with a paean to the supra-linguistic powers and pleasures of memory and dance: 'Dancing as if the very heart of life and all its hopes might be found in those

29 *Dancing at Lughnasa*, 70–71

assuaging notes and those hushed rhythms and in those silent and hypnotic movements. Dancing as if language no longer existed because words were no longer necessary ...'[30] While memory, dance and the rituals of art carry a certain utopian charge in the play, this is nevertheless only a de-energized and aestheticized utopianism detached from any conviction in the possibility of social transformation.

Uninterested in the epic or tragic thunder that Sheridan's *The Field* strains after, less weighed down by the naturalistic grimness and the sense of history as trauma that is McGahern's trademark signature even in the somewhat similarly autumnal *Amongst Women*, *Dancing at Lughnasa* achieves on a formal level a wonderfully balletic equipoise and a sense of grace and beauty that materializes the ideal of dance that inspires the imagination of the play. But like these other two works, it, too, is, for all its beauty, essentially a drama of lost faiths — the lost faith of Irish Catholicism, the lost faith of Irish nationalism, the lost faiths of history and of modernity as progress also — and it is this combination of lost faith, history volatilized into subjective memory, and bitter-sweet nostalgia that makes *Dancing at Lughnasa* one of those works where Irish naturalism shades into a post-naturalist postmodernism of a distinctly late twentieth-century kind.

5

The works of Sheridan, McGahern and Friel all re-create different versions of de Valera's Ireland, but these are differences that operate, nonetheless, within restricted parameters. Though *The Field* reaches towards a mythopoeic register that strains to go beyond naturalism, though *Amongst Women* displays a serenity quite different to the much more darkly naturalistic novels of McGahern's early career, though *Dancing at Lughnasa* deploys a variety of modestly Brechtian techniques to undercut the play's essentially naturalist conventions, all three works remain rooted in a naturalist aesthetic that emphasizes the disenchanted and anti-romantic qualities of the rural Ireland they each depict. None can be said to be conservative in the sense that they, in the manner of *Brideshead Revisited* or the British Merchant Ivory heritage films or mainstream Hollywood 'nostalgia films', construct the past as a desirable civilizational state to be hankered after or as a world whose loss we are likely to lament. Because they are not straightforwardly conservative narratives in this fashion, many critics will ascribe them a critical function. But while these works are certainly not without some critical impulse (as has been shown here), the degree to which they also serve to reinforce the dominant structures of feelings and ideologies of their own late twentieth-century moment ought not to be underestimated.

The story that all these narratives rehearse, each according to its own formal grammar, is the story of the death of de Valera's Ireland. However, the construction of that world as one of economic failure, cultural narrowness and social repressiveness can hardly be

30 *Dancing at Lughnasa*, 71

deemed either controversial or radical at the end of the twentieth century, because this sense of the period between independence and the sixties had long since congealed into a 'just-so' stereotype and only the most perversely conservative factions in Ireland could by the century's end construe the period as any kind of idyll. Yet however much these fictions work to reassure us at a narrative and cognitive level that this whole world of de Valera's Ireland is now coming to an end, or is already ended and being subsumed into memory as in Friel's *Dancing at Lughnasa*, they also display a remarkable tendency to cleave at the sensorial level to that world and to avoid and evade any other. Hence there is a recurring dissonance in these works between the cognitive message that they transmit, which is that the Irish have finally come through the sterility of de Valera's Ireland and are ready to move into some new dispensation, and the sensorial dimension, which operates at the level of thick description or the reconstruction of visual landscape to transport us back into a world whose texture and temporality is not our own.

At the level of narrative, these works are all about how an arthritic old world collapses in the face of the irresistible encroachments of the modern, but on an aesthetic level they actually constitute a kind of resistance to the emergent order by restoring to us the older sensorial world that has supposedly been lost. It can scarcely be doubted, therefore, that at least one of the major attractions of these texts is that they allow their audiences or readers to have things both ways. They all to some degree strike a psychic compromise that reassures the reader or spectator that the old world of de Valera's Ireland is being swept away and that some new — but never at all clearly identified — order is imminent, while at the same time the readership or audience is allowed to immerse itself once again in a non-modern aural and visual landscape still immune from the noisy routines of industrial agriculture, let alone the roar of motorways or the cybernetic hum of transnationalized, globalized communications systems. Cognitively confirming a sense of national progress by reassuring us that the old Ireland of the past is about to disappear or has disappeared already, the narratives also shelter us sensorially from the consequences of that progress by keeping its whole sensorial economy at bay.

It has been taken as a given here that these works are not in any simple manner about the past, and that in some fundamental ways they are more about the Ireland of the 1990s than about the early or mid-century decades they depict. But while it can be allowed that these narratives are of their own end-of-century moment, it is harder to see how they can be said to offer any really intellectually vigorous or assertively radical cognitive mapping of that world and time. Recurrently depicting the collapse of some narrowly insular autarkic Ireland, these works nevertheless belong to a moment when Ireland was already changing rapidly in a rapidly changing post-Cold War world, a condition which made it urgent for its people to be able to cognitively and critically find their bearings. Viewed from this perspective, the early 1990s works discussed here seem to be characterized by a rather tentative uncertainty about Ireland's past and future that was (for better or worse) to prove more symptomatic of the Celtic Tiger at its inception rather than in its full flush.

As compared with anything to be found in *The Field*, *Amongst Women* or *Dancing at Lughnasa*, Frank McCourt's *Angela's Ashes*, which appeared only a few years later in 1996, represented an intensified no-holds-barred naturalism that offered a much more scorchingly negative and unequivocal indictment of de Valera's Ireland and an altogether more uncritically and unabashedly gung-ho embrace of the American dream as the obvious alternative. In the same year, *Riverdance*, transformed from the seven-minute interlude that concluded the 1994 Eurovision Song Contest into a full-length Busby Berkeley-type show, opened, after hugely successful runs in Dublin and London, at the Radio City Music Hall in New York. If McCourt's memoir took naturalism to extremes in order to exorcize de Valera's Ireland without pretence of balance or regret, *Riverdance* took matters in an entirely different direction by ripping the Dionysian dance scene in *Dancing at Lughnasa* out of its naturalistic casing and offering instead what one critic has rightly described as 'a version of energetic Irishness' that 'bespoke rude health, stamina and stomping self-assertion'.[31]

The works of Sheridan, McGahern or Friel might have forecast (after the event) the death of de Valera's Ireland and intimated the emergence of some new order, but when that new order was actually installed the uncertainty and fatalism of these works would themselves quite rapidly seem the sentiments of a different time. McCourt's unqualified embrace of America as the land of opportunity or *Riverdance*'s ebullient celebration of a new syncretic globalized Irishness might each be highly commodified products and be disdained by the Irish intelligentsia for their lack of critical ambiguity. But maybe Ireland had now had more than its share of the autumn of the de Valera patriarchy and the rechronicling of deaths long foretold. The new entrepreneurial world of Celtic Tiger Ireland had a dream to chase and had at least the virtue of being prepared energetically to chase it. Those sceptical of that dream would now either have to develop their own alternative dreamworld or accommodate themselves to the new order.

31 Joan Fitzpatrick Dean, *Dancing at Lughnasa* (Cork, 2003), 78

Domestic Troubles:
Tragedy and the Northern Ireland Conflict

Domestic tragedy, historically associated with the sensibility of the emergent metropolitan middle classes, has never been held in high esteem by Marxian critics. In recent times, many critics on the left have tended to regard the whole genre of tragedy — with its supposedly élitist sensibility and its leaning towards an apocalyptic conception of history — in a somewhat dim light. It was not always so. Marx shared the enthusiasm of his age and class for classical Greek and Shakespearean tragedy, and some of the greatest Marxist cultural critics of the twentieth century, including Georg Lukács, Walter Benjamin and Raymond Williams, have written about tragedy in quite positive terms.

This chapter will examine three twentieth-century 'Protestant' dramas, all of a tragic character or design, which deal with the conflict in Northern Ireland. The first and earliest of these plays, St. John Ervine's *Mixed Marriage* (1911), can be considered a domestic tragedy. The second, Sam Thompson's *Over the Bridge* (1960), differs from Ervine's in that it is set in the more 'masculine' and public space of the Belfast shipyards, but, like *Mixed Marriage*, it also explores how sectarianism impedes the development of class politics in Northern Ireland. The third, Tom Paulin's *The Riot Act: A Version of Sophocles'* Antigone (1984), differs from the earlier two in that it adapts one of the great Greek tragedies to the northern situation, and in that its focus is not class and sectarianism but republican and unionist conceptions of duty and the state. Viewed in conjunction, these plays usefully demonstrate that different categories of tragic drama deploy the tropes of kinship and family and the distinction between public and private spheres in significantly different ways. From a distance, all forms of tragic drama may seem to rehearse a similarly bleak politics, an indifferently catastrophic conception of things. However, the basic thesis to be developed here is that it is important to discriminate between diverse forms of tragic narrative that have their own distinct histories and morphologies, since these distinct forms structure perceptions of class and sectarian conflict that are, in some ways at least, interestingly at odds with each other.

2

Some commentators on Irish theatre have suggested that a tragic conception of the Northern Irish conflict will almost inevitably lend itself to a reactionary politics. Noting the bland facility with which the term 'tragic' has been applied to the northern situation in the international media, Shaun Richards, for example, has argued that a tragic theatre will tend to construct a disabling sense of Northern Ireland as a cursed House of Atreus fated to incessant cycles of violence, the origins of which remain incomprehensible and irrational. Such a theatre, he suggests, must essentially bolster an already entrenched conception of Northern Ireland as inexplicable, as a place doomed to play out its 'luckless and predetermined fate' to a grand catastrophic finale.[1]

This argument against any fatalistic conception of the Northern Irish conflict is important, but the idea that tragic form must automatically lend itself to a reactionary or fatalistic conception of the North can also be somewhat reductive. Richards cites Brecht's arguments against traditional tragedy to support his case, but there is also a long Marxian tradition that conceives of tragedy, rather differently, as a form that tends to emerge in convulsive moments when societies undergo a wrenching process of transition from one kind of dispensation to another. In his comments on tragedy and historical drama, Lukács writes that

> the dramatic collision and its tragic outcome must not be conceived in an abstract pessimistic sense. Naturally, an abstract denial of the pessimistic elements in the drama given to us by the history of class society would be senseless. The horror of the conflicts in class society, the fact that for most people there is clearly no solution to them, is certainly *one* motif, and by no means and unimportant one, in the rise of drama. But it is by no means supreme. Every really great drama expresses, amid horror at the necessary downfall of the best representatives of human society, amid the apparently inescapable mutual destruction of men, an *affirmation of life*. It is a *glorification of human greatness*.[2]

---

1 Shaun Richards 'In the Border Country: Greek Tragedy and Contemporary Irish Drama', in C. C. Barfoot and Rias van den Doel, eds., *Ritual Rememberings: History, Myth and Politics in Anglo-Irish Drama* (Leiden, 1995), 191–200. My argument, I should make clear, is not with Richards's assessments of individual works nor indeed with his strictures against fatalistic or catastrophic conceptions of the northern situation, but only with his tendency to equate tragic narrative as such with a resigned or reactionary political outlook.
2 Georg Lukács, *The Historical Novel*, trans. Hannah Mitchell and Stanley Mitchell (Lincoln and London, 1962[1937]), 121–22. Italics in the original.

Benjamin's conception of tragedy, similarly dialectical, asserts that the death of the tragic hero does not represent a surrender to despair; on the contrary, that death 'offers up the hero to the unknown god as *the first fruits of a new harvest of humanity*'.[3] In short, the emphasis in both Lukács and Benjamin is on a tragic dialectic in which struggle and destruction are part of a dynamic process that leads ultimately toward a new social order. Finally, taking quite a different approach to the issue, Raymond Williams's study, *Modern Tragedy*, also demonstrates the limitations of any wholesale endorsement or rejection of the genre. For Williams, the category of tragedy can neither be endorsed nor rejected in the abstract, but must always be historically contextualized. Accordingly, the values inscribed within specific tragic genres can only be disclosed by way of an analysis that would take into account the political and intellectual milieu in which specific types of tragedy have been elaborated.[4]

Several different kinds of 'tragic' narrative have been adapted to the Northern Irish situation. Genres such as revenge tragedy, romantic tragedy, domestic tragedy and versions of classical Greek tragedy have all shaped the imagination of the conflict. Depending on their historical moment of emergence, some of these genres will clearly have much closer links with realist and naturalistic modes of narrative and stage presentation than others. Greek tragedy, for instance, deploys stylized modes of action indebted to mythic narrative, whereas the conventions of domestic tragedy have closer links to the those of the realist novel and stage melodrama. Moreover, the meaning ascribed to 'the family' — which tends to provide the social basis for nearly all modes of tragic narrative — can vary significantly. In a classical work such as *Antigone*, for instance, the family demands weighty duties even when these come into irreconcilable conflict with other obligations. However, in romantic tragedies, the family is commonly negatively construed as something that stands in the way of the future of the star-crossed lovers who defy parental will. In domestic tragedy, the milieu of a middle-class family, which may be either stifling or consoling, is the fundamental site of action, but the world beyond is almost invariably oppressive. The family, in short, is a critical site of meaning in nearly all modes of tragedy, but its function differs from one mode to another.

During the course of the 'Troubles', the Northern Irish conflict was viewed mainly within standard variations of romantic and domestic tragedy. In the theatre, as in other modes of fiction, and indeed in actual fact, the cutting edge of the political conflict in the region tended to be associated with working-class Catholics and Protestants rather than with their middle-class counterparts. So, domestic tragedy was typically set in a working-class rather than a middle-class environment or milieu. The development of this kind of drama owes a great deal to the influence of Sean O'Casey on contemporary political theatre in Ireland. In the early O'Casey plays, the setting is usually a working-

---

3 Walter Benjamin, *The Origin of German Tragic Drama*, trans. John Osborne (London and New York, 1985), 107. My emphasis.
4 Raymond Williams, *Modern Tragedy*, rev. edn. (London, 1979 [1966]), *passim*

class tenement, the social situation one of political turmoil and rebellion, and the theatrical conventions, though eclectic and drawing on a variety of dramatic genres and styles, are considerably indebted to nineteenth-century melodrama and to middle-class romantic and domestic tragedy.

One of the questions that might be asked of O'Casey's early theatre, as indeed of the more recent theatre of the Troubles which his work has helped to shape, is what precisely happens when middle-class or domestic tragedy is adapted to working-class situations? Can the form be reworked successfully to serve the interests of the working classes rather than those of the bourgeoisie? Or will a genre so closely wedded in its origins and ideals to the emergent middle classes operate in such a way that, even when employed consciously against the middle class, it is the values and sensibility of that class that will still tend to be endorsed?

Marxian reservations about domestic tragedy have centred on two objections: first, that the genre has typically rehearsed a humanist worldview in which specifically middle-class interests are mystified as universal human values; and, second, that it almost invariably privileges the private over the public sphere as the basis of human value. In 1973, shortly after another phase of open political conflict had swept across Northern Ireland, Seamus Deane published a searching critique of Sean O'Casey's theatre expressed in more or less these terms. Deane argued that the theatrical paradigms established by O'Casey were not ones equipped to meet the demands of the contemporary situation in the North. Given O'Casey's status and his extensive dramatic engagement with Irish nationalist politics, it was inevitable, Deane observed, that in the heat of the immediate northern crisis many dramatists would look to O'Casey as a model to be emulated or adapted. But it was, he argued, a mode that would prove disabling.[5] The major limitation of O'Casey's work, Deane proposed, is that it turns on a recurrent opposition between politics (whether nationalist or socialist, but especially when it is nationalist) conceived as a distortion or coarsening of the human, and a humanism associated with 'ordinary' people uninvolved in political pursuits. This separation between Irish politics, legitimately subjected to critical pressure by the playwright, and a humanism, unjustifiably exempted from the same critical pressure, is reinforced by the gendered axis on which it turns: in that work humanism is recurrently associated with female characters, while the apparently inevitable distortion of politics into egoism, fanaticism and sterile cant is identified with males. O'Casey's drama, Deane argued, reiterates two constants: first, the dehumanizing effects of visionary dreaming, especially when it takes a political form; second, the humanizing effects of being involved in people rather than ideas or ideologies — best expressed in the desire for domestic security and the capacity for deep human feeling exemplified by his womenfolk.

5   Seamus Deane, 'Irish Politics and O'Casey's Theatre', Threshold, 24 (1973), 5–16. The essay later reappeared, with some alterations and elisions, as the chapter 'O'Casey and Yeats: Exemplary Dramatists' in Deane's Celtic Revivals: Essays in Modern Irish Literature, 1880–1980 (London, 1985), 108–22.

   In its general outline at least, Deane's thesis about the limitations of the political vision
inscribed in O'Casey's theatre anticipates some of the arguments this chapter will want
to develop by way of readings of Ervine's *Mixed Marriage* and Thompson's *Over the Bridge*.
Both works deal with tragically failed attempts to forge an alliance between working-
class Catholics and Protestants within a state order dependent for its survival on the
maintenance of sectarian division. Yet despite the different perspectives and political
sympathies of Ervine and Thompson, and despite the fact that each play registers quite
a strong indictment of sectarianism, in the end both still see the divisions that threaten
to split the Protestant community if the struggle against sectarianism is pushed too far
as the real source of tragedy; it is this, and not the fate of the subaltern Catholic working
class, the class most oppressed by sectarian social structures, that is cathected as the
proper object of the audience's sympathy and concern.

   Nevertheless, and (parting company with both the standard Marxian critique of
domestic tragedy and with Deane's essay on O'Casey on this point), the argument here
is not that the chief weakness of these plays is that they privilege the domestic over
the political sphere. On the contrary, taking quite a different tack, it might better be
argued perhaps that in the context of Northern Ireland domestic tragedy may well have
an unexpected or even inadvertent radical potential, since that form by its very nature
fixes attention on issues that socialist politics has too often preferred to sidestep.
What I mean by this is that domestic tragedy has some potential at least to act as a
corrective to the more crudely economistic or 'bread and butter' forms of labour and
socialist politics in Northern Ireland, since these have frequently been premised on the
assumption that Catholic and Protestant working-class alliances can best be developed
by concentrating on workers' shared economic interests and downplaying more divisive
'emotional' matters (such as religious or national identity, state allegiance, gender,
interdenominational marriage or residential segregation) that might only inflame
intra-class divisions. A formal analysis of Ervine's and Thompson's works will show,
I hope, that those very elements of domestic tragedy that are usually seen to hinder the
genre from dealing adequately with social and historical problems — namely, the fact
that it is 'wedded to the personal, the domestic, the touching, and the sentimental'
— may, paradoxically, press into visibility issues that overly economistic conceptions
of class tend to suppress.[6] The idea is not to valorize domestic tragedy as such as a
radical form. However, in a situation where attempts to build working-class alliances
across the sectarian divide have too often proceeded on the basis that it is necessary to
subordinate 'secondary' matters to supposedly more fundamental economic interests,
domestic tragedy, despite its inherent limitations, can at least serve as a useful corrective
by demonstrating that attempts to separate spheres such as the public and the private
usually work against, not for, the interests of the oppressed.

6   Erich Auerbach, *Mimesis: The Representation of Reality in Western Literature*, trans. Willard R. Trask (Princeton,
    1974 [1946]), 441

To widen the debate on tragedy, the closing section of this chapter deals with Tom Paulin's adaptation of Sophocles' *Antigone* in *The Riot Act*. The full significance of Paulin's turn to Sophocles is best gauged by attending to the ways in which Greek tragedy unsettles perceptions of the northern conflict made available through the more familiar domestic tragedies. Yet though Paulin's Greek tragedy offers in many ways a more intricate take on the conflict than that expressed by either romantic or domestic modes of tragedy, it too will lend itself to a reading in which the essential tragic conflict turns out to be that within the Protestant-unionist community itself and not that between unionist and nationalist. In this respect at least, if not in others, Paulin's work reveals some unexpected continuities with the vision of things that informs both *Mixed Marriage* and *Over the Bridge*.

3

St. John Ervine's *Mixed Marriage*, first performed in the Abbey Theatre in Dublin in 1911, can be considered a seminal play in the development of modern northern drama.[7] Organized in terms of a 'love across the divide', the play tells the story of the collapse of a tentative alliance between Catholic and Protestant workers as a consequence of sectarianism. The play's basic plot situation, its 'Romeo and Juliet' narrative device, and its working-class domestic setting all became staple elements of late twentieth-century representations of the northern conflict.

Set in the month of July (the climax of the Orange marching season and consequently the period in which sectarian tensions are usually most acute), the action of *Mixed Marriage* unfolds within the Rainey family home. The play begins with John Rainey's announcement to his wife that the local workers have gone on strike for better wages. Rainey, charismatic but headstrong and authoritarian in personality, staunchly Protestant and unionist in allegiance, and a member of the local Orange Lodge, supports the strike. But his solidarity with Catholics ends there, since he is strongly opposed to any kind of social interaction between Catholics and Protestants outside the workplace: 'A don't like Cathliks an' Prodesans mixin' thegither. No good ivir comes o' the like o' that.'[8] His eldest son Hugh, on the other hand, is not only on friendly terms with Michael O'Hara, a socialist republican, but is also (unknown to Rainey) in love with Nora Murray, a local Catholic girl. Despite Rainey's distrust of Catholics, he is persuaded by Michael's and Hugh's arguments that the employers will try to sow division between the striking workers by playing the Orange card and by insinuating that the strike is simply the work of nationalist agitators and Home Rulers. Knowing that Rainey is a member of the Orange Order, and that as such he will have more influence with his co-religionists than

---

7   St. John Ervine, *Mixed Marriage*, in *Selected Plays of St. John Ervine*, ed. John Cronin (Gerrards Cross, 1988)
8   *Mixed Marriage*, 20

they will, Hugh and Michael manage to convince him to urge the Protestant workers to keep solidarity with their Catholic comrades and to resist the employers' attempts to divide them by stoking religious bigotry.

Initially, the strategy works well. Enjoying the sense of power he experiences as mediator and guarantor of working-class solidarity, and relishing the fact that the Protestant workers heed him more than they do his opponent, Hand (a unionist agitator brought up from Dublin by the Belfast employers), Rainey takes enthusiastically to his new task. However, the crisis in the play is precipitated when he accidentally overhears that Hugh and Nora are engaged and that, at Mrs. Rainey's prompting, they had planned to keep the engagement secret until the success of the strike was assured, lest news of it should cause Rainey to change his mind about the consequences of Catholic and Protestant solidarity. Horrified at the prospect that Hugh is to marry a Catholic, and convinced now that he is being used as a dupe to undermine the wider interests of his own community, Rainey declares that he will denounce the strike to the Protestant workers unless Hugh and Nora agree to end their engagement. Michael, represented as a political idealist willing to sacrifice everything to the higher cause of working-class solidarity and Irish national unity, pleads with Nora and Hugh to concede to Rainey's demand, since the wider good of society must take precedence over personal desire. When Hugh and Nora refuse, Rainey exits to tell the Protestant workers that he can no longer support the strike.

All through the closing act of the play, the Rainey house is besieged by an Orange mob protesting the marriage of Hugh and Nora. The door is bolted, stones are pelted against the shuttered windows, the background din of the mob is constant. Later, Catholic and Protestant mobs clash offstage, the sound of their collision interrupted only by Michael's unavailing calls for reason and moderation. Inside, Nora, unhinged by the terrible consequences of her love for Hugh, becomes increasingly hysterical and blames the whole situation on her own selfishness. Hearing that the army is about to open fire to clear the streets outside, she rushes out of doors to proclaim her guilt, is accidentally shot, and falls dead across the threshold. Rebuked by his younger son, Tom, for causing her death, Rainey, dazed and 'as if in a dream', still maintains that what he had done was right. In the closing lines of the play, Mrs. Rainey, weeping and patting her husband gently, laments: 'Aw, my poor man, my poor man.'[9]

The subject matter of Ervine's play is explicitly political. Its main concerns include the ways in which sectarian resentments can suddenly capsize labour solidarity, the capacity of the business and establishment interests to exploit that sectarianism for their own ends, and the wider contest between unionism and nationalism. These political issues are usually associated with the public sphere, but in Mixed Marriage they attain dramatic life only as they are mediated through the private sphere of the Rainey living room. All of the major actions that take place beyond that space — Rainey's addresses to the Orangemen

9   Mixed Marriage, 63

in their lodge, the Sinn Féin hall where Hugh and Michael meet, the Orange diatribes against Catholics and Home Rule on the Custom House Steps, the mob protests — are merely reported. Since public spaces are not actually staged, everything that happens in the play happens 'inside' and there alone.

The narrative structure of Ervine's play, in a manner typical of domestic tragedy, requires that the 'hard' currency of the political subject matter must be converted into the 'softer', more affective, currency of an Oedipalized family narrative, the allegorical framework of which requires that social transformation must be imagined primarily in terms of some sort of overthrow or relaxation of paternal authority. But the intriguing thing about Ervine's plot is that it is a given of the piece from the outset that social transformation can only be accomplished if the father lends it his support, not if he is overthrown. In other words, the starting premise in *Mixed Marriage* is that the strike will only succeed if Rainey supports it; without his support, a brittle working-class solidarity will collapse into sectarian anarchy. Since his commitment to radical social change in the 'public' political sphere effectively entails, within the logic of the 'private' Oedipalized framework of the play, a corresponding commitment to the diminution of his own paternal authority, the narrative is structured in such a way that Rainey's symbolic position as authoritarian paterfamilias, and his political commitment to the strike, are set at tragic cross-purposes from the start. The bind in which Rainey finds himself can be read as a nicely compressed dramatic metaphor for a wider political one. Can the northern Protestant working class commit itself to radical social transformation without surrendering its own paternalist privileges in the process?

For some critics, *Mixed Marriage* offers a rather straightforward liberal social critique of sectarianism.[10] On this reading, Rainey is the moral culprit of the piece. It is his inability to overcome his personal prejudices against Catholics that destroys the strike and withers the hope for a brave new world beyond sectarianism that Nora's and Hugh's love allegorically prefigures. However, the emotional drama of *Mixed Marriage* is ultimately a good deal more complex than this, since Rainey's support for the strike is represented in the play as principled and sincere. When he discovers Hugh's engagement to Nora and decides, after some irresolution, that he can no longer give his support to the strike, it is not simply, or at least not only, as Norman Vance puts it, that 'atavistic sectarianism reasserts itself'.[11] This is indeed how the other characters in the play see things, but from Rainey's own perspective the proposed mixed marriage between Hugh and Nora is objectionable because, in the first instance, it violates the social segregation between Catholics and Protestants that he upholds and, in the second instance, by relaxing such boundaries it prefigures an assimilation of the two communities that might ultimately pave the way for a united Ireland. The crux that binds him, in other words, is that he is

10 See Norman Vance, *Irish Literature: A Social History* (Oxford, 1990), 179–80, and Christopher Murray, *Twentieth-Century Irish Drama* (Manchester, 1997), 192.
11 Vance, *Irish Literature*, 180

willing to support the working-class alliance, but only on condition that such an alliance is devoted to workers' common economic improvement and does not go beyond that. But what the alliance between Hugh and Nora brings home to him, is that there can be no such thing as a purely economic solidarity between Catholic and Protestant; no economic solidarity that will not have wider social and political consequences. Will an empowered Catholic working class not advance its own national interests? Moreover, what starts out as a cross-community solidarity on a purely economic level might always lead sooner or later to other forms of interaction and affective bonds as well, and these in turn might eventually undermine the commitment to Protestant separatism and to the Union with Britain so dear to Rainey.

Mixed Marriage should be understood not simply as a 'thesis play' that offers a banal ethical or moral critique of individualized sectarianism, but as a more complex work in which Rainey's dilemma ultimately takes on a more tragic dimension because mutually compromising commitments are at issue. This tragic conception of Rainey's situation reflects a more significant social and historical truth than any moral critique of individual bigotry could do. A moral critique will conceive of sectarianism essentially in terms of personal limitation; sectarianism persists, that is, because unenlightened individuals fail to overcome their atavistic prejudices. The construction of Rainey's predicament as a tragic one stemming from mutually irreconcilable commitments, on the other hand, works towards a more materialist diagnosis, because it starts from the assumption that sectarianism persists not simply because of personal weakness, but because it is imbricated in real structures of power.

In the North, whether before or after partition, the Protestant community has always enjoyed a privileged relationship to the state. For this reason, the situations of the Catholic nationalist and Protestant unionist or loyalist working classes have never been symmetrical (though Protestant working-class organizations have consistently failed to confront this fact).[12] The relative advantages enjoyed by the Protestant working class, because of its affiliation with the state, have constituted a persistent obstacle to any genuinely radical working-class politics in the northern state, since real solidarity with Catholic workers would require their Protestant counterparts to commit themselves to the construction of a new social order which would dissolve their own privileged relationship to the current order. The tragic construction of Rainey's dilemma, one in which his willingness to work to improve the shared economic interests of Catholic and Protestant workers comes into irresolvable conflict with his desire to maintain

---

12 Frank Wright's *Two Lands on One Soil: Ulster Politics Before Home Rule* (Dublin, 1996) offers a useful analysis of some of the ways in which the British state maintained Protestant supremacy in northern Ireland in the period before partition. For a succinct and cogent summary of the ways in which the northern state privileged the interests of the Protestant over the Catholic working class in the period since partition, see Mark McGovern and Peter Shirlow, 'Counter-Insurgency: Deindustrialisation and the Political Economy of Ulster Loyalism', in *Who are 'The People'?: Unionism, Protestantism and Loyalism in Northern Ireland* (London, 1997), 176–98.

Protestant hegemony in all other social domains, reflects a genuinely materialist and structural grasp of the nature of Protestant sectarianism — something that goes well beyond any conception of that sectarianism as a matter of personal prejudice or communal atavism.

4

Sam Thompson's *Over the Bridge*, another landmark text in the development of modern Northern Irish drama, and one also written by a Protestant of working-class background, offers an instructive contrast with Ervine's *Mixed Marriage*.[13] Thompson's play is set in the offices of the Belfast shipyards, a workplace historically dominated by a largely Protestant 'labour aristocracy' and the site of recurrent pogroms against the few Catholics employed there. Thompson's play, like Ervine's, deals with the difficulties involved in developing any kind of trade-unionist solidarity in a context where workers are bitterly divided along sectarian lines. Davy Mitchell, a legendary and now elderly Protestant trade-unionist, has given his life to the cause of working-class advancement, but his efforts are constantly hindered by all sorts of obstacles: by Orange and republican antagonisms; by the opposition of the more fundamentalist strands of Protestantism to any kind of socialism; by the difficulty of reconciling the sometimes 'illiberal' *realpolitik* measures needed to maintain trade-union discipline with the union's wider commitment to the development a more tolerant and liberal society.

When an explosion occurs in the shipyard, the Protestants accuse the Catholic workers of republican sympathies and have them expelled from the workplace. Initially, Davy Mitchell, like most of the other Protestant trade-union officials, believes that the best way to deal with the situation is the conventional one; the Catholic workers should remain at home, keeping their heads down for a few days until Protestant tempers cool and things can return to normal. Peter O'Boyle, a stubborn Catholic with a long involvement in trade unionism, complicates things for everyone, however, when he insists on returning to work the next day. His action makes embarrassingly clear the gap between the social democratic ideals of the trade-union movement and the *realpolitik* of the situation whereby its leadership tacitly endorses Protestant supremacy. When a Protestant mob threatens O'Boyle's life unless he agrees to return home, the other trade-union leaders succumb to the intimidation and are prepared to leave O'Boyle to his fate. However, Davy Mitchell decides that in this situation he has no other option but to take a principled stand alongside O'Boyle. In the mob violence that follows (which takes place offstage to 'a terrific din of hammers and voices' and is reported to the audience by an onlooker) we learn that O'Boyle is mauled and injured and that Mitchell, sacrificing his

---

13 Sam Thompson, *Over the Bridge* (Dublin, 1970); the play was first staged in 1960. For a more extended study of Thompson, see Hagal Mengel, *Sam Thompson and Modern Drama in Ulster* (Frankfurt am Main, 1986).

life for the principle of solidarity, is killed.

The plays of Ervine and Thompson share a commitment to working-class solidarity and a conviction that the primary impediment to that solidarity is a conservative paternalist attitude toward Catholics on the part of Protestant labour leaders. Even Davy Mitchell, Thompson's heroically virtuous and self-sacrificing labour veteran, is initially willing to condone the discriminatory practice whereby Catholic workers are expected to lie low and wait for Protestant consent to their returning to the shipyards. It is only when O'Boyle takes a stand against such intimidation, and against the expression of Protestant supremacy it nakedly asserts, that Mitchell is forced to acknowledge the shortcomings of established trade-unionist practice and to adopt a more principled position.

The most obvious difference between Ervine's and Thompson's protagonists is that Mitchell, when forced to choose between communal and class solidarity, unlike Rainey, opts for the latter. Nevertheless, the whole pattern of Davy's tragic sacrifice in *Over the Bridge* is one heavily accented in Christian terms, suggesting that while his stand is exemplary, it is a uniquely heroic action on the part of an exceptional individual; it is, in other words, not an act that the other labour leaders, who are all represented as men of much lesser stature or calibre, are likely to emulate. Davy's death, then, is depicted as a form of martyrdom or tragic sacrifice which consecrates the ideal of principled working-class solidarity, but which simultaneously acknowledges the sorry gap between the high ideal and the compromised mundane actuality. The manner of Mitchell's death suggests that Thompson had very little expectation that in the world beyond the theatre the trade-unionist leadership would live up to the high principles the play wants to endorse. [14] In sum, Thompson's play might be read as an attempt to consecrate, at the level of tragic art, values that are patently absent in the society to which the play addresses itself; the life of one good man is offered up simultaneously as an example to, an indictment of, and perhaps an act of atonement for the rest.

That Thompson's Mitchell ultimately opts for class over communal solidarity, whereas Ervine's Rainey makes the opposite choice, suggests that Thompson's work offers the more radical critique of Protestant supremacy and paternalism. In Ervine's play it is Nora, the Catholic who transgresses the sectarian divide by her love for Hugh, who is the victim sacrificed to sectarian violence at the end, while the Protestant father is saved; in Thompson's work, it is O'Boyle, the oppressed Catholic, who survives, while Mitchell, the venerable Protestant father figure, makes the supreme sacrifice for his comrade.

---

14 The distinction between Davy Mitchell and the other Protestant trade unionists is reinforced in several ways. Davy belongs to an older generation than his fellow union members and he has a stature that none of the rest possess. His oldest comrade, Rabbie White, is basically honest, but is evasive on the matter of sectarianism and he is also a 'ruleatarain' (43) who relies in a bureaucratic manner on the union rule-book. Warren Baxter, who is engaged to Davy's daughter, is more willing than Rabbie to acknowledge that the trade-union movement depends on a tacit acceptance of Protestant supremacy, but he is also, quite cynically, prepared to profit from this: he accepts that the only reason he will be elected to the post as union organizer is that his opponent is Catholic. His breakdown at the end is a dramatic expression of the 'bad conscience' inherent in his position.

Nevertheless, the reality is much more complex than this because even though Thompson's *Over the Bridge* offers the more explicit critique of Protestant working-class paternalism on a thematic level, in terms of the ideology of form it remains in many ways much more tied to a Protestant paternalist conception of the northern situation than Ervine's play does. In *Mixed Marriage*, the story of the strike cannot be detached from the love story of Hugh and Nora; the two narratives are inextricably intertwined. The effect of the device of the twinned love and strike plots in Ervine's play is to insist, rightly, that working-class politics (having to do with questions of exploitation and the distribution of economic resources) and national and state politics (having to do with modes of social and economic regulation and the institutionalization of collective communal recognition and identity) cannot simply be separated or detached. There can be no purely 'economic domain' where workers can pursue their interests that does not have consequences for other social 'domains'. The love affair between Hugh and Nora serves as a 'national romance' in which the erotic embrace of the lovers operates as an allegorical projection of a desire for reconciliation between historically antagonistic communities.[15]

By intertwining the story of the strike with that of the national romance, Ervine's play implies that any genuine solidarity between Catholic and Protestant built in the workplace must inevitably extend into domestic space as well. The difficulty for Rainey is that real non-sectarian class solidarity between Catholic and Protestant workers seems likely to lead, logically, and inevitably, towards intermixing beyond the workplace and hence to the establishment of some kind of common Irish national identity, which might ultimately undermine a separate Protestant identity on an island. It is precisely this prospect that plagues Rainey's fantasy and that ultimately causes him to break the strike. While he accepts that '[t]he workin' class has got t' hing thegither' (the irony requires no comment), his opposition to 'Catliks an' Prodesans mixin' thegither' outside of the workplace is resolute.[16] However, what the play as whole suggests is the tragic inadequacy of this conception of things. Rainey's commitment to uphold Protestant and unionist interests is allowed its dignity, but the tragic dénouement also insists that such commitment can only be maintained at the cost of genuine cross-class solidarity. Protestant workers, Ervine's play seems to infer, must decide whether they want real solidarity with their Catholic counterparts and risk the attendant dangers, or to safeguard their traditional privileges and separate identity. What they cannot do — the play insists — is to choose both at once.

The strangely ambivalent status and function of the romance between Hugh and Nora in *Mixed Marriage* requires some comment here. As mentioned earlier, that romance seems at one level to work as a national romance: in the erotic embrace of the lovers,

15 For more on such romances-across-the-divide, see Joe Cleary, *Literature, Partition and the Nation-State: Culture and Conflict in Ireland, Israel and Palestine* (Cambridge, 2002), 97–141.
16 *Mixed Marriage*, 24, 20

traditionally antagonistic communities come to recognize each other as political allies. Yet, within the structure of the plot, that same romance also serves, paradoxically, as the critical obstacle to class and national unity: when Hugh and Nora refuse to give each other up for the common good, Rainey feels he has no option but to scupper the strike. In a pivotal scene, Rainey pleads with Hugh and Nora to give each other up in order to maintain separation between Catholic and Protestant, while, from the opposite side of the political spectrum, Michael, the socialist republican, also pleads with them to give each other up, lest their union jeopardize Rainey's support for the strike and the promise of eventual national unity that might develop out of its success. Strangely, the romance seems to demand interpretation on one level as an allegory of national unity and on another as its immediate practical impediment. This disjunctive status is well captured in an exchange between Michael and Mrs. Rainey. When Michael pleads the need to put collective national good before private interest, Mrs. Rainey protests: 'Ye're wrong til be suggestin' partin' til them. Can't ye see, they're doin' the very thing ye want Irelan' t' do. It's Cathlik an' Prodesan joinin' han's thegither. It's quare ye shoud be wantin' til separate them.' To which Michael responds: 'It's acause a want a bigger joinin' o' han's. It's not enough fur a man an' a wumman til join han's. A want to see the whole wurl' at peace.'[17] While Mrs. Rainey reads the proposed marriage between Hugh and Nora as an omen of a wider political marriage between Catholic and Protestant in a united Ireland, Michael reads it, in the immediate context at least, as an impediment or threat to that same ultimately desired end.

How are we to interpret this curious romance, which seems to function simultaneously as a symbol of a desired union between Catholic and Protestant and as the very thing that destroys Protestant support for the solidarity of working communities expressed in the strike? The best way to do so, perhaps, is to see the ambivalent status of the romance as a symptom of a genuine Protestant dilemma in Ireland in the pre-partition period. That is, while the romance of a genuine marriage between Catholic and Protestant is attractive as an ideal, the difficulty from a Protestant perspective is how to ensure that one of the practical consequences of such an union would not be an assimilationist erosion of a distinct Protestant identity over the longer term? Unable to square the desire for authentic solidarity across the communal divide with the terror of assimilation and the loss of distinct identity, Ervine's romance of reconciliation slips irrevocably into a tragedy of doomed love. In historical terms, of course, the Protestant terrors that aggravate Ervine's play were to be appeased by the partitioning of the island of Ireland and the establishment of Northern Ireland as a separate state in those six northern counties where Protestants constituted a safe demographic majority.

Thompson's *Over the Bridge* was produced in 1960, several decades after the establishment of the northern state, which was at that time aggressively Protestant and British in its structures and symbols, despite its substantial Catholic and Irish

17 *Mixed Marriage*, 50

nationalist minority. Given that northern Protestants had monopolized political power and had been a secure majority within that state for several decades by 1960, it might reasonably be expected that the task of imagining solidarity between Catholic and Protestant workers would have to engage the fact that Catholics now occupied a vulnerable minority position within the northern state structurally similar in some ways to that occupied by Protestants island-wide before partition. However, Thompson's play suggests that once northern Protestants themselves became the majority community, the preservation of minority ethnic or communal identity was no longer regarded as a serious or legitimate concern. Indeed, in *Over the Bridge* such matters are dismissed as a distraction to a genuine socialist solidarity between workers.

The shape of Thompson's narrative, as well as its orchestration of stage space, attests to this dismissal. In Ervine's play the action unfolds within the Raineys' domestic living room and, as argued earlier, the narrative of the strike and that of Hugh and Nora's love affair are braided together so that what happens in the public and private spheres cannot be separated. In contrast, except for two scenes set in Davy Mitchell's home, most of the action in Thompson's play is set within the shipyard offices and thus among an exclusively male workforce. Moreover, the only romantic interest in *Over the Bridge*, a minor element in the play as a whole, is an exclusively Protestant affair. Warren Baxter, a young Protestant trade-union official who admires Davy Mitchell's principles, but who lacks the elder man's moral courage, is engaged to marry Davy's daughter, Marion. However, in an act of daughterly devotion Marion eventually rejects Baxter at the end of the play because he has failed to live up to her father's standards. In Thompson's play, the development of working-class politics is what happens in the masculine workplace and the general attitude towards the domestic sphere tends on the whole to be hostile and negative. The world of domesticity is associatively linked with Davy's brother, George, and especially with the latter's unattractively bossy wife, whose aggressive socialclimbing brings George into repeated conflict with Davy's union politics. Consequently, the domestic sphere is associated in *Over the Bridge* with selfish private interests that only get in the way of a masculine or fraternally-conceived working-class unity.

Although Thompson's play does include a minor romantic plot, the affair between Marion and Warren Baxter is restricted to issues of succession and inheritance *within* the Protestant community. By associating domestic space with selfish private interests, and by ignoring anything to do with Catholic and Protestant social relations outside the workplace, Thompson's play implies that social solidarity can be developed solely in some discrete economic sphere, and that the building of class alliances between Protestant and Catholic workers need not have implications for the domestic or civic spheres nor raise awkward political matters about nationality and state.

In other words, the social vision that shapes Thompson's play ultimately rests on a rather crude version of socialism that clings to the notion that working-class politics can be detached from questions of nation and state. In *Over the Bridge*, identity politics of any kind and national politics, particularly, are conceived, in a manner that is conceptually naïve, and within the Northern Irish context distinctly disingenuous, as either a secondary distraction from authentic class politics or as a trivial particularism. In marked contrast with Ervine's play, then, Thompson's *Over the Bridge* conceives of cross-class solidarity only along the axis of a single subject position (the economic solidarity of the male worker); other subject positions (based on nationality or gender) that might mediate and complicate such solidarity are not engaged.

Since one of the essential functions of the Northern Irish state system in the period when Thompson's play was produced was to regulate the local economy in order to maintain the coherence of the unionist bloc — which required the state to try to maintain the relative advantage of the Protestant working class over its Catholic counterpart — the assumption that Catholic nationalist or republican politics represented merely a diversion from or distortion of authentic working-class concerns is untenable. *Over the Bridge*, however, depends on precisely this assumption, and the critique of Protestant paternalism expressed in that play on a thematic level is thus compromised by a deeper paternalism implicit in the overall structure of the narrative. On the other hand, by insisting that it is impossible to detach the narrative of the strike from the story of the love affair between Hugh and Nora, Ervine's domestic tragedy rightly asserts that in the last analysis economic, domestic and wider socio-political matters will not be detached from each other. By assuming that class alliances can and ought to be articulated solely within the economic sphere of the workplace, without wider reference to other socio-political matters, Thompson's play succumbs to the illusion that these spheres can indeed be detached. On the whole, then, Ervine's work, despite appearances to the contrary, offers the more tough-minded appreciation of the nature of the obstacles to be overcome on the way to establishing genuine equality and solidarity between Catholic and Protestant in the North.

5

In a classic essay on family melodrama, Thomas Elsaesser draws attention to an important distinction between that genre and more 'masculine' action-oriented genres such as the Western or adventure movie. In the latter, Elsaesser observes, the assumption of 'open' spaces is axiomatic; the hero is usually defined dynamically as the centre of continuous movement; and suspense is generated by the linear organization of the plot and the action, together with the kind of 'pressure' the expectant spectator brings to the film. The family melodrama, in contrast, is typically set in the middle-class home, weighed down with objects. While in action-oriented genres, violence is externalized and suspense maintained through dynamic movement, in the more constricted 'inside' space of family melodrama, there is no outside world to be acted on. Since violence cannot find legitimate outlet within the closed space of the home, the range of 'strong' actions that the genre can accommodate is limited. Violence consequently is directed inwards or against the self or finds outlet only in moments of 'excess', such as outbursts of anger or hysteria. For Elsaesser, then, family melodrama is a masochistic form that records 'the failure of the protagonist to act in a way that could shape ... events and influence the emotional environment, let alone change the stifling social milieu. The world is closed, and the characters are acted upon.'[18]

In Ervine's *Mixed Marriage* or Thompson's *Over the Bridge* the settings may be working class rather than middle class, but the worlds imagined are consonant with the 'closed' and centripetal ones Elsaesser describes. Despite the different patterning of social space in Ervine's and Thompson's plays discussed earlier, in one respect at least their works display a notable similarity: as each play comes to its climax, the 'inside' space where everything happens (the place of the stage proper) is completely besieged by a hostile 'outside' space (the offstage world). In Ervine's *Mixed Marriage* the opening stage directions tell us that when the action commences it is 'the evening of a warm summer day at the beginning of July'. Despite the warmth, however, '[t]he living room of John Rainey's house is intolerably heated; to counteract this, the door leading to the street is partly open, and the scullery door, leading to the open yard, is open to its widest'.[19] At the start of the play this suffocatingly overheated interior, clearly a metaphor for the explosive political emotions that will devastate this domestic space later on, is ventilated to some extent by the fact that the private living room still remains open on to the public world beyond it. And even if everything happens inside, forward plot movement is sustained, during the first three acts at least, by the constant traffic passing through those open doors between domestic and public space.

In the final act, everything changes. Now the stage directions stipulate that: 'The kitchen shows signs of unusual agitation. The window-shutters are closely barred, and the street door is well fastened. Outside is heard the noise of people shouting, occasionally a stone strikes the shutters or the door.'[20] Literally besieged by a terrifically threatening exterior world (the rising and falling din of the mob outside is maintained offstage throughout this act), domestic space is now hermetically sealed off from the world outside. What goes on in that sinister and nightmarish space outside the home exists for the audience as something that cannot directly be apprehended but only imperfectly imagined. From an upstairs window (offstage), Tom calls down snatched reports of the tumultuous scenes outside to those in the kitchen below (the stage area). The whole construction of things here emphasizes the distance between interior and exterior worlds and implies that what goes on outside has passed beyond the limits of realist representation and that those inside are no longer real social agents but are reduced to the passivity of spectators or the helplessness of victims.

18 Thomas Elsaesser, 'Tales of Sound and Fury: Observations on the Family Melodrama', in Christine Gledhill, ed., *Home is Where the Heart Is: Studies in Melodrama and the Woman's Film* (London, 1987), 43–69, 55
19 *Mixed Marriage*, 19
20 *Mixed Marriage*, 56

The scene that brings Thompson's *Over the Bridge* to its climax is similar.[21] In that scene all of the principal characters are besieged in a shipyard office by a sinister mob of Protestant workers who demand that Peter O'Boyle be sent home. As in *Mixed Marriage*, the vulnerability of this precarious space inside to the threatening outside world is highlighted in terms of a communicative crisis: when the office manager decides that matters are out of hand and it is time to telephone the police, he lifts the receiver to find that the line has already been cut. In both plays, then, communication between inside and outside eventually becomes impossible; all access between them having been suspended. Again, in Thompson's play as in Ervine's, the mob exists primarily as a cacophonous offstage presence (that 'terrifying din of hammers and voices').[22] When Mitchell and O'Boyle exit the office to make their stand against intimidation, the violence inflicted on them by the mob is reported to those who remain inside by Warren Baxter, who witnesses their fate, helplessly and hysterically, through an office window. In each case, once sectarian conflict openly erupts into violence, the little band of people crowded into the space inside lose all effective agency and, in doing so, acquire the pathos of victims.

This Manichaean construction of stage space encourages a paranoid and reactionary conception of the world, one which rests on a division of humanity between the besieged civilized few 'inside' and the anonymous brute multitude 'outside'. The trope is one most commonly found perhaps in narratives of the colonial frontier, that exemplary space where civilization and savagery meet. A high-culture example can be found in the opening chapters of Joseph Conrad's *Nostromo*, where the reader sees the world from the perspective of the besieged household of the sympathetically-drawn European family of Georgio Viola as it is attacked by a faceless mob of native 'scoundrels' and '*leperos*' outside. The standard mass culture equivalent appears in the Western in the image of American Indians attacking a huddled homestead of terrified white settlers. In the closing act of *Mixed Marriage*, Mrs, Rainey's description of the mob predictably enough equates its behaviour with that of savage indigenes: 'Ye would think they wur wil' savages thrum the heart of Africa, the way they're goin' on.'[23]

By any standards, the Protestant pogroms that Ervine and Thompson refer to in these works were, of course, politically reactionary phenomena. Nevertheless, the way in which the plays depict such events is also reactionary, since they construct the behaviour of those involved as brute atavism. Conversely, the audience is sutured into a point of view whereby it inevitably identifies with the beleaguered minority 'inside'

21 Although in both plays these 'siege' scenes are climactic, *Mixed Marriage* concludes with this scene, whereas it constitutes the penultimate scene in *Over the Bridge*. Thompson's play closes with a scene set in the Mitchell home where Davy's family and fellow workers, all Protestant, have gathered for his funeral.
22 In Thompson's play there is one brief scene in which the mob is represented onstage when its leader enters to give O'Boyle a final warning. But that scene does not individualize the Protestant characters issuing the threat and does not represent any real break with offstage representations of the mob in plays such as Ervine's.
23 *Mixed Marriage*, 56

— which in each case also proves to be exclusively (or mainly) Protestant. In short, the audience in the theatre is willy-nilly corralled into a liberal élitist position in which a sense of victimization at the hands of a barbarous multitude is combined with a sense of superiority that derives from belonging to the 'civilized' world.[24]

Despite the working-class sympathies of Ervine and Thompson, their works are able to construe working-class collective action only within a constrictively bourgeois humanist structure of feeling that habitually conceives of sectarianism primarily in terms of the mob actions of the working classes. In reality, working-class sectarian disputes are common, yet sectarian violence has never been the preserve of these classes; it has operated across all classes, and the various apparatuses of the Northern Ireland and British states (civil and military) have often been utilized as instruments of sectarianism. But if these climactic collective scenes tend to reproduce dismissive conceptions of both the Catholic and Protestant working classes, in both plays it is the subaltern Catholic working class that is most severely compromised. In Ervine's play, the offstage clash between Catholic and Protestant mobs insinuates a false, though obdurately conventional, symmetry in which the violence of Catholics and Protestants is constructed as that of two equally reactionary sectarian forces, thus occluding the fact that within the northern region Protestant riots against Catholics were intended to uphold sectarian social structures, whereas the object of Catholic rioting was to protest that community's oppression by such structures. In some ways Thompson seems to come closer to acknowledging this historical or structural difference between the two classes, since in his work Catholics are clearly the victims of Protestant violence. Nevertheless, in Over the Bridge, the plot is constructed so that the whole stress of the action is not on the suffering (or on the courageous stand) of the Catholic worker O'Boyle, who is only injured by the mob, but on the nobly self-sacrificing Mitchell, who dies in the same incident. Once injured, O'Boyle, never more than a minor character, disappears from the plot altogether. In contrast, the entire final scene is set in Mitchell's home, where his death is mourned by an exclusively Protestant set of characters.

Thus, in both Mixed Marriage and Over the Bridge the narrative develops towards a situation in which a Catholic is a tragic victim of mob violence (Nora is shot dead; O'Boyle is injured), yet the audience is invited to see the 'real' tragedy as a Protestant one. Ervine's play closes with Mrs. Rainey's plangent cry for her husband: 'Aw, my poor man, my poor man.' The cry mixes empathy with a note of rebuke, perhaps, but its effect is surely to fix the audience's attention on the sorrowful case of her husband, who must bear the bitter

24 In the works of Ervine and Thompson the split between 'inside' and 'outside' is obviously much less rigid in both ethnic and moral terms than in the Western, for example. In Mixed Marriage there is a Protestant mob outside as well as a Catholic one, and in Over the Bridge the mob outside is exclusively Protestant. Moreover, in each play the division between inside and outside is not absolute in moral terms: some of those inside, such as Ervine's Rainey or Thompson's Archie Kerr, are at least partly to blame for triggering the mayhem without. Even if the division between inside and outside is less absolute than it is in genres such as the Western, these northern dramas still rest on a dichotomy between the humane few and the dehumanized lumpen masses beyond.

burden of his decision to elevate communal over class loyalty. Thompson's *Over the Bridge* manages audience sympathy in such a way that it is much more completely monopolized by the Protestant characters. Concluding with a tableau in which Protestant mourners bow in reverence before a clergyman reading the prayers of the dead over the corpse of Mitchell, the scene ensures that it is the fallen Protestant hero who commands the grief and empathy of the theatre audience. In both works, Catholics are acknowledged as the actual victims of sectarianism, but it is Protestant suffering that is cathected as the stuff of tragedy. Whether it is Rainey, who must bear the burden of his decisions, or Mitchell, who takes the sins of his community on his own back, tragic destiny is essentially Protestant.

Elsaesser's distinction between action-oriented genres, which assume open spaces and dynamic heroes who can use violence legitimately, and genres such as family melodrama and domestic tragedy, which operate within a more enclosed and immobilized environment where the characters tend to be acted upon and violence is directed inwards, is useful here. As Elsaesser notes, whatever their other limitations, these latter genres typically make greater provision for women protagonists, and they cannot simply affirm masculine fantasies of potency and the disavowal of the feminine that more action-oriented genres do. Still, in so far as activity in these more domestic genres continues to be equated with masculinity and passivity with femininity, the greater scope they allow for women characters and for the expression of passion inevitably creates its own problems. 'Masculinity,' Geoffrey Nowell-Smith writes, though usually impaired and rarely attainable within these genres, is at least known as an ideal. 'Femininity', on the other hand, 'within the terms of the argument, is not only unknown but unknowable', since social efficacy is recognizable only in a 'masculine' form. Thus, the contradictions facing the women characters are more acutely posed from the outset, and women's protests against the restrictions of their situation tend to assume various forms of hysterical excess or masochism.[25]

These observations on the relationship of gender and genre throw useful light on the constrictions that govern not only the representation of women but also of Catholics in Ervine's and Thompson's plays, and in others of their kind. Indeed, Catholics in these plays are essentially 'feminized', in the sense that they share many of the constraints that usually apply to women characters in such genres. Since in each play effective social agency is restricted to patriarchal Protestant males (in Ervine's play, the success of the strike depends totally on Rainey; in Thompson's, only Mitchell has enough credit with the workers to solve problems), the Catholic characters are implicitly aligned with women. Hence, although their oppression within the given social structure is recognized, any strong actions that they themselves might undertake to undo that oppression are not considered acceptable; Catholics, like women, are most sympathetic, in other words, when they remain passive and impotent victims. When they individually protest their situation, their behaviour is registered as feminized hysteria, but, if the protest takes a

25 Geoffrey Nowell-Smith, 'Minelli and Melodrama', in Gledhill, *Home is Where the Heart Is*, 70–74, 72

militant collective expression, it is depicted as brute mob activity that cannot be approved. In Ervine's *Mixed Marriage*, Nora Murray is the principal Catholic character in the play and her role allows Catholic and feminine positions to be conflated. Despite her initially spirited defence of her love for Hugh, Nora's behaviour becomes progressively more hysterical as the consequences of that transgressive love are visited upon the Raineys, and the manner of her death, when she runs into the street and is shot, has a patently masochistic quality.[26] Similarly, in Thompson's *Over the Bridge*, O'Boyle's complaints about his harassment and his insistence on returning to work in a way that puts everyone at risk are, as Lionel Pilkington has noted, depicted as a mixture of 'petulant and violent obduracy'.[27] As the play reaches its climax, O'Boyle's whinginess slides into an explicitly feminized excess. When the office is besieged by the mob, he panics and becomes hysterical and: 'Davy smacks him across the face. Peter stares back in shock and then slumps into the chair.'[28] Davy's self-command here is stereotypically 'masculine', Peter's lack of it characteristically associated with a 'womanish' loss of control.[29]

The crux here is that these plays operate in terms of conventions in which activity, control and social efficacy are associated exclusively with masculinity and Protestantism, while passivity, domesticity and hysteria are associated with women and Catholics. Once Catholics actively protest their oppression, they are caught in a double bind whereby their actions are construed as hysterical and masochistic or else, if they take a more aggressive form, slide into a kind of criminalized violence, which supposedly mirrors the violence visited upon them. Essentially, then, Catholics, like women, are sympathetic so long as they remain passive, the worthy recipients of liberal Protestant benevolence. Once they step out of this role, or are foolhardy enough to venture out from the (oppressive) security of private domestic space — as Nora does when she crosses over the threshold of the living room into the street or as O'Boyle does when he refuses to stay at home with the other Catholics — into the dangerous and militantly masculinized public sphere, they court destruction for themselves and sow dissension, which brings destruction on civilized society as a whole.

Writing about eighteenth-century German middle-class tragedy in *Mimesis*, Erich Auerbach comments that the world revealed to the spectator in such works is 'desperately narrow, both spatially and ethically'. The genre, he remarks, was

wedded to the personal, the domestic, the touching, and the sentimental, and it could not relinquish them. And this, through the tone and level of style which it

---

26 The only other Catholic in *Mixed Marriage*, Michael O'Hara, has a lesser role than Nora. Although he is politically motivated, he has no real agency, since all his plans depend on Rainey's support for the strike.

27 Lionel Pilkington, 'Theatre and Cultural Politics in Northern Ireland: The *Over the Bridge* Controversy, 1959', *Éire-Ireland*, 30 (1996), 76–93, 83

28 Thompson, *Over the Bridge*, 99

29 In a scene included in the rehearsal copy of the play but later excised, the parallel between Catholics and women was even more explicit, since O'Boyle's hysteria anticipates Marion's 'hysterical' language when she breaks her engagement with Warren Baxter.

implied, was unfavorable to a broadening of the social setting and the inclusion of general political and social problems. And yet it was in just this way that the break-through to things political and generally social was achieved: for the touching and, in essence, wholly personal love alliance now no longer clashed with the opposition of ill-willed relatives, parents, and guardians, or with private moral obstacles, but instead with a public enemy, with the unnatural class structure of society.[30]

Something similar might be concluded about Northern Irish tragedies such as Ervine's and Thompson's. These plays are strongest when they insist, with the rigour of tragedy, that the realization of desire, whether it be love across the sectarian divide or working-class unity, is ultimately impeded not by individual villainy or the machinations of small élites in power, but by the whole structure of a society that rests on a vicious interweave of working-class exploitation and sectarian domination. At the same time, the limitations of the genre are such that this insight is seldom more than fleetingly grasped, and almost never opens out into any kind of radical understanding of the situation. Instead, the plays too often lapse into a kind of besieged liberal self-pity, in which the Catholic and Protestant working classes prove intractably wedded to their bigotries, or else into a kind of sentimentality that, in order to square accounts, acknowledges compassion for Catholics only at the price of representing Protestants as even more tragic victims.

6

Though he shares with Ervine and Thompson an Ulster unionist upbringing, Tom Paulin's commitment to republicanism distinguishes him from such precursors, and The Riot Act: A Version of Sophocles' Antigone, was first produced by the republican-identified Field Day Theatre Company in Derry in 1984.[31] Paulin was not the first to see in Sophocles' tragedy a mythic paradigm for the northern struggle. In 1968, when the Royal Ulster Constabulary was brutally repressing civil rights demonstrations, Conor Cruise O'Brien gave a lecture in which he used Sophocles' play to ponder the political and ethical complexities of the Northern situation. Arguing that 'it was Antigone's free decision, and that alone, which precipitated the tragedy', O'Brien concluded his deliberation by asserting that, whatever her personal appeal, the actions of Antigone are ultimately indefensible, since she brings disaster not only on herself but on everyone else as well.[32] In O'Brien's reading, Antigone becomes, in ways that recall Ervine's Nora Murray or Thompson's whiny Peter O'Boyle, the hysterical feminine Catholic culprit

---

30 Auerbach, Mimesis, 439, 441

31 Tom Paulin, The Riot Act: A Version of Sophocles' Antigone (London, 1985)

32 The lecture was printed in The Listener (London), 24 Oct. 1968. The text was later included, in abridged version, in O'Brien's States of Ireland (London, 1972), 152–59. The reference is to this edition, 157. See also George Steiner's comments on O'Brien's interpretation in Antigones (Oxford, 1984), 190–91.

whose selfish agency visits chaos on all. The shifting emotional trajectory of the lecture — initially registering some sympathy for Antigone, but then dismissing her assertion of individual conscience at the expense of social order as too costly, and thus siding with Creon — anticipates that of the lecturer's own political career. Having written against partition as a young civil servant some decades earlier, once the northern conflict erupted O'Brien went on to become a vigorous defender of the northern state, and adopted an increasingly rigid pro-unionist line, eventually joining the United Kingdom Unionist Party. On one level at least, Paulin's version of *Antigone* can be read as part of his ongoing imaginative engagement with O'Brien, a southern intellectual whose migration from Irish nationalism to Ulster unionism ran in inverse direction to Paulin's own political development.

Paulin's *Riot Act* appeared just three years after the 1981 hunger strike in which ten men in the H-Block prison camps starved themselves to death to protest the British government's attempts to deny republican prisoners political status. The contest between the hunger-strikers and the British government had convulsed Northern Ireland and it had also transformed republican strategy, setting in motion a shift away from an exclusively military struggle with the state towards the building of a mass political movement. Coming in the immediate wake of these events, Paulin's rewriting of Sophocles' tragedy addressed itself to a society still traumatized by a powerful collision of wills and by antithetical concepts of justice, a collision so intense that it had threatened at certain moments to precipitate outright civil war.

In Paulin's play, Creon is identified with northern unionism and Antigone with republicanism. Creon justifies his refusal of proper burial to Polynices and the severity of his response to Antigone on the grounds that she had 'levelled [Eteocles] with a state traitor'.[33] This inevitably recalled the recent hunger strike episode, since the British government's attempt, strongly backed by unionists, to deny the republican prisoners political status rested on a similar insistence that it was imperative to maintain a categorical distinction between the violence of the security forces, who upheld the state, and that of 'terrorist' paramilitaries, whose actions tried to undermine it. Like the republican campaign against criminalization, Antigone's actions serve to destabilize Creon's categorical distinction between Eteocles (the representative of legitimate state violence) and Polynices (who rebels against state authority), as does her insistence that there are some laws higher than those of the state.

Although its local political resonance was unmistakable, the significance of Paulin's *Riot Act* is not reducible to such one-to-one correspondences. Sophocles' tragedy, after all, does not reduce to the struggle between Creon and Antigone. There is also the contest between Antigone, with her tendency to exalt what she sees as her higher calling, and her sister, Ismene, who asserts the values of compromise and the imperatives of survival. There is, as well, the struggle between Creon and his son, Haemon, whose

33 *The Riot Act*, 29

appeals to his father to act with greater judiciousness go unheeded until it is too late. In the circumstances, then, the Sophoclean text — or, more precisely, the complex of difficult moral choices, equally legitimate claims, and the indeterminacies of feeling which it engenders — was deployed by Paulin to speak to a society recently shaken by the traumas of the hunger strikes, and the northern conflict more generally, in a way that alluded to recent events, but tried to get beyond any kind of polemical 'blame-game' in order to diagnose the complex ethical imperatives at work on each side of the divide.

A sceptical critic might argue that Paulin's adaptation of Sophoclean tragedy simply translated conventional constructions of the Troubles in 'lowbrow' domestic tragedies such as Ervine's *Mixed Marriage* into a more prestigious 'highbrow' literary idiom or register. After all, many of the formulaic structural devices that shape romantic and domestic tragedies about the Troubles seem to resemble those that appear in *The Riot Act*.[34] For example, the opposition between Creon as paternal masculine unionist and Antigone as feminized republican seems to repeat the same gendered patterning of the communal conflict that we have already noted in Ervine and Thompson. Similarly, the love of Haemon for Antigone might be seen as merely a variant on the romantic 'Romeo and Juliet' or love-across-the-divide device that appears in Ervine's play, as well as in so many other recent Troubles narratives. Don't both Ervine's *Mixed Marriage* and Paulin's *The Riot Act* translate the Ulster unionist predicament — the son forced to choose between a forward-looking love for the Other and filial loyalty to his father — into the same Oedipal dilemma?

These correspondences have their interest, but the overall dynamic of Paulin's narrative is nevertheless quite different. The 'Romeo and Juliet' or love-across-the-divide device that structures plays such as *Mixed Marriage* is one in which the drive towards reconciliation represented by the lovers from hostile communities can only succeed if they first detach themselves from their respective families. In the Shakespearean prototype, the love of Romeo and Juliet develops against the background of the perpetually quarrelling Montagues and Capulets; if that love is to triumph over inherited circumstance, the two young people must first rise above their own family allegiances. In Shakespeare's romantic tragedy, the conflict is essentially between extended kinship allegiances, represented by the rival clans, and the values of the privatized bourgeois couple, mythically self-contained and supposedly outside of all social determination.[35] Adapted to the contemporary Northern Irish situation, the effect of this device is to depict the Catholic and Protestant communities generally as symmetrical tribal and atavistic

---

34 Paulin's play and Ervine's share some interesting things in common. The most obvious is their respective uses of Ulster dialect. Paulin's title may obliquely refer to Ervine's play; the following lines are in the closing act of *Mixed Marriage*:

   TOM (*from the stairs*): There's a magistrate outside readin' the Riot Act.
   NORA: The Riot Act!

35 For a carefully argued interpretation of *Romeo and Juliet* along these lines, see Dympna Callaghan, 'The Ideology of Romantic Love', in Dympna Callaghan, Lorraine Helms and Jyotsna Singh, eds., *The Weyward Sisters: Shakespeare and Feminist Politics* (Oxford, 1994), 59–101.

entities, and the two young lovers then come to represent a more modern-minded, liberal minority, struggling heroically to overcome the entrenched sectarian attitudes associated with the opposing factions. The device, in short, is one that constructs the northern situation in such a way that an enlightened liberal vanguard, personified by the tragic couple, is seen to be involved in a desperate struggle (doomed for now but nevertheless noble and future-oriented) to overcome the supposedly twin sectarianisms of the broad mass of the two communities.

The degree to which this compositional structure expresses a deeply negative attitude to the wider body of both Protestant and Catholic communities can best be gauged by comparing it with Georg Lukács's account of the representation of antagonistic political communities in the classical historical novel. For Lukács, the 'wavering' hero in the classical historical novel (Scott's Edward Waverley is the exemplary instance) sides completely with neither of the warring camps in the great crisis of his time. But for all his vacillations, the hero does have strong emotional ties to both sides in the dispute, and his meandering progress through the novel sees him involve himself for a time with each of the rival parties. These interactions with each side are essential, Lukács argues, since they ensure that the reader 'enter[s] into human contact with both camps'. Unless imaginative involvements of this kind are established, Lukács stresses, the historical clash between warring forces will be reduced to 'a merely external picture of mutual destruction incapable of arousing the human sympathies and enthusiasms of the reader'.[36]

The sympathetic involvement of the reader with both sides that Lukács applauds in the classical historical novel is at odds with the 'Romeo and Juliet' device. By inviting the reader to empathize exclusively with the humane and enlightened lovers and to take an essentially negative attitude towards their wider families and communities, the latter compositional structure sponsors exactly the kind of alienated and morally superior standpoint towards historical conflict that Lukács praises the historical novel for circumventing. Where the historical novel encourages the reader to weigh up dialectically the wider social losses and gains at stake in violent and explosive moments of societal transformation, and to try to avoid the easy consolations of praise and blame, the 'Romeo and Juliet' plot empties social collision of all political significance and dismisses it as a meaningless cycle of mutual destruction. Since the wider social world represented by the warring communities is conceived so reductively — the two 'warring tribes' merely impeding the future world that wants to be born — the privatized interiority and mutually self-enclosed passion of the bourgeois couple is endorsed as the only substantive value.

The real significance of Paulin's use of *Antigone* lies in its capacity to estrange or defamiliarize the construction of the northern situation that romantic tragedies have established as normative. Where the latter confer on the romantic couple a lyrico-tragical

36 Lukács, *The Historical Novel*, 36

halo while damning the wider communities as regressive, the effect of the Antigone narrative is to restore to the antagonistic parties in the northern situation some less condescending sense of their historical struggle with each other. When viewed through the lens of Sophoclean tragedy, the conflict no longer appears as a meaningless clash of rival atavisms, but instead as one that grows out of antithetical ethical claims, each of which has some justice on its side and legitimate claim to recognition. In Sophocles' narrative, the love of Haemon and Antigone emotionally and ethically complicates the struggle between Creon and Antigone, but romantic love is not detached from all other obligations and values and enshrined as a transcendent absolute.

The 'Romeo and Juliet' narratives operate in terms of a moralized dichotomy that pits a superior humane élite against the regressive mass of the community as a whole, but *Antigone* accords the greater body of the population, which tries to steer somewhere between the polarities represented by Antigone and Creon, a far less derisory status. As embodied in the persons of Ismene and the Chorus, the general body of the population is allowed its own worth, though the play does not extol or sentimentalize the average either. In short, what distinguishes Sophocles' *Antigone* is that the very different values and moral imperatives represented by Creon and Antigone are each allowed strong claim on the audience's respect.[37] Each side to the dispute has a genuine claim to justice, but by pushing its own claim to such an extreme that the claim of the other side is entirely negated, assertions of justice lead unwittingly to catastrophe for all. By adapting the *Antigone* narrative to the northern situation, Paulin allows the conflicting parties in the northern struggle (to each of which he personally has conflicting ancestral and ideological ties) what Winston Churchill once referred to, though with a patrician British sneer, as 'the integrity of their quarrel'.[38]

That said, some caveats possibly need to be entered. Paulin's version of *Antigone* does indeed work to rescue Northern Irish society from the liberal condescension to which it is commonly subjected, but his actual handling of the material suggests some unease and misgivings on his part, some difficulty in breaking with the very assumptions the play seems to want to contest. One of the more obvious signs of tension is the disjunction between the elevated classical style of the original and Paulin's use of northern vernacular — his translation of the Greek is heavily colloquial, slangy, often jokey — and his modes of characterization, which tend towards caricature at times, steering very close in the case of Creon and the Messenger to satiric unionist stereotype. The deliberate mixing of high tragedy and slangy colloquialism 'lowers' the overall tone of Paulin's *Antigone* and

---

37 However much they differ otherwise, the most sophisticated readings of the play, from Goethe to Hegel to Hölderlin, respect this dialectical character of the drama (in a way that O'Brien's unequivocal partisanship of Creon does not). Steiner's *Antigones* provides valuable commentary on the different ways in which European critics have read Sophocles' tragedy.

38 Cited in Tom Nairn, *The Break-Up of Britain* (London, 1981), 223. It has to be acknowledged, however, that if Paulin's tragedy restores to the warring communities 'the integrity of their quarrel', it does so by translating it out of the dynamic realm of the historical altogether and into an abstract ethical metaphysic.

seems to indicate a degree of uncertainty: it is as though the work can never quite decide whether it really wishes to achieve an 'elevated' and 'heroic' tragic effect — that would register a conception of the northern conflict as a terrible collision of irreconcilable rights — or a more 'democratic' comic-satiric effect — that would suggest that with a little more pragmatic 'give and take' matters might be more readily resolved — and hence veers somewhat unsteadily between the two. Thus while the plot turns on an exemplary tragic situation in which two irreconcilable imperatives trigger a collision in which something has to give way, the moral thrust of Paulin's version seems to insist, in a spirit nearer to comedy, that a greater capacity for compromise might have resolved everything. Compromise, after all, is what Haemon counsels: 'Be firm sometimes, / then give a little — that's wise.' The Messenger's verdict on Creon underscores the same point: 'He could neither bend nor listen. He held firm just that shade too long. There was no joy nor give in him ever.' A few lines later, the Chorus reiterate the same message: 'It was too late you changed your mind.'[39] The Riot Act, in short, seems to contain a frustrated comic-satiric soul trapped within a tragic body, and this stylistic 'identity crisis' is indicative of an unresolved attitude to the communities and conflict it depicts.

The stylistic mixing that characterizes Paulin's treatment of his material may ultimately be only surface symptoms of an even odder incongruity or identity crisis at the core of this play. In the standard allegorical interpretations of The Riot Act, Paulin's Creon is identified with the Ulster unionists and Antigone with Northern Irish republicans. Given that Paulin's own political allegiances were republican, the extent to which his identification of Antigone with republicans seems to concede so much to hostile revisionist stereotypes of republicanism is perhaps rather surprising. In The Riot Act version at least, what Antigone reveres are the primordial values of kith and kin. Against Creon's exaltation of the reason of state and Ismene's pragmatic common sense, Antigone asserts the duty owed to the dead and to blood ties. Her behaviour, moreover, exhibits a certain morbid fascination with her own martyrdom. Whether or not the Sophoclean original supports such a conception of the heroine, this means that if she is intended to express republican value, then Paulin's Antigone seems in many ways a curious choice. After all, the identification tends to support the notion that Irish republicanism is a form of primordialist ethnic nationalism committed to the call of ancestral voices — in other words, a conception of republicanism closer in conception to O'Brien's caricature than to the ways in which republicans typically understand their own ideology. For republicans, the essence of republicanism is its opposition to ethnic nationalism and to the idea that the state should privilege any one sect or creed. The republican credo is, in principle at least, essentially a civic and secular nationalist one, which sponsors the idea of a common citizenship that would make no distinction between Catholic, Protestant and Dissenter. What has happened then? How can this Antigone, so strangely at odds in many ways with values that one might associate with

39 The Riot Act, 38, 56, 60

secular republicanism, be reconciled with Paulin's declared republican commitments?

In order to answer this question, it may be necessary to pursue a reading that suggests that Paulin's version of *Antigone* is only on one level, and not necessarily the most compelling one at that, an allegory of the wider communal conflict in the North. The play's 'deeper' emotional energy may be charged by an unresolved Oedipal conflict (one generated and shaped by the actual historical situation, thus not familial in any narrow sense) within the author himself. On such a reading, Antigone would not represent Irish republicanism, but rather those instinctive or emotional claims to loyalty that Paulin's natal Ulster Protestant culture still continues to exert on him (as he himself has allowed) despite his rejection of Ulster unionism and intellectual conversion to republicanism. Creon (a rather heavy-handed Paisleyite caricature in Paulin's version) would, in this reading, express all the more unappealing aspects of Ulster unionism that have compelled Paulin to reject the political culture within which he was raised: its self-righteous intransigence, its puritanical severity, its triumphalist swagger, its exaggerated and even 'blasphemous' fetishism of the state. The real predicament, if we accept this reading, is not whether the ethical deadlock represented by Creon and Antigone can ever be resolved. Instead, the play can better be read as a psychodrama in which Antigone acts as a figure for the compelling emotional loyalites that continue to bind Paulin to his ancestral community, while Creon stands for everything that repels and makes it impossible to accede to those forces of attraction. Accordingly, Haemon, the tormented liberal son torn between Antigone and Creon, may well be the figure within the play whose predicament most nearly approximates that of the author himself. If only Haemon's father were not so bloody intransigent and severe, if only he could learn to compromise and to share power ('That's no city / where one man only / has all the power'), then Haemon's would be much less tormented by self-division and he might have had his Antigone.[40] Or, to put it another way, if only Ulster unionism were not so uncompromising, then Paulin's relationship to the Ulster Protestant community might have been a lot less painfully self-divided, and the bonds of primordial obligation and allegiance represented by Antigone more easily acknowledged.

If we credit this reading, Paulin's play seems, in this one respect at least, broadly similar to those by Ervine and Thomspon examined earlier. Their plays, we recall, start out as critical reflections on sectarian relations, but the focus gradually mutates so that the dilemma turns out to be the crisis of Protestant self-identity (collective and individual) set in motion whenever the issue of Protestant sectarianism is pressed home. In Ervine's *Mixed Marriage*, the failure of working-class solidarity between Catholic and Protestant gives the play its theme, but as the action develops the tragedy becomes the divisions within Rainey's family and especially within Rainey himself. Thompson's *Over the Bridge* also begins as a drama about the obstacles to working-class solidarity, but modulates eventually into a tragedy where the pathos is reserved for the moral dilemmas that

---

40 *The Riot Act*, 40

sectarianism poses for Protestants, not for the material ones it inflicts on the subaltern Catholic community. Likewise, while Paulin's *Riot Act* works on one level as a more intellectually complex play about the antithetical claims to justice that put unionists and republicans at odds with each other, it may also be contrapuntally inflected by an existential narrative of Protestant self-division.

7

Tragedy, to paraphrase Raymond Williams, can inhere in many shapes of the historical process, and the social situation that has long prevailed in Northern Ireland is one in which several of these overlap: in the failed revolution; in the deep internal divisions and self-contradictions within both communities at a time of shock and loss; in the deadlock or stalemate of a blocked and apparently static period; in the difficulty in reconciling equal and yet antithetical rights.[41] In the circumstances, the emergence of a variety of tragic forms to depict the Troubles is hardly surprising. While a tragic conception of the situation cannot be privileged over any other, it might be argued that its distinctive contribution lies in its stark, uncompromising insistence that a new social order can only emerge after a painful period of crisis and rupture in which many old allegiances must be abandoned, and many new kinds of recognition attained.

When an old social order is dying, as Williams observes, it grieves for itself.[42] For those invested in that order, its disintegration will inevitably be conceived in terms of tragic loss. For those for whom it was hurtful and oppressive, it will not be the disintegration of the old, but the slowness with which the new emerges, if it emerges at all, that will appear the real calamity. In all of the tragic narratives discussed here, a certain grieving for the failure of the new to emerge is audible. However, what cannot be overlooked is the contrapuntal movement in which this grief for the obstruction of the new can also modulate into a sense of mourning for the old that is perceived to be dying. The plays examined here all attribute responsibility for the crisis of community relations within Northern Ireland to Protestant sectarianism. To this extent, all three works discussed represent a break with and challenge to the ideology of traditional unionism since it has never been able to bring itself to acknowledge even that much. Nevertheless, what these plays also show, in various ways and to different degrees to be sure, is that in the catastrophe that follows from the collision between the two communities, the internal divisions opened up within Protestant identity tend to be cathected as the true source or motor of tragic suffering, and the standpoint of the victims of state sectarianism is steered, wittingly or not, into the background. It is here that the plays come nearest to expressing a structure of feeling that tends to inform various shades of liberal unionism.

41 Williams, *Modern Tragedy*, 218
42 Williams, *Modern Tragedy*, 209

When the plight of the oppressed northern nationalist community is acknowledged in this structure of feeling, the emphasis usually shifts to the parity of suffering endured by both communities in the nearly three decades of vicious struggle to overthrow the structures of state oppression.[43] But this insistence on parity of suffering during the Troubles obscures the fact that the weight of state oppression has never, either under the centuries of British rule or in the several decades since the foundation of the northern state, fallen equally on both communities. Unless this limit of the liberal unionist imagination is superseded, the emergence of the new will continue to be impeded.

43 The tendency within liberal unionism that I am referring to here is neatly summed up in a post-ceasefire radio interview which Ken Maginnis, Ulster Unionist MP, gave in 1994. Maginnis, widely considered too liberal to become leader of his party, expressed the view that the Northern Irish Protestant community generally considered itself 'more sinned against than sinning'. Cited in Duncan Morrow, 'Suffering for Righteousness' Sake: Fundamental Protestantism in Ulster Politics', in Shirlow and McGovern, Who are 'The People'?, 55–71, 55. The issue, surely, is not which community sinned or suffered most, but to understand the forces and structures that conditioned both communities' actions and dispositions.

The Pogues and the Spirit of Capitalism

Shane MacGowan and the Pogues were one of the most flamboyant forces in late twentieth-century Irish popular culture. Notoriety alone assures them a place in the history of modern Irish popular music, and even in dilapidated middle age MacGowan remains a cult figure, yet critical opinion on the band's achievements is divided. When they first appeared in the early 1980s, the Pogues seemed to many to be just another boozy ballad group content to exploit a cod-Irish confection of drunken emigrant nostalgia, blowhard republicanism, and hooliganish hedonism. Their first album, *Red Roses for Me* (1984) — its title taken from Sean O'Casey's 1943 play of that name, and featuring songs such as 'Waxie's Dargle', 'Poor Paddy', 'Streams of Whiskey', 'Boys from the County Hell', and Brendan Behan's 'The Auld Triangle' — did much to create this impression. However, subsequent albums, especially *Rum, Sodomy & the Lash* (1985) and *If I Should Fall from Grace with God* (1988), complicated matters by winning critical acclaim in Ireland and beyond. 'Fairytale of New York' (1987), the famous MacGowan/Kirsty MacColl duet that featured on *If I Should Fall from Grace with God*, was the band's most successful single and it has remained one of the most popular Christmas songs of our times. MacGowan has penned many other fine songs over his career, such as 'A Pair of Brown Eyes', 'The Sick Bed of Cuchulainn', 'The Broad Majestic Shannon', 'The Old Main Drag', 'Rainy Night in Soho', and the exquisite 'Summer in Siam', and is widely recognized as a songwriter of genuine ability. But he and the Pogues were also able to take popular 'classics' and make them their own. Ewan MacColl's 'Dirty Old Town', Eric Bogle's 'And the Band Played Waltzing Matilda', and several well-known popular ballads, notably 'The Galway Races' and 'The Irish Rover', were given memorable treatments by the band.

Despite these achievements, the Pogues were a short-lived, essentially 1980s phenomenon. Their last album to feature MacGowan, *Hell's Ditch*, was released in 1990. Since the split in 1991, the Pogues have continued to tour and MacGowan established a new band, the Popes, in 1994. But neither he nor the Pogues ever regained the musical heights they reached in the mid to late eighties nor have they managed to dispel the sense that latterly they continue to trade chiefly on those glory days. Today, the Pogues seem essentially a tribute band to their former selves and MacGowan's post-Pogues 'legend' rests less on new albums than on his having survived decades of apparently massive alcohol and drug consumption.

In these circumstances the tendency to reduce the artistic achievements of the Pogues and MacGowan to drunken rabble-rousing and sentimental nostalgia has reasserted itself. In his recent *Noisy Island: A Short History of Irish Popular Music* (2005), one of the few scholarly studies of this form of Irish culture, Gerry Smyth compares the Pogues unfavourably with Van Morrison, and suggests that the latter's music displays 'levels of musical authenticity, skill and subtlety' and 'forms of Irish identity generally more complex and more resonant' than those associated with the Pogues. For Smyth,

> the image purveyed by the Pogues, and most especially by MacGowan, pandered to all the stereotypes regarding the Irish in Britain, the drunkenness, the aggression (as found in a track such as 'Sally MacLennane' or 'Boys from the County Hell', for example), and beneath it all, the hint of Celtic wistfulness and poetry ('A Pair of Brown Eyes' or 'A Rainy Night in Soho').

Some of those drawn to this version of Irishness might, Smyth surmises, 'lose this identity next day as they would a hangover', but 'for those who felt compelled to embrace it because of their nationality it could become a badge of permanent cultural disability'.[1]

Smyth's argument is consistent with a hostile line of assessment that attended the Pogues from the start. In 1985, for example, the band confronted an inquisitorial panel of traditional musicians and rock journalists on leading disc jockey B. P. Fallon's radio show, where they were roundly rebuked for their retrograde version of Irishness. On that occasion, former Planxty member Noel Hill dismissed their music (along with the whole ballad tradition represented by the Clancy Brothers and the Dubliners) as 'a terrible abortion of Irish music'.[2] Irish rock pundits were scarcely more sympathetic:

1   Gerry Smyth, *Noisy Island: A Short History of Irish Popular Music* (Cork, 2005), 75–77. See also the judgement in his earlier article 'Who's the Greenest of Them All? Irishness and Popular Music', *Irish Studies Review*, 2 (1992), 3–5, which he cites and reaffirms in the book. Smyth modifies his evaluation later in *Noisy Island*, acknowledging that the music of the Pogues or the Dubliners might well 'provide access to estimable discourses, such as honesty, loyalty, community, and a generally affirmative attitude towards life' (77). But the overall assessment remains fundamentally negative.

2   On this episode and on the Irish rock establishment's initial reaction to the Pogues, see Joe Merrick, *Shane MacGowan: London Irish Punk Life and Music* (London, 1991), 63–66. On the equally hostile reaction of the folk world, see Ann Scanlon, *The Pogues: The Lost Decade* (London, 1988), 71–75. See also the short chapter on the Pogues, in Sean Campbell and Gerry Smyth, *Beautiful Day: Forty Years of Irish Rock Music* (Cork, 2005), 97–99.

writing in the *Irish Times*, Joe Breen suggested that his distaste for the Pogues resembled the attitude of contemporary African-Americans who preferred contemporary music to a blues tradition obsessed with the miseries of slavery and Jim Crow.[3] Of course, not all early assessments were so negative and, particularly after the release of *Rum, Sodomy & the Lash* and *If I Should Fall from Grace with God*, many of the Pogues' peers were complimentary. Thus, for Elvis Costello, the band's real achievement was to have 'saved folk from the folkies'; Christy Moore and Sinéad O'Connor have praised MacGowan as one of the greatest Irish songwriters of the twentieth century; and Bob Geldof has described how the Pogues's music opened his eyes to a rebelliousness in Irish popular culture to which his disdain for Irish cultural nationalism had blinded him.[4]

The range and contradictory nature of these assessments beg several questions. Critics can approach popular cultural phenomena such as the Pogues in a variety of ways, each requiring different research strategies, specialist knowledge, and evaluative criteria. However, given that the study of popular culture in Ireland is underdeveloped, existing modes of analysis tend to be rather narrow, and much of the current scholarship on Irish popular music, as in Irish studies generally, is absorbed with issues of identity. This is problematic, especially when considering a very protean medium like popular music in which 'image' (or 'Irishness-as-image') may be important but is not necessarily the crucial key to understanding what the music culturally means or how it socially functions, and it may ultimately privilege the issue of stereotypes or images of Irishness over other elements of the overall cultural package. In other words, the analysis of image and stereotype obviously allows music studies to build on scholarship in literary, visual and media studies, often in useful and interesting ways, but it can also obscure concerns specific to music in its own right, diverting attention from matters such as songwriting, the development of a band's music over time, or more 'specialist' questions such as instrumentation, orchestration and technique.

Music is usually evaluated with reference to genres and traditions or histories. But in which musical tradition should a band like the Pogues be situated? Is it really the case, as Costello's remarks seem to imply, that MacGowan and the Pogues accomplished something for folk music, but not for Irish or British rock music? Or does it make sense to locate them in an essentially Irish rock tradition, as Smyth effectively does when he contrasts them with Van Morrison? After all, the Pogues were in no simple sense either an Irish or an English band; their music, too, was a product of an eclectic mixing of traditions. The argument here is that to comprehend the Pogues it is necessary to consider their relationship to both Irish music and to British punk, and also to attend to the curious ways in which they merged the 'modernist'- and 'avant-garde'-coded aesthetics of punk with the 'romantically'-coded idioms of the Irish musical forms they

---

3 Cited in Scanlon, *The Pogues*, 76
4 Elvis Costello is cited in Nuala O'Connor, *Bringing It All Back Home: The Influence of Irish Music at Home and Overseas* (Dublin, 2001), 159, and Moore and O'Connor in Campbell and Smyth, *Beautiful Day*, 99. Geldof's essay on the Pogues can be accessed at www.pogues.com

cultivated. To say that the Pogues were defined by a fusion of British punk and Irish folk is a commonplace, but to fully grasp what was involved — conceptually and semantically as well as musically — one needs to appreciate not only the historical particularities of the various musical milieux between which the Pogues operated, but also their capacity to play havoc with the self-legitimizing metanarratives on which those milieux typically depended for meaning.

Images of drunken, brawling Paddies have loomed large in racist English or American stereotypes of the Irish. Certainly, no thorough discussion of the Pogues can avoid their engagement with such representations. The matter is typically posed, as it is by Smyth, in terms of 'stereotypes of Irishness'. But might not such issues be as usefully considered in terms of capitalism, the carnivalesque and consumer excess? After all, commentary, not all of it by outsiders and not all of it disapproving, on the communal licentiousness of wakes and patterns, fairs, faction fights and Donnybrooks dates from before as well as during the colonial period, and many motifs in early reports recur insistently in modern anthropological or quasi-anthropological writings on the lower-class or 'slum Irish' communities in England or America.[5] Rowdy binge-drinking, hell-raising subcultures — those of eighteenth-century 'rakes', nineteenth-century navvies, mid-twentieth-century poets and novelists, and the pub ballad singers of the 1960s and 1970s — are a recurrent feature of the country's history. Moreover, variant images of Irish sociability and excess have proven highly marketable, featuring in tourist advertising campaigns from the 1950s through to the present. However we assess traditions of popular bibulousness, festivity or misrule, they have left their mark on contemporary popular culture, most obviously in a vast repertoire of (often highly self-conscious and self-parodying) drinking songs, and also in film where Donnybrook scenes serve not as motifs of social breakdown but as antic expressions of communal harmony and rejuvenation.[6] For the more respectably inclined, these dissolute versions of Irishness — at odds variously with more desirable images of modernizing improvement, religious or cultural purity, industrial discipline or cosmopolitan sophistication — have long been an embarrassment, and contemporary scholarly discussions of the stereotype do not always escape a similar prissiness.

The Pogues are certainly not unique in exploiting this carnivalesque seam in Irish popular culture; numerous Irish writers, from James Joyce to Flann O'Brien to J. P. Donleavy, or musicians, from the Clancy Brothers to the Dubliners to Planxty, have done

---

5   On stereotypes of Irishness in British culture, see L. Perry Curtis, Jr., *Apes and Angels: The Irishman in Victorian Caricature* (Washington, 1997) and Michael de Nie, *The Eternal Paddy: Irish Identity in the British Press, 1798–1882* (Madison, 2004). On the carnivalesque in Irish literary culture, see Vivian Mercier, *The Irish Comic Tradition* (Oxford, 1962), and for associations between the Irish and carnivalesque misrule more generally, see Peter Stallybrass and Allon White, *The Politics and Poetics of Transgression* (Ithaca, 1986).

6   On the comic Irish party and drinking song, see Mick Moloney, *Irish Music on the American Stage* (Cork, 1993), 12. On the Donnybrook in films about Ireland, see Luke Gibbons, 'Romanticism, Realism, and Irish Cinema', in Kevin Rockett, Luke Gibbons and John Hill, *Cinema and Ireland* (London, 1987), 194–257, 237–39.

the same. What was unusual, perhaps, was the gusto with which the Pogues, and, again, MacGowan in particular, committed themselves to this version of Irishness, making it not simply one element of their music or image (as many Irish bands before them had done), but pushing it to such extravagant extremes that it defined them. But does this mean that we can make sense of the Pogues, or the cult of the Pogues, only in terms of the backward look? Hardly. Excess alcohol and drug consumption has long been a source of anxiety in societies, like Ireland, traumatized by the brutality of their initial insertion into the capitalist system, but these and other forms of hedonistic extravagance also remain an abiding obsession in comfortably prosperous late capitalist consumer societies. It might be argued, therefore, that where drunkenness and a rowdy hedonism are in question, the Pogues represented not simply a throwback to the 'old Ireland' of James Clarence Mangan, Brendan Behan, Flann O'Brien or Luke Kelly (all acknowledged by MacGowan as tutelary heroes), but also an anticipation of the swinging 'new Ireland' of the 'Celtic Tiger', when the country ceased to be regarded as a byword for repression, poverty and sexual starvation and was rebranded instead as an affluently consumerist home of the *craic*.[7]

The approach here is to examine the different musical traditions that went into the making of the Pogues, before considering how some of their songs articulate particular versions of the Irish carnivalesque. Unlike either punk bands such as the Clash and the Gang of Four or the more campaigning figures associated with the Irish ballad scene such as Luke Kelly and Christy Moore, the Pogues never had a distinct political profile. They did sing songs associated with the Irish rebel and republican tradition (such as 'Kitty', 'Young Ned of the Hill' or 'The Auld Triangle') and MacGowan's own compositions sometimes refer to more internationally-minded Irish republican figures such as Frank Ryan or to sexual- and political-outlaw types such as Federico García Lorca or Jean Genet. Likewise, in 1988, the Terry Woods/MacGowan medley 'Streets of Sorrow/Birmingham Six', included on *If I Should Fall from Grace with God*, was the subject of considerable controversy when the British Broadcasting Authority banned it from the airwaves. Yet despite these elements of their repertoire and MacGowan's well-publicized republican sympathies, the Pogues were more associated with wild Rabelaisian mayhem than with any 'serious' political programme. One could conclude, therefore, that the Pogues' aesthetic of festive Irish excess was simply a hibernicized version of late capitalist rock-and-roll debauchery. Yet excess and debauchery have their own histories and politics, and, taken as a whole, the Pogues' albums display a highly diverse range of songs of usually anarchic and distinctly subaltern excess, extending from pre-industrial celebrations of license through to ballads of nineteenth-century industrial navvying and soldiering to late twentieth-century songs of physical and spiritual exhaustion in

7   On MacGowan's conception of Irish literary and musical history, see Victoria Mary Clarke and Shane MacGowan, *A Drink with Shane MacGowan* (London, 2001), 251–71, and *passim*. A series of interviews dealing with MacGowan's life and interests, this work self-consciously affects an *At Swim-Two-Birds* style, linking it to an Irish comic literary tradition rather than to the 'memoir' in some 'straighter' form.

the seedier sides of London, New York and Thailand. In their own ways, then, these albums track a peculiar mini-history of modern subaltern carnival and consumerist excess that stretches from pre-modern to postmodern times.[8] To put it another way, what is significant about the Pogues is not their rowdy, drunken Irishness as such, but the manner in which they articulated this sense of hedonism and mayhem. Too easily dismissed as buffoonery or an ignorant embrace of crude Irish stereotypes, the lunatic binge-drinking consumerist/anti-consumerist excess in their work is actually key to adducing what might be called their 'politics'.[9] However, while this articulation of excess was radical in the broader socio-historical context of the depressed 1980s, it inevitably lost much of its transgressive edge in the affluent 1990s.

2

British punk, the foundational subculture that shaped the Pogues, was possibly the last significant rock movement on the British side of the Atlantic to define itself in explicitly modernist and avant-garde terms.[10] Starting in the mid-1970s, punk took shape in the final crisis-ridden years of the last 'Old Labour' government and in a United Kingdom soon to experience the shock waves of Thatcherite economic and social overhaul. In some ways, punk — with its bellicose assault on received establishments and traditions

8   This takes its cue partly at least from MacGowan's own sense of the band's development when he commented laconically that 'Yeah, we started out in the fucking 18th century with the Pogues first album [Red Roses for Me] ... then the 19th century with the second LP [Rum, Sodomy & the Lash]. [But] we got up to the 1950s with the third one [If I Should Fall from Grace with God]!'. Quoted in Merrick, Shane MacGowan, 66.

9   In contrast to Smyth, who contends that the Pogues were simply mesmerized by debilitating Irish stereotypes, Noel McLaughlin and Martin McLoone argue that 'while blatant Irish stereotypes are present, these are rearticulated in interesting ways. In music and performance, the nostalgic associations are wrenched out of their context both by the irreverent way that folk forms are played (and played with) and in the lyrical associations that are attached to them. The Pogues parody and interrogate aspects of Irishness in complex and confusing ways, and to see in them only a lack of positive stereotypes is to miss the point'. See their 'Hybridity and National Musics: The Case of Irish Rock Music', Popular Music, 19, 2 (2000), 181–99, 191. My own analysis of the Pogues in terms of the carnivalesque is closer to that of McLaughlin and McLoone than to Smyth's. But while they, to my mind, correctly identify the self-consciously parodic and burlesque elements in the Pogues that Smyth misses, they understand this parodic impulse in formalist terms only, dissociating it from a broader politics of the carnivalesque.

10   The most radical post-punk forms, such as rave, house and hip-hop are all dance-and-beat oriented and more postmodernist than modernist in their aesthetics. The literature on punk is extensive, but some standard texts are: Dick Hebdige's Subculture: The Meaning of a Style (London, 1979); Ian Chambers, Urban Rhythms: Pop Music and Popular Culture (London, 1985); David Laing, One Chord Wonders: Power and Meaning in Punk Rock (Milton Keynes, 1985); Peter Wicke, Rock Music: Culture, Aesthetics and Sociology, trans. Rachel Fogg (Cambridge, 1990), esp. ch. 7 '"Anarchy in the UK": The Punk Rebellion'; Roger Sabin, ed., Punk Rock: So What?: The Cultural Legacy of Punk (London, 1999); and Dave Laing, 'Listening to Punk Music', in K. Gelder and J. Thornton, eds., The Subcultures Reader (London, 1997), 406–19. See also Jon Savage, England's Dreaming and Punk Rock (London, 1991); and Adrian Boot and Chris Salewicz, Punk: The Illustrated History of a Music Revolution (London, 1997) for more general overviews.

(musical and otherwise) and its desire to return a commercially compromised rock and roll to its primitive roots — rhetorically anticipated the Conservative 'revolution' of the 1980s, which also combined a belligerently 'modernizing' progressivism with a 'back to basics' rhetoric. Yet though it had its reactionary strands, the punk movement's animus was not directed against the unions or welfare dependants — the Conservatives' primary targets — but against things like the monarchy, the police, and the stultifying complacency of Middle England. From its inception with the Sex Pistols, it was self-consciously modernist in its aesthetics; indeed, Malcolm McLaren, Vivienne Westwood and others who helped to develop the concept had trained in art school and thus had some familiarity with the various avant-garde movements. McLaren, for example, had attended the St. Martin School of Art, and was familiar with Dada and the Situationists as well as with the anti-music experiments of the New York 'New Wave'.[11] As punk's tonal cacophony, hostility to the big music corporations, and the cultivation of an aesthetics of shock tactics all illustrate, it drew on an assortment of Euro-American avant-garde ideas and promoted a sensibility so militantly pugnacious that it made all other modes of rock appear tame or anachronistic. Some of the movement's iconic singles, such as the Sex Pistols' 'Anarchy in the UK' and 'God Save the Queen' or the Clash's 'White Riot' and 'London's Burning' or the Gang of Four's 'Love Like Anthrax', expressed a mood of anarchic rage and alienation that remains unmatched in its intensity in late twentieth-century British popular culture.

In musical terms, then, punk was essentially an anti-music — a deliberately jarring, improvised and unrefined, high-volume, low-tech 'bad music', calculated to negate the 'epic' sound structures and the high-technology flashiness of stadium rock as well as the melodic harmonies of mainstream pop. Punk songs were cynically anti-lyrical, either parodying or repudiating the received pop lexicons of 'love' and 'desire' in favour of more stripped-down or nihilistic lexicons charged with violence, mayhem and obscenity.[12] The punk 'dance' style, called the pogo, was, in like manner, a spasmodic anti-dance: a deliberately jerky and graceless tangling, pushing and jumping that contrasted starkly with the sexualized self-display of disco. The term 'punk' suggested something like 'muck, trash, rubbish, even whore', and the punk 'look' or 'style' likewise aspired to be an ostentatiously loud anti-fashion.[13] The look comprised spiked Mohican haircuts, garish hair dyes, bondage trousers, and slashed or mutilated clothing studded with accessories that were either a bricolage of the quotidian trivia and waste of late consumer capitalism (clothes pegs, paper clips, lavatory chains, bin-liners) or strongly suggested abjection and bondage (cadaverous makeup, safety pins and razor blades, studded belts, dog collars, chains and leads). Sometimes described as an 'aggressive cult of the ugly' (the phrase is Peter Wicke's), it mixed elements of 'urban primitive' and 'decadence',

11 On the European and US avant-garde influences on punk, see Wicke, *Rock Music*, esp. ch. 7. The Sex Pistols first took stage at St. Martin's School of Art in London.
12 On punk's vocal and musical styles, see Laing, 'Listening to Punk Music', 406–19.
13 Wicke, *Rock Music*, 138

and was resolutely hostile to the late twentieth-century idea of the body beautiful.[14]

What the Pogues borrowed from punk is evident enough — a sense of low-tech but high-energy rough musical improvisation; a demotic taste for the trashy and vulgar; a tendency to favour cacophonous and abrasive musical textures over refinement and melody (a feature of their style that extended to MacGowan's smoke-scarred, alcohol-slurred vocals); near-chaotic sets; shock tactics; and a backbeat dominated, hook/riff-based musical language. Nevertheless, from a punk purist perspective, this merger of punk and an 'ethnic' Irish folk music might appear a 'domesticating' appropriation that brought punk closer to the musical mainstream. After all, there is in much of the music of the Pogues a return to the lyrical note that punk proper had abhorred. The classic punk 'songs' are typically extremely brief and fiercely declamatory (discarding narrative for expressionistic intensity) and lacking in tonal variety (few shifts of tonal gear from high to low pitch; little variety in accent and intonation), but the Pogues' songs generally take more conventionally structured ballad forms. And whereas many punk bands had attempted to frustrate the audience's tendency to identify with the vocals of the lead singer by dispensing with any clear centre of vocal authority, MacGowan often fulfilled a more conventional lead-singer role in the Pogues' sets, his voice functioning (in the band's most popular 'hits' at least) as a point of lyric identification that established some sort of vocal core to an otherwise shambolically centrifugal line-up.

Still, the argument that the Pogues essentially domesticated punk misses far too much to be persuasive. Punk's essential strength may have been its capacity for a remorseless blasting of everything in its sights. But if this was a powerful short-term shock tactic, it was also a fatal weakness, since such an indiscriminate berserker scything inevitably cuts the ground from under itself, severing any connection with older traditions and their resources. Seen thus, one of the real achievements of MacGowan and the Pogues was that they took what was by the early 1980s an already fading punk and connected it to older vernacular Irish and British musical forms that were in their own ways aggressively 'low cultural' and trashy, and also intensely rebellious and anti-authoritarian. Trained in the 'high culture' aesthetic histories of the art schools, McLaren or Westwood may have plundered the continental avant-garde movements or the New York experimental music subcultures for inspiration, but what MacGowan and the Pogues did was to wire punk's energies into an indigenous local history of British and Irish lower-class and lumpen rebelliousness. Punk had mixed a curious blend of futuristic contempt for the conservatism of British tradition with a late modernist or postmodernist scepticism about the possibility of all futures (an apocalyptic mentality expressed in the Sex Pistols' anthemic 'No future, no future' in 'God Save the Queen' or the Clash's 'London's Burning'). But it had only an abbreviated historical consciousness that did not stretch

---

14 Wicke, *Rock Music*, 145. The seminal text on punk style is Hebdige's *Subculture*, which construes punk as a working-class subculture of resistance. For a more sceptical account, which posits a degree of symbiotic interplay between punk fashion and a broader commodity culture, see Frank Cartledge, 'Distress to Impress?: Local Punk Fashion and Commodity Exchange', in Sabin, *Punk Rock*, 143–53.

much further back than the emergence of rock itself. Thus, by grafting punk onto folk (or, particularly, low cultural folk), the Pogues connected it to an historical sensibility that had been shaped, not in the bohemian high culture of the art schools, but in the rough and tumble subaltern subcultures of the Irish and British-Irish lumpenproletariat.

The Irish forms to which the Pogues married punk were, strictly speaking, neither traditional nor folk but *céilí* and pub-ballad music.[15] By the time the Pogues adopted it, *céilí* was regarded by most young Irish people as the epitome of a 'hick' backwoods Irish traditionalism. Ironically, perhaps, it was historically a metropolitan-born confection of recent vintage: the London Gaelic League had hosted the first Irish *céilí* social evening, modelled on Scottish *céilidh* houses, in Bloomsbury Hall in London in 1897. *Céilí's* origins, then, were in the Gaelic Revival's drive to combat the anglicization of Irish culture and to promote distinctively Irish art forms, and in that context anything that seemed to be too English or to smack of 'stage Irishness' or indecency was frowned upon. Thus, Percy French's 'Phil the Fluter's Ball', for example, was deemed unacceptable at the first Bloomsbury event because it was supposedly too stage Irish, but the composer's Anglo-Irish background and the song's sexual innuendo and references to collective drunkenness probably also counted against it. The *céilí* phenomenon quickly spread from London to Ireland and its popularity created the need for specialist Irish *céilí* bands, groups of musicians (usually eight or nine) that typically played fiddle, flute, button accordion, bass and snare drum, banjo, and occasionally piano or double bass.[16]

Accredited and incorporated as a version of traditional Irish music in post-independent Ireland by the newly established Irish broadcasting service under Seamus Clandillon, *céilí* reached the zenith of its popularity in the 1940s and 1950s. However, by the end of the latter decade, *céilí* bands were beginning to be eclipsed both by the new electric-guitar based showbands and by the emerging folk revival. In his *Our Musical Heritage*, a series of lectures delivered in the 1960s, Seán Ó Riada (1931–71) decried *céilí* as a form in which 'everyone takes hold of a tune and belts away with it without stopping', the result being, he concluded, 'a rhythmic but meaningless noise with about as much relation to music as the buzzing of a bluebottle in an upturned jamjar'.[17] By the 1980s, then, *céilí* was

---

15 The term 'folk music' is mobile and never innocently descriptive. It usually points to modes of music that are orally transmitted, ideally non-commercial, and connected to older rural or urban working-class communities. But it is also a regulative term, designating certain kinds of music, on the basis of instrumentation or commercialism or some other criteria, as not authentically 'folk.' The term 'rock' is never descriptively neutral either, and rock is consistently defined by separating it off from whatever is deemed to be a more mainstream and more thoroughly commodified 'pop' music. For an excellent overview of the politics of terminology and categorization, see Keir Keightly, 'Reconsidering Rock', in Simon Frith, Will Straw and John Street, eds., *The Cambridge Companion to Pop and Rock* (Cambridge, 2001), 109–42.

16 Fintan Vallely, *The Companion to Irish Traditional Music* (Cork, 1999), 60–64

17 Seán Ó Riada, *Our Musical Heritage* (Mountrath, 1982), 74. Ó Riada's critique of *céilí* is premised on his view that the Irish musical tradition 'is not a group activity', but 'is essentially a solo effort, a matter of the individual player or singer giving free rein, within the limits of the art, to his own musical personality' and he also felt that *céilí* had succumbed to an excess of eclectic instrumentation: 'One might have expected

decidedly *déclassé*, satisfying neither the dons of Irish musical nationalism nor a younger generation increasingly attracted either to a more modern international rock music or to the more authentic forms of traditional music associated with the folk revival. Only in the backwaters of the parish halls of rural Ireland and in the Irish centres of London, Birmingham, Liverpool, Manchester, Coventry and Glasgow — the cities in which the displaced Irish of the 1950s had congregated — did *céilí* music retain any significant presence, usually as an end-piece at community social functions. But the punk sensibility had always prized things generally deemed to be tacky or an affront to sophisticated good taste and high culture. And in the late 1970s and early 1980s, there was no form of Irish music that better fitted this description than *céilí*.

If *céilí* gave to the Pogues much of their basic instrumentation, a pounding collective beat, and a flair for musical speed that prized vigour and verve above polish and sophistication, it was the Irish ballad groups that had emerged during the 'second' folk revival of the 1960s that gave them their song repertoire.[18] A low cultural spin-off of the various American and English folk revivals associated with left-wing singers, songwriters and collectors such as Woody Guthrie, Pete Seeger, Alan Lomax, Bob Dylan, Ewan MacColl and A. L. Lloyd, the Irish ballad scene combined a curious mixture of old street songs, rural and industrial folk songs, nationalist rebel music, and a broadly leftist or populist politics.[19] The most popular of these groups were the Dubliners, whose formative influence on the Pogues, 'especially the dirty songs', MacGowan has always acknowledged.[20] In its early

that, after a certain time, the *céilí* bands would have managed to work out some sort of a compromise between the solo traditional idea and group activity. But instead of developing this kind of compromise, the *céilí* band leaders took the easy and wrong way out, tending more and more to imitate swing or jazz bands, which play an entirely different kind of music and are organized on a different principle. First they added piano and drums, then double-bass, then the final insult: saxophones, guitars and banjos. The most important principles of traditional music — the whole idea of variation, the whole idea of personal utterance — are abandoned' (73–74).

18 Reared in London, MacGowan may well have been drawn to *céilí* and to pub-ballad music because his family roots were in Dublin and in the Irish midlands, and not in the western seaboard counties commonly, if romantically, identified with the more authentic and prestigious or 'high' forms of traditional or folk music. Commenting on the accordion and concertina music played in the family kitchen in County Tipperary, where he spent his early youth, MacGowan notes that the folk and traditional revival of the 1960s and 1970s had reconfirmed the idea that 'real' Irish music belonged only in the West: '[T]he ballad groups had brought back interest in traditional Irish music, and people were rushing around the countryside going, "Everybody go to Clare! Everybody go to Clare!"', Clarke and MacGowan, *A Drink with Shane MacGowan*, 208.

19 The 'first' folk revival, during the 1930s and 1940s, was closely linked to left-wing organizations that emerged during the Great Depression when the American Communist Party shifted its focus from mass to vernacular musics. The 'second' revival, extending over the 1950s and 1960s, also had a strong political impetus, but it became, in the US and the UK at any rate, a more college-based movement, and took more intellectual, 'New Left' or 'New Age' and sometimes quite purist directions. But there were strong links between the two revivals, and figures with connections to both (such as Seeger, MacColl, Lomax and Lloyd) all had Communist or left-wing backgrounds. For a review of this history and the evolution of folk rock, see Britta Sweers, *Electric Folk: The Changing Face of English Traditional Music* (Oxford, 2005), 20–43.

20 See Merrick, *Shane MacGowan*, 8, and Clarke and MacGowan, *A Drink with Shane MacGowan*, 169.

days, the ballad scene was closely linked to the establishment of 'lounge-bars', venues that catered to women as well as men, thus breaking down an older, more exclusively male pub culture; in other words, the ballad scene — centred on mixed gender pubs, sometimes involving electric instruments and tipping its hat to the sixties folk revival in the United States — was in some ways 'modern', despite its 'romantic' or 'old world' image. Politically, the scene cohered as the IRA bombing campaigns in Northern Ireland and in England were reaching their height and when Irish republican or 'rebel music' was, first informally and then formally, excluded from the airwaves by both the British and Irish states. Several of the leading figures in Irish rock music, notably Bob Geldof, Bono and Paul Brady, had also become vocal critics of militant nationalism and in this climate the unreconstructed republican-nationalist repertoires favoured by many ballad groups were seriously out of favour in 'right thinking' or 'responsible' circles. But the rabble-rousing music had tenacious roots in certain constituencies. And, in the context of civil and military conflict in the North and the targeting of the Irish community in Britain by both media and police in their campaigns against 'welfare sponging' and 'terrorism', 'rebel songs' retained a sharply contemporary political edge, rarely heard in the antiquarian or purist refinement of English or Scottish folk songs.

Yet though the ballad scene had a distinct political dimension, it was not political in any narrow sense. In the noisy public houses where ballad sessions were played, the atmosphere was often raucous and audiences regularly became active participants in the sessions, calling out requests, singing along to favourite numbers, or joining in rousing choruses. Sometimes the music might well be ignored altogether as the crowds moved about to buy drink or shift conversations. Thus, the milieu was less disciplined and the interaction between performers and audience much more intimate and interactive than either more high art concert halls or the more serious folk clubs tended to allow. Another notable feature of the ballad session scene was the promiscuity of the repertoire. The groups typically played a wide variety of songs — bawdy and burlesque ballads, songs of emigration and political protest, outlaw elegies and sea shanties, drinking and working come-all-yehs, romantic love and rebel songs — that spoke both to rural and urban experiences and to the immediate moment as well as the longer historical past. Thus, overtly 'rebel' songs were not necessarily segregated from songs about domestic matters such as courting and adultery or songs about the hardships of work and the loneliness of emigration or the excitements of horse-racing and the tavern.

For the Pogues to yoke together in this context the avant-garde future-oriented metropolitan aesthetics of punk, the retro-aesthetics of céilí and the broadly political edginess of the pub-ballad scene was an inspired act not only of musical synthesis but of semantic sabotage as well. To merge these three kinds of music was to produce not only an unexpected aesthetic combination of different musical styles and techniques, but also seriously to mess with the regulative metanarratives that ascribed meaning to both rock and folk music in Ireland. Ever since the 1960s, when the second Irish folk revival got under way and Irish rock music also began to take off, most commentators represented these developments as either entirely discrete or even antithetical — a musical contest between two distinct Irelands, one traditional and inward-looking, the other modern and cosmopolitan, pulling in radically different directions. As established by their respective metanarratives, Irish folk music was commonly understood (and understood itself) in terms of conserving and building up a long indigenous cultural 'heritage', while Irish rock music was understood (and understood itself) in terms of the quintessentially new and 'modern' — the music that expressed the sentiments of an increasingly urban and industrial society trying to cast off an oppressively ruralist cultural nationalism so as to discover its own more internationalist idiom.

Still, in the regulative logic of these metanarratives, if folk music tended to be identified with the countryside and continuity with the past, and rock music with the city and change and progress into the future, each mode insisted on its own counter-cultural radicalism. Thus, if rock music's self-identity was tied to the notion that it expressed a modernizing youthful rebellion against an old puritanical Catholic Ireland, Irish folk music (like folk more generally) conceived of itself as an antidote to the rank commercialism of rock music. Rock and pop historians, therefore, recurrently narrate the development of Irish rock and pop music in 'heroic' terms as a radical awakening from the dogmatic slumber of de Valera's Ireland to the sexual and other excitements of a more metropolitan world, but commentators on folk music elaborate an equally 'heroic' metanarrative in which it figures as an antidote to Anglo-American cultural imperialism and commercial blandness. Consequently, rock and folk music were always more than simply different musical styles or tastes; they were positioned differently within the national cultural field, defined by different aesthetic value-systems, and freighted with discrepant social meanings. Rock music depended on a 'modernist' and future-oriented aesthetic value-system that associated musical worth and authenticity with avant-garde experiment and progress, with radical stylistic change and constant innovation, and with an extroverted cosmopolitanism. The production and reception of the various forms of folk and traditional music tended, on the other hand, to be mediated through a more 'romantic' idiom that typically valued gradual stylistic innovation within received forms rather than an aesthetic of radical rupture, and that stressed rootedness in deep vernacular traditions rather than a capacity to keep pace with metropolitan novelty or fashion.

However valid or deceptive these self-legitimizing metanarratives might have been in the 1960s, the reality was that by the 1980s both rock and folk music in Ireland were increasingly attached to modes of production, distribution and consumption that were equally (if not identically) regulated by corporate organizations. Folk music might believe itself to be working at a greater distance than rock from commodity culture and the big corporations, but it was still closely linked to tourist and other service and heritage industries that were themselves increasingly corporatized. Moreover, to view these two types of music in fundamentally antagonistic terms was also to miss the various ways they had sometimes converged to energize each other — most obviously perhaps in the variants of 'Celtic rock' essayed by Thin Lizzy, Horslips, Clannad, Stockton's Wing or

Moving Hearts in the late 1970s and early 1980s or, when the Pogues were in their prime a few years later, in the work of Van Morrison, Paul Brady or Sinéad O'Connor, all of whom experimented in both traditional and rock formats.

Hence, when the Pogues combined punk with céilí and ballad music in the early 1980s, crossover forms were not without precedent. However, the manner in which they transacted the crossover managed to be more outrageously offensive to the regnant ideologies of both rock and folk than anything attempted earlier. The earliest hybrid developed by Horslips had used instrumentation that came from both musics — uilleann pipes, bodhráns and acoustic fiddle arranged with electric guitars, drums, bass and keyboards — but the general aesthetic aimed for was essentially a Celtic version of progressive rock, with the latter's high art or rock-symphonic ambitions. Similarly, when Morrison's early 1980s experiments with Irish traditional materials culminated with his 1988 *Irish Heartbeat* album, that merger of his blues-rock and the Big House traditional music of the Chieftains was also clearly aimed at the more refined or 'arty' end of the market. The same attempt to cross folk and rock in mutually refining ways was even more pronounced in the more unabashedly commercial crossovers, as when Clannad and later Enya mixed etherealized songs or refrains in Irish with electric synthesizer and acoustics to produce self-consciously New Age or 'world music' effects. In other words, in all of these experiments, the crossover was governed essentially by a logic of harmonization — by attempts, that is, to find arrangements that would best allow rock and folk musics mutually to complement, refine and 'beautify' each other.

The difference with the Pogues was that in their work the sounds and styles, the instrumentation and tempos of Irish traditional and rock music did not meld or fuse into each other in some harmonic fashion so much as collide with and disfigure each other. By merging an extremely irreverent punk-derived delivery style with low-tech instruments such as the accordion, tin whistle, harmonica, mandolin or banjo (as opposed to the acoustic fiddles and pipes of Horslips or the even more 'aristocratic' harps and uilleann pipes of the Chieftains), the Pogues produced a folk- rather than a hard rock-type acoustic, but one that was patently more plebian or 'grungy' and unrefined than anything essayed elsewhere. Thus, even though the Pogues drew on folk, they did not follow Clannad or the Morrison/Chieftains and O'Connor/Chieftains collaborations and use it to lend 'colour' or a fey exoticism or an archaicizing mythological or mystic-ethereal grandeur or a 'softer' or more decorative tonality to rock. Instead, working very much with the 'rougher' ends of both the rock and folk worlds, they combined punk rock and céilí-cum-ballad music with such reciprocally distressing panache that elective affinities between the two modes never hitherto fathomed became apparent and the one type of music was transmogrified almost as much as the other. Thus, in achieving a late modern *Verfremdungseffekt*, governed by a logic of dissonance rather than of harmonization, the Pogues stripped both rock and folk traditions of much of their 'classier' refinements and, in so doing, mined a kind of raw anarchic baseline energy common to both.

The Pogues' crossover offended because it was transacted at the rougher rather than the refined end of both rock and folk aesthetics; but it cannot be understood by regarding it as a form of crudity. Given the regulative norms of Irish musical culture, crossovers between the two modes might always be deemed political (the 1988 collaboration between the northern Protestant Morrison and the southern 'Gaelic' Chieftains provoked much comment in this regard), yet few of the other hybrid forms had much explicit political content. The pioneering work of Horslips was undoubtedly aesthetically radical, but that formal experimentation was not matched by any corresponding political radicalism. Most of the later hybrids could even be argued to have depoliticized both rock and Irish folk music, since they deliberately avoided contemporary social or political comment of almost any kind. The Pogues, in contrast, drew on those elements of the punk and folk ballad traditions that had much grittier political components. Sometimes they drew directly on the protest wings of those traditions, as when they covered songs by socially committed folk figures such as Ewan MacColl or Eric Bogle, but they also recorded new compositions such as 'The Old Main Drag' and 'Thousands are Sailing' that expressed contemporary social concerns in traditional forms. Still, it was their charging of the social commentary element of the folk ballad with the more rawly aggressive delivery style of punk that constituted their most decisive political innovation. By combining the two, they achieved an altogether more militantly 'in your face' and irreverent type of folk-rock than had previously been produced.

The band's look or image aggravated the jarring effect of this new musical mix. In the 1980s, the Irish political, intellectual and cultural élites were struggling, in the very frustrating circumstances of severe economic depression in the South and war in the North, to present Ireland as a progressive, outward-looking, secular European or Euro-American country. As the newest and most future-oriented of Irish musical forms, rock music carried a special burden in this context to be modern, since part of its whole raison d'être was to manumit the country from its oppressive history. Yet at a time when all the superstars in the Irish rock firmament cultivated looks indebted to some or other version of modern Americana, the Pogues, despite their impressively metropolitan punk-rock credentials, sported not only an 'old time' céilí band look, but also invoked a whole array of caricatures of Irishness that modern Ireland would gladly have relegated to the museum basements of national character. In the Pogues' on- and off-stage behaviour it was as if a whole gallery of hoary old Irish types — the drunken navvy Paddy, the brawling slum Paddy, the melancholic emigrant Paddy, the militant republican Paddy — acquired a frenetic new life.

Rock-star fashion, as exemplified by Van Morrison and U2 especially, was supposed to be the very epitome of the metropolitan and the modern. But even when not disporting themselves like escapees from Punch, the Pogues deliberately cultivated a 1950s look, something that implicitly identified them with a moment before the 1960s (the decade synonymous with modernity, sexual liberation and rock music) and thus with the de Valera's Ireland — the very antithesis or negation of the modern. Eschewing the more spectacularly outrageous urban-decadent styles of the punks or the 'mid-Atlantic' T-shirts, jeans and leather standard to classical rock fashion but steering clear also of the more homespun natural look favoured by 'romantic' subcultures such as folkies, hippies or even reggae fans, the Pogues adopted the two-piece suits, white open-necked shirts, and tidy haircuts that MacGowan has described as a distinctly cross-generational 'Irish look':

> The suits, black suits with white shirts which we wore, were Brendan Behan uniform and that's why we chose them, not to look smart, but to look like as if we could have come from any decade ... We could have looked like people from the fifties, sixties, or seventies ... we just looked like classic Paddys.[21]

In some circumstances, a mid-century retro-style like this might be deemed nostalgic and conservative. But in Ireland at least, the mid-century look could never mean the same thing that it did for conservatives in the United States for example. There, the fifties might well be idealized as some prelapsarian moment of conservative rectitude and tranquillity before the fall into decadence and mayhem of the sixties, but in Ireland the fifties summoned up something very different — a dead-end decade of national economic crisis and social failure that had seen the poorer classes of Irish society forced to emigrate in vast numbers. In the context of the 1980s, with emigration levels again reaching such crisis proportions that the 1950s were commonly evoked as precedent and parallel, the 'classic Paddy' look essentially stopped time in its tracks — suspending any sense of linear progress, it signified neither the consolations of some better past nor any reassurance that the modern was really leaving that troubled past behind.

The Pogues, then, represented a form of musical and cultural experimentation that amounted to more than a banal 'clash of cultures' or some merely formalist parody or hyridization of musical styles. By yoking an aggressively modernist and avant-garde British punk to the retro or traditional aesthetics of Irish céilí and pub-ballad forms, the band disaggregated the received metanarratives that conditioned the production and reception of popular music in Ireland. As a band schooled in the English punk scene, they brought to Irish music a noisily brutalist aesthetics of excess that suggested neither 'continuity' nor 'revival' (key terms in any 'romantic' lexicon), but radical rupture and a pugnacious disrespect for tradition. To compound matters, several of the band's members either had no ethnic Irish connections or only tenuous ones, and thus as

---

21 Clarke and MacGowan, *A Drink with Shane MacGowan*, 168. In the same text, MacGowan elaborates further on the appeal of the band's look for the fans: 'They wanted that Paddy chic. That is an Irish look. I mean, recently it's gone out of date ... it's disappeared to a large extent. But then you could still spot an Irishman a hundred yards away. The haircut, quite apart from the racial features; the haircut, and the two-piece suit and the high open-necked shirt. Not dirty or anything, but like sort of casually worn. No t-shirts, no jeans, no fucking ties. That was our dress code, know what I mean? Time had frozen still since 1957. The year of my birth. Like the Beatles had never happened.' (213).

ostentatiously 'plastic Paddys' (a derogatory term used to dismiss second-generation Irish people in England as imitation-Irish or 'not the real thing'), they also violated the codes of authenticity or organicism or continuity conventional to any romantic value-system. But while bringing with them punk's vanguardist bravado and spectacular impurity, the Pogues also subverted the normative temporalities of the avant-gardes, which are supposed to annihilate and not resurrect the past. With their classic Paddy image, low-tech céilí instrumentation and pub-ballad repertoires, they reclaimed identification with previous generations and with a long historical past — thereby expressing a commitment to communal populism rather than to the anti-populist, subcultural minoritarianism of classical avant-garde rock. The result was a music and a style that fused folk and rock in strange combinations but refused to genuflect to the regulative norms of either, and to this extent the Pogues expressed, more extravagantly than anyone else, a moment in Irish musical history when the capacity of the older metanarratives of cultural nationalism or modernization theory, of romanticism or modernism, of tradition or modernity, all began to exhaust their capacities to organize the musical field.

A sceptic might reasonably object that the breakdown of the older metanarratives was disabling, as it was not at all clear what (if anything) might ever prove viable in their place. Viewed thus, the Pogues' comedic scrambling of musical and semiotic codes might be regarded as symptomatic of a typical postmodern impasse, one in which they would be interpreted as a retro/avant-garde band destined to live in a world of copies and repetitions, doomed to be able to generate 'novelty' only by ever more antic recyclings of the now-exhausted styles of the past in a world without belief in a substantively transformed future. Yet even if they could not escape this impasse, the Pogues still exploited it with an exuberant and unapologetic bravado, helping to create an Irish (and British) musical scene less dogmatically in thrall to the old tradition/modernity opposition than before.

3

The Pogues' repertoire, like that of the ballad groups, was heterogeneous. It included drinking songs, songs of rakes and delinquents, songs of communal festivity, songs of pre-industrial and industrial male labour, outlaw and rapparee songs, rebel songs, anti-recruiting songs, emigrant songs, industrial folk songs and songs of post-industrial urban despair, love songs, and dinnseanchas or place-praise songs. Many of the band's own compositions were modelled on traditional forms, though the tempos were usually speeded up and the idioms were more raucous. 'Bottle of Smoke', for example, is a manic racing song in the style of 'The Galway Races' but with more vulgar or 'loutish' language. Similarly, 'The Old Main Drag' recalls any number of old-style ballads about a young person who goes to the city in search of fortune only to meet with hardship and death, but the references to rent boys, drug addiction and police brutality give it a raw contemporary edge.

Taken collectively, the ambience evoked by the albums is distinctly seedy and plebian: the songs continually return to a world of lower-class bars and race tracks, of red-light districts and drunk tanks, of emigrant quarters and low-market foreign holidays. The landscapes described range historically from the pre-modern taverns of the rake songs to the railways or famine ships of nineteenth-century emigrants up to the late twentieth-century New York of *If I Should Fall from Grace with God* or the Thai bars and beaches of *Hell's Ditch*. But however varied the settings, they are invariably peopled by the same subaltern and usually delinquent types (navvies, soldiers, emigrants, drug addicts, rent boys, exiled republicans, priests with clap, alcoholics and psychotics) and the general atmospheric effect veers between carnivalesque exuberance and physical and emotional burn-out. The manic-depressive swings between exuberance and exhaustion that shape the tempos of many of the songs individually are accentuated by the arrangements of numbers on the various albums, where the slower melancholy tunes are nearly always interleaved between others that are particularly boisterous. Thus, for instance, the tired downbeat mood of 'The Old Main Drag' gives way to the antic instrumentals of 'Wild Cats of Kilkenny' on *Rum, Sodomy & the Lash* and the plaintive emigrant lament 'Thousands are Sailing' is followed by the joyously rambunctious 'South Australia' on *If I Should Fall from Grace with God*. The band's major albums across the 1980s might even be said to follow a rather similar tonal trajectory. *Red Roses for Me* is musically the crudest and narrowest of their collections, ranging little beyond drinking songs, but it is also the most consistently and collectively rumbustious of their works. *Rum, Sodomy & the Lash* and *If I Should Fall from Grace with God* are both much more experimental and wider-ranging in ambition, but the overall tonal 'mood' in each swings between exuberantly Stakhanovite feats of excess consumption and a sense of burn-out and enervation. *Hell's Ditch*, with its low-oriental 'Third World' pleasure periphery Thai 'feel', also alternates hallucinatory 'bad trip' numbers (such as the title song or 'Lorca's Novena') with some very trippy 'blissed-out' songs ('Sunnyside of the Street', '5 Green Queens & Jean' and 'Summer in Siam'). But on this late album the foot-stomping dance beat of the earlier works has virtually disappeared, and this creates a sense that the business of excess has become less communal and has moved more into the subjective domain of the interior consciousness.

This capacity to deliver sudden, disorientating or estranging lurches in tone is one of the more innovative aspects of the Pogues' music and it can be considered key to what might be called the 'politics' of their work. Their music summons up a rowdy world of subaltern excess and mayhem, but this version of carnival is never allowed to become cosily celebratory because it is always shot through with sentiments of anger and aggression, sometimes strident, sometimes more muted. The result is a music that leans heavily on the established aesthetics of folk music and the ballad scene, but which, in combining the tempo of *céilí* with the belligerence of punk, creates an entirely new structure of feeling all of its own.

The estrangement effect achieved by this dissonant conjunction of folk and punk aesthetics is very dramatically illustrated by 'Streets of Sorrow/Birmingham Six', the Pogues' most overtly political song. Several of their other political songs, such as the redactions of MacColl's 'Dirty Old Town' or Bogle's 'Waltzing Matilda', were old-style industrial folk or protest songs delivered in a relatively conventional left-folkie manner, and others, such as Philip Chevron's 'Thousands are Sailing', used the inherited compositional structures of the Irish emigration song but updated the imagery. 'Streets of Sorrow/Birmingham Six' produces a more startling effect than any of these numbers, because what starts out as a fairly standard folk-protest number abruptly transmogrifies into something altogether more abrasively pugnacious and confrontational. Penned and sung by Terry Woods, who had had a distinguished career on the traditional folk circuit before coming to the Pogues, 'Streets of Sorrow', the first section of the recording, is delivered in a slow, down-tempo manner and the vocals express the sentiments of a morose, emotionally drained, war-weary man no longer able to cope with violence, and thus bidding a despondent goodbye:

O farewell you streets of sorrow
O farewell you streets of pain
I'll not return to feel more sorrow
Nor to see more young men slain.

There is at this point no explicit reference to Irish politics. Then, after only two brief verses, this folk-dirge is brutally stopped short when MacGowan's stridently incendiary voice cuts across it in tones of furious indignation and denunciation, explicitly referring to Ireland:

There were six men in Birmingham
In Guildford there's four
They were picked up and tortured
And framed by the law
And the filth got promotion
But they're still doing time
For being Irish in the wrong place
And at the wrong time

In Ireland they'll put you away in the Maze
In England they'll keep you for several long days
God help you if ever you're caught on these shores
And the coppers need someone
And they walk through that door
(chorus)

You'll be counting years
First five, then ten
Growing old in a lonely cell
Round the yard and back again

A curse on the judges, the coppers and screws
Who tortured the innocent, wrongly accused,
For the price of promotion
And justice to sell
May the judged be their judges when they rot down in Hell

(chorus)

May the whores of the empire lie awake in their beds
And sweat as they count out the sins on their heads
While over in Ireland eight more men lie dead
Kicked down and shot in the back of the head.

The recording may well have been banned due to the content of its lyrics, which refer not just to the cases of the wrongfully imprisoned Birmingham Six and Guildford Four but also to the killing of an eight-man IRA active-service unit in an SAS ambush in Loughgall, County Armagh, on 8 May 1987. But it is the running together of the two sections — essentially two songs — that tests the limits of political acceptability.

Thus, Woods's 'Streets of Sorrow' begins as a mordant complaint about terrible conditions, but it does so in a manner so generalized in its reference and so passive in its sentiments as to be almost completely uncontroversial. However, MacGowan's opening of the 'Birmingham Six' section vaporizes the complaint mode and replaces it with a much more punk-style accusatory diatribe against the British establishment's miscarriages of justice. The limits of political consensus are tested even more severely when what begins as accusation about wrongfully imprisoned innocents transmutes into a protest about the killing of armed IRA men. The song, in other words, pushes things further and further so that, while the initial complaint is so abstract as to be acceptable to almost any kind of liberal humanism, and the references to the wrongfully imprisoned express a sense of justice flouted that might still appeal on the same basis, by the end the audience is expected to indict the state assassination of even armed (and hence 'non-innocent') militants as well. In short, as the song progresses, it repeatedly ups the ante, first inviting an identification with 'the young men slain' in a non-specific sense, then railing against the British establishment's responsibility for imprisoning innocent men until it finally protests at the state killing of eight armed militants at Loughgall.

But if the 'Brechtian' effect achieved by scorching the passive complaint mode of 'Streets of Sorrow' with the aggressive punk-delivery style of 'Birmingham Six' is shocking enough, the intransigent vulgarity of the language ratchets things up even more. Thus, a song that starts out in a very non-militant old-style romantic folk register (with its banally poeticized idiom of 'streets of sorrow, streets of shame' and its archaic-sounding 'farewells') very quickly slides into a foul-mouthed demotically republican argot that spits out a poisonous hatred at 'the whores of the empire' and at the 'filth' at the top of the legal system and the 'coppers and screws' who are its executives. As the accents of the opening folk-dirge cede to those of lower-class Irish republicanism, the whole narrative stance and mode of address shifts too. In the standard folk-protest song, the singer appeals to the audience's humanitarian empathy for the oppressed and downtrodden whose story is narrated. Here, things are different. There is no plaintive narrative that tries to win over the audience to identify with the wrongfully imprisoned men. Instead, the tone is stridently accusatory and abrasively incensed from the outset, and the narrative stance is one that makes no attempt to win the sympathy of the listening audience, but simply assumes that it will already share its incendiary outrage. In 'Birmingham Six', in other words, the sense of protest is not conveyed in the humanitarian accents of some 'reasonable' observer; instead, it is delivered in the voice of a demotic republicanism that dismisses the entire British state as rotten to its core. To do so, was to deliver the song in the accent of a subaltern community every bit as 'foreign' and frightening to Irish as to British political and cultural establishments.

Although 'Birmigham Six' adopted a particularly strident republican stance, the Pogues tended to eschew political commentary in such an overt and aggressive mode. In their repertoire as a whole, there are scarcely any of the laments for nationalist martyrs or working-class heroes that are common in the repertoire of conventional republican or left-wing ballad groups. References to republicans (Irish, Spanish, and other) recur, but the majority of their songs concentrate not on the politics of specific situations but on a more antic world of subaltern carnival and mayhem. To the unsympathetic listener, these songs might seem entirely apolitical, even crudely boorish and 'laddish'. But in fact it is arguable that the cult of uninhibited indulgence celebrated in such songs simply translates the same plebian republicanism that is expressed in tones of outrage in 'Birmingham Six' into a more festive or utopian mode. The Pogues' celebratory songs, that is to say, express a commitment to a bibulous national popular *communitas* that is fundamentally both republican and anarchic in its value-system.

It is, curiously enough, in their adaptations of traditional rake songs that the Pogues come nearest to the 1980s 'lad culture' and rock decadence of their own epoch.[22] Within

---

22 For some suggestive remarks on 'New Lad' culture of the 1980s, see Jeremy Gilbert and Ewan Pearson, *Discographies: Dance Music, Culture and the Politics of Sound* (London, 1999), 174–79. My argument here acknowledges that the carnivalesque in the Pogues is distinctly masculinist, as seems to be the case with carnival historically, and that it also intersects with British New Lad culture of its own time. But I would also suggest that in the Pogues this laddishness is given an anti-capitalist inflection that is largely at odds with New Lad culture generally. One would also have to take account of MacGowan's several references in his work to gay men, whether in 'The Old Main Drag' or the references to Lorca and Genet.

the Irish musical tradition, these songs often deal with Anglo-Irish lower-gentry or British military subcultures that celebrated philandering, horse-racing, gambling, feckless spending, and a general disdain for orderliness, restraint and domesticity. Only a small number of songs on the Pogues' albums actually belong to this tradition. The best-known, both on *Rum, Sodomy & the Lash*, the title of which is taken from Winston Churchill's evocative summary of subaltern life in the British navy, include 'A Gentleman Soldier', which tells, with a politically incorrect gusto, the tale of a militiaman who impregnates a young woman and then blithely abandons her, and, in a different register, the more melancholic 'I'm a Man You Don't Meet Everyday'. 'The Gentleman Soldier' displays all of the laddish boorishness typical of the rake songs at their worst, but MacGowan's draglike falsetto vocals and manic over-the-top delivery, as he switches between the contemptuously haughty voice of male seducer and the wretchedly pleading female victim, results in a comical send-up of the genre. Similarly, the only overtly aristocratic song in their repertoire, 'I'm a Man You Don't Meet Every Day', is sung by Cáit O'Riordan, her feminine vocals conveying but also complicating the cocky sense of male swagger that gives the song its distinctive mood. This is not a rowdily boisterous tavern ballad of 'The Rakes of Mallow' kind that celebrates the antics of a class that prides itself on being above menial labour or that vaunts male fecklessness, but it does convey a rather similar sense of social superiority ('I have acres of land, I have men I command / I have always a shilling to spare'). Even so, the narrator's sense of his own status is expressed, not by his pride in his possessions, to which he affects a careless indifference, but by his capacity for a liberal open-handedness contemptuous of cost-counting ('So be easy and free when you're drinking with me / I'm a man you don't meet every day'). The rake or 'wild rover' songs typically extol either an aristocratic transcendence of the servile routines of lower-class restraint or the dissolute fecklessness of (only partially repentant) prodigal sons who have squandered themselves and their fortunes. They express an aristocratic disdain for the drudgeries of labour. Such songs are fundamentally pre-capitalist or even anti-capitalist in their core value-systems and extol neither the production nor the accumulation of wealth or assets, but an economy of extravagant and sometimes ruinous display and (self-)expenditure in a masculine world that values good company and conviviality rather than any kind of enterprise or work ethic.

Notwithstanding these rake songs in the Pogues' repertoire, a festivity of a lower-class and communal type is more frequently heard on their albums. Played to a frenetic *céilí* beat, these songs are not delivered in the voice of the rakish individual who has detached himself from the quotidian norms of toil and routine. They express, rather, a collective overturning of that world, as society *en masse* abandons its daily disciplines and gives itself over to a promiscuous social mingling in a common pursuit of pleasure. Their basis is an entirely primitive and carnal sense of Cockaigne, in which all the bodily delights — eating, drinking, gambling, fighting, fucking, singing, music-making — are indulged with abandon. Several recordings, including 'Streams of Whiskey', 'Bottle of Smoke', 'The Irish Rover' and 'Fiesta' belong to this category, but their version of 'The

Galway Races' conveys the general atmosphere:

> As I went down to Galway town
> To seek for recreation on the 17th of August
> Me mind being elevated
> There were passengers assembled
> With their tickets at the station
> And me eyes begin to dazzle
> And they off to see the races
> *With me wack fol do fol*
> *The diddle idle day*
>
> There were passengers from Limerick
> And passengers from Nenagh
> The boys from Connemara
> And the Clare unmarried maiden
> There were people from Cork city
> Who were loyal, true and faithful
> Who brought home the Fenian prisoners
> From dying in foreign nations
>
> And it's there you'll see the pipers
> And the fiddlers competing
> And the sporting wheel of fortune
> And the four and twenty quarters
> And there's others without scruple
> Pelting wattles at poor Maggie
> And he gazing at his daughter ...
> There was half a million people there
> Of all denominations
> The Catholic, the Protestant, the Jew,
> The Presbyterian
> There was yet no animosity
> No matter what persuasion
> But failte hospitality
> Inducing fresh acquaintance
> *With me wack fol do fol*
> *The diddle idle day.*

Unlike the tavern-located rake or wild rover songs, these communal holiday songs usually have out-of-doors settings and tend to be more proto-industrial and more national-popular in their imaginings. Here, for example the excitement of the railway contributes to the overall festive thrill, and though the recitation of place-names recalls the *dinnseanchas* tradition, there is no loving recreation of small local intimacies. Instead, the song summons up a more expansive national geography where the fraternity of distant counties and the mingling of all classes and 'all denominations' celebrate not the intimate geography of the familiar homely site or the reassurance of the well-known neighbour, but the dizzier mix of 'fresh acquaintance'. The nation is imagined as a kind of extended fairground; it is conceived not (to recall Benedict Anderson's terms) as a singular entity moving soberly up or down history, but as a demotic collective thrilling in the immediate here-and-now to the excitements of its own heterogeneity and plenitude. Discourses of the nation are often anxious about difference, fearing it as a threat to political coherence, but in 'The Galway Races' the mingling of different regional and religious identities offers itself as an intoxicating source of excitement and pleasure.[23] What appears, then, from a distance only as a completely apolitical holiday song actually conveys a radical democratic plebian republicanism (as the allusions to the Fenians and to the mingling not only of rival Christian denominations but also of Jews indicates) that is the more, and not the less, politically charged because of its bibulous bonhomie.

The carnival and Cockaigne these songs celebrate are always counterposed against the harsher realities of the industrial and post-industrial worlds of Great Britain and the United States. Within this Anglo-American world the Irish have historically served as an 'unskilled' migrant lumpenproletariat and, as cultural historians have extensively documented, went on there to acquire a reputation both for a capacity for hard manual labour as well as considerable notoriety for their association with drunkenness, squalor, filth, laziness, violence and excess of all sorts. This history features very strongly in the Pogues' imaginary. 'Navigator', their recording of a Phil Gaston song, celebrates both the navvies' extravagant feats of labour ('The canals and the bridges, the embankments and cuts / They blasted and dug with their sweat and their guts') and their no less outsize excesses ('They never drank water but whiskey by pints / And the shanty towns rang with their songs and their fights'). It issues a protest against lower-class exploitation ('They died in their hundreds no sign to mark where, / Save the brass in the pockets of the entrepreneur'), but at the same time it also underlines that the navvies' achievements have actually outlasted those of their betters ('The supply of an Empire where the sun never set / That's now deep in darkness but the railway's there yet'). MacGowan's own songs display a similar kind of worldview, one as alert to the loneliness of exile as to the heady excitements of the emigrant's escape from home and the opportunities of the bright city, sometimes underlining the destruction and self-damage that follows from emigrant failure ('Lullaby of London', 'Fairytale of New York', 'The Old Main Drag'), but

23 The sense of demotic celebration in the ballad version becomes very apparent when contrasted, for example, with W. B. Yeat's poem 'At Galway Races', published in *The Green Helmet and other Poems* (1910). For Yeats, the race meet becomes a pretext to mourn the loss of aristocratic value, an occasion for lamenting the fall of horsemen. The races also feature, in a rather different manner, in the work of Jack B. Yeats.

as commonly expressing a kind of high-spirited, lumpenproletarian joyous disdain for good order.

In contrast to most songwriters who dealt with the travails of industrial or post-industrial working-class life in 1980s, the Pogues, and particularly MacGowan, scarcely ever pleaded for sympathy or presented the people they depicted primarily as victims. Several of the most popular and commercially successful songs of this type of the period, such as Bruce Springsteen's 'The River', Peter Gabriel and Kate Bush's duet 'Don't Give Up', or Christy Moore's 'Ordinary Man', are essentially melancholy 'rustbelt laments': the male worker is a misfortunate but decent and deserving type with whom the listener is asked to identify. However, the Pogues' presentation is typically much more complex and stresses not the helplessness and despair of the lower classes but their latent anarchy and combativeness. A song such as 'The Sick Bed of Cuchulainn' provides a useful example:

McCormack and Richard Tauber are singing by the bed
There's glass of punch below your feet and an angel at your head
There's devils on each side of you with bottles in their hands
You need one more drop of poison and you'll dream of foreign lands
When you pissed yourself in Frankfurt and got syph down in Cologne
And you heard the rattling death trains as you lay there all alone
Frank Ryan bought you whiskey in a brothel in Madrid
And you decked some fucking blackshirt who was cursing all the Yids
At the sick bed of Cuchulainn we'll kneel and say a prayer
And the ghosts are rattling at the door and the devils in the chair
And in the Euston Tavern you screamed it was your shout
But they wouldn't give you service so you kicked the windows out
They took you out into the street and kicked you in the brains
So you walked back in through a bolted door and did it all again
At the sick bed of Cuchulainn we'll kneel and say a prayer
And the ghosts are rattling at the door and the devil's in the chair
You remember that foul evening when you heard the banshees howl
There was lousy drunken bastards singing Billy is in the bowl
They took you up to midnight mass and left you in the lurch
So you dropped a button in the plate and spewed up in the church
Now you'll sing a song of liberty for blacks and paks and jocks
And they'll take you from this place and stick you in a box
They'll take you to Cloughprior and shove you in the ground
But you'll stick your head back up and shout we'll have another round
At the graveside of Cuchulainn we'll kneel around and pray
And God is in heaven, and Billy's down the bay.

There is a comic-grotesque mock-epic quality here to the protagonist's masochistically cyclical compulsion to drunkenness and violence. But there is also something magnificently ebullient in the crazed energy of the lyrics and in the gusto of MacGowan's delivery. The narrative is ostensibly funereal, but, as is usual in a wake song, what is really celebrated is an inexhaustible appetite for life, manifest in the corpse's return from the dead so as not to miss out on the carousing and conviviality of his own burial. The drunken and belligerent Paddy — an old republican socialist bruiser and comrade to Frank Ryan, who had fought against the Fascists in Spain — appears neither in conventionally heroic nor conventionally wretched terms, but as a lunatic figure for some sort of ineducable spirit of defiance that revels in taking on all comers. Things reach a nadir of abjection when MacGowan's voice slows to relate how the old drunk spews up in the church, but immediately the tempo of the song picks itself up again and dashes off in a breakneck gallop to the end when the old combatant belts out his defiant song of liberty for the other wretched races of the earth ('the blacks and paks and jocks'). In this, as in several other of MacGowan's compositions, a 'politically incorrect' hooligan mayhem is rendered in a spirit of abrasive exuberance, a mood-tone quite different to that of the typical folk song or leftist ballad, where the emphasis is usually on the 'deserving poor' rather than on the feckless but also rather dangerous *lazzaroni* types that populate the Pogues' imaginary.

Whereas songs like 'The Galway Races' or 'Streams of Whiskey' or 'Fiesta' or 'The Irish Rover' offer a version of carnival in its most life-affirming, festive and comic sense, 'The Sick Bed of Cuchulainn', and similar songs, such as 'Sally MacLennane' or 'Billy's Bones', present a version that is more riotous and hooligan in character. The former mode is the more benign and affirmative, but the latter needs to be situated in the broader social context of the 1980s to be fully appreciated. The discourses of the drunken and fighting Irish that these songs mine have deep historical roots, and for the Pogues to be rehearsing them in the late twentieth century might seem a belated plundering of a stale hoard rather than an intelligent engagement with the realities of their own moment. However, a conjuncture of forces in the 1980s had served to reactivate these discourses. For one thing, the economic depression (and the war in the North) had triggered a new wave of emigration that sent hundreds of thousands of young people to Britain or the United States, the vast majority working in broadly the same unskilled vocations in the construction industry or service sectors (baby-minding, gardening, cleaning, catering and hotel work) that previous waves of migrants had occupied. For most, this would have involved an abrupt shift from subsisting on the dole in an austerely conservative social and sexual world at home to a sudden acquisition of new 'affluence' in more permissive and less regulated urban worlds abroad: hence a tendency to 'live it up' with often hectic feats of partying and binge-drinking that would, for many onlookers, call to mind the feckless habits that had made the Irish notorious in previous centuries. In the same decade, the Reaganite and Thatcherite right were ratcheting up campaigns against 'spongers' as part of a strategy to downsize the welfare state, and deploying the discourses of 'terrorism' to strengthen the apparatuses of state repression. At a time when many young 'underclass' Irish had indeed moved to Britain to take advantage of its better welfare system, when the republican 'dirty protests' and hunger strikes were still topical, and when the IRA campaign was still generating headlines around the world, older associations of Irishness with sponging and squalor and with violence and mayhem acquired a new life, most luridly in tabloid media such as the *Sun*.

In this context, the types of music and song that the Pogues performed, as well as the band's own self-dramatization, obviously tapped not only into potent reservoirs of historical memory but also into quite immediate cultural concerns. In a whole series of songs, the Pogues actually celebrated those very qualities of Irish drunken rowdiness and lumpen anarchy that many were anxious to disown as the stigmata of racism. Clearly, the embrace of these versions of Irishness always risked sliding into a kind of 'frat-boy' delinquency. But by defiantly converting the supposed 'vices' of the Irish into 'virtues', the Pogues could also be seen to be inverting the official culture's values of good order and discipline and to be elaborating versions of festively anarchic Irishness that were not without a political charge. In nineteenth-century Britain, when tirades against Irish anarchy, fecklessness and indiscipline were at their most virulent, Friedrich Engels had taken a rather unorthodox view by arguing that the greatest contribution that the Irish brought to the class struggle was their 'passionate, mercurial Irish temperament', adding that 'the mixing of the more facile, excitable, fiery Irish temperament with the stable, reasoning, perverse English must, in the long run, be productive only for the good of both'.[24] Engels's language of 'race' and 'nature' belongs to the essentialist racial vocabularies of the time, but, even so, a structurally parallel inversion of received value-schemas might be seen to operate in the Pogues. Unlike classic punk bands, most obviously the Sex Pistols and the Clash, the Pogues did not as a rule vent their rage in declamatory mode against the state establishment or scream about having no future or conjure up apocalyptic images of race riots and cities burning. Unlike the Irish ballad-bands, they did not sing of heroic wars of independence or gallant working-class struggles. However, drawing creatively on both of these musical aesthetics, they tilted the emphasis instead towards an aesthetic of a rowdy subaltern collective exuberance that was simultaneously anti-authoritarian and festive, but also infused with a kind of rough-house republican pugnacity. That shift of emphasis away from either folk protest and complaint or punk rage against the establishment towards a mode of carnivalesque festivity and riot might seem to be a defusing of direct social engagement, but it might better be interpreted as an ambitiously innovative and renovative attempt to buck or enliven some of the prevailing dissident politico-aesthetic agendas that dominated the musical world of the 1980s.

Since their identity was always connected to ideas of carnival and excess, it is appropriate that the Pogues' single greatest 'hit' should be a song about New York, the capital of

---

24 Friedrich Engels, cited in E. P. Thompson, *The Making of the English Working Class* (New York, 1963), 435

capital, on Christmas Eve, that late twentieth-century carnival of carnivals that has become a byword for demented extravaganzas of shop-till-you-drop fervour and mass consumption. 'Fairytale of New York' is a tribute to New York and by extension to 'the American Dream' that the city epitomizes. In many ways, the city's allure, like that of the American Dream, depends on the idea that the United States represents the abolition of 'Old World' scarcity and indeed the abundance beyond appetite that were always central to carnival's appeal. Yet though its emotional tribute to the allure of America's most iconic city is sincere enough, 'Fairytale' also shows the Pogues at their slyly subversive best. The song's lush orchestral soundtrack clearly makes concessions to the feel-good schmaltziness of the Christmas-song genre, and the mixing together of the 'magic' of New York, romantic love and the America Dream is obviously a potent one. But the tribute to all these things is double-edged. 'Fairytale' is, after all, a Christmas song that simultaneously manages to be an exceptionally foul-mouthed anti-Christmas song:

> You scumbag
> You maggot
> You cheap lousy faggot
> Happy Christmas your arse
> I pray God
> It's our last.

It is a tender love song that is also a biting duet of mutually reciprocated disappointment ('I could have been some one / So could anyone'), and an aria that invokes the city it hymns not as a place where emigrant dreams are realized, but as a wasteland of the down-and-out — the lonely, the drug-addicted, the drunken, the homeless, the old, the incarcerated. The magic of New York is that it offers all of the extravagantly exaggerated carnal promise of the old lands of Cockaigne ('They've got cars / Big as bars / They've got rivers of gold'), yet while acknowledging this, 'Fairytale' is never so mesmerized by the city's spell as to loose sight of the alienation behind all the hype ('But the wind / Blows right through you / It's no place for the old'). 'Fairytale' is emotionally 'softer' and musically more melodic than most of the Pogues' best songs and this partly at least accounts for its commercial success and staying power. But it ought not to be forgotten that this duet by an English socialist (MacColl) and an Irish republican (MacGowan) is less a hymn to America than to the emigrant dream of abundance — a dream that the Empire State has always successfully exploited, yet never quite redeemed.

4

The classic studies of carnival, including Mikhail Bakhtin's seminal work, are almost invariably histories of *the end* or *the death* of carnival rather than accounts of carnival as it exists in the contemporary world.[25] The history rehearsed by Bakhtin and his successors describes how carnival is vitiated in the transition from the medieval to the modern period as the old communally sanctioned holidays are swept aside when a Protestant ethic of self-improvement, hard work and deferred gratification ushers in an increasingly capitalistic world. According to these accounts, carnival survives (when it survives at all) in the more labour-intensive societies of modern capitalism only within marginal bohemian enclaves and subcultural ghettos or the individualized domains of bourgeois literature and the private neuroses of the bourgeois subconscious.[26]

One of the limitations of the Bakhtinian school of thought is that its essentially Weberian conception of modernity causes it to accentuate the dour, repressive and pleasure-negating dimensions of capitalist society. Conceived thus, capitalism becomes synonymous with puritanical new regimens of self-discipline and deferred gratification and the development of new technologies for the maximization of labour. However, this emphasizes only the productive side of capitalism, whereas contemporary consumer theories offer quite a different stress, asserting that capitalism needs to be understood not simply as a revolutionary new mode of production, but also as a revolutionary new mode of consumption. So, if the middle and working classes had to undergo long historical processes of resocialization to internalize the new entrepreneurial mentalities and work disciplines that were essential for the Industrial Revolution, the same classes had equally to internalize the new consumer mentalities that would condition them to want to consume the vast quantities of mass-produced goods made available by that revolution. Simply put, what contemporary consumer theories underline is that the emergence of modern capitalism required not just the development of a new regimens of labour and accumulation, but also the abolition of those non-modern cultural beliefs that had inhibited the kinds of mass consumerism that advanced capitalism requires to reproduce itself.[27] Non-modern modes of consumption had generally been tied to either

25 Some of the key works on this topic include Mikhail Bakhtin, *Rabelais and His World*, trans. Hélène Iswolsky (Bloomington, 1984); Emmanuel Le Roy Ladurie, *Carnival: A People's Uprising at Romans, 1579–80*, trans. M. Feeney (Harmondsworth, 1981); Natalie Zemon Davis, *Society and Culture in Early Modern France* (Stanford, 1955), and Stallybrass and White, *Politics and Poetics*.

26 For a useful overview, see Allon White, 'Pigs and Pierrots: The Politics of Transgression in Modern Fiction', *Raritan*, 2 (1982), 51–70. White suggests the old medieval forms of popular carnival begin to wilt during the Protestant Reformation, and that the decline thereafter advances most swiftly over the following centuries in the industrial north-west of Europe 'roughly in line with the Protestant/Catholic split'. For White, carnival survives into late twentieth-century society essentially in individualized neurotic forms that are cut off from 'social celebration and communal pleasures', manifesting themselves most commonly as 'emblems of alienated desire, paranoid fantasy, and the individual will-to-power' (55).

27 Some key works in the vast literature on the development of modern consumer society include Jean Baudrillard, 'Consumer Society', in *Selected Writings*, ed. Mark Poster (Cambridge, 1988 [1970]); Pierre Bourdieu, *Distinction: A Social Critique on the Judgement of Taste* (London, 1984 [1979]); Neil McKendrick, John Brewer and J. H. Plumb, *The Birth of a Consumer Society: The Commercialisation of Eighteenth-Century England* (London, 1982); Colin Campbell, *The Romantic Ethic and the Spirit of Modern Consumerism* (Oxford, 1987); and Arjun Appadurai, *The Social Life of Things: Commodities in Cultural Perspective* (Cambridge, 1986). For a useful overview of the scholarly field, see Peter Corrigan, *The Sociology of Consumption* (London, 1997).

fixed quantities or specific kinds of prestige goods. But the distinguishing feature of 'the modern consumer is the primary obligation to want to want under all circumstances and at all times irrespective of what goods and services are actually desired and consumed'.[28]

If modern capitalism is conceived in this more dialectical manner, then it seems reasonable to surmise that carnival loses much of its socially transgressive quality in modern times not simply because — as Bakhtin's followers tend to suggest — the old carnival practices were outlawed or driven underground (though this did take place), but also because successful capitalist societies eventually created an affluent world of prodigious mass consumption to which appetites of continuous consumerist hedonism eventually became culturally indispensable. Carnival, that is to say, gradually ceded its original communal functions not because a neurotically kill-joy and work-addicted bourgeois world annulled the old festivals of licence and misrule, but because the modes of excess and extravagant consumption associated in non-modern societies with limited periods of communal licence now became virtually routinized and individualized in late capitalist consumer societies. Capitalism, so viewed, does not 'kill' carnival so much by abolishing it as by attempting to canalize its celebration of abundance and uninhibited indulgence into the very different routines of the consumer society.

To understand what this means for the Pogues' version of carnival, we need to dispense with a priori conceptions of carnival as innately socially transgressive or as merely conservative and cathartic, and to situate it in the immediate historical context of the 1980s. As argued above, this period was defined internationally by a New Right assumption of power, most especially in the United States and in the United Kingdom, that mobilized the 'respectable' middle and working classes by promising tough new 'no nonsense' approaches to all those social segments that could be characterized as parasites and freeloaders on the body politic. In the Republic of Ireland, all social debate at the time was cast in terms of a rigid Kulturkampf between Catholic traditionalists and social liberals and political debate was articulated in terms that suggested that the only choice was between an inherited economic-and-cultural nationalism and an emergent economic neo-liberalism. Against this backdrop, the culture of rowdily aggressive subaltern hedonism and exuberant excess cultivated by the Pogues appears essentially progressive. In an international context, their music celebrated the excesses and the unruly impulses of those very subaltern strata that were targeted by the New Right, and thus constituted a sometimes humorous, sometimes belligerent refusal of the New Right's sanctimonious moral authoritarianism. And in an economically depressed and war-torn Ireland, their plebian-carnivalesque aesthetic discombobulated traditionalists and modernizers alike.

Ever since the Great Famine and the Devotional Revolution, and especially when they came to power after the establishment of the Free State, the traditionalists had

---

28 See Colin Campbell, 'Romanticism and the Consumer Ethic: Intimations of a Weber-style Thesis', Sociological Analysis, 44, 4 (1983), 279–96, 282.

been concerned to make Irish culture more refined and respectable by filtering out, as 'inauthentic' or 'degraded', all its more licentious and anarchic or uncouth elements — those very elements that were to make such a whoopingly triumphant return of the repressed in the Pogues' music. Since Irish modernizers were themselves hostile to cultural nationalist puritanism — the latter initially essential to inculcating capitalist mentalities and disciplines in Ireland, but long since become an impediment to the system's further development — this constituency might be expected to be more receptive to the Pogues. But since modernization required Ireland to become not just more socially liberal but also a more hardworking, disciplined and entrepreneurial society, the Pogues' espousal of a recalcitrant and retro 'classic Paddy' image of hard-drinking fecklessness, hooligan rowdiness and Fenian-republican rebelliousness sat very awkwardly with this ideological worldview too. Thus, from the modernizing perspective, the Pogues' whole aesthetic would inevitably appear a throwback to the undisciplined, trashy, slovenly and rebellious old nationalist Ireland they wanted to leave behind. Accommodating neither the cultural agendas of the already waning old cultural nationalist régime nor those of the official modernizing opposition already coming to power, the Pogues represented an antinomian radicalism that was, for a time at least, shocking.

Yet what was awkwardly antinomian in the 1980s became something quite different in the changed context of the 1990s. Under Thatcher and Reagan, the 1980s was a decade of repressive labour-discipline and general belt-tightening for all but the wealthiest classes. However, after the defeat of Communism in 1989, a more confidently expansionist and 'globalized' capitalism — with much less to fear now from any challenge from either the political left or from organized labour — set the scene for a new international political order in which the capacity to achieve or sustain conditions of mass consumerist affluence was now consolidated as the only criterion of political legitimacy. As one commentator put it, when the peoples of the formerly Communist Eastern European states came flocking over the rubble of the Berlin Wall, the lesson drawn was that 'civil society [now] meant consumer society, civic freedom the freedom to shop freely'.[29]

In this changed context, the excesses associated with rock and roll generally, and the Pogues specifically, meant something different to what they had done previously. Since its inception, rock and roll's culture of licence and excess had legitimated itself as a counter-cultural riposte to a puritanical official culture. But by the 1990s the capitalist world was no longer nearly so 'puritanical' as it had been even a few decades earlier (much to the chagrin of back-to-basics-conservatives everywhere), and, at least where sexual expression was concerned, a new permissiveness now prevailed in the more affluent capitalist zones. In such circumstances, the rank hedonism and excess of rock and roll was much more likely to appear either as a 'tolerated transgression' or even as an endorsement of the mass consumerist ethos rather than as any kind of iconoclastic challenge to the dominant culture.

29 See Don Slater, *Consumer Culture and Modernity* (Cambridge, 1997), 37. For a supplementary account, see Donald M. Lowe, *The Body in Late-Capitalist USA* (Durham, 1995), esp. chs. 1–3.

As an economic beneficiary of this broader global moment of capitalist expansion, Ireland too, of course, was transformed and the distressed capitalist society of the 1980s would become by the late 1990s one of the models of late twentieth-century capitalist prosperity. A country notorious in the 1980s for massive international debt and exceptionally high unemployment levels was now experiencing an extended economic boom and almost full employment. From being a society that had always exported emigrants to the advanced capitalist centres, Ireland now became an economic magnet for migrants from elsewhere. In the North, the long republican war against the British state also drew to a close with the initiation of the 'peace process'. In this dramatically altered socio-cultural landscape, the whole iconography of the Pogues inevitably lost much of its charge. By the mid-1990s, certainly by the new century, 'republicanism', 'emigration' and 'excess' all meant something quite different to what they had meant a decade earlier. Even before then, the physical rigours of carnival had exacted a personal toll on the band members generally. But it is doubtful anyway if the band could have continued to mean the same thing in the 1990s that it had done in the 1980s. Very simply, in non-affluent and socially conservative societies of scarcity and want, carnival serves functions quite different from those that it fulfils in societies of permissive consumerist affluence. Whereas in the former its licence and revelry functions as a sign of some utopian alternative to the penurious social norm, in commodity-rich consumer societies its celebration of excess inevitably cedes much of its utopian dimensions. To this extent, it can be said that the Pogues succumbed not so much (or not only) to the toll of their own vices, but to a wider historical sea change as well.[30]

To acknowledge this is in no way to diminish the Pogues' many achievements. As has been argued earlier, the band's entirely novel combination of English punk and Irish céilí and ballad music did much to complicate, even confound, the established metanarratives that had conditioned the reception of Irish popular music. In loosening these, the Pogues made an important contribution to the establishment of a more genuinely pluralistic music scene and prepared the ground for less rigid conceptions of genre and tradition in Ireland. In broader cultural terms, the band's commitment to a distinctively plebian version of carnival that had long roots in Irish culture challenges the notion that Irish society was simply grey, grim and repressively puritanical before it was belatedly 'rescued' from its miseries by neoliberal capitalism. For many historians

---

30 The final irony here is that it was this same sea change that would eventually transform MacGowan into the harmless and rather sadly anachronistic cult figure he now is. In the 1980s, his combination of unapologetic republicanism and general debauchery made him (along with, for different reasons, Sinéad O'Connor) the most genuinely non-conformist and eccentric of the stars in the Irish rock firmament. As the republican threat receded in the 1990s and as rock-and roll debauchery was upstaged by its more clerical versions, the climate eventually altered sufficiently for MacGowan to become more fully integrated into the rock pantheon. Today, in an Irish rock world that has cleaned up its 'hard-living' and 'hedonistic' image, and embraces instead a more 'mature' and socially responsible liberal humanist philanthropy, he seems to function more as a quaint historical curiosity than as the subversively potent figure he once was.

of the twentieth century, it has become almost axiomatic that Ireland before the 1960s, or even before the 1990s, was essentially a dourly purgatorial society — a place defined not just by its political and economic failure, but by an utterly joyless puritanism as well.[31] The trouble with these accounts is not that they are wrong — the poverty and hardship, the crass authoritarianism of Church and state, the moral puritanism are all patently obvious — but that they elide those more unruly elements in Irish society that were recalcitrant to the dominant culture of the time.[32]

If the 'miserabilist' conception of post-Treaty Ireland found its most distinguished artistic expression in some versions of Irish modernism and its most sustained expression in Irish naturalist literature, it was also fundamental to the self-understanding of Irish rock music. In the 1980s, Bob Geldof expressed this worldview with admirable clarity when he dismissed modern Ireland as a misbegotten 'banana republic' of 'priests and police', which the rock artist — like the literary modernists of an earlier era — had to leave if he were to succeed. To Shane MacGowan, born in Turnbridge Wells in Kent in 1957, who spent his early youth living with maternal aunts and uncles in Puckane, near Borrisokane, County Tipperary, things were very different. Though born into a family considerably less affluent than Geldof's, which lived in Dublin's prosperous southside, MacGowan's memories of his childhood in the Irish midlands were altogether more positive. As MacGowan narrated it, the society in which he had spent his formative childhood years was not the redneck heart of darkness it had become in the liberal and literary imagination. For him, it was, rather, a place of almost scandalous freedom where he had been introduced at a prodigiously early age to the pleasures of alcohol, gambling, hurling, horse-racing, music, story-telling and song. In his narrative, the defining trauma of his youth was not the mauling of his spirit by the Catholic Church or the cultural or libidinal miseries of Irish provincialism, but rather his family's relocation to a 1960s England that he had experienced as cold, grey, racist and regimented. When

---

31 See, for example, Tom Inglis, *Moral Monopoly: The Rise and Fall of the Catholic Church in Modern Ireland* (Dublin, 1998) and Tom Garvin, *Preventing the Future? Why was Ireland Poor for so Long?* (Dublin, 2004). See also Terence Brown's *Ireland: A Social and Cultural History 1922–2002*, rev. edn. (London, 2004). Unlike Inglis and Garvin, who stress only the oppressive dimensions of post-independence Irish society before the 1960s, Brown's work does not neglect internal forces of resistance and opposition. But in Brown's case, opposition is conceived essentially in terms of the élite classes and confined mainly to writers and intellectuals. Popular culture receives little attention in his work.

32 The novelist John McGahern made the point effectively, and with humour, when reflecting on the 1950s in a 1999 article in the *Irish Times*: 'That the climate was insular, repressive and sectarian is hardly in doubt, but there is also little doubt that many drew solace from its authoritarian certainties. And, in a society where the local and individual were more powerful than any national identity, much of what went on was given no more than routine lip service. The people it affected most were the new emerging classes closely linked to Church and State — civil servants, teachers, doctors, nurses, policemen, tillage inspectors. Most ordinary people went about their sensible pagan lives as they had done for centuries, seeing all this as just another veneer they had to pretend to wear like all the others they had worn since the time of the Druids.' See John McGahern, 'Whatever You Say, Say Nothing', *Irish Times*, 26 Oct. 1999. McGahern's own novels reflect little of this 'pagan' culture; they are preoccupied instead with the emerging middle classes he discusses here.

compared to the larger-than-life Irish rural folk that had populated his early childhood years, MacGowan remarked, the English that he encountered later 'just don't measure up to those people'.[33]

The point here is not that MacGowan's experience of Ireland is somehow more valid or more 'true' than Geldof's. Rather, it is that if Geldof's portrait of the artist as a young punk rocker deploys the conventions of an essentially 'modernist' or 'naturalist' conception of Irish society, MacGowan's account of his early life in the countryside espouses a more 'romantic' version of things. Thus, whereas for Geldof Ireland was essentially a static and stultifying world from which it was necessary to escape to emancipate and fulfil oneself, for MacGowan it was essentially a place of indulgence and rebellion, to be exiled from which represented some kind of fall into modern alienation. Sceptics will inevitably argue that this merely confirms that MacGowan, like many a second-generation emigrant before him, succumbed to a regressive nostalgia that lends unwarrantedly a colourful tint to what was in reality an exceptionally repressive mode of life. The self-consciously Rabelaisian colouring of this account would suggest, however, that what MacGowan was essentially rejecting in his depiction of his early childhood was a 'naturalistic' conception of rural Ireland that tended to inventory only the ways in which that society crushed and maimed, but failed to register any form of popular resistance to the repressive forces.[34] For MacGowan, the mundane things within this world that had allowed it to preserve its spirit and energy — the ordinary drinking, singing, sporting, gambling, fighting, and other recreational practices — mattered as much as the repression itself.[35] The songs and the music of the Pogues would continually

33 For MacGowan's account of his early years in Ireland and relocation to England, see Clarke and MacGowan, *A Drink with Shane MacGowan*, 1–36, 3.

34 In a laconic but telling review of the Irish literary tradition, MacGowan expresses particular admiration for Joyce, O'Casey, Behan, and Heaney. Heaney is admired as a better writer of 'Bogman Poetry' than Kavanagh, because 'He is quintessentially Irish, but he doesn't go on about being beaten up by the Christian Brothers all the time', Clarke and MacGowan, *A Drink with Shane MacGowan*, 268. Expressing little affection for modern Irish poetry, he declares greater affection for the old Irish-language tradition, especially Aogán Ó Rathaille and Brian Merriman's *Midnight Court*. Several naturalistic writers — including Frank O'Connor, Edna O'Brien, John McGahern and Frank McCourt — get positive mention and McCourt's *Angela's Ashes* is even described as 'the greatest Irish novel ever' (262). For MacGowan, it is 'absolutely truthful, totally lacking in O'Casey style romanticism' and yet 'hysterically funny all the way through'. That MacGowan's taste consistently gravitates away from the naturalistic and towards the more carnivalesque strands in Irish writing is clear and it colours even his appreciation of McCourt (252–71).

35 The contrast between MacGowan's Rabelaisian version of his Irish childhood and the more standard repressive versions associated in recent times with figures as diverse as Bob Geldof, Frank McCourt or John McGahern is worth citing at some length, if only to underline the different aesthetics of Irishness involved. Asked to describe his early years in the midlands, MacGowan responds: 'I was allowed to smoke, drink, and bet, as a child, all of which are regarded by puritans as bad habits, because I came from a very anti-puritan background. Sex was the one thing that was a no-no, sex and blasphemy. You were allowed to say fuck as much as you wanted to, but that isn't blasphemy, that isn't saying anything against Jesus or His Holy Mother. Fuck, itself, is the most popular word in the Irish vocabulary. And I was brought up to say it from an early age. And I was smoking and drinking and gambling before I could hardly talk. The first horse I ever bet on was called Maxwell House and he came in at 10–1. I was five years old. So I

return to the quotidian recalcitrance and defiance of lower-class rural and urban Ireland, both at home and abroad. By so doing, they drew attention to a dimension of Irish subaltern cultural history neglected in conventional scholarship, whether of the cultural nationalist or liberal modernizing variety.

Finally, it is worth remembering that even in the 'failure' of the Pogues there is a stubborn integrity. What punters have always wanted from the Pogues was the headily collective experience of carnival that the band created in its concerts. It was the pursuit of this, and not any specific politics or worldview, that won the Pogues their following. But the crux was that to deliver that experience of carnival regularly to the punters in the manner they desired, the Pogues as an outfit would have had to function with all of the self-discipline and well-regulated efficiency of an industrial machine. Carnival may be about suspending self-discipline and celebrating natural abundance and uninhibited indulgence and topsy-turvy. But to transmit that experience in the form of a mass commodity to the fans, the Pogues would have had to commit to long months of endless touring across Europe and America, to rigidly planned and punctually kept bus and airline schedules, and to endlessly simulated repetitions of supposedly spontaneous experiences of partying and mayhem.[36] In short, carnival could not be delivered to the punters as a mass commodity on an industrial scale except by espousing an entrepreneurial ethic that was anathema to it. The band's *de facto* collapse in 1991, having never really 'cracked' the United States market (the criterion of rock success), is usually attributed to MacGowan's chronic alcoholism. But the contradiction between a commitment to the values of collective hedonistic excess and the music industry's commitment to the well-regulated delivery of carnival on a vast scale is one that has bedevilled modern music for decades. An efficiently administered carnival is a contradiction in terms. It is a dilemma that cannot be resolved. For all their antinomianism, this was an antinomy that the Pogues, no more than any other band, could not overcome. That MacGowan knew as much suggests that he may have been cannier than those who argue that he simply blew it.

was a regular gambler after that. And the way my Auntie Nora taught me the gospel was we used to do the Irish Sweepstake together and she used to buy me packets of cigarettes. She was a heavy smoker, she didn't drink but she allowed the men to buy me drink, she told me there was no crime in having a drink, she told me the crime was in worshipping the devil. So with one hand she was dishing out cigarettes and the Irish Sweepstake, which we used to do religiously every week, the two of us and we used to win again and again because it involves a certain amount of intelligence, the Irish Sweepstake, because it involves a crossword puzzle, and then when she had me pissed and smoking like a chimney, she'd start teaching me the gospels. Hideously devious. Jesuits couldn't touch it. So I became a religious maniac at the same time as becoming a total hedonist. And it worked because I'm still a religious maniac and a total hedonist.' See Clarke and MacGowan, *A Drink with Shane MacGowan*, 15.

36 It may be worth leaving the last word to MacGowan on this: 'It was the touring that made me ill ... America was where I started getting ill. I always got ill in America. A fifty-two-date tour. Not eating properly. Psychosomatic I think it was, as well. I just wanted to be at home. Night after night after night, repeating the same routine. I felt like I was acting. I felt like I was faking, you know. I felt like the audience could see through it. So I got really paranoid. And I knew the band had nothing but contempt for me ... I'd become institutionalised into touring with that group.' See Clarke and MacGowan, *A Drink with Shane MacGowan*, 241–42.

Index

Melville, Herman, 65, 66n
Memmi, Albert, 46n
Mengel, Hagal, 185n
Mercier, Vivian, 241n
Merrick, Joe, 262n, 266n, 270n
Merriman, Brian, 293n
Middle East, 10, 24n, 30, 46, 58
Mitchel, John, 27, 43
modernism (and modernists), 4, 22, 49,
    66, 69, 73, 75, 79–87, 89–96, 98–
    99, 101, 103–06, 108–110, 111–12,
    117–120, 122–24, 130, 132, 137, 138,
    139, 141, 148, 152, 154, 155, 157,
    175, 212–14, 263, 266–68, 272, 275,
    276, 292–93
  Perry Anderson on, 79, 82–83
  Marshall Berman on, 212
  Terry Eagleton on, 86, 92
  in Ireland, 49, 86–94, 100–02, 108–110
  and Irish Literary Revival, 89–94, 139
  Fredric Jameson on, 80–81
  and postmodernism, 82–83, 103–06
  and primitivism, 132
  See also Irish Literary Revival;
    modernity; modernization;
    naturalism.
modernity, 5–6, 8–9, 17, 22, 33–34,
    53, 64–66, 78, 86, 88–89, 92–93,
    97, 98, 101, 141, 133, 169, 174, 183,
    185, 191–203, 205–06, 212–215,
    224–29, 274, 276, 288
  alternative modernities, 5–6
  and carnival, 288
  consequences in Ireland, 78
  Terry Eagleton on, 86
  Rita Felski on, 183n, 197
  and gender of, 196–97
  Fredric Jameson on, 6n
  and loss, 184–85
  and matriarchate, 182–83
  Francis Mulhern on, 17

  and music, 228–29, 275–76
  and postcolonial studies, 33
  and religion, 183–85
  and tradition, 5–9
  See also Catholicism; de Valera's
    Ireland; modernism;
    modernization; Protestantism.
modernization, 5, 6, 191, 196–97,
    203–231
  and aesthetic ideology, 203–231
  as Americanization in cinema, 191
  in Cathal Black's Korea, 203–06
  discourses of, 6, 217n
  Terry Eagleton on, 86
  Rita Felski on, 197, 201
  gendered discourses of, 196–97
  in Irish studies, 5
  in Brian Friel's Dancing at Lughnasa,
    225–31
  in John McGahern's Amongst Women,
    209, 211, 215–17, 221–25, 229, 231
  in Pat O'Connor's The Ballroom of
    Romance, 215
  opposition to official versions of,
    207–08
  and periodizations of twentieth
    century, 8–9
  and reception of the Pogues, 289–90
  and religion, 199–200
  in Jim Sheridan's The Field, 215–21,
    222–25
  and social anxiety, 183–84, 189–90
  See also de Valera's Ireland;
    modernism; modernity.
Moloney, Mick, 264n
Moore, Brian, 100, 154, 155n, 157–58,
    165–66, 173, 175
  The Feast of Lupercal, 157, 165
  The Lonely Passion of Judith Hearne, 154,
    157–59
  compared to James Joyce, 157–58

rising, of 1798, 38, 39, 63
Riverdance, 231
Robinson, Mary, 220, 225
Roediger, David, 40, 41n
Roman Empire, 77
Romanov court, 90
Romeo and Juliet (Shakespeare), 254–56
  compared to historical novel, 255
  compared to Sophocles' Antigone,
    254–56
  and representations of Northern
    Ireland, 255–56
  See also domestic tragedy; tragedy.
Royal Ulster Constabulary, 252
Ruane, Joseph, 23–25, 46n
Russia, 24n, 26, 58n, 77, 82, 86, 87, 89,
  90, 91, 113, 205, 213
Russian realism, 58n
Russian Revolution, 82
Ryan, Frank, 265, 285

Said, Edward, 14–15, 55–56
  Culture and Imperialism, 55–56
  Orientalism, 15
  Yeats and Decolonization, 14
Salewicz, Chris, 266n
Sampson, Denis, 158n
Saunders, David, 117n
Savage, Jon, 266n
Savage, Mike, 52n, 67n, 68n
Savage, Robert J., 8n
Sayers, Peig, 152n
Scandinavia, 112, 113, 134
Scanlon, Ann, 262n, 263n
Schwarz, Roberto, 22, 57
Scotland, 41–42, 45, 55, 56, 69, 73
Scott, Derek, 106
Scott, Malcolm, 63n
Scott, Walter, 69, 122, 189, 255
Scully, Sean, 104
Second World, 86

sectarianism
  in St. John Ervine's Mixed Marriage,
    232–33, 236–43, 248–50, 258
  in Tom Paulin's The Riot Act, 254–55
  in Sam Thompson's Over the Bridge,
    241–52
Seeger, Pete, 270
Sex Pistols, the, 267–68, 286
Shafir, Gershon, 32n
Shakespeare, William, 4n, 221, 232, 254
  Romeo and Juliet, 254–56
  See also domestic tragedy; tragedy.
Shaw, George Bernard, 103, 117n, 124,
  128–32, 138, 140
  The Quintessence of Ibsenism, 124, 128–29
  critical assessments of, 129
  compartmentalization in, 129
  in Eleanor Marx's 'Nora', 128
  and naturalism, 128–130
Shergar, 188n
Sheridan, Jim, 184–85, 186n, 187,
  190–99, 209, 211, 215–21, 220, 224,
  225, 229–31
  Into the West (film), 184–99, 169, 202,
    220
  The Field (film), 194n, 209, 211, 215–21,
    220, 224, 225, 229–31
  compared to John McGahern, 231
  and conflicts of modernization, 199,
    217–221
  and Travellers, 187–88, 190, 192,
    195–98, 218, 220–21
Shirlow, Peter, 240n, 260n
Siberia, 24n
Simmel, Georg, 182
Sinn Féin, 3, 69, 96, 131, 141, 207,
  208, 239
  See also republicanism.
situationism, 267
Slater, Don, 11n, 290n
Slater, Eamonn, 27, 35, 36n